. White grub

17. Japanese beetle

18. Annual white grub adult

. Grub damage pattern

20. Black turfgrass ataenius - adult, pupa, larva

21. Billbug damage

. Sod webworm damage

23. Sod webworm larva

24. Sod webworm adult

. Bluegrass webworm adult

26. Black cutworm

27. Greenbug damage

. Greenbugs on leaf

29. Spittlebug nymph and spittle

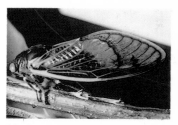

30. Periodical cicada laying eggs

Controlling Turfgrass Pests

MALCOLM C. SHURTLEFF
Plant Pathologist

THOMAS W. FERMANIAN
Turfgrass Scientist

ROSCOE RANDELL
Entomologist

University of Illinois
Urbana, Illinois

A RESTON BOOK
Prentice Hall Career & Technology
Englewood Cliffs, New Jersey 07632

Library of Congress Cataloging-in-Publication Data

SHURTLEFF, MALCOLM C.
    Controlling turfgrass pests.

    "A Reston book."
    Bibliography
    Includes index.
    1. Turfgrasses—Diseases and pests. 2. Turf
management. I. Fermanian, Thomas W. II. Randell, Roscoe
W. III. Title.
SB608.T87S48 1987   635.9'642   86-16975
ISBN 0-8359-1017-2

Editorial/production supervision
and interior design: *Theresa A. Soler*
Cover design: *Photo Plus Art*
Manufacturing buyer: *John Hall*

 © 1987 by Prentice-Hall, Inc.
A Simon & Schuster Company
Englewood Cliffs, New Jersey 07632

Printed in the United States of America

10 9 8 7 6

ISBN 0-8359-1017-2

Prentice-Hall International (UK) Limited, *London*
Prentice-Hall of Australia Pty. Limited, *Sydney*
Prentice-Hall Canada Inc., *Toronto*
Prentice-Hall Hispanoamericana, S.A., *Mexico*
Prentice-Hall of India Private Limited, *New Delhi*
Prentice-Hall of Japan, Inc., *Tokyo*
Prentice-Hall of Southeast Asia Pte. Ltd., *Singapore*
Editora Prentice-Hall do Brasil, Ltda., *Rio de Janeiro*

Contents

6   APPLICATION EQUIPMENT AND CALIBRATION   330

7   INTEGRATED PEST MANAGEMENT   361

Contents

Preface

This book is an up-to-date account of the current state of the art and science of turfgrass pest management. It is designed as a comprehensive reference for the professional turfgrass manager which includes golf course superintendents, lawn care company personnel, park and cemetery officials, those responsible for maintaining turf on sports fields, at airports, and along highways, seed and sod growers, and landscapers. The book has also been written as a basic text for undergraduate and graduate students in turfgrass management, landscape architecture, turfgrass pathology, and economic entomology. It should prove a valuable reference to turfgrass consultants, representatives of a variety of agribusinesses that serve the turfgrass industry, county, area, and state Extension (Advisory) personnel involved in diagnosis and control of turfgrass pests, officers in state and federal departments of agriculture and regulatory agencies, vocational agriculture and biology teachers, garden center personnel, garden writers, and home lawn enthusiasts. The book contains both the technical and practical information necessary for decision-making and the day-to-day operation in all areas of turfgrass culture and management.

The stimulus for writing this book has come from the rapid expansion of the turfgrass industry in the past 10 to 20 years and a tremendous increase in the numbers of professional turfgrass managers responsible for maintaining turf as free as possible of weeds, insects, diseases, and other pests. There are a number of excellent books available on turfgrass management and culture. However, a reference-textbook was needed that concentrates on the diagnosis, fundamental biology and control of turfgrass weeds, insects and other animal pests, and diseases.

Emphasis is placed on how to identify turfgrass pests, where and why they occur, the damage that may take place, the life cycles of pests, plus cultural, chemical, and other control measures designed to keep pest damage to a minimum. A chapter on integrated pest control blends the various control strategies and general turfgrass maintenance practices into a unified whole. The recommendations made take into account all the cultural aspects of turfgrass management (e.g., proper establishment, watering, fertilization, mowing, dethatching, aerification). Successful turfgrass management, including pest control, is an art based on sound scientific knowledge. Because of the frequent changes in pesticides and other chemicals used in turfgrass culture, climatic variations, and the turfs grown, this book should be supplemented by current pest control programs and bulletins available in each state or country from the local county Extension (Advisory) office or state agricultural experiment station.

Accurate diagnosis is the first step in the control of any pest. The detailed keys in Chapters 3, 4, and 5, plus the numerous illustrations, are designed to make positive diagnosis as simple as possible. The extensive index should also be helpful.

Much of the research information concerning turfgrass culture, including the biology and control of weeds, insects and plant diseases, is scattered throughout thousands of scientific journals, trade publications, turfgrass conference proceedings, and field day programs, and therefore not generally available to turfgrass managers, students, and others interested in controlling turfgrass pests. Many thousands of references were reviewed during the preparation of this text. Each of the major chapters ends with a list of the more pertinent and widely available references for those wishing to study a pest or area in more detail. The text is complemented by numerous line drawings, photographs, and color plates which have been carefully selected to illustrate all of the common and uncommon pests and even the rare and nuisance ones. In writing this book, the authors assume that the reader possesses an elementary knowledge of such basic sciences as botany, chemistry, and soil science.

Comments regarding the general usefulness and/or any errors or omissions in the text are always welcome. With your suggestions, future editions can become even more valuable for the diagnosis and control of turfgrass pests.

ACKNOWLEDGMENTS

The authors wish to express their gratitude to the following colleagues for adding breadth, accuracy, and value when reviewing parts or all of the manuscript: R.C. Avenius, D.J. Blasingame, L.E. Bode, T.H. Bowyer, L.L. Burpee III, J.D. Butler, G.A. Chastagner, P.F. Colbaugh, J.L. Dale, P.H. Dernoeden, J.M. Dipola, R.L. Goss, C.F. Hodges, Noel Jackson, B.G. Joyner, G.M. Kozelnicky, P.O. Larson, L.T. Lucas, T.A. Melton, W.A. Meyer, H.D. Niemczyk, D.L. Roberts, J.L. Saladini, G.W. Simone, R.W. Smiley, J.D. Smith, W.C. Stienstra, R.W. Toler, A.J. Turgeon, J.M. Vargas, Jr., J.E. Watkins, H.T. Wilkinson, and G.L. Worf.

Individuals, institutions, and companies who so willingly provided illustrations or photographs are given specific credit following the illustration legend.

Limitations of space make it impossible to acknowledge adequately our indebtedness to the hundreds of research scientists, extension specialists, and writers for the enormous storehouse of information from which we drew the material presented.

We are also grateful to Patricia C. Novak, Dorothea M. Grider, and Mary Jo Mahannah for typing the manuscript throughout the several tedious revisions. A special thanks goes to artists George Mayer, Earl Mayer, and Nancy Fermanian who drew a number of the weed species and, especially to Lenore Gray who did some of the maintenance and equipment art work, weed species, plus all of the drawings of insects, other animal pests, and plant pathogens. Finally, we thank our wives who were quietly patient and supportive during the long hours we neglected them while referencing and writing this book. Our indebtedness to all of these persons is gratefully acknowledged.

Malcolm C. Shurtleff
Thomas W. Fermanian
Roscoe Randell

Kneeling: Malcolm C. Shurtleff (left) and Thomas W. Fermanian (right); standing: Roscoe Randell.

—————————————————— 1 ——————

Introduction

This book is written for anyone who enjoys beautiful turf as free as possible of weeds, insects, diseases, and other pests. It is written for professional lawn care company personnel; home lawn enthusiasts; golf course superintendents; park and cemetery officials; managers of athletic fields; commercial seed and sod growers; students in turfgrass management, landscape architecture, plant pathology, and economic entomology classes; turfgrass consultants; agribusiness research and sales representatives; county extension agents; officials in state and federal departments of agriculture and regulatory agencies; those in charge of maintaining turf at airports and along highways; area and state extension turfgrass specialists, entomologists, weed specialists, and plant pathologists involved in diagnosis and control of turfgrass problems; garden store personnel; vocational agriculture and biology teachers; garden writers; and others who grow, know, and love turfgrasses. You will find this book not only invaluable as a reference, but easy to use.

An attempt has been made to write in everyday language, omitting as much of the scientific terminology as practical. Scientific names of weeds, insects, and disease-causing agents are included. There is a comprehensive glossary to help with technical terms. This book blends descriptive terminology with the more technical language of weed science, entomology, nematology, plant pathology, and turfgrass management to better serve the diverse levels of knowledge and skills of a wide variety of turfgrass managers and consultants. Each chapter ends with some selected reference books found in many public libraries where more detailed information may be obtained.

Three questions invariably asked about a turfgrass problem are, "What's wrong?" or "What is it?" and "What should I do about it?" Sometimes such questions as "How serious is it?" or "Will it kill my turf?" follow. This book helps to answer these basic questions.

In Chapter 2 we cover integrated turfgrass management starting with selecting seed or other plant materials, establishing and maintaining turf, plus common problems that arise and their solutions. A healthy and vigorous turf is basic to controlling weeds, insects, diseases, and other pests.

In Chapters 3, 4, and 5 each weed, insect, or other animal pest, and each disease (including nematodes) is described; how serious it may become; where and when it can be expected to be a problem in the United States; symptoms of damage are given; life cycles are described; and cultural control measures that will keep damage to a minimum are outlined. For quick reference, chemical controls are presented in tables at the ends of Chapters 3, 4, and 5. The simplified but comprehensive keys at the beginning of the chapters covering weeds, insects and other animal pests, and diseases, plus the many photographs and line drawings will help you diagnose essentially any turfgrass problem in the United States from southern Florida to northern Maine to Washington state and the arid southwest.

More detailed information follows in each chapter discussing the grasses most susceptible and resistant to injury, and the environmental conditions that favor or check each pest. Also included is information on "turf protection chemicals," including their common and trade names and principal uses.

Chapter 6 covers the selection, use, and calibration of various types of equipment used for application of fertilizers and pesticides to commercial, public, and private turf. Tips are given on how to make spray and granular applications most effective.

Chapter 7 is an integrated (IPM) approach to controlling all types of turf pests under three levels of management: low, medium, and high.

Appendices A through D provide a wealth of information on where and who to write to in each state for additional information on weeds, insects, diseases, and other turfgrass problems; a wide variety of useful calculations and units of measurement; conversion tables for measuring dry and liquid chemicals; measurement and rates of application equivalents; a conversion table for using fertilizers and pesticides on small areas; calculating land areas of various shapes; calibrating compressed-air sprayers and granular applicators; how to calculate nozzle flow rates; tractor speed conversions; an operating chart for tractor boom sprayers; and many other calculations that you will find useful. A complete glossary defines the technical and nontechnical terms used in the text.

The information you seek should be easy to find, especially with the extensive index.

WHERE TO FIND ADDITIONAL HELP

You can get help on lawn and fine-turf problems by contacting your county extension agent or adviser (listed under the county name in the telephone directory) or, when local assistance is not available from extension specialists at your state land-grant university. A list of these institutions and their addresses is given in Appendix D, page 397.

Write to the extension turfgrass specialist (in the Department of Horticulture or Agronomy, Plant Science, or Plant and Soil Science) regarding turfgrass management problems and weeds and their control; the extension entomologist for information about insects, mites, and other animals; and the extension plant pathologist concerning diseases and their control.

When writing to an extension specialist at your land-grant university, provide as much background information as you can about the problem or pest. Include the date collected if samples are submitted; extent of the turf area affected; cultivar and species of grass(es) affected; degree of severity; description of the problem; date when first observed; weather and soil conditions for the past several weeks or longer; recent fertilization, watering, and pest control measures taken; color photographs showing the problem; and other facts that you believe may aid in the diagnosis. Do not forget your name and return address! Remember that a correct diagnosis is essential before control measures can be suggested. A diagnosis can be only as good as the specimen(s) and/or information you send.

Most county extension offices have "Plant Clinic" or "Specimen Forms" available that cover much of the background information outlined above. Many offices also have mailing boxes or tubes available, which will save you the trouble of finding a suitable container.

For weed identification.   Correct identification of weeds is dependent on fresh, structurally intact samples. The identification of both broadleaf and grassy weeds is largely conducted by examining the floral or seedhead portion of the plant. If specimens without flowers or seeds are submitted, positive identification can sometimes be difficult. Find one to three samples of the weed which appear the most mature. Dig out the plant, retaining all portions possible (roots, rhizomes, stolons, etc.). If the weeds are extremely large, take a representative portion. If the turf is very droughty or dry, water locally around the weeds and let them absorb water before sampling (digging). Shake loose as much soil as possible from the root system and wrap the weed(s) in newspaper, then place the plant loosely in an open, plastic bag. If the roots are attached to the plant, moisten a paper towel, remove the excess moisture, and wrap the root section before wrapping with newspaper. The sample and other moistened material must be damp and *not* wet. Mail the weed sample in a crush-proof carton or mailing tube. The samples will only remain in a condition suitable for identification for a period of 2 to 3 days. Make certain that the mailing procedure chosen will deliver the samples promptly. If seeds are present and loose, they can be pasted to a piece of paper or cardboard and submitted along with the sample. It is helpful to enclose a note, explaining when the weed first appeared in the lawn, how long it has persisted, and whether it is in small clumps or has spread throughout the entire turf area. If flowers are not present but were visible previously, provide a description of the flower and when it first appeared.

For insect identification.   Collect more than one insect specimen found in the affected area. If possible, include more than one size or stage of the insect. Place the specimens in a pill bottle, plastic vial, or other durable small container. Wrap the container with paper or enclose in a small box. Enclose a sheet of paper with your name, address, where the insect was found, type of damage observed, and how numerous the insects were in the area affected. Mail or take the package to your county extension agent, or mail to the extension entomologist at your land-grant university. Do *not* tape the insects to a sheet of paper and place inside an envelope. The insects will be flattened beyond recognition before they can be identified.

For nematode assay.   Carefully collect one or more plugs of growing turfgrass and underlying soil (up to 4 to 8 in. deep). Include as many feeder roots as possible. Sample a half dozen or more places in the suspicious area, as well as from nearby "healthy" grass, saving about ½ to 1 cup of soil from each spot. Thoroughly mix the soil and save 1 to 2 quarts for mailing. Mark the specimens either "healthy" or "suspicious." Place the soil and plugs in sturdy plastic freezer bags, close the open ends securely, and place in a *strong* container. Be sure to include with the package your name and address, turf location, species and cultivar of grass sampled, symptoms observed, cultural management program being followed, and the approximate size of the area sampled. Mail the package as soon after collecting as possible. Do *not* let it sit overnight except in a refrigerator. Keep it cool. Nematodes are living animals and must reach the laboratory alive.

For disease analysis.   Carefully collect one or more plugs of growing turfgrass and underlying soil (up to 1 in. or more deep). The plugs should be taken at the *margin* of the diseased and healthy turf and, where possible, show a range of symptoms. Wrap or pack the turf securely in a plastic bag (so that soil will not spread over the grass surface) and mail in a crush-proof carton or mailing tube. Do *not* add moisture to the turf before mailing—otherwise, the grass will probably arrive in a badly rotted condition, making diagnosis impossible.

All states publish turfgrass management and pest control recommendations. Many of these publications are free. A wide variety of printed information on turfgrass problems may be obtained from your county extension office or land-grant institution. Supplement this information with the suggestions and recommendations you find in the following chapters.

2

Maintenance of Turfgrasses

INTRODUCTION

Turfgrass pests cannot be controlled over long periods solely through the use of pesticides. For a healthy, vigorous turfgrass stand, it is necessary to use pesticides in combination with sound cultural practices. This integrated pest management (IPM) system not only controls existing pests but helps prevent the reoccurrence of those pests and the regeneration of new ones.

Of all the activities related to turfgrass management, the establishment period of a turf is the most critical to its long-term success. Proper establishment has the greatest influence over the future quality of the site. The soil environment is developed largely during establishment. Since a healthy, deep root system is the principal means for turfgrass survival during periods of stress, the preparation of the soil environment will be one of the limiting factors in the long-term success of the turf. Improper establishment can nullify even the best maintenance practices.

The initial step in the establishment of a turf is the careful planning and consideration for the future use and objectives of the site. Local and regional climatic conditions, the final soil environment, and the intensity and duration of traffic expected on the turf will largely determine the maintenance requirements after establishment. A very stressful climate can limit the use of a fine turf, due to the extensive maintenance requirement.

The level of traffic on a turf can increase continuously. For planning purposes, traffic levels can be simplified to three basic groups. An area receiving minimal traffic, such as infrequent foot traffic and little vehicle traffic, would probably require low levels of maintenance. With increasing foot traffic such as a home lawn or public park might receive, but without extensive vehicle traffic, the turf could be maintained at a medium level. For intensely trafficked areas, receiving daily or hourly foot and vehicle traffic (soccer fields, golf course greens, tees, and to a lesser extent, fairways), the turf would require a high level of maintenance. The possibility exists to extend a low level of maintenance to an area that might receive greater traffic. In most instances, however, the quality of the turf will also diminish.

Each level of maintenance may require that the turfgrasses chosen exhibit unique attributes. Low-maintenance turf requires plants that show thriftiness with water, growth at minimal fertilization, and hardiness to extreme hot and/or cold temperatures. Medium-maintenance turf requires a compromise between resistance to wear or traffic and the ability to withstand low-moisture and low-fertility situations. It is generally kept at a higher mowing height than high-maintenance turf to help provide resistance to injury and minimize overall plant stress. Turfgrasses growing under high-maintenance conditions must exhibit a rapid rate of growth to replace injured tissue. Often they must withstand low mowing heights and exhibit a prostrate growth habit. Grasses with a high resistance to shearing or tearing are often selected for high-maintenance areas.

ZONES OF ADAPTATION

Turfgrasses are adapted for optimum growth to a limited range of climatic conditions. This adaptation gives the plant a competitive edge over weeds. Climatic adaptation must be balanced with the expected maintenance level of a given turf. Turfgrasses grown under low-maintenance levels must be well adapted to the prevailing local climate. Since little maintenance is provided, selected turfgrasses must be strongly competitive to dominate in the site. Zones of adaptation for a turf can often be expanded beyond their normal range when the turf is placed under high maintenance. An excellent example of this is the range of adaptation for creeping bentgrass used for golf course greens. With proper maintenance techniques, bentgrass greens can survive in Maine or Minnesota and as far south as Florida.

Temperature and precipitation have the greatest influence of climatic factors on the extent of adaptation for turfgrass species. Turfgrasses can be divided into two groups; those growing at an optimum rate in warm to hot temperatures (80 to 95 °F) and those growing at an optimum rate during cool periods of the year (60 to 75 °F). Similarly, moist, humid areas will limit the growth of some turf species, while semiarid regions might be more suitable for others. Grasses used for turf are divided into two groups, cool-season and warm-season. Generally, warm-season grasses are grown in the south and cool-season grasses in the north.

The United States can be split roughly into four large regions, as illustrated in Figure 2.1. The upper midwest and northeastern United States, together with western Oregon and Washington, comprise an area known as the cool, humid region. The southern United States, from eastern Texas to Florida, composes the warm, humid belt. In the western United States, the area north of a line from Denver to San Francisco is referred to as the cool, semiarid region; the area south of this line often experiences a warm, arid climate. Although this artificial division of the United States can serve as an approximation for determining the adaptation of turf species, the localized environment often supersedes regional conditions. An illustration of this might be high-elevation sites in

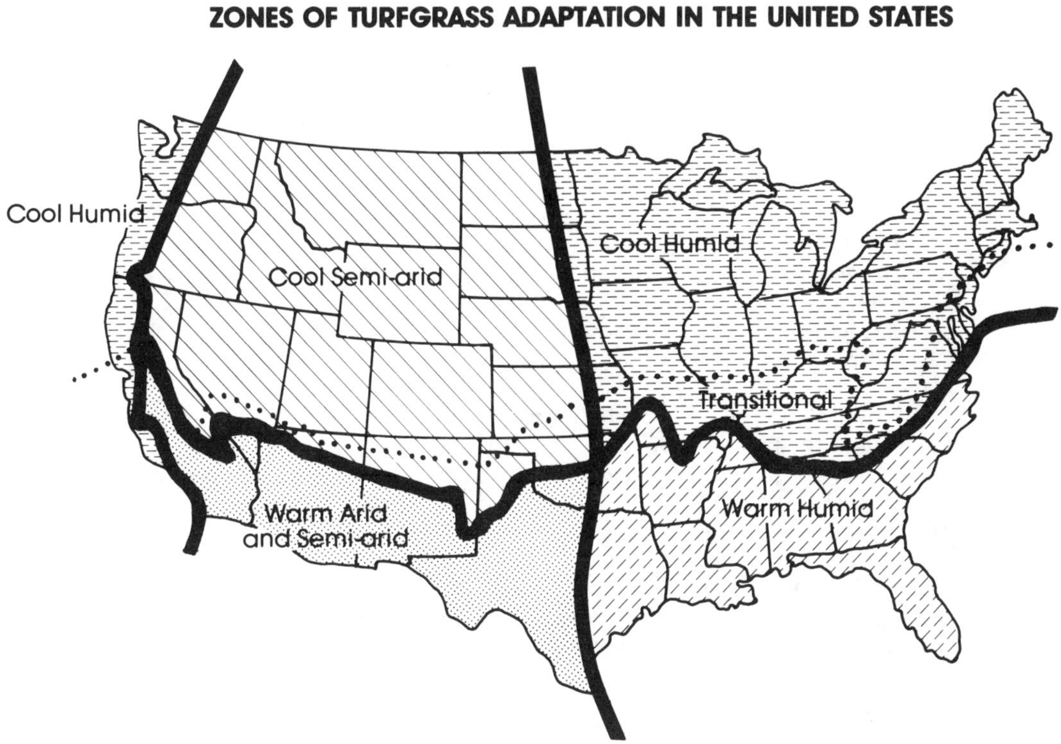

ZONES OF TURFGRASS ADAPTATION IN THE UNITED STATES

Figure 2–1   Zones of turfgrass adaptation in the United States.

the western United States, which often support cool-season turfs, whereas only warm-season turfgrasses perform well at lower elevations. A similar situation exists in the upper warm, humid region, where a warm-season species may survive on south-facing slopes but show little or no hardiness on a north-facing site. Table 2.1 lists turfgrass species for zones of adaptation in the United States.

TABLE 2.1   ADAPTATION OF TURFGRASS SPECIES TO THE UNITED STATES

Turfgrass species	Growth habit	Cultural intensity	Leaf texture
Cool, Humid Region			
Colonial bentgrass *Agrostis tenuis*	Short stolons or rhizomes	Medium to medium high	Medium fine to fine
Creeping bentgrass *Agrostis palustris*	Stoloniferous	Medium high to high	Fine
Velvet bentgrass *Agrostis canina*	Stoloniferous	High	Fine
Annual bluegrass *Poa annua*	Bunch-type to stoloniferous	Medium high to high	Medium to fine
Canada bluegrass *Poa compressa*	Rhizomatous	Low to medium	Medium to fine

Turfgrass species	Growth habit	Cultural intensity	Leaf texture
Cool, Humid Region			
Kentucky bluegrass *Poa pratensis*	Rhizomatous	Low to medium	Medium to fine
Rough bluegrass *Poa trivialis*	Short stolons	Low	Medium
Smooth brome *Bromus inermis*	Rhizomatous	Low	Coarse
Chewings fescue *Festuca rubra* ssp. *commutata*	Bunch-type	Low to medium	Very fine
Red fescue *Festuca rubra*	Short rhizomes	Low to medium	Very fine
Sheep fescue *Festuca ovina*	Bunch-type	Low	Very fine
Hard fescue *Festuca longifolia* (*F. ovina* ssp. *duriuscula*)	Bunch-type	Low to medium	Very fine
Tall fescue *Festuca arundinacea*	Bunch-type	Low to medium	Medium to coarse
Orchardgrass *Dactylis glomerata*	Bunch-type	Low	Coarse
Perennial ryegrass *Lolium perenne*	Bunch-type	Medium to medium high	Medium to fine
Timothy *Phleum pratense*	Bunch-type	Low	Coarse
Cool and Warm-Arid Regions			
Blue grama *Bouteloua gracilis*	Short rhizomes	Low to medium low	Fine to medium
Buffalograss *Buchloe dactyloides*	Stoloniferous	Low to medium	Fine to medium
Sideoats grama *Bouteloua curtipendula*	Short rhizomes	Low	Fine to medium
Fairway wheatgrass *Agropyron cristatum*	Bunch-type	Low to medium	Medium to coarse
Western wheatgrass *Agropyron smithii*	Rhizomatous	Low to medium	Medium fine to coarse
Warm, Humid Region			
Bahiagrass *Paspalum notatum*	Short rhizomes and stolons	Low to medium	Medium to coarse
Bermudagrasses *Cynodon* spp.	Stoloniferous and rhizo- matous	Low to high	Medium to fine
Carpetgrasses *Axonopus* spp.	Stoloniferous	Low to medium	Medium coarse to coarse
Centipedegrass *Eremochloa ophiuroides*	Stoloniferous	Medium	Medium to medium coarse

Turfgrass species	Growth habit	Cultural intensity	Leaf texture
Warm, Humid Region			
Kikuyugrass *Pennisetum clandestinum*	Rhizomatous and stoloniferous	Medium	Medium to coarse
St. Augustinegrass *Stenotaphrum secundatum*	Stoloniferous	Medium	Coarse
Zoysiagrasses *Zoysia* spp.	Stoloniferous and rhizomatous	Medium to high	Medium to fine

BLENDS AND MIXTURES

With few exceptions, turf sites are generally planted with more than one cultivar or species of turfgrass. Frequently, a blend of two or more cultivars of the same species of grass are utilized or a mixture of two or more species are combined for the final plant selection. For low-maintenance areas, turfgrass mixtures are often advantageous due to their wide adaptability to various environmental conditions. Table 2.2 lists suggested species and mixtures for turf use. Several turfgrass species, such as Kentucky bluegrass, have cultivars which are particularly adapted to low-maintenance conditions. Many cultivars of Kentucky bluegrass are particularly adapted to medium or medium-high maintenance levels. Due to the wider range of maintenance techniques, medium-maintained turf provides greater flexibility in the selection of turfgrass species and cultivars. A state turfgrass extension specialist or county extension adviser (often called a county agent) is a good source for information on locally adapted turfgrass cultivars.

TABLE 2.2 SUGGESTED TURFGRASS BLENDS AND MIXTURES

Blend or mixture	Potential turf quality	Maintenance level	Adapted environment	Suggested seeding rate (lb/1000 sq ft)
Cool-Arid or Cool-Humid Regions				
Kentucky bluegrass				
Improved varieties	Good to excellent	Medium to high	Full sun	1 to 2
Common types	Fair to good	Low to medium	Full sun	1 to 2
Kentucky bluegrass[a]/ fine fescue 50:50	Fair to good	Low to medium	Partial shade	3 to 4
Fine fescue	Poor to fair	Low	Partial shade to full sun	3 to 5
Kentucky bluegrass/ perennial ryegrass 75:25	Good	Medium to high	Full sun	2 to 3
Rough bluegrass	Fair	Low	Partial shade	1 to 3
Tall fescue	Fair to good	Low to medium	Partial shade to full sun	4 to 7
Fairway wheatgrass	Fair	Low	Full sun	3 to 5

TABLE 2.2 SUGGESTED TURFGRASS BLENDS AND MIXTURES (continued)

Blend or mixture	Potential turf quality	Maintenance level	Adapted environment	Suggested seeding rate (lb/1000 sq ft)
Cool-Arid or Cool-Humid Regions				
Bentgrass	Excellent	High	Partial shade to full sun	0.5 to 1
Zoysiagrass	Good to excellent	Medium to high	Full sun	Vegetatively established, (occasionally seeded)
Transition Regions				
Kentucky bluegrass/ perennial ryegrass 75:25	Good	Low to medium	Full sun	2 to 3
Tall fescue	Fair to good	Low to medium	Partial shade to full sun	4 to 7
Tall fescue/ Kentucky bluegrass 90:10	Fair to good	Low to medium	Partial shade to full sun	4 to 7
Zoysiagrass	Good to excellent	Medium to high	Full sun	Vegetatively established
Warm-Arid or Warm-Humid Regions				
Bermudagrass				
Hybrid	Excellent	Medium to high	Full sun	Vegetatively established
Common type	Good	Low to medium	Full sun	1 to 2
Tall fescue	Fair to good	Low to medium	Partial shade to full sun	5 to 7
Bahiagrass	Fair	Low	Full sun	4 to 6
Buffalograss	Fair to good	Low to medium	Full sun	3 to 6
Centipedegrass	Fair to good	Low	Full sun	¼ to ½
Zoysiagrass	Good to excellent	Medium to high	Partial shade to full sun	Vegetatively established
St. Augustinegrass	Fair to good	Low to medium	Partial shade to full sun	Vegetatively established

[a]Select Kentucky bluegrass cultivars which have been judged to be partially adapted to shade. Consult with state turfgrass extension specialist.

SEEDING OR VEGETATIVE ESTABLISHMENT

Before selecting the appropriate blend or mixture of turfgrass, it is necessary to determine which types of planting materials are available. Many turfgrass species, particularly in the warm-season group, do not produce adequate seed for commercial production. These grasses are available only as vegetative material and must be transplanted in some way. Although seed is available for some species, such as Kentucky bluegrass, vegetative planting through the use of sod can offer a much reduced time interval for establishment.

The time interval for establishment is reduced due to the fact that mature turfgrass plants are installed. It is erroneous to surmise that less site preparation is necessary than would be appropriate for seeding. When the proper sod bed is not provided, it is only a matter of time before the quality of the turf declines (*Color plate 1*). While the cost of site preparation is similar for either seeding or vegetative propagation, material cost is generally less for seeding. Seeding provides a greater cultivar selection for many species. Seeding also minimizes thatch-accumulation problems. Any thatch present on the site can be removed prior to seeding. Establishment is more rapid, however, through vegetative propagation, particularly with sod. The interval of development necessary for sod to provide usable turf is minimal—in many cases, only a few days.

The notion of an instant turf with sod installation is realistic, but as with all plants, a period of initial growth and rooting is necessary. This solid or continuous covering of the surface minimizes competition from germinating annual weeds and provides for lower water requirements than is necessary for seeded areas.

Along with the advantages of vegetative propagation, there are distinct disadvantages. Sodding generally represents a much higher establishment cost per square foot compared to seeding. Although properly produced sod presents a minimal thatch layer, some organic debris will be placed on the soil surface. Seeding, however, can present a susceptible host for seedling diseases and cause a greater threat of soil erosion. Table 2.3 illustrates the advantages and disadvantages for either seeding and vegetative establishment.

TABLE 2.3 COMPARISON OF SEEDING OR VEGETATIVE ESTABLISHMENT OF TURFGRASSES

Establishment method	Advantages	Disadvantages
Seeding	Less costly, greater varietal selection in mixture design, no initial thatch	Slow to establish, high initial water requirements, greater possibility of erosion, susceptibility to seedling pests, weeds present until cover established
Vegetative propagation	Rapid establishment, good soil erosion protection, minimizes potential for competing weeds, lower water requirements than seed, assurance of a stand	High cost, heavy weight, introduction of thatch layer, potential soil-layering problems, limited varietal or species selection

PREPARING THE SITE

Many future problems in the care of a new turf can be avoided by following the appropriate steps in establishment for the site:

1. Control perennial grasses.
2. Rough-grade the area to be planted for the desired slope and uniformity of the surface.

3. Make soil modifications if appropriate and install drainage systems when necessary.
4. Apply pH amendments and basic fertilizer as indicated by soil tests.
5. Plow, rototill, disc, or otherwise work the soil to a depth of at least 6 in.
6. Remove stones, stumps, dead roots, masonry, boards, or other debris.
7. Grade the area to a smooth, uniform surface free of depressions or high spots.
8. Apply nitrogen fertilizer and rake into the soil surface.
9. Plant seeds or vegetative materials, providing firm contact with the soil.
10. Roll with a weighted roller to provide contact of the seed or vegetative material with the soil.
11. Mulch the seedbed with weed-free straw or other suitable material.
12. Irrigate to provide uniform moisture at the soil surface for proper establishment.

Weed Control

One of the largest causes of seedling failure is competition by weeds. Often in the renovation of an existing turf, the old turfgrass can survive if not properly controlled, and become a troublesome weed in the newly established turf. Perennial weedy grasses such as bentgrass, quackgrass, and bermudagrass can persist throughout the life of the new turf. Effective control measures for removing these weeds in an established turf are not available. An application of a suitable nonselective herbicide (see Table 3.5 for chemical weed control recommendations) may be adequate to control most perennial grasses. However, repeat applications may be necessary. For the renovation of established turf, the dead plant material may need to be removed from the site to allow preparation of a suitable seedbed.

Soil Testing

Prior to disturbing the soil on the site, representative soil samples should be obtained to determine the need for soil amendments. Soil under turf should be tested routinely every 3 to 5 years by a reputable laboratory. Test results can be utilized to determine necessary fertilization needs. Changes in pH can also be detected. If the pH is found to be excessively high, acidifying materials such as elemental sulfur, sulfuric acid, aluminum sulfate, or iron sulfate may be utilized to lower the pH. The quantity of materials required will depend on the targeted pH level and the soil's resistance to the change in pH (buffering capacity). Contact your state turfgrass extension specialist for recommendations on pH amendments for your state.

Soil samples should be taken when the soil temperature is above 50°F. This will ensure an accurate potassium test, which may report an elevated level from cold soil. Collect a soil sample from several locations in each area in which turfgrass will be planted. Do *not* take samples after recent additions of lime or immediately after fertilizer applications. Samples may be collected with a soil probe or by inserting a spade deeply into the ground and taking a vertical slice of the soil. Discard roots or other debris. The vertical slice should be approximately ½ in. in thickness, and 4 to 6 in. deep. Separate the thatch from the underlying soil and submit it as a separate sample. Obtain vertical slices from at least six to eight areas. These cores should be mixed in a nonmetallic container and a representative sample of approximately ½ pint of soil can be removed for submission to a soil testing laboratory. Enclose the sample in a soil testing sack or other nonglass container and pack in a sturdy carton. Mail the sample to a soil testing laboratory for a routine analysis. A routine analysis of soil includes tests for current levels of soil phosphorus, potassium, and a measurement of the soil reaction (pH). Valid interpretation of the soil test results is often dependent on accurate historical information of the site. Submit all pertinent information on the maintenance and care of the turf or any activities on the site over the past several seasons. The test results may indicate whether pH adjustment is required and if fertilization is necessary. For further information about soil tests and their interpretation, consult a county extension adviser in your area or the state turfgrass extension specialist.

Irrigation and Drainage

To maintain a medium- or high-level turf, supplemental irrigation during drought periods will be necessary. Irrigation can range from hand-set, flexible hose irrigation to a below-ground, automated system. The major difference is in convenience and efficiency. A good system, however, should be able to uniformly deliver 1 in. of water to all areas within a 24-hour period. The ability to provide moisture to the root zone can be limited largely by the rate at which the water will drain through the soil.

For medium- and high-maintenance areas, it might be necessary to install a drainage system to promote adequate movement of the water through the soil. Proper drainage for turf areas is important in the control of pests and proper root function. Any drainage system needs to provide for rapid removal of excessive water from the root zone after irrigation or rain. Drainage should be provided for at both surface and subsurface areas. Surface runoff should be diverted to collecting channels and then moved away from the turf site. For athletic fields, proper crowning of the field will ensure adequate surface drainage. Most drainage systems generally consist of a perforated drainage pipe on a bed of large aggregate materials such as pea gravel at the base of a trench. Several inches of pea gravel, and a layer of sand and/or topsoil, is then added to fill the trench. The distance between drain tiles is dependent on soil type; generally, 10- to 30-ft spacing is needed. To ensure that water can be moved rapidly away from the turf surface, French or open drains can be used. In this drainage system, the gravel layer is brought to the surface, which must remain open for efficient use of the system. A poorly installed drainage system can cause many future problems.

Modifying the Soil

Turfgrasses can survive and persist on almost any soil if adequate nutrients, water, and aeration are provided. Although turf can be grown on a heavy clay soil, a sandy loam soil is preferred, because turfgrass quality is generally better and management requirements are less. On turfs subject to heavy traffic, resistance to compaction is a highly desirable soil characteristic. Sand is usually resistant to compaction due to its large particle size and is used often in high-maintenance turfs. Most soils can be modified to improve their physical properties.

When soils are high in clay content, organic matter (peat, rotted sawdust, etc.) or sand can be mixed with the soil to improve aeration and drainage and reduce the potential for compaction. When adding organic matter, plan to add 10 to 15% by volume of material to the soil. Muck should be avoided because it frequently contains large amounts of dispersed clay and silt which will reduce the infiltration rate. When sand is utilized to increase the pore space in clay soils, it should be added in large enough quantities to be effective. The mixture should contain at least 80% sand. A choice of sands is not always possible, but if available, a fine sand with particles between 0.10 and 0.35 mm in diameter should be selected. Small additions of sand may be less effective and even harmful.

For high-maintenance turfs, root zones have been designed by extensive soil modification. Most root zones incorporate the use of large quantities of sand, from 80 to 100% of the total mixture. They require careful planning and construction but will provide a wear-resistant turf with the least maintenance outlay.

Droughty, sandy soils may be improved with the addition of organic matter or finer-textured soil. Four to six inches of loam soil, low in clay content, and uniformly incorporated into the top 6 in. of sand will substantially improve the water-holding capacity of the original soil. It will also provide better storage of essential plant nutrients. Any additional material added to the site should be free of perennial grass rhizomes, roots, or vegetative plant parts which might persist and increase in the newly establishing turf. Under a vigorously growing turf, soil conditions are generally improved without soil modification. This process, however, is relatively slow and may be offset by the compacting effects of severe traffic.

Droughty, sandy soils require a different fertilization program than would normally be used on a finer-textured soil. Due to the low water retention capacity of droughty soils, frequent light applications of soluble fertilizer or the use of slow-release fertilizers is necessary for uniform nutrient release. Deeper-rooted turfgrasses (i.e., tall fescue) may be selected to obtain water from a greater volume of soil when the water-holding capacity is low.

Adding Basic Fertilizer Requirements

Following the recommendations based on the soil test, any fertilizers and amendments should be added to the surface prior to tilling operations. Lime or sulfur used to adjust the pH to within the recommended range can be added in greater quantities than would normally be safe on the established turf. The pH amendment should be incorporated into the soil in a separate operation from the addition of basic fertilizers. Additions of phosphorus and potassium from either single or combined sources should also be thoroughly incorporated in the soil. (For details on fertilizer application and packaging, see page 27.) All materials should be mixed into the upper 6 in. of the soil. The use of a plow, disc, harrow, or rotary tiller will help to ensure thorough incorporation. After the addition of fertilizer materials, the rough or subsurface grade should be considered. A slope of 2 to 6% should be designed to allow surface runoff away from structures on the site. In areas with slopes greater than 25%, alternative methods such as terracing should be considered. Steep slopes are dangerous to mow. Constructing a terrace with a retaining wall, or landscaping the slope with ground covers, will provide an attractive alternative to the turf.

When extensive recontouring or modification of the soil takes place, special care is needed to ensure that the original soil level is retained around the base of existing trees. Construction of a stone-lined well or elevated terrace is necessary for the survival of trees.

After the rough slope is prepared, surface irregularities should be minimized to prevent low spots that might collect water and remain wet longer than surrounding areas. Surface irregularities can be minimized by rolling the area with a weighted roller prior to final grading.

Final Grade

After the incorporation of any soil amendment, a final grade should be prepared for the seed or sod bed. Final grading is similar to the subgrading, where gentle slopes of less than 6% should remain and slope away from existing structures. For seeding or vegetative plantings, a powdery surface is not beneficial. Remove all stones, soil clods greater than 1 in. in diameter, and any organic debris (sticks, twigs, or dead grass) that might interfere with the young seedlings. After the final raking of a surface, if the soil footprints more than 1 in., roll once with a weighted roller to minimize footprinting when the area is seeded or planted. The completed final grade should be level with or slightly below any paved walkways or road surfaces. For vegetatively established sites, the surface should be moist just prior to planting. It is advisable to plan to complete the final grade immediately prior to the planting period.

For high-maintenance turfs requiring an absolutely level surface, work should proceed while standing on large sheets of plywood or other suitable material to prevent changing the contour of the surface.

Nitrogen Fertilizer

A nitrogen fertilizer can be added after the final grade is prepared to help the young seedlings through the initial stages of establishment. A complete fertilizer containing nitrogen, phosphorus, and potassium may be applied at the rate of ½ lb of nitrogen per 1000 sq ft. Complete fertilizer rates are based on nitrogen because phosphorus and potassium vary a great deal in basic fertilizers.

Seeding

The best time for seeding is during late summer to early fall for cool-season turfs and late spring to early summer for warm-season turfs. Soil moisture and temperature are most favorable in the fall for rapid cool-season grass establishment and weed competition during early development of the turf is usually less severe. Early spring seeding is an alternative, but excessive soil moisture and severe competition from annual weeds can threaten successful establishment of cool-season turfs during the spring. Use of the selective preemergence herbicide Siduron can minimize competition from annual grasses (see Table 3.1), and some broadleaf weeds. Siduron is the only preemergence herbicide available that will selectively control summer annual grasses without injuring newly seeded turf. Midsummer plantings are frequently unsuccessful, due to high temperatures, drought, weed competition, or diseases.

When purchasing seed, the label should be examined to ensure adequate quality. The percentage of included turfgrass species and cultivars will be clearly listed on the label together with their tested percentage of germination. The percent germination is an indication of the seeds that can be expected to germinate under optimum conditions.

Together with germination, seed purity is important in determining the necessary seeding rate. Seed purity indicates the ratio of seed to other ingredients, which are also listed on the tag. Two important "other ingredients" are the percent crop and percent weed seed in the mixture. This seed can often be a source of weed problems after establishment. These contaminants should not be tolerated in the chosen seed for medium to highly maintained turfs. Certified seed ensures genetic purity and usually good quality.

The seeding rate may have to be increased if the germination or purity percentage is low or if unfavorable growing conditions are anticipated. For rapid establishment with minimum weed competition, plant approximately 10 to 15 seeds per square inch.

For uniform growth, distribute the seed evenly across the soil surface with the recommended rate range for the blend or mixture selected (see Table 2.2). A mechanical seeder or fertilizer spreader should be used for best distribution. Hand application of seed is an alternative but is generally less uniform. To ensure even distribution, apply one-half the recommended seeding rate in an east-west direction and one-half in a north-south direction. After seeding, rake the area lightly to cover the seed partially. For small areas, dragging the surface with the back side of a rake provides good seed/soil contact. An alternative to raking is the use of a weighted roller, metal door mat, or chain-link fence, which will ensure good seed/soil contact. Rollers using water for ballast should be checked for leaks to minimize the tracking or bunching of seed. Finally, the site should be irrigated after mulching, if necessary, (page 18) to provide adequate germination (page 19).

Hydroseeding.   An alternative to dry application of seed is hydroseeding. Seeds, together with fertilizer and a pulp fiber mulch, may be suspended in water and applied to the seedbed in a high-pressure stream of water. This method is very useful for establishing difficult-to-reach sites such as slopes or rocky areas. Hydroseeding can save considerable time in establishment by combining seeding and mulching operations. Hydroseeding is most successful on sites with adequate soil moisture.

Vegetative Planting

Sodding.   The installation of sod is an alternative to seeding, but is generally more costly. Table 2.3 compares the advantages and disadvantages of seeding or sodding. The major advantage of this alternative is the rapid establishment of turf and/or the short interval before the site becomes usable. One can install sod any time during the growing season. A sod bed is similar to a seedbed except the surface of the latter should be moist when the sod is laid, to promote rapid rooting. A leading cause of failure with sod establishment is improper preparation of the sod bed. Laying sod on a nonprepared, compacted soil will prevent root extension and causes rapid desiccation during stressful periods (*Color plate 1*). Lay the sod pieces with the edges snugly fitting and with ends staggered so that there are no cracks in the surface or overlapping. Stretching the sod excessively may result in shrinkage and openings in the surface during drying. Roll the sod at a 90° angle to the direction it was placed to ensure close contact with the underlying soil. This removes air pockets that would cause drying of the roots. On steep slopes, the sod should be pegged in place to prevent slippage. Water the sod thoroughly as soon as possible after laying. Daily watering during hot, dry weather, for the next 2 to 3 weeks, can provide adequate moisture during the rooting period. Less frequent watering after the sod is well knitted is required. It may take from 4 to 8 weeks for proper rooting of the newly installed sod. After that a sodded turf may be handled as an established turf. Sods that have been produced rapidly under good growing conditions will generally root much more slowly than sods that have been grown at a slower rate under moderate fertilization.

Although sod provides the most rapid cover, other vegetative planting techniques are available. Various methods of planting are often required for turfs that form poor or loose sods or for a more economical approach to establishment. Many turfgrasses, particularly the warm-season hybrids, do not produce fertile seed, and therefore vegetative methods of establishment must be used.

Establishment by plugs. Plugs are small pieces of sod, 2 or more inches wide, which are usually placed 1 to 2 in. in the soil and spaced 6 to 12 in. apart (Table 2.4).

TABLE 2.4 ESTABLISHMENT OF TURFGRASSES BY SPRIGS OR PLUGS

Turfgrass species	Planting method	Rate per/1000 sq ft
Bermudagrass	Sprigs or plugs in rows by hand or machine, 6 to 12 in. apart in 12-in. rows	1 bu of sprigs or 2-in. plugs on 6-in. spacings requiring 55 sq ft of sod
		2-in. plugs on 12-in. spacings requiring 28 sq ft of sod
Buffalograss	Seeding is usual method of establishment but can be plugged with 3- or 4-in. plugs by hand or machine	3-in. plugs on 12-in. spacing in rows 12 in. apart requiring 63 sq ft of sod
		4-in. plugs on 12-in. spacings in rows 12 in. apart requiring 112 sq ft of sod
Centipedegrass	Sprigs or plugs in rows 6 in. apart in 6-in. rows	Sprigs from 8 to 10 sq ft of sod or 2-in. plugs requiring 55 sq ft of sod
St. Augustinegrass	Sprigs or plugs, 6 to 12 in. apart, 6- to 12-in. row spacing	6 to 8 sq ft of sod if sprigging or 2-in. plugs on 6-in. spacing in rows 6 in. apart requiring 55 sq ft of sod
Zoysiagrass	Plugs 2 in. square, or sprigs 6 to 12 in. apart, 6- to 12-in. row spacing by hand or machine	6 to 8 sq ft of sod if sprigging or 2-in. plugs on 6-in. spacing in rows 6 in. apart requiring 55 sq ft of sod
		2-in. plugs on 12-in. spacing, rows 12 in. apart requiring 28 sq ft of sod

Many warm-season and some cool-season turfgrasses are available as plugs. Plugging tools may be purchased to simplify the extraction of soil and the insertion of a new plug. After planting, soil sould be packed firmly around the plugs and the area must be extensively watered. Moderate watering every day or two is usually adequate for proper establishment.

Establishment by sprigs.   Sprigs are individual stems, or small clusters of stems, used for vegetative establishment. They are planted in slits 2 to 3 in. deep and 6 to 12 in. apart (Table 2.4). The sprigs should be arranged in more-or-less continuous lines and placed in the slit so that the upper one-half of the stems is above the soil level. The slit should be backfilled with soil and then rolled to ensure close soil contact with the plant material. The water requirements are essentially the same as for plugs.

Establishment by broadcast sprigging.   Sod is shredded to produce large numbers of individual pieces of lateral stems. The sod should be shredded as fine as possible. Generally, 1 sq yd of bermudagrass or zoysiagrass sod will produce 1 bu of sprigs. However, the resulting sprigs should have at least two nodes on each stem. These stems should be applied uniformly over the area at a rate of 8 to 10 bu per 1000 sq ft, depending on the species (Table 2.4). Place additional soil over the sprigs or incorporate them into the existing soil by tilling or crimping to cover them partially. Whereas common bermudagrass sprigs can be buried, bermudagrass hybrid or other turfgrass sprigs must be exposed to the surface for their survival.

Rolling the area to firm the surface and ensure contact with the sprigs is essential. This method requires more water than other vegetative planting methods but provides the most rapid cover.

Mulching

Mulching after seeding or vegetative planting is recommended to reduce drying of the seedbed and provide a more suitable microenvironment for germination and early seedling development. Mulching also helps reduce erosion caused by wind or rain. One of the most common and effective sources of mulch is cereal straw (wheat, oats, rye, etc.). It can be spread uniformly over the seeded area at the rate of 25 to 50 lb per 1000 sq ft. Subsequent weed problems can occur when weed seed is brought to the site in the straw. Inspect all straw to ensure that it is free of weed pests. Even in a gentle breeze, keeping the straw in place can be a problem. Watering the straw immediately after distribution and rolling can help prevent bunching or movement of straw off the site. Nylon or jute netting can be put over the straw to help tack it down. The netting usually needs to be fastened or pegged to the soil. For large sloped areas, equipment that applies asphalt or other adhesive can be utilized to help tack down the straw.

Other organic materials can be used as mulches. Wood chips or shredded bark have proven to be effective as mulches and can represent an economical choice if available near the site of establishment. Fiberous peat, ground corncobs, and sawdust can also be used as mulches but should be partially rotted to prevent the tie-up of nutrients. These materials, if dry, also compete for water, adding to the irrigation requirement normally necessary.

Many synthetic mulches are commercially available. These may be shredded paper, woven paper net, burlap, fiberglass, wood pulp, or similar material. These mulches are particularly useful in hydroseeding. Their relative effectiveness in providing protection and preventing water evaporation is generally no better than that of natural materials such as straw.

Watering

Regardless of the method of establishment, watering is critical immediately following planting. The amount and frequency will depend on the soil type, wind, temperature, infiltration rate of the soil, and the duration and intensity of sunlight. Light daily watering for the first 2 to 3 weeks should be adequate for most times of the year. The crucial zone to keep damp is the upper inch of soil. More frequent watering may be necessary on hot, windy days to compensate for faster evaporation of water from the soil surface. The seedbed surface is extremely vulnerable to runoff or erosion during the initial period of germination. To ensure an even, light watering, use a mist nozzle to break up the water spray. Once the plant has established an extensive root system, frequent watering is no longer required.

MOWING

Start mowing a newly planted turfgrass area after the foliage has grown approximately 50% higher than the desired mowing height. This will remove not more than 33% of the leaf tissue at any one time. For example, a lawn maintained at a height of 2 in. should receive its first and all subsequent mowings when it reaches 3 in. in height. Approximate mowing heights for turfgrass blends and mixtures are given in Table 2.5. For the first several mowings after establishment, the mower blades should be kept extremely sharp

TABLE 2.5 SUGGESTED MOWING HEIGHTS FOR COMMON TURFGRASSES, BLENDS, AND MIXTURES

Blend or mixture	Cutting height (in.)
Bahiagrass	2 to 2½
Bermudagrass	³⁄₁₆ to 1
Buffalograss	1 to 2
Centipedegrass	1 to 1½
Creeping bentgrass	⅛ to ¾
Fine fescues	2 to 2½
Kentucky bluegrass/perennial ryegrass	1 to 2
Kentucky bluegrass	
Improved varieties	1 to 2
Common types	1½ to 2½
Kentucky bluegrass/red fescue	1½ to 2½
Tall fescue	1½ to 3
Zoysiagrass	½ to 1

to help prevent the seedlings from being pulled out of the soil. A high-quality turf requires regular mowing at the correct height with proper equipment. Mowing is essential to the development and maintenance of a dense, uniform surface and can effectively reduce the number of weed species (Chapter 3) that might invade a turfgrass stand.

Cutting Height

The correct cutting height depends primarily on the turfgrass species and cultivar used, environment (shade, etc.), and the intensity of management. Generally, the lower the cut of height, the higher the level of management required. Appropriate cutting heights for common turfgrasses and mixtures are listed in Table 2.5. A cutting-height range is presented in the table for each species or mixture, to account for variation in environments. For shaded or little-used turfs, the taller figure is appropriate. With the added stress of medium to high use and the potential for rapid growth in full sun, the shorter figure is preferred.

Cutting the grass too short weakens the turf and increases its susceptibility to weed invasions, disease and insect damage, injury from drought, and temperature extremes. Short mowing can also substantially reduce root, rhizome, and stolon development, particularly in the summer months, as well as minimize the ability of the turf to withstand stress. If the grass is cut too high, it often has a shaggy appearance that detracts from turf appearance.

Mowing Frequency

High, infrequent mowings can also reduce the density of most turf. Mowing frequency is dependent on the cutting height chosen and the rate of growth of the turf, rather than by fixed time intervals. Removal of more than one-third the total foliage of the turf in a single mowing can be detrimental. Scalping, or excessive defoliation of the turf, occurs when mowing removes more than 33% of the foliage, thus reducing the amount of leaves available for photosynthesis. For optimum growth, mow the turf when it exceeds 33% of the mowing height (Figure 2.2). Short mowing can also substantially reduce root development, particularly in summer months, as well as minimize the ability of the turf to withstand stress. Clippings are beneficial because they return essential plant elements and organic matter to the soil. If they are not excessively long and do not cover the turf surface after the mowing, it is unnecessary to remove clippings. They will generally sift down into the turf when dry. Mowing at the proper frequency will minimize the amount of grass clippings that remain on the turf surface. However, if there are large clumps of clippings, remove them to avoid smothering the turf.

Mowing Pattern

Alternating the pattern of mowing over the turf will cause the turf to grow more upright, providing a cleaner cut and enhanced appearance. A distinctive striped or checkerboard appearance will result, particularly with a reel-type mower and alternated patterns. If at all possible, 180 to 360° turns should be made off the mowing surface.

MOWING FREQUENCY

Figure 2–2 Mowing frequency based on growth rate.

Mowing Equipment

Reel mowers. There are two principal types of mowers for use on turf: reel and rotary. Reel mowers cut with a shearing action (Figure 2.3). If properly sharpened and adjusted, they provide the highest-quality cut available. Improper adjustment, however, leaves the turf surface with an uneven appearance and the grass leaves appear gray to brown and/or stringy. Grass leaves may also have a similar appearance if the reel or other cutting edge (bed knife) is dull. One disadvantage of reel-type mowers is the difficulty in mowing high-cut turf. Reel mowers cannot effectively mow turf that exceeds the center line of the reel. Mowing action is also disrupted on rough or irregular surfaces. Turfs with irregular surfaces should be smoothed through topdressing (page 26). Small pieces of debris such as stones and other hard objects can nick or mar cutting edges. Reel mowers also generally require more maintenance. Check the adjustment and sharpness of the cutting edge using the following steps:

1. Mount the mower stationary, allowing the reel to turn fully.
2. Place a strip of newspaper between the reel and the bed knife and rotate the reel slowly to cut the paper. The reel should rotate very smoothly with very little pressure, cutting the paper cleanly.
3. If the reel does not rotate or cut smoothly, adjust the movement by following the directions on the instructions that came with the mower.

Check the mowing height of the mower frequently. To ensure proper mowing heights, place the mower on a flat surface and measure the distance between the surface and the upper edge of bed knife with a small ruler. On most mowers, the cutting height

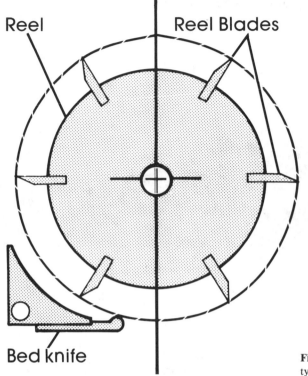

Reel

Reel Blades

Bed knife

Figure 2-3   Reel and bed knife of reel-type mower.

may be changed by raising or lowering the castings that hold the roller at the rear of the unit. If unable to adjust mowing height, consult the instructions that were included with the mower.

Rotary mowers.   Rotary mowers are an alternative to reel-type mowers and they have become quite popular because of their lower cost and ease of maintenance. These mowers can be dangerous, however, if not used properly. The rotary motion of the blade can project stones, pieces of metal, and other debris quite forcibly for long distances, possibly injuring the operator or other persons or animals in the area. To prevent accidents, check for loose debris in the area prior to mowing; always keep fingers and feet well away from the rotary mower housing when the engine is running. A good safety measure is to detach the spark plug wire from the spark plug after use and before any adjustments are made to the mower. Rotary mowers are more versatile than reel-type mowers. They have the ability to mow not only tall turf but also weeds and to mulch dry leaves. They are, however, not suitable for mowing turfs below 1 in.

The cutting height of rotary mowers can be adjusted by raising or lowering the wheels. Place the mower on a flat surface, measure the height of the cutting blade from the surface, and raise or lower until the desired height is reached. To ensure a uniform, clean cut, rotary blades should be removed and sharpened periodically. Dull blades tend to tear the grass leaves, eventually causing deterioration of the turf (*Color plate 2*).

Flail and sickle-bar mowers. Two additional mower types are often used on low-maintenance turf. Flail mowers have a horizontally aligned shaft with vertical rotating blades. This type of mower will provide some give when coming in contact with a solid object and is used to cut tall growth up to 12 in. above the cutting height. A sickle-bar mower provides a finer cut through a scissors action between a moving cutting blade and a stationary one. The movement between blades is in a horizontal plane. Sickle-bar mowers are generally used to cut tall turf with the cutting units extended off the side of a tractor. One typical use is on highway rights-of-way.

Growth Retardation of Turf

Several chemical growth inhibitors of turfgrasses are currently available. These materials, when applied at the appropriate time, can help reduce the normal mowing frequency during periods of maximum growth. Many variables must be anticipated for the successful application of a growth retardant. The rate and timing of the application of a retardant is dependent on the turf species. The competitive nature of turf, through its rapid growth, provides a means for pest control and resistance to stress. Retarded turfs generally require pest control and are not effective during stressful periods. Table 2.6 lists currently available growth retardants and some of the necessary information for their use.

The successful application of a growth retardant is dependent on environmental conditions both at the time of application and for the period of growth reduction. In general, the turf to be treated must be actively growing and totally free of signs of winter dormancy. In most cases, growth and development stops soon after application. For turfs in a stage of change from winter dormancy to full green-up, this will leave the dead or dying older leaves visible, providing a reduction in quality.

Turfgrass growth retardants can be grouped according to their mode of action. The first group includes those retardants that suppress both the development and growth of a plant, preventing the normal transition of vegetative growth to a mature flowering plant. The growth retardants melfluidide, maleic hydrazide, and amidochlor are examples of this group and will reduce or eliminate the production of seedheads if applied prior to their development. It is important to apply the retardant while the turf is still in a vegetative stage of growth. If any portion of a seedhead is visible from the tip of the sheath, the effectiveness of the growth retardant in reducing seedhead production will be minimized.

The second group of growth retardants are those that suppress growth only. This is generally achieved by reducing the production of gibberellic acid, a plant hormone necessary for shoot growth. While growth is suppressed, the plant generally matures and produces an inflorescence but the whole plant is a much reduced size. Flurprimidol, paclobutrazol, and other experimental growth retardants exhibit these characteristics. Flurprimidol has varying effects on different species and is most often used in mixed bentgrass and *Poa annua* turfs to provide a competitive advantage for growth of creeping bentgrass through greater growth suppression of the *Poa annua*.

Although sequential or repeat applications of growth retardants can be effective for long-term growth suppression, the possibility of injury to the turf is enhanced. Growth retardants are generally used to minimize the mowing requirements during peak periods of mowing in spring or summer. The response of the turf to an application of a growth

TABLE 2.6 TURFGRASS GROWTH RETARDANTS AND THEIR PROPERTIES

Trade name	Common name	Mode of action	Formula-tion	Site of uptake in plant	Labeled species
Royal Slo-Gro, MH-30	Maleic hydrazide	Growth and develop-ment	1.5S	Foliar	Kentucky bluegrass, fescues, bromegrass, orchardgrass, quackgrass, and perennial ryegrass
Embark	Melfluidide	Growth and develop-ment	2S	Foliar	Kentucky and annual bluegrass, fescues, perennial ryegrass, timothy, reed canarygrass, quackgrass, kikuyugrass, crested wheatgrass, orchard-grass, smooth bromegrass, centipedegrass, and St. Augustinegrass
Limit	Amidochlor	Growth and develop-ment	4F	Roots	Kentucky bluegrass, fescues, and perennial ryegrass
Cutless[b]	Flurprimidol	Growth suppres-sion only	50WP	Roots	Annual bluegrass and creeping bentgrass
Maintain CF 125	Chlorflurenol	Growth and develop-ment		Foliar	Kentucky bluegrass, fescues, and perennial ryegrass

[a]AI, active ingredient.

[b]Cutless is not currently labeled for use on turf. However, a turf label is expected in the near future.

retardant will often depend on the local environment. Consult your state turfgrass extension specialist for the optimal use of a growth retardant in your area.

Research in the area of turfgrass growth retardants is rapidly expanding and many materials, such as paclobutrazol (PP333, Parlay), EPTC (Short-stop), and ethephon (Ethrel), are being evaluated for their effectiveness on turf. It is important to remember that chemical growth inhibitors or retardants will not totally substitute for mowing and should be used in integration with normal maintenance.

Application rate (lb AI/acre)[a]	Weeks of effective growth reduction	Seedhead suppression	Comments
2.25 to 3	4 to 8	Good	Bentgrass may be inhibited but often shows discoloration effects. Do not use on St. Augustinegrass. Not recommended as mowing reduction treatment for fine turf areas.
0.063 to 0.126 and 0.25 to 0.38	4 to 8	Excellent	Lower rates are for seedhead control of *Poa annua,* without growth reduction for fine turf areas. Rates in excess of those recommended can cause discoloration or severe injury to turf. Surfactant should be added to Embark except for *Poa annua* seedhead control.
2.5	4 to 8	Very good	Effectiveness of Limit can be reduced if not watered in within a short period of time after application. Application during rain is optimum.
0.5 to 1.0	6 to 10	None	Cutless can provide greater growth suppression of annual bluegrass rather than creeping bentgrass in mixed turfs providing for the eventual elimination of annual bluegrass. The growth-suppression effects of Cutless can be minimized through the application of gibberellic acid.
	4 to 8	Good	

LEVELING THE SITE

With proper establishment of a firm, uniform seedbed, leveling should not be required. However, when irregularities do occur in the surface of a newly planted or established turf, several techniques for leveling can be utilized. For small irregularities, a weighted roller can be used to aid in removing the depressions. To avoid severe compaction, however, the ground should be moist but not wet when rolled. For large ridges or depressions, rolling is of very little value. After full establishment of the turf, the sod can be cut and removed. The area underneath can then be leveled before replacing the sod.

Topdressing

Topdressing, the application of a light layer of soil to the surface of the turf, can also be used to smooth irregularities. The key to efficient topdressing is through repeated light applications of soil over an extended period. The texture of materials chosen for topdressing should closely resemble the texture of the underlying soil. No more than ¼ in. of topdressing material should be applied at any time. The best rule of thumb in topdressing is "light and often."

IRRIGATION

Rainfall usually provides adequate moisture for cool-season turfgrass growth during cool spring and fall periods for many areas of the country. Extended drought periods during summer and early fall, however, may cause the grass to wilt and turn brown. In the arid and semiarid west, natural rainfall is both limited and frequently poorly distributed when it occurs. Irrigation is mandatory for much of the turf in this area. Soil moisture is crucial for active growth of warm-season turfs during the warm months of summer (April through October). Unfortunately, in most warm-season areas, rainfall is minimal during the summer months. Therefore, supplemental irrigation is usually necessary for suitable turf. Many turfs, while maintaining adequate cover under natural precipitation only, provide superior turf with supplemental irrigation. Turfgrasses such as Kentucky bluegrass may turn brown and go dormant in summer months without supplemental irrigation. These grasses generally recover and return to normal levels of quality in cooler weather. The decision as to when to irrigate will depend on the quality of the turf desired, the availability of water, the probable duration and severity of the drought conditions, and probably most important, the budget.

Duration of Irrigation

To maintain a high-quality appearance throughout the growing season, an area should be irrigated as soon as the turf shows symptoms of wilting. Visual symptoms can be a rapid darkening in color or grayish appearance. Other symptoms include the lack of resilience when the turf receives traffic (i.e., the appearance of footprints). Ideally, all turfs should be irrigated to saturate the root-zone area thoroughly. Following irrigation, the turf should not receive water until further signs of wilting appear. Apply enough water to moisten the soil to a depth of at least 6 in. For a medium-textured soil, this might be equivalent to 1 in. of water (approximately 600 gal per 1000 sq ft). The amount of water received by the soil surface can be measured simply by placing several coffee cans or other receptacles within the irrigation zone. The time interval required to apply the recommended quantity of water can then be used as a "yardstick" for future irrigations.

Frequency of Irrigation

Surface runoff can be a problem in soil with a low infiltration rate. Dividing the total irrigation requirement into several shorter intervals allows a slow wetting of the soil and minimizes runoff. Light, frequent irrigations can lead to turf deterioration as a result of high moisture levels in the upper root zone. Soil saturated for extended periods places stress on the turf, which can lead to direct damage by diseases, insects, and weed competition. Damage can also result from the proliferation of roots in this restricted surface area, preventing the plant from obtaining moisture from lower soil areas during drought periods. The turf may receive irrigation any time during the day as long as the rate of application does not exceed the infiltration rate. Irrigation during periods of bright sunlight is inefficient, with up to 40% water losses due to evaporation. The potential for disease is reduced by irrigating from early morning to midday to minimize the time interval during which leaf surfaces remain wet.

Water Quality

The benefits of irrigation are limited by the quality of the water supplied to the turf area. The quality requirements for irrigation water are not nearly as stringent as those for human consumption. A few basic problems can occur with low-quality water. When the water source lacks clarity due to the suspension of soil particles, (silts, clays, or sand) the soil can become impervious to further watering, due to the clogging of pore spaces from the introduced particles. Sand suspended in irrigation water has an abrasive effect on irrigation equipment, quickly reducing the accuracy of the delivery system.

Often, irrigation reservoirs, ponds, lakes, streams, and so on, receive runoff from surrounding agricultural areas. Pesticides in the runoff can be transported to the turf through irrigation, causing severe damage. Periodic appraisal of the irrigation source from freedom of pesticides or other toxic chemicals is a good practice. The last area of concern for the quality of irrigation water is the transmission of salts to the turfgrass site. Even dilute concentrations of salts, particularly sodium salts, added to a turf with a low infiltration rate can cause the gradual breakdown of soil structure. The analysis of salt or salt-related materials in water is a simple and inexpensive procedure.

Irrigation Methods

Irrigation systems come in many different shapes and sizes. The majority of components in the system can be placed either above or below ground. Second, water flow and distribution patterns can be controlled manually or automatically. Medium-maintained turf can sometimes be conveniently irrigated with aboveground manual systems. With higher maintenance requirements, below-ground automatic irrigation systems are necessary to deliver the required water. Regardless of the system chosen, the design and installation should be left to a qualified professional.

TURFGRASS NUTRITION

Turfgrasses, like all plant life, require varying amounts of up to 16 common elements for optimum development and growth. When the soil pH is between 6.0 and 7.0, many if not most of these essential elements are supplied by the natural weathering and decomposition process of native soil. Soils in many areas of the United States, however, do not supply adequate quantities of nitrogen, phosphorus, potassium, and certain other elements, resulting in a loss of turfgrass quality.

Proper fertilization is important, therefore, for a healthy dense stand of turf that will resist weeds and recover quickly from disease or insect injury. Table 2.7 lists the essential elements necessary for turfgrass growth. Nitrogen (N), phosphorus (P), and potassium (K) are required in the largest quantities and are the three basic components of many turf fertilizers. When all three elements are included in a material, it is said to be a complete fertilizer. Phosphorus (P) and potassium (K) requirements vary widely across the United States. The status of P and K in the soil can easily be determined through soil analysis. Soil tests will point out the relative requirements of P and K needed for optimum turfgrass growth. Consult the state turfgrass extension specialist or county extension adviser for interpretation of soil test results to determine the proper fertilization rates for phosphorus or potassium.

TABLE 2.7 ESSENTIAL ELEMENTS FOR TURFGRASS GROWTH

Element	Symbol	Source
Nitrogen	N	Fertilizer, soil organic matter
Phosphorus	P	Fertilizer, soil, soil organic matter
Potassium	K	Fertilizer, soil
Magnesium	Mg	Fertilizer, liming materials, soil
Calcium	Ca	Fertilizer, liming materials, soil
Sulfur	S	Fertilizer, soil, soil organic matter
Iron	Fe	Fertilizer, soil
Manganese	Mn	Generally soil only
Zinc	Zn	Generally soil only
Copper	Cu	Generally soil only
Boron	B	Generally soil only
Molybdenum	Mo	Generally soil only
Chlorine	Cl	Generally soil only
Carbon	C	Atmosphere
Hydrogen	H	Water
Oxygen	O	Water

pH Amendments

The normal pH range for soil is 4.0 to 8.0. In general, turfgrasses will grow best when the pH is between 6.0 and 7.0. Some turf species (fescues, centipedegrass, etc.), however, thrive well at a pH lower than 6.0. Corrective materials can be added to a soil when pH levels are outside this range. The effectiveness of pH amendments is less throughout the root zone when surface applied than when incorporated during establishment.

If the soils are excessively acid (below pH 5.5), ground limestone or other liming materials can be added to the surface in small amounts. The material and quantities to be added to the turf will vary depending on the soil. When lime additions are required, the soil testing laboratory will usually provide a local recommendation. If this is not available, contact the state extension turfgrass specialist.

For soils that are alkaline, acidifying materials such as elemental sulfur, sulfuric acid, aluminum sulfate, and iron sulfate can be used to lower the pH. These materials potentially have toxic effects on the turf if added in large quantities. The total requirements, as indicated by the soil test recommendations, should be split into smaller amounts and applied in several applications. If soil pH is amended, additional testing to ensure changes in the soil reaction is necessary. The soil pH should be tested every 6 months until the pH is within the recommended range.

Nitrogen, the element required in the largest quantity, is less stable in soil and can easily be removed through leaching with the application of water. Soil test levels of available nitrates can vary widely even in a short period of time. Soil tests for nitrogen are therefore of very little value in determining the nitrogen requirements of an actively growing turf. Nitrogen is generally applied on a scheduled basis to provide a uniform, timely release of nitrogen.

Nitrogen can comprise up to 5% of the total weight of a turfgrass after the water is removed. This large requirement makes turfgrasses more responsive to nitrogen than to any other mineral nutrient. Nitrogen is taken up by roots and used by the plant in the nitrate (NO_3) or ammonium (NH_4) form.

Nitrogen Sources

Any nitrogen fertilizer applied to the turf must therefore be converted into NO_3 and/or NH_4 before it can be utilized. The complexity of this conversion to nitrate or ammonium will largely determine how quickly the turfgrass responds to an application of fertilizer and also how persistent this effect will be. Turfgrass fertilizers can be grouped into three broad sources, depending on the relative speed of conversion to a usable form. Table 2.8 lists the common turfgrass fertilizer sources.

TABLE 2.8 COMMON TURF FERTILIZER SOURCES

Source	Usual analysis ($N-P_2O_5-K_2O$)
Water-soluble	
Ammonium nitrate	33-0-0
Ammonium sulfate	21-0-0
Diammonium phosphate	20-50-0
Monoammonium phosphate	11-48-0
Muriate of potash	0-0-60
Potassium nitrate	13-0-44
Sulfate of potash	0-0-50
Superphosphate	0-20-0
Treble superphosphate	0-45-0
Urea	45-0-0
Slowly soluble	
IBDU (isobutylidine diurea)	31-0-0
Oxamide	32-0-0
Urea formaldehyde (UF)	38-0-0
Slow-release	
Milorganite	6-4-0
SCU (sulfur-coated urea)	32-0-0 to 36-0-0[a]

[a]Nitrogen content is dependent on the sulfur shell thickness.

Water-soluble nitrogen.   Water-soluble or rapidly available nitrogen, which occurs in such common materials as ammonium nitrate, ammonium sulfate, and urea, provides the quickest response after application. In most cases, one of the two plant available compounds (NO_3^- or NH_4^+) is provided by the simple dissolution of the material. Urea conversion processes take slightly longer but still occur within a few days under most conditions. These materials are also the least expensive fertilizer sources, due to their relative ease of manufacture, but have the high potential for causing chemical or fertilizer injury to turf when not properly applied (see Chemical Injury, page 39).

Slowly soluble nitrogen.   Slowly soluble forms of nitrogen include natural organic materials (activated sewage sludge and animal by-products) and synthetic organic materials which are largely urea derivatives. Slowly soluble sources either have a low degree of solubility, allowing gradual dissolution over an extended period, or require some breakdown or conversion by native soil microorganisms. The latter is greatly influenced by the soil temperature. As the soil warms through the season, populations of microorganisms increase, releasing greater amounts of plant-available nitrogen.

Nitrogen sources such as IBDU and Oxamide are more efficient during cooler periods of the year because they are not dependent on microbial activity as ureaform sources. Although these materials are more expensive per pound of nitrogen, due to higher manufacturing costs, they are highly efficient as a result of minimal nitrogen losses through leaching. An additional benefit of slowly soluble forms of nitrogen is the relative safety from chemical injury to the turf during application. This is a necessity when irrigation is not available.

Slow-release nitrogen.   This source of nitrogen is actually a water-soluble or rapidly available form, but it is encapsulated to prevent its rapid dissolution. Plastic and/or sulfur is the most common encapsulating material. These form a continuous membrane around a soluble form of fertilizer, allowing a gradual diffusion of fertilizer into the soil solution. If the coating material becomes cracked or split, rapid dissolution occurs and the material responds like a water-soluble source. Careful application techniques are imperative to ensure the coating integrity of particles during application. Generally, a rotary-type spreader (see Fertilizer Spreaders, page 33, and Figure 6.12) will minimize the breakage of these materials. Slow-release nitrogen forms are also more expensive per pound of nitrogen than water-soluble nitrogen forms. However, they generally provide a greater degree of safety with an extended period of nitrogen release.

Liquid Fertilizer Sources

The use of liquid fertilizer is new to the turfgrass industry. Such fertilizers have been widely used for less than 10 years. Prior to 1978, liquid fertilizer solutions were combinations of urea or nitrogen salts and water, targeted for foliar uptake. As the professional lawn care industry developed, many of the larger companies expanded nationally. Their areas of operation encompassed a wide variety of turfs and soil types. This brought about the need for greater control of the fertilizer materials and the ability to adapt application programs to a particular environment. Liquid-applied fertilizers offer both ease of handling and versatility of materials adjustment for each application. New sources of fluid fertilizer were developed to meet this demand. Materials such as Formolene, FLUF,

FAN, and others were developed for the professional lawn care market. Although most of the materials (Formolene, Folian, etc.) are a soluble source, the potential for turfgrass injury with these materials has been reduced. Formolene is a urea formaldehyde solution which offers greater safety in application than that of other soluble sources.

In addition to the soluble sources, several true liquid slow-release sources have become available. FLUF, flowable urea formaldehyde, is a stable suspension of ureaform that will provide a gradual release of nitrogen over an 8- to 10-week period. Slower-release sources such as Nitroform, with hot-water-insoluble nitrogen (HWIN), are available for liquid application in the form of a powder. These suspensions are much less stable, however, and require constant agitation for proper application. As with granular applications of Nitroform, some of the nitrogen is carried over into future growing seasons.

Research has shown little difference in fertilizer efficiency between liquid or dry application. The use of a fluid-applied fertilizer is a matter of convenience and versatility. This type of formulation allows for the easy addition of other fertilizer nutrients or pesticides and is widely accepted in the professional lawn care service industry.

Turfgrass Nitrogen Requirements

The total nitrogen requirement for any turf varies widely according to the turfgrasses used, maintenance level, and whether clippings are removed or allowed to remain on the site. Table 2.9 lists the range of nitrogen fertilizer needs for common turfgrasses. The suggested amounts reflect the soluble nitrogen necessary to support high-quality turf growth. If slowly soluble or slow-release forms are utilized, larger quantities can be added to the turf for longer persistence.

TABLE 2.9 NITROGEN FERTILIZER RATES FOR COMMON TURFGRASSES

Turfgrass	lb N/1000 sq ft/year
Bahiagrass	0 to 1
Bermudagrass	4 to 8
Buffalograss	1 to 2
Carpetgrass	0 to 1
Centipedegrass	0 to 1
Creeping bentgrass	4 to 6
Dichondra	2 to 4
Fine-leaf fescues	1 to 2
Kentucky bluegrass	
Improved varieties	2 to 4
Common types	1 to 2
Perennial ryegrass	2 to 4
St. Augustinegrass	2 to 4
Tall fescue	2 to 4
Zoysiagrass	2 to 4

Any single application of fertilizer should deliver no more than 2 lb of soluble nitrogen per 1000 sq ft to the turf. For sensitive turfgrasses such as bentgrasses, fine fescues, and so on, this rate can be excessive and lower rates are generally recommended. Always apply the fertilizer uniformly when the foliage is dry. To ensure even distribution, apply one-half of the fertilizer application in a north-south direction and the other half in an east-west direction. This technique will also minimize any streaking or overlapping appearance that might otherwise occur with a single-pass application. After distribution, irrigate the area thoroughly to remove all fertilizer from the leaf tissue.

Since fertilizer elements must eventually enter the soil solution, there is little difference between liquid or dry fertilizer sources. Liquid-applied urea, however, is more susceptible to loss through volatilization if allowed to remain on the leaf blades for extended periods of time. It is advisable to irrigate immediately after the application of a liquid fertilizer. This will help to minimize volatilization losses and will also ensure a rapid turf response to the fertilizer by moving it to the root zone, where it can be absorbed. The rinsing of leaf blades will prevent damage from fertilizer injury which can easily occur during hot days.

Application Schedules

Regardless of the type of nitrogen used, fertilizer applications should be applied at scheduled intervals to provide maximum benefit to the turf with minimum risk of plant injury. Generally, fertilizers are applied in the greatest quantity and frequency during periods of rapid growth. For cool-season turfs, spring and fall are the optimum times for fertilization, whereas summer fertilization is of greatest value to warm-season turf. Table 2.10 lists a generalized fertilizer schedule for most turfs. The suggested schedules are based on the use of water-soluble nitrogen and can be adjusted accordingly if a slow-release material is used. When soil test results are not available, a general ratio to follow might be a complete fertilizer with a 3:1:2 ratio of N, P_2O_5, and K_2O, respectively. Frequent light applications of fertilizer will generally result in optimum turfgrass quality.

TABLE 2.10 FERTILIZER APPLICATION SCHEDULES FOR COMMON TURFGRASSES

Turfgrass mixture or blend	Application (lb N/1000 sq ft)		
	Spring	Summer	Fall
Bahiagrass		0 to 1	
Bermudagrass		4 to 8[a]	
Buffalograss	0 to 1	0 to 1	
Carpetgrass		0 to 1	
Centipedegrass		0 to 1	
Creeping bentgrass	1 to 2	1 to 2[a, b]	2
Dichondra		2 to 4	
Fine fescues	0 to 1		1
Kentucky bluegrass/fine fescue	0 to 1		1
Kentucky bluegrass			
Improved varieties	1	0 to 1[b]	1 to 2
Common types	0 to 1		1
Perennial ryegrass	1	0 to 1[b]	1 to 2
St. Augustinegrass		2 to 4	
Tall fescue	1	0 to 1[b]	1 to 2
Zoysiagrass	0 to 1	1 to 3	

[a]For high-maintenance turfs, apply no more than ¾ N/1000 sq ft for each application in hot weather, thus reducing the possibility of injury.

[b]Avoid summer fertilization of cool-season turfgrass grown in the transition or warm-humid zones.

Fertilizer Calculations

Converting recommended nitrogen application rates (pounds of nitrogen (N) per 1000 sq ft) into quantities of actual fertilizer is relatively simple but requires some explanation. For example, an application of 1 lb of nitrogen per 1000 sq ft of turfgrass area requires 10 lb of a 10-6-4 fertilizer, 5 lb of a 20-5-10 fertilizer, or 3 lb of 33-0-0. These amounts are determined by dividing the desired nitrogen application rate by the nitrogen percentage of the fertilizer and multiplying by 100. To apply a 23-7-7 fertilizer at the rate of 1.5 lb of nitrogen per 1000 sq ft, calculate as follows:

$$\frac{1.5 \text{ lb N}}{23} \times 100 = 6.5 \text{ lb of 23-7-7 fertilizer}$$

For a turf area that measures 8500 sq ft, continue the calculation as follows:

$$\frac{6.5 \text{ lb 23-7-7}}{1000 \text{ sq ft}} \times 8500 \text{ sq ft} = 55 \text{ lb of 23-7-7 fertilizer for the total area}$$

The same method of calculation applies to other nutrients in a fertilizer. For example, a 0-20-0 fertilizer contains 20% phosphoric acid (P_2O_5) but does not contain nitrogen or potassium. The amount of this fertilizer required to apply 1 lb of phosphoric acid per 1000 sq ft of turf is calculated as follows:

$$\frac{1 \text{ lb } P_2O_5}{20} \times 100 = 5 \text{ lb of 0-20-0 fertilizer}$$

It is important to note that the fertilizer analysis to represent phosphorus indicates the percentage of phosphoric acid that is less than half phosphorus. If fertilizer recommendations are given in pounds of phosphorus, they must be converted to the equivalent rate of P_2O_5. To do this, multiply the recommended rate of phosphorus by 2.29 to obtain the recommended quantity of phosphoric acid.

The third number listed in a fertilizer analysis represents the total amount of potash (K_2O) contained in the fertilizer material. Like phosphorus, when potassium requirements are suggested in pounds of potassium per 1000 sq ft, the value must be multiplied by 1.20 to convert to pounds of potash. Potassium may also be found alone or in a mixed fertilizer. Muriate of potash 0-0-60 may be used when only potassium is desired. For example, to apply 1 lb of potash per 1000 sq ft, use the following calculation:

$$\frac{1 \text{ lb } K_2O}{60} \times 100 = 1.7 \text{ lb of 0-0-60 fertilizer}$$

Fertilizer Spreaders

Fertilizer spreaders are of two principal types: rotary (broadcast) or drop type. The rotary spreader (Figure 6.12) employs a rotating disc to distribute fertilizer well beyond the width of the spreader, thus allowing coverage of a large area in a relatively short time. The drop type (Figure 6.11), in contrast, applies fertilizer directly beneath the spreader. Accuracy of application is generally better with the drop-type spreader than with the rotary type. Care should be taken to avoid overlapping or missing areas. Both types of spreaders should be kept in good mechanical condition and should be cleaned immediately after use to avoid rusting or other deterioration of parts due to the buildup of salts from fertilizers. Periodic calibration can help to ensure uniform fertilizer distribution and point out areas of wear or mechanical breakdown. Calibration simply means determining the application rate of the spreader at a specific setting. For accurate application, the spreader must be calibrated for each fertilizer used. Fertilizer spreader calibration techniques are outlined in Chapter 6, page 358.

Secondary Nutrients

Calcium (Ca), magnesium (Mg), and sulfur (S) are also necessary for optimum turf growth but are required in lesser amounts than N, P, and K. These elements are generally in short supply when the pH is outside the range for optimum growth (6.0 to 7.0). When pH amendments are added to the soil, Ca, Mg, and S, which were previously unavailable, will be converted to an available form. These elements are often found in fertilizers as contaminants or impurities in the mixture. Sulfur is an added component of many complete fertilizers and may be listed on the label.

Minor Nutrients

Minor nutrients, also referred to as micronutrients or trace elements, are required for optimum turfgrass growth. They need be present in smaller quantities than the major nutrients. In most medium- to fine-textured soils, there are available sufficient supplies of micronutrients for turfgrass needs. The minor nutrients, like secondary nutrients, can be in plant-unavailable forms when the pH is outside the range for optimum turf growth. In the arid and semiarid western United States, it is not uncommon to experience minor nutrient deficiencies on alkaline soils. Due to the high buffering capacity, pH adjustment in these soils may not be practical. In this situation, for high-quality turf, additions of minor elements through fertilizers is necessary. Coarse-textured soils, such as sand with its inherently low buffering capacity, also tend to exhibit extremes in pH. Coarse-textured soil may also benefit from the addition of minor-nutrient fertilizers. Since minor-nutrient deficiencies tend to be a localized problem in many regions, it is best to consult the county extension adviser for recommendations or corrective measures.

Foliar application of iron may be used to rapidly increase the color of light green turfgrasses. Although the effect is rapid, it is often short in duration. The iron does not move far from the site of absorption in the plant and is generally removed with mowing. Foliar applications are not suitable for the long-term correction of chlorosis (see page 39), because they are not intended to reach the soil. Both salt and chelated forms of iron are effective; however, salt formulations (e.g., iron sulfate) may stain building materials.

THATCH

Many turfgrasses species, when grown at rapid rates, accumulate thatch at the soil surface. Thatch is a tightly intermingled layer of living and dead stems, leaves, and roots of grasses that can develop between the actively growing vegetation and the soil surface

TURF PROFILE

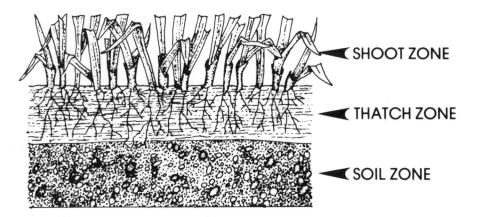

Figure 2-4 Profile of established turf.

(Figure 2.4). Thatch is undesirable because it increases the disease susceptibility of the turf, reduces tolerance to drought, cold, and heat, and can minimize the movement of air, water, fertilizers, and some pesticides through the turf into the soil. Thatch also tends to decrease the turf's capacity for growth, resulting in an all-round deterioration of turf quality. Some buildup of thatch is desirable, however, because it increases the resiliency of the turf and provides a source of nutrients through the breakdown of organic matter. An increase in thatch is directly related to the rate at which dead plant materials accumulate. If the production of dead material exceeds the ability of microorganisms to break down the material into its elemental components, thatch accumulates. Therefore, vigorously growing grass cultivars, heavy fertilization, excessive soil acidity (which inhibits bacterial activity), poor soil aeration and drainage, cold soils, and some pesticides are all contributors to thatch buildup.

The depth of thatch can be determined by cutting a wedge of turf and examining the profile of green vegetation, thatch, and soil (Figure 2.4). If the compressed layer of dead materials just above the soil surface is greater than ½ in. in thickness, it should be controlled.

Two basic methods are used to control excessive thatch: (1) physical removal of the thatch by various types of machinery, and (2) modification of the environment to encourage rapid bacterial activity, reduce the growth rate of the turfgrass, or both. Although effective in thatch control, physical removal of thatch, can be destructive to living turf. Therefore, physical thatch removal should occur only during peak grass-growing periods. Dethatching machines are often utilized for this process. A vertical mower represents one type of dethatching machine. It contains a rotating shaft with evenly spaced, vertically oriented solid blades. A power rake, which is similar, has hinged or springlike teeth. These machines can often be obtained at garden supply stores or equipment rental companies. Similar to the height-setting mechanism on a rotary mower, most dethatching machines have adjustable wheel heights to allow various depth penetrations of the turf by the blades. The blades should be set deep enough to penetrate the soil surface slightly. As much thatch as possible should be removed. Extensive removal of a thatch layer greater than ¾ inch is excessively destructive to the turf, minimizing its ability for recovery. In this situation, less thatch should be removed at one time but additional dethatching should continue during future periods of rapid growth. Because dethatching procedures open up the soil surface for invasion by annual grassy weeds during early spring, applications of preemergence herbicides should always follow this cultivation technique.

Modifying the turf environment to remove the thatch layer slowly is generally more effective for long-term control. When thatch tends to accumulate, it can rapidly decrease the pH. Acidic conditions minimize the growth and reproduction of bacteria and other microorganisms, thus reducing their ability to degrade thatch. The addition of lime to raise the pH within the thatch will promote rapid degradation. Thatch tends to reduce air, water, and fertilizer movements to the soil surface. It also decreases the ability for microorganisms to multiply. Core aerification (*Color plate 3*) provides conduction channels for the movement of air and water to the soil throughout the thatch. Core aerification is a process of removing small cylinders of soil and turf in a uniform pattern through the turf. Several different types of equipment are available to remove cores over large areas in a relatively short time. The majority of the machines deposit the cylinder of turf and soil onto the surface. If these cylinders are then broken up or left to disintegrate, allowing the soil to sift down into the thatch layer, an increase in thatch degradation will result. This can be attributed to the increase in microorganism activity in the soil-enriched environment.

One of the oldest practices in turfgrass management, next to mowing, is the application of fine layers of soil to the turf surface to provide a smooth, firm, even turf (page 26). Light, frequent topdressings also aid in the degradation of thatch by introducing soil into the thatch layer. The soil-enriched environment can now support larger populations of soil microorganisms. Topdressing also tends to minimize the rate of thatch accumulation. As mentioned previously, it is important to closely match the texture of the topdressing mixture with the underlying soil. This helps prevent any problems in the ability of the turf to absorb water.

SOIL COMPACTION

Compacted soils are characterized by poor aeration and drainage, poor surface-water infiltration, shallow root growth, and reduced overall quality. Turfgrasses in compacted soils grow slowly, lack vigor, and become thin or do not grow at all. Soil compaction is more prominent on fine-textured soils subjected to concentrated foot and/or vehicle traffic. Soil compaction can be reduced by cultivation with machines that create openings extending into the underlying soil. The two principal types of mechanical cultivators to alleviate compaction are core aerifiers and spikers. Core aerification machines remove small cores of soil (see above), depositing them on the surface of the turf or collecting them for removal from the site. For simple alleviation of compaction, these cores can be removed or chopped or matted into the grass to provide topdressing. Spikers and slicers employ solid spines or knives, respectively, to create narrow openings in the turf. These machines, although not as effective as core aerifiers, generally are less destructive to turf growth and can be used during periods when core aerification would otherwise cause injury. Usually, cultivation should be carried out only during periods of rapid turf growth.

If the soil is seriously waterlogged, drainage tiles can be installed where feasible. Foot and/or vehicle traffic can be reduced or redirected by constructing walks or fences, or by planting shrubs.

Because soil is more conducive to compaction when it is very moist or wet, it is crucial to minimize traffic on a turf after a heavy rainfall or irrigation. Moderately moist or dry soils are much less prone to compaction.

MAINTENANCE CALENDAR

Using all the technical information available for turfgrass growth still cannot ensure optimum turfgrass quality. The quality of a turfgrass site is largely the reflection of the timely application of turfgrass management techniques in a consistent and repetitive manner. Variations in climate and uses of the site can mandate great fluctuations in the scheduling of management techniques. All good turf managers, however, must work from a basic maintenance schedule to provide the consistent uniformity necessary for high-quality turf. Table 2.11

TABLE 2.11 GENERALIZED MAINTENANCE SCHEDULES FOR COOL-SEASON AND WARM-SEASON TURFGRASSES

Month	Operation	Comments	Page
		Cool-Season	
March–April	Rolling	Use only for correction of small surface irregularities.	25
April (cool, humid and arid zones only)	Dethatching	Delay dethatching until the turf has resumed active growth. Spring dethatching is not recommended for the transition and warm-humid zones.	35
February–March (transition and warm-humid zones April–mid-June (cool-humid and cool-arid zones)	Fertilization	One to two fertilizer applications can be made at this time. Delay first application until after the second mowing.	32
April–mid-May	Weed control	Application of preemergence herbicide should be made in advance of summer annual grass germination. Postemergence broadleaf herbicide should be applied after the resumption of active growth. Turfgrass growth retardants should be applied after the second mowing.	142
February–March (transition and warm-humid zones)	Reseeding	Thin areas that require reseeding should be seeded as early as possible. Seed when soil conditions permit.	15
Mid-April–May (cool-humid and cool-arid zones)	Renovation or establishment	If perennial grass weeds are present, delay renovation or establishment until they are controlled.	9

Month	Operation	Comments	Page
June–mid-August	Mowing, irrigation, and pest control	Conduct maintenance practices only as necessary to ensure survival and desired turf quality.	19
Mid-August–mid-September	Renovation, establishment, and reseeding.	Delay renovation or establishment until perennial grass weeds have been controlled.	9
September–mid-October	Fertilization	One to two fertilizer applications should be made as early in fall as possible. Avoid midfall applications of fertilizer. If soils are deficient in P or K, incorporate with fall application.	32
September–mid-October	Cultivation and dethatching	Delay cultivation or dethatching until turf resumes rapid growth.	35
Mid-September–October	Weed control	Delay the application of postemergence broadleaf herbicides until weeds are rapidly growing.	142
Mid-October–November	Fertilization	Delay late fall fertilization until after turf stops growing. Late fall fertilization helps to promote early spring green-up.	32
Warm-Season			
January–February	Weed control	A nonselective herbicide with no soil residual activity may be applied to existing weeds in dormant warm-season turfs.	149
April–August	Fertilization	Delay first application of fertilizer until after full green-up. Additional applications can be applied monthly. If P or K is required, spread the application over the entire season.	32
March–July	Cultivation and dethatching	Dethatch warm-season turfs well in advance of green-up or delay until active growth resumes. Other cultivation techniques should be applied only after resumption of growth.	35
March–mid-April	Weed control	Apply preemergence herbicides prior to germination of summer annual grasses. Postemergence broadleaf herbicide applications should be delayed until weeds are actively growing.	2
May–July	Renovation, establishment, and planting	Delay renovation or establishment of warm-season turf until similar turfs in the area have resumed full growth.	9
September–October	Winter overseeding	Dormant warm-season turf may be overseeded with cool-season turfgrasses to provide color through the winter months.	142

documents two basic maintenance schedules for cool-season and warm-season turfs. It is important to emphasize that these schedules should represent the rough outline of a *final* maintenance calendar. Local conditions and use will justify appropriate changes in these basic schedules. Again, the state turfgrass extension specialist is an excellent source for localized maintenance scheduling. Even with these resources, maintenance schedules will change periodically. Experience is often the best source of information for accurate scheduling.

ADDITIONAL TURFGRASS PROBLEMS

Chlorosis

A general yellowing or chlorosis of small to large areas of turf can often be attributed to a nutrient deficiency. Chlorosis often reflects a lack of nitrogen. However, several turfgrass species, such as centipedegrass, are very susceptible to a deficiency of iron. Although not harmful on a short-term basis, chlorosis can reduce shoot growth and cause thinning when extended over a long period of time. Application of the appropriate fertilizer nutrient can quickly rectify chlorotic turf.

Chlorosis can, however, persist even when the total nutrients available are above turfgrass requirements. Saturated soils, a highly alkaline or acid soil, and excessive salt(s) in the soil can prevent the turf from absorbing the necessary nutrient requirements. Turfs that are chlorotic in the fall can be injured during the winter due to low food reserves and a weakened root system.

Chlorosis is generally controlled through application of the appropriate nutrient in the form of fertilizer. Some soils, however, such as those in dry areas of the west, are alkaline and cannot be corrected easily (page 28). Nutrients applied to these soils may be converted to nonavailable sources. Iron, however, may be effective in correcting chlorosis when applied in the form of an iron salt (ferrous sulfate, ferrous ammonium sulfate, etc.). Iron can also be temporarily introduced into the turfgrass plant through foliar applications of iron sulfate or iron chelate, to provide a rapid greening of foliar tissue. This technique, however, is temporary at best. Should the turf not respond to the application of the corrective fertilizer nutrient, the chlorosis could be a symptom of another problem.

Chemical Burns

Fertilizers, pesticides, lime, sulfur, soaps, gasoline, hydraulic fluids, oils, and so on, can cause rapid discoloration and injury to turfgrass tissue (Figure 2.5). In excess, these materials cause a rapid loss of water from leaf tissues, resulting in dehydration and death of the grass, usually in patches or streaks. When applying fertilizers, herbicides, insecticides, fungicides, and other turf chemicals, the directions and precautions on package labels must be followed strictly (see Chapter 6). To prevent the dissolution of fertilizer materials on the foliage, apply fertilizer only to dry foliage and then water it in immediately. If the safety of an application of material is in question, apply smaller amounts over an extended period of time or test it on a small area. Always calibrate spreaders and sprayers to ensure uniform and accurate application of materials (see Chapter 6 and Appendix B).

Symptoms of pesticide damage often appear as broad swaths, narrow streaks, or

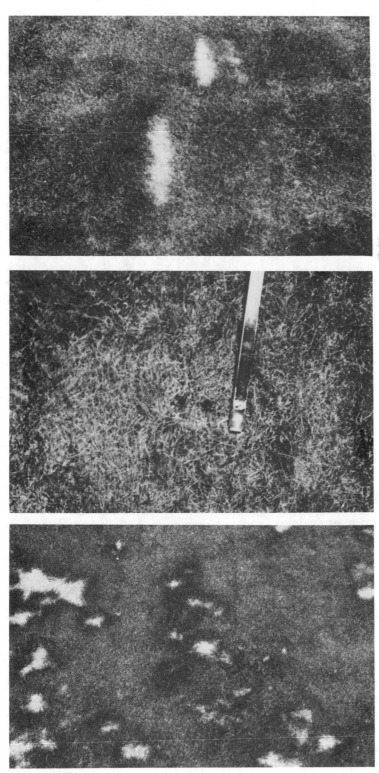

Figure 2-5 Injury from the overapplication of fertilizer.

Figure 2-6 Buried debris (plaster) from building contractor.

Figure 2-7 Injury from dog urine.

other regular patterns in which the pesticide was applied. Specific symptoms might include leaf speckling, yellowing, or death soon after application—or even after an extended period during which other growth conditions were optimal.

Buried Debris

Materials buried beneath the turf's surface (often left by the building contractor) which are impervious to water shorten the active root zone of the turf above it (Figure 2.6). During extended droughts, the turf will wilt or die more rapidly than in surrounding areas. These brown patches are often confused with turf diseases or other pest damage. Probe the area to locate buried debris, remove it, and replace the debris with a comparable soil.

Dog Injury

Dogs and high quality-turf do not mix. Although this is unfortunate for the dog-loving segment of our society, it is true. Urine-soaked spots can rapidly desiccate turfgrass tissue, killing the foliage (Figure 2.7). Urine, especially in the same spot, can kill the crown and all tissues above ground. The more-or-less circular patches are from several inches to 2 ft in diameter. These spots may superficially resemble diseases such as fairy rings, brown patch, or dollar spot (see Chapter 5). When fertility is suboptimal, the spots are often surrounded by a ring of darker-green, faster-growing grass due to the release of nitrates from the urine. Although heavy irrigation of the area can help promote recovery of injured spots, the only long-lasting control is the removal of "man's best friend." Generally, turf quality loses out to this method of control. One possibility is to try to train the dog to use a certain area of the yard in an out-of-the-way location. Fencing the turf, or the establishment and enforcement of leash regulations, is often needed. Symptoms similar to dog injury may be caused by fertilizer spills (page 39).

Moss

Mosses form tangled green mats composed of a branched, threadlike growth over the turf surface. Closely mowed and thatched turfs, composed largely of nonaggressive turfgrasses, are most prone to invasion by mosses. These plants grow in neglected turf areas low in fertility, with poor soil aeration and drainage. Highly acid, excessively shady, improperly watered, or heavily compacted soil, or a combination of these factors, encourages the growth of mosses. The best control is to keep the grass growing vigorously following the steps outlined for algae (below) and for compacted areas (page 36). Other useful controls include raising the height of cut, controlling thatch (page 34), adjusting the pH to between 6 and 7 (page 28), and the establishment of a more vigorous and better adapted turfgrass species or cultivar. Moss can be removed by hand raking and the site can be made unfavorable for moss growth by treating when first seen with ferrous ammonium sulfate, ferrous sulfate, or ammonium sulfate (see Table 5.4 on page 327).

Algae

Algae are a group of small, primitive, filamentous, green plants that manufacture their own food. Under *very wet* surface conditions, they can form a thick, slimy, greenish-to-

Figure 2-8 Algal scum in a thin bentgrass turf.

brownish scum on bare soil or in thin turf (Figure 2.8). High fertility and a weak, thin turf encourage their growth. Algae occur in low, shaded, heavily tracked, or compacted turfgrass areas. Algal scum can dry to form a tough black crust that later cracks and peels. Algae may also induce iron-deficiency chlorosis in plants.

To prevent algal scums, establish a thick stand of healthy, vigorous turf. Provide for good surface and subsurface drainage when establishing new turf areas. Avoid frequent waterings, especially in late afternoon or early evening. Avoid overwatering and waterlogged soil. Aerify compacted turf areas using hand or power equipment (page 36). Eliminate heavily trafficked areas by providing walks, paths, or traffic guidelines such as fences or shrubs. Increase light penetration and air movement over the area and speed drying of the turf surface by thinning dense trees or shrubs in nearby areas. When designing the landscape, space plantings to avoid too much shade. In partial shade, use shade-tolerant turfgrasses or ground covers that persist well in low-light situations. Algacides or fungicides that control algae can be applied to the area as recommended in Table 5.4. Correct the pH if necessary (page 28). Applications of dilute solutions of sodium hypochlorite or liquid household bleach (0.01%), copper sulfate (2 to 3 oz per 1000 sq ft), or some fungicides (see Table 5.4) will help control algae when combined with the cultural practices outlined above.

Summer Drought or Desiccation

Dry winds during the summer months, when air temperatures are above 80°F, can rapidly wilt and desiccate turf areas (Figure 2.9). When water is applied shortly after the wilting *first* appears, prompt recovery usually results. Common turfgrasses with medium to excellent resistance to drought include buffalograss, bermudagrass, zoysiagrass, bahiagrass, most fescues, Kentucky bluegrass, and perennial ryegrass. Bentgrasses, St. Augustinegrass, centipedegrass, and meadow fescue are less resistant to drought. Deep-rooted species, such as tall fescue, bermudagrass, and zoysiagrass, will maintain their color and growth better than most other desirable grasses before summer dormancy from drought occurs. These species are able to utilize water from a greater volume of soil, thus taking longer to deplete soil reserves.

For high-quality turf, a temporary reduction in the surface temperature results in reduced water transpiration, reducing the amount of wilting. Surface temperatures can be reduced for a short period through the temporary application of small amounts of

Figure 2–9 Injury from summer drought or desiccation.

water. This method is called syringing. The effectiveness is short-lived, however. To aid in minimizing the extent of wilt through drought, promote a deep root system through infrequent, thorough watering. Apply soluble nitrogen sparingly during stressful summer months to reduce shoot growth. Reduce compacting forces, such as foot and vehicle traffic, to minimize turf injury.

Scald

Death of turfgrasses as a result of submergence under water during hot, sunny weather is called scald. Damage usually occurs in low areas following a heavy rain or excessive irrigation. Most widely grown turfgrasses can tolerate 5 to 10 days of being submerged if the water temperature is below 80°F. On a hot, sunny day, being under water even a half-hour around noon can kill individual grass shoots. To prevent scald, proper surface and subsurface drainage is a necessity through contouring and installation of drain tiles or the placement of dry wells in sunken areas that cannot be corrected by surface grading. Naturally, do not apply more water than can enter the soil. Shallow pools can be removed with a squeegee if the practices outlined above are insufficient.

Winter Drying Out or Desiccation

Winter desiccation (*Color plate 4*), which causes the leaves to turn white to brown in affected areas, is most severe on elevated sites and sloped areas where the grass is exposed to drying winter winds and there is little accumulation of snow. These areas also have a large surface runoff and low rates of infiltration. When air temperatures are above freezing and the soil is frozen, water is lost from foliar tissue, causing desiccation and death.

A certain amount of winter desiccation occurs in turfs annually. This is commonly called "wind burn" and results in the leaves turning some shade of brown. The brown leaves are mowed off during the first two or three mowings in the spring and little damage remains. However, a severe winter drought may dry out and kill the crowns and nodes of turfgrass plants, resulting in serious winter kill.

To help prevent winter desiccation, irrigate dry soils thoroughly to a depth of 6 to 8 in. in late autumn or early winter. Help to ensure uniform infiltration on sloped areas by removing excessive thatch and alleviate compaction. Fertilize lightly during the last 6 weeks of the growing season to allow a hardening-off period to take place. Turfgrasses should enter winter dormancy at a moderate nutritional level or snow-mold damage (see Chapter 5) or other severe injury may result.

Heaving

Repeated freezing and thawing from late autumn into early spring shears off turfgrass roots and pushes the grass plants up to an inch or more above their normal position in the soil. Crowns and roots are exposed to desiccation. Seeds planted late in the fall will not produce plants well rooted. These are very susceptible to heavy damage. To minimize injury, apply a light surface mulch of straw and possibly erect snow fences or other barriers to promote snow accumulation. Established turfs are seldom damaged by heaving. Control by lightly rolling the area in early spring once the soil has dried out somewhat (page 25).

Ice Injury

Thick layers of ice for prolonged periods may cause suffocation of turf, even though respiratory processes are greatly reduced during freezing weather. Most injury occurs when standing water covers the turf and then freezes. Should this happen, the turf may winter kill. Unless the ice layer remains in place for more than 3 months, removal will probably not be necessary. Whenever possible, drain any excess water from the ice as it thaws. Fortunately, well-adapted, perennial, cool-season turfgrasses are seldom injured by ice covers.

Late-Spring Frosts

Cool temperatures that kill new spring growth of warm-season grasses destroy the food reserves stored in live portions of the plant. Several frosts, separated by warm periods that stimulate new growth, can completely exhaust the food reserves, killing grass plants. When less severe, the root systems do not develop sufficiently to absorb water and minerals, resulting in thin, nonthrifty turf. If not too severe, the grass will gradually recover.

Air Pollution

Several air pollutants, including ozone, peroxyacetyl nitrates (PAN), sulfur dioxide, nitrogen dioxide, fluorides, chlorine, hydrogen chloride, ethylene, and toxic dusts, can cause turfgrass leaf blades to become bleached, chlorotic, or die back from the tips or margins. Other symptoms include bands across the leaf blades, a yellow to brown striping of the leaves, a glossy brown discoloration before the leaves die, or reduced foliar growth without visible symptoms. Injury from air pollutants is most common near industrial and urban areas where electric power plants, incinerators and refuse dumps, pulp and paper mills, smelters, refineries, a variety of chemical plants, and much-traveled highways are located. Turfgrass species and cultivars differ greatly in symptom expression and growth responses to the various air pollutants. Turfgrasses usually recover after a mowing or two unless there are a series of air pollution "alerts."

Salt Injury

The application of salt (sodium chloride or calcium chloride) to roadways, walks, and drives can injure adjacent turf. With adequate drainage, most salts can be flushed through the soil profile. If salt injury persists, the use of salt-tolerant turf species can help minimize damage. One of the most salt-tolerant grasses is alkaligrass (*Puccinellia distans*). Other salt-tolerant species include bermudagrass, creeping bentgrass, and St. Augustinegrass; Kentucky bluegrass, red fescue, and colonial bentgrass are salt-intolerant species.

SELECTED REFERENCES

BEARD, H. J., J. E. BEARD, and D. P. MARTIN. 1977. *Turfgrass Bibliography from 1672 to 1972.* East Lansing, MI: Michigan State University Press. 730 pages.

BEARD, J. B. 1973. *Turfgrass Science and Culture.* Englewood Cliffs, NJ: Prentice-Hall, Inc. 658 pages.

BEARD, J. B. 1982. *Turf Management for Golf Courses.* Burgess Publishing Co., 7100 Ohms Lane, Edina, MN. 642 pages.

COLLINGS, G. H. 1955. *Commercial Fertilizers,* 5th ed. New York: McGraw-Hill Book Company. 617 pages.

DANIEL, W. H., and R. P. FREEBORG. 1979. *Turf Managers Handbook.* New York: Harvest Publishing Company, 423 pages.

ETTER, A. G. 1951. "How Kentucky bluegrass grows," *Annual of Missouri Botanical Gardens,* 38: 293–375.

HANSON, A. A., and F. V. JUSKA, eds. 1969. *Turfgrass Science.* Agronomy Monograph 14. Madison, WI: American Society of Agronomy, Inc. 713 pages.

MADISON, J. H. 1971. *Principles of Turfgrass Culture.* New York: Van Nostrand Reinhold Company, Inc. 420 pages.

SPRAGUE, H. B. 1976. *Turf Management Handbook,* rev. ed. Danville, IL: The Interstate Printers and Publishers, Inc. 253 pages.

TURGEON, A. J. 1985. *Turfgrass Management, Second Edition.* Prentice-Hall, Inc., Englewood Cliffs, N.J. 391 pages.

VENGRIS, J. 1973. *Lawns,* rev. ed. Fresno, CA: Thompson Publications. 240 pages.

3

Biology and Control
of Weeds in Turfgrasses

INTRODUCTION

The prime objective in managing a turf is to establish and maintain a uniform living plant cover for recreational use and/or aesthetic enjoyment. Uniformity of color, leaf texture, and plant density of the turfgrass stand is of the utmost importance for consistent playability and enjoyment. To achieve uniformity, a select group of plants must exist throughout the turf and must be growing at similar rates (Chapter 2).

Any other plant that might grow and persist in the turf would, for the most part, deviate from the color, texture, or density of the turf. These plants are considered weeds in the turf even if they are turfgrass species! Weeds detract from the overall appearance of the turf and compete for light, water, minerals, and space, reducing the vigor of the turf.

Weeds in turf, like all plants, have a minimum set of requirements for their establishment and growth. Turfgrasses are excellent competitors which under optimum growing conditions will often outcompete weeds for necessary resources.

TYPES OF WEEDS

Plants from many diverse families comprise the weeds that are found in turf. Turfgrass weeds can be grouped into two major categories: (1) plants that are true grasses or appear grasslike, and (2) broadleaf weeds. The term "broadleaf" weeds can be misleading. Several weed species grouped in this classification have narrow leaves and somewhat resemble grasses. Their control, however, is similar to other broadleaf weeds.

Weeds are also categorized by their life cycle and growth habit. Annual weeds complete their life cycle in 1 year. Biennials complete their life cycle in 2 years, developing to partial maturity during the first growing season, with flowering and eventual death during the second season. Perennial plants can persist over long periods of time, usually overwintering in a dormant state. These species resume growth the following season from stored energy. They may also reproduce from seed.

Weed taxonomy and biology are used extensively in determining effective control methods. In general, the more closely a weed's growth habit resembles that of the chosen turfgrass or mixture of turfgrasses, the more difficult its control.

WINTER ANNUAL

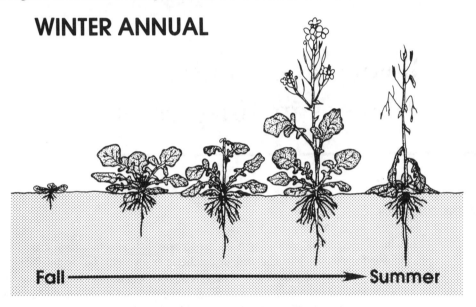

Figure 3.1 Life cycle of a winter annual weed.

SUMMER ANNUAL

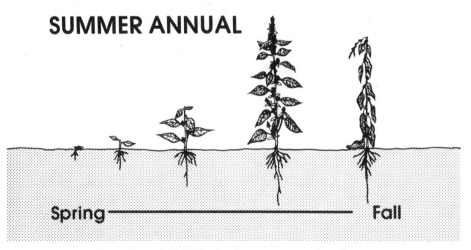

Figure 3.2 Life cycle of a summer annual weed.

BIENNIAL

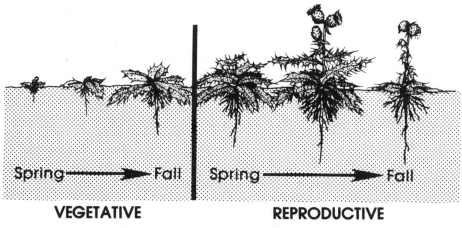

Figure 3.3 Life cycle of a biennial weed.

WEED BIOLOGY

Annual weeds can be classified by the season when their seed normally germinates. Winter annuals germinate during late summer or fall, persist as an immature plant throughout the winter months, and produce more vegetative growth and flowers and seed in the spring (Figure 3.1). Summer annuals germinate in the spring and produce seed in summer or fall (Figure 3.2). Biennial plants may have seeds that germinate in either the spring or fall (Figure 3.3). Perennial plants persist over many growing seasons (Figure 3.4).

PERENNIAL

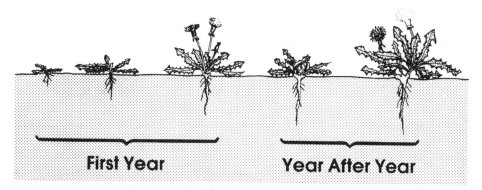

Figure 3.4 Life cycle of a perennial weed.

WEED ECOLOGY

The degree to which a weed adapts to the turf environment determines its persistence in a turf. Several factors influence the growth of each species, including climate, soil, and cultural or maintenance operations. Cultural operations applied to the turf during routine maintenance exerts the greatest influence on weed persistence. For example, over-application of water during irrigation promotes the germination of weed seeds such as annual bluegrass or crabgrass that thrive in a moist habitat. The timing and intensity of aerification or vertical mowing can influence the germination of these same weeds. The turfgrass manager also has limited control over existing soil conditions. Soil fertility can affect the growth of certain weed species. Annual bluegrass responds positively to high levels of soil phosphorus.

Climatic factors also influence weed populations. Weeds and turfgrasses have specific zones of adaptation. These are largely regulated by climate. In addition, dormancy mechanisms of each weed species influences its role in the turfgrass community.

Dormancy is a physical method by which a plant persists during periods of stress. To survive stressful periods, turfgrass weeds have developed to allow the plant to resume a full growth rate when conditions return to normal. Through the production of seeds or vegetative organs such as stolons, rhizomes, tubers, corms, or bulbs, a weed can persist at a minimal metabolic rate, preserving the necessary tissue and food reserves for regrowth after the dormant period.

Annual weeds are prolific seed producers, ensuring future generations of the species. Perennial weeds, while producing some seed, may rely more on storage organs to persist from season to season. Several conditions can prevent the immediate germination of weed seeds. These include a hard seed coat which mechanically prevents the imbibition of water or expansion of the seed within the seed coat. Some species produce inhibitors which must be leached from the seed coat before germination can begin. Other turfgrass weed species require short periods of light exposure to initiate the germination process. Some species shed seed from the plant before it is fully mature, requiring an after-ripening period before germination can occur. Seeds of certain species have been shown to survive in soil for long periods of time. Lotus seeds, found in a lake bed in Manchuria, were approximately 1000 years old, still viable and capable of germinating. Several turf weeds, such as green foxtail and curly dock, have germinated after 38 years of dormancy.

INFLUENCE OF WEEDS ON TURF

The greatest influence weeds exhibit on turf is through direct competition for water, light, space, and nutrients. Weeds also influence turf in other important ways. Turf injured from insects or other animals, diseases, excessive wear, compaction, or misuse of fertilizers or pesticides results in weakened turf and thin or bare areas. Weeds often occupy these areas more rapidly than the desired turfgrass. Loss of turf cover greatly reduces overall quality and the turf's ability to compete.

If weeds persist for long periods, they can often be a good indicator of unsuitable growing conditions for the turf. A physical soil problem (compaction, poor drainage or structure, etc.) can often prevent turfgrasses from obtaining a competitive edge, allowing the further development of weeds. An example is the extensive development of prostrate knotweed (page 90) in severely compacted soil. Prostrate knotweed can persist and spread under conditions of low oxygen potential, typically found in compacted soils. Most turfgrasses, however, do not grow well under these conditions. Therefore, the persistence and growth of prostrate knotweed in an area might indicate a compacted condition. The alleviation of compaction through core aerification can often reverse the balance, giving the turfgrass a new competitive edge (page 36).

Weeds, during normal development, can produce chemicals which, when exuded into the soil solution, are toxic to surrounding turfgrass plants. These allelopathic compounds can have a tremendous impact on the balance of plant species in a given area. For example, chemical compounds produced by members of the walnut family can strongly inhibit turfgrass growth. Research is being conducted to examine the effects of allelopathic compounds produced by weeds and turfgrasses which might influence turf development. Initial experiments would suggest that turfgrass species such as perennial ryegrass have the ability to inhibit the growth of other grasses. The collection and concentration of these compounds might someday prove to be beneficial for direct weed control.

WEED IDENTIFICATION

To apply accurate and timely control methods to turfgrass weeds, it is first necessary to identify the species of weeds present. First, determine whether the weed is a grass or a nongrass broadleaf plant. All grasses have relatively narrow (longer than wide) leaves with veins running parallel to each other. Single simple leaves, in alternate groups of two, arise from the stem, which is generally round or slightly flattened (compressed) but never triangular. Most grasses have a fibrous or multibranching root system with all stems meeting at the crown. Nongrass monocotyledonous plants are often confused with grasses. Wild onion and wild garlic, while resembling grasses, are more closely related to other plants. The sedges and rushes, which are close relatives of the grass family, are, on occasion, controlled in a fashion similar to broadleaf weeds (application of a selective postemergence herbicide).

Broadleaf Weed Identification

Descriptions of broadleaf weeds without using extensive technical terms is difficult. Many broadleaf turfgrass weeds have showy, colorful flowers, which can be used as a simple means of separating these weeds into smaller groups. The identification of broadleaf weeds by floral characters is convenient. Flowers are often not present on turfgrass weeds, so the use of floral parts for identification will be minimal.

It is necessary to use a few technical terms in any basic discussion on plant structure. Just as it is impossible to describe a lawn mower without describing some of the mechanical parts (i.e., reel, bed knife, blade, motor, etc.), it is also impossible to describe a weed accurately without a minimal reference to descriptive terminology. Most of the terms used in the description of individual weeds or in the key (page 61) are included

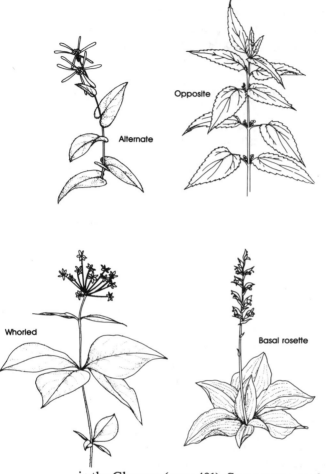

Figure 3.5 Arrangement of leaves.

in the Glossary (page 401). Some terms used extensively throughout the descriptions of broadleaf weeds help to describe the arrangement of leaves on the stem or the basic shape of the leaf. The arrangement of leaves on stems can be divided into four basic groups (Figure 3.5): (1) an alternate arrangement where one leaf arises from the stem and another is attached farther up the stem but on the opposite side; (2) an opposite arrangement where two leaves appear together at the same point on opposite sides of the stem; (3) in some cases, leaves are found to be whorled, where three or more leaves are attached to the stem at the same site; and (4) leaves arranged in a basal rosette are all attached to the stem near ground level.

A leaf can be described as being simple (Figure 3.6), in which it is not divided into smaller portions and forms one mass, or it can be compound (Figure 3.7), such as that found on a locust or elm tree, in which a single leaf is the combination of many smaller leaflets. Although the diversity of leaf size and shape for broadleaf plants is great, most broadleaf weeds found in turf can be described by the leaf shapes shown in Figures 3.6 and 3.7. Figure 3.6 illustrates the eight basic shapes for simple leaves. Unfortunately, a species growing under different conditions can exhibit variations in leaf shape. The shapes illustrated should be used

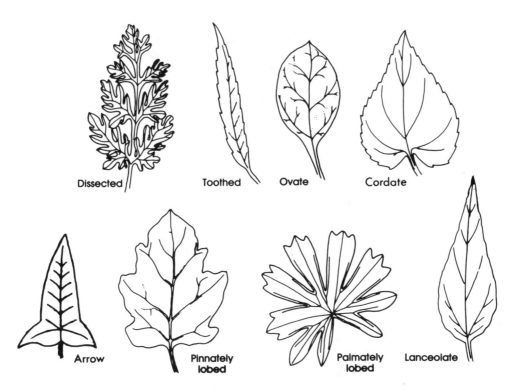

Dissected   Toothed   Ovate   Cordate

Arrow   Pinnately lobed   Palmately lobed   Lanceolate

Figure 3.6 Simple leaf types.

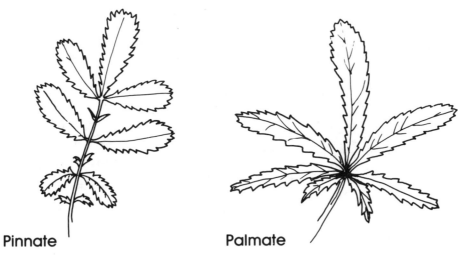

Pinnate   Palmate

Figure 3.7 Compound leaf types.

Weed Identification   **53**

only as a guide in the identification of a species. When a leaf is described as serrate, or toothed, the indentations on the leaf margin are generally uniform and shallow, much like teeth on a handsaw. If a leaf margin is described as lobed, it is generally rounded, varying in the depth of the indentation. Pinnate leaves branch from different parts of the midvein, while palmate leaf veins all branch from a central connecting point. A compound, dissected leaf is often mistaken for a pinnately lobed, simple leaf. The difference lies in the relative size of the lobes. If the lobe spaces are as large as, or larger than, the leaf surfaces which they separate, the leaf is considered compoundly dissected.

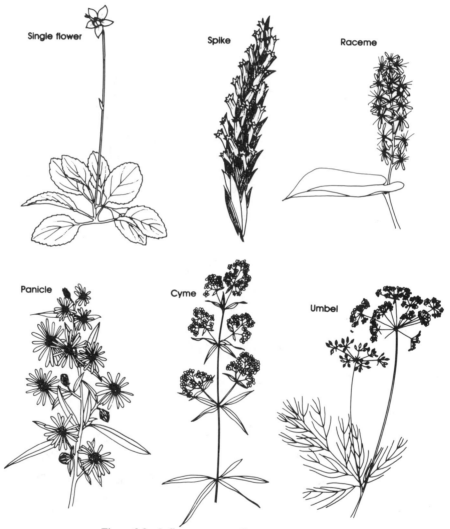

Figure 3.8   Inflorescences or flower arrangements.

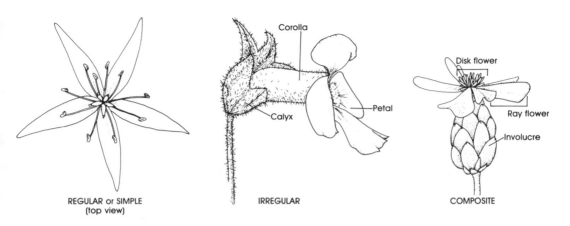

Figure 3.9 Parts of a flower.

When comparisons of vegetative characteristics fail to identify a weed, the arrangements of the flowering portion (inflorescence) of the plant can be helpful in its identification (Figure 3.8). Some weeds develop a single flower at the end of a terminal stem, also known as an apical inflorescence. When a number of flowers are attached to the terminal stem, without branching, they are called a spike. If a group of flowers are attached to the main stem by a single shorter stem, they are referred to as a raceme. Plants that exhibit some secondary branching in the flower attachment, can be described as a panicle. When the branching always results in a terminal flower, either arising from the apex of the stem or from the axils of leaves, it is described as a cyme arrangement. The final arrangement in Figure 3.8 is an umbel, where all branching of the inflorescence arises from the terminal end or apex of stems.

The flowers themselves also provide clues to the identification of a weed (Figure 3.9). If both stamens and pistils are present, the flowers are described as perfect (e.g., bedstraw, prostrate knotweed). If either structure is missing, the flower is considered imperfect (e.g., plantains, pigweed). When a portion of a flower differs in shape, the flower is considered irregular (e.g., henbit, red sorrel). When all portions of a flower are similar, or can be dissected into equal halves, it is considered regular (e.g., chickweed, moneywort). Petal color is often useful in the identification of a weed. Composite flowers, such as the English daisy or sunflower, while resembling a single flower, actually are comprised of numerous, smaller, individual flowers. Those tightly grouped in the center are called disk flowers, while those flowers with a large petal, radiating around the outside of the disk flowers, are called ray flowers. Seed structures can also be utilized in the identification of weeds in turf; however, these structures have not been incorporated in the key.

Grass Identification Features

If an unknown weed is determined to be a grass (main key, page 61), the easiest identification is often through characteristics of the inflorescence. In turf, however, this portion of the plant is usually not available or does not persist under normal mowing heights.

Weed Identification

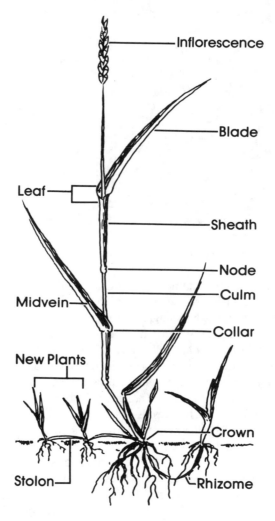

Figure 3.10 Parts of a grass plant.

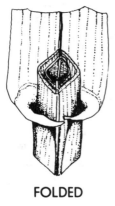

FOLDED

ROLLED

Figure 3.11 Vernation of a bud shoot.

Thus you must rely on vegetative (Figure 3.10) features for identification. The following features, listed in order of their relative importance for identification, are used in the grass key (page 67).

Vernation. Vernation (Figure 3.11) is the arrangement of the young leaf in the bud shoot. In general, leaves may be classified as rolled or folded. Kentucky bluegrass is an example of folded vernation, whereas the bud shoots of tall fescue are rolled.

Ligule. A ligule (Figure 3.12) is a light, translucent membrane or ring of hairs which encloses the stem at the junction of the leaf blade and sheath, remaining fairly uniform and consistent within each species. The ligule is on the inside of the blade between the stem and blade. When the ligule is a group or ring of hairs, it is referred to as ciliate. When the ligule is a fine papery membrane, it is considered membranous and can be identified by the shape of its margin. Although the length or height of the ligule varies from one species to another, this character was not used in the key.

Collar. The collar (Figure 3.13) is an area where the leaf blade and sheath join. It is generally lighter in color than the blade. It may be divided into two sections by the midvein. The collar is also distinctively narrow or broad for each grass species.

 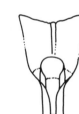 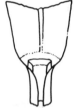 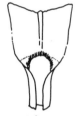 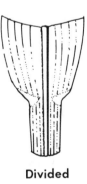 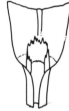

| Acuminate | Acute | Rounded | Truncate | Ciliate | Toothed |

Figure 3.12 Ligule margins.

 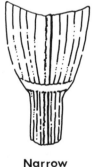

| Broad | Narrow | Divided |

Figure 3.13 Collar types.

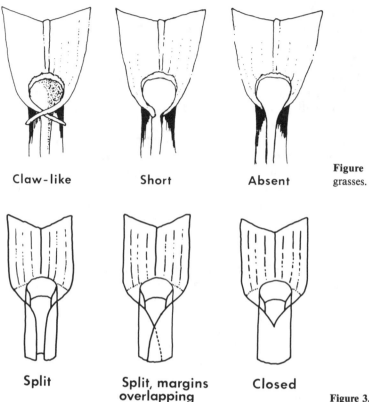

| Claw-like | Short | Absent |

Figure 3.14 Auricle arrangements of grasses.

| Split | Split, margins overlapping | Closed |

Figure 3.15 Sheath margins.

Auricles. Auricles (Figure 3.14) are green appendages projecting from either side of the collar to the inside of the leaf blade. They range in size from small stubs to those which fully encompass the stem. Quackgrass is an example of a species with clasping auricles.

Sheath. The sheath is the lower portion of the grass leaf which usually encloses the stem. It begins at the junction of the blade and collar extending downward to the next lower node. The sheath is considered a portion of the leaf, but generally adheres tightly to the stem or expanding leaves. The margin of a sheath (Figure 3.15) can be split, just touching or slightly separated from the stem. More often, they are split and overlap. Rarely, the sheath is entirely fused or closed.

Blade. The blade is the upper portion of a leaf which begins at the sheath, extending outward from the stem. The length, width, type of tip, and general roughness or smoothness of the blade can be used for identification. The grass key (page 67) uses a generalized blade width to aid in identifying a grass weed. For each species, the blade can vary in width under different growing conditions (mowing height, soil moisture, age, etc.). Blade width should therefore be used cautiously and only in combination with several other identifying characteristics. The following apply to mature plants growing under optimum conditions. If the blade width averages less than 5 mm, it may be considered fine. For blade widths from 5 to 10 mm, the blade texture is considered medium, while coarse-textured blade leaves are more than 10 mm wide.

Rhizomes. A rhizome (Figure 3.16, 2) is an underground lateral stem with the capacity to produce a new plant. Rhizomes are present or absent and can be termed strong (numerous and rapidly growing) or weak (few and often short). They are similar to aerial stems but grow laterally. In some species they turn upward, producing new plants.

Stolons. A stolon (Figure 3.16, 3) is a horizontal, aboveground stem that produces roots from the nodes and provides new vertical growth for plant propagation. Stolons start from the same growing point as rhizomes but have an aboveground growth habit.

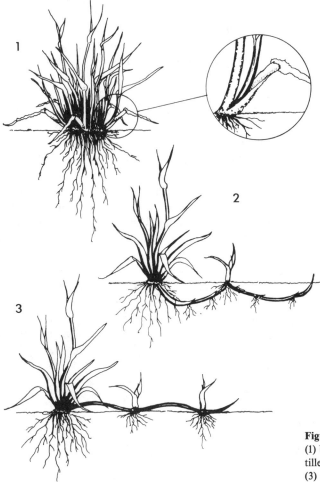

Figure 3.16 Growth habits of grasses: (1) bunch type with close-up of a new tiller; (2) rhizomatous growth habit; (3) stoloniferous growth habit.

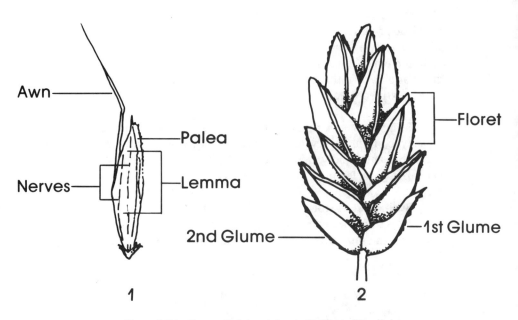

Figure 3.17 Grass spikelet and floret: (1) floret; (2) spikelet.

Seedhead. The seedhead (inflorescence) is a total collection of flowers or seed-bearing portions of the plant arranged in various configurations (Figure 3.8). The basic flower of a grass plant is called a floret (Figure 3.17, 1). It consists of stamens and/or pistils in association but, unlike broadleaf plants, the surrounding modified leaves or bracts are highly specialized. The innermost bract is called the palea. Opposite the palea is the lemma, which occasionally has a long pointed tip known as an awn. When the awn is attached to the center of the lemma, dividing the lemma tip into two portions, it is considered a bifid awn. Depending on the grass species, any number of florets can be grouped together in a spikelet (Figure 3.17, 2). The glumes, which are without other floral parts, are generally present under the lowest florets. The glumes are generally much shorter than the whole spikelet but in some species may extend past the outer florets, encompassing the entire spikelet. There are two distinctive ways in which florets break away from the stem to distribute the enclosed seed, known as disarticulation. It can be either below the glumes (Figure 3.18, 1) or above the glumes (Figure 3.18, 2), leaving the glumes attached to the seedhead. While the grass inflorescence is not always present in grassy weeds in turf, it can be a more reliable source for identification than vegetative characteristics. The key has been arranged to allow for identification by floral parts if they are present.

KEY TO TURFGRASS WEEDS

The identification of a turfgrass weed from a mature, intact specimen can be both time consuming and laborious. When one or more essential plant parts are underdeveloped or are missing from the plant, the task becomes even more difficult. To simplify iden-

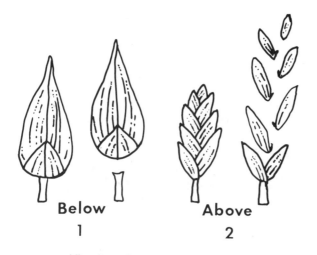

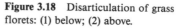

Figure 3.18 Disarticulation of grass florets: (1) below; (2) above.

tification, the structures normally found on weeds in mowed turf are utilized together with floral or seedhead parts for identification process.

The key is organized to present pairs of possible identifying structures. After you have a representative weed available for identification, select the statement that best describes or applies to the plant you wish to identify. Your choice directs you to the next appropriate subordinate pair of statements. Again, select between the two statements. Proper choices direct you until a choice ends with the identification of any weed included in the key.

Main Key

1. Plant not appearing grasslike, leaves sometimes wider than long, leaf veins generally branched . . . . *Broadleaf key,* page 62

1. Plant appears grasslike, leaves longer than wide, leaf veins generally parallel 2

   2. Leaves long, narrow, in groups of two, stems, if present, are flat, round, or hollow . . . . *Grass key,* page 67

   2. Leaves long, narrow, in groups of two or three; stems triangular or round 3

      3. Leaves long, slender, somewhat thickened with a white underground bulb, with garlic odor or taste 4

         4. Narrow, nearly round stem, hollow (at least toward base); aboveground bulblets present in clusters at top of stem or greenish-to-white flowers . . . . *Wild garlic,* page 109

         4. Narrow, flat leaves arising from base of plant only, few flowers or aboveground bulblets . . . . *Wild onion,* page 109

      3. Leaves long, narrow, thin, and grasslike, in whorls of three around a triangular stem 4

         4. Grasslike, three-sided stem, corms present, closed sheath, ⅛ to ⅖ in. wide, sheath approximately as wide as mature stem; flowers yellow-brown in narrow spikelets in an umbel-like inflorescence . . . . *Yellow nutsedge,* page 112

         4. Grasslike, three-sided stem, corms absent, closed sheath which is generally shorter than stem when mature; flowers dark brown or purple . . . . *Purple nutsedge,* page 112

Broadleaf Key

Grass Key

Annual Grasses

Barnyardgrass, *Echinochloa crus-galli.*   Barnyardgrass (Figure 3.19) is a coarse annual with broad, compressed purple sheaths. In closely mowed turfs, it lies flat on the ground and can spread out in a semicircular pattern. The absence of a ligule distinguishes barnyardgrass from many similar grasses.

Figure 3.19 Barnyardgrass, *Echinochloa crus-galli:* (1) whole plant; (2) two views of spikelets.

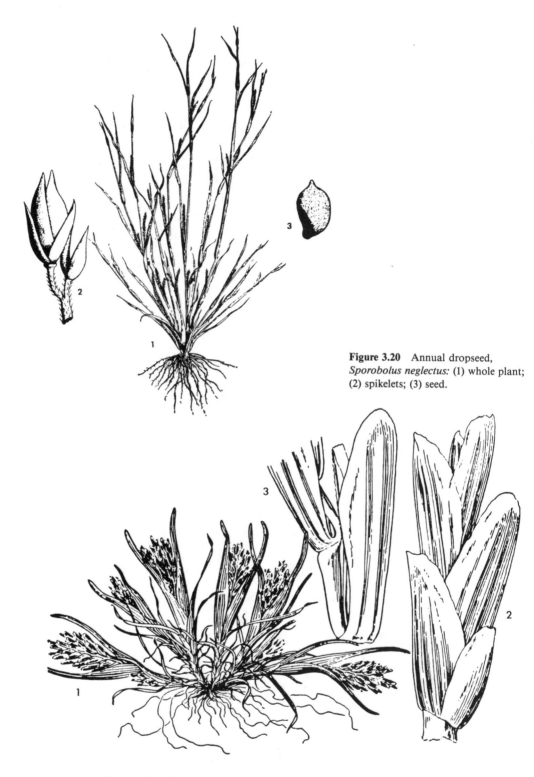

Figure 3.20 Annual dropseed, *Sporobolus neglectus:* (1) whole plant; (2) spikelets; (3) seed.

Figure 3.21 Hardgrass, *Sclerochola dura:* (1) whole plant; (2) spikelet; (3) floret.

Figure 3.22 Junglerice, *Echinochloa colonum:* (1) emerging inflorescence; (2) panicle.

Annual dropseed, *Sporobolus neglectus.*   Annual dropseed (Figure 3.20) is an annual grass with short stems 6 to 12 in. high found throughout the midwestern and western states. The leaf blades are long and narrow with a tapering tip and somewhat hairy at the base. Annual dropseed is a late germinator but can persist in low-maintenance turf.

Hardgrass, *Sclerochola dura.*   Hardgrass (Figure 3.21) is a cool-season annual grass that closely resembles annual bluegrass. It is most common in the west but has been identified in Illinois. This grass has short, narrow leaf blades with boat-shaped tips. The seedheads are tightly bunched racemes with awnless, three-flowered spikelets. Unlike annual bluegrass, hardgrass thrives well in sandy or coarse soils.

Junglerice, *Echinochloa colonum.*   Junglerice (Figure 3.22) is an annual grass, distributed throughout the southern United States. This species is often mistaken for barn-yardgrass. However, the spikelets do not have awns. The leaf blades are medium in width and the flowers are borne on a tight panicle with tightly bunched small spikelets. Junglerice is an occasional weed in turf, and often presents a problem in newly established areas.

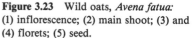

Figure 3.23 Wild oats, *Avena fatua:*
(1) inflorescence; (2) main shoot; (3) and
(4) florets; (5) seed.

Wild oats, *Avena fatua.* Wild oats (Figure 3.23) is an annual grass. It is found throughout the western United States. The stems are smooth and large, reaching a height of 1 to 4 ft where left unmowed. The leaves are coarse and long. The seedhead is an open, multibranched panicle with a spikelet at the end of each branch. The flowers have a distinctive long awn which is twisted. Wild oats will not long survive constant mowing and presents a problem only in newly established sites.

Fall panicum, *Panicum dichotomiflorum.* Fall panicum (Figure 3.24) is a late-germinating, cool-season annual grass. It has a short, purplish sheath with a medium-width leaf blade. The seedhead is an open panicle with the small, awned spikelets borne on secondary branches. This species is sometimes confused with witchgrass (page 80).

Rescuegrass, *Bromus catharticus.* Rescuegrass (Figure 3.25) is an annual or biennial grass distributed throughout most of the United States, being particularly common in the warm, humid, and arid regions. Its cool-season growth habits make it particularly troublesome in dormant, warm-season grasses. It has sparingly hairy, V-shaped, medium-width leaf blades. The spikelets are tightly grouped with 6 to 12 flowers on an open panicle seedhead. Rescuegrass has little tolerance to hot weather.

Figure 3.24 Fall panicum, *Panicum dichotomiflorum:* (1) whole plant; (2) branching panicle; (3) and (4) spikelets; (5) fertile floret.

Figure 3.25 Rescuegrass, *Bromus catharticus:* (1) leaf sheath and blade; (2) portion of panicle with spikelets.

Weeds That First Germinate in Spring

Italian ryegrass, *Lolium multiflorum.* Italian ryegrass (Figure 3.26), or annual ryegrass, is a cool-season, often annual, grass. It is generally introduced to turf through seed in inexpensive seed mixtures. Italian ryegrass is a medium- to coarse-bladed grass with prominent veins. The seedhead is a true spike with the spikelets attached directly to a single terminal stem. The flowers of annual ryegrass have prominent awns in comparison to the awnless flowers of perennial ryegrass. An additional distinctive characteristic of annual ryegrass is the long, pointed, clawlike auricles. It is found throughout the United States, where it is introduced through seeding.

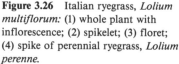

Figure 3.26 Italian ryegrass, *Lolium multiflorum:* (1) whole plant with inflorescence; (2) spikelet; (3) floret; (4) spike of perennial ryegrass, *Lolium perenne.*

Figure 3.27 Field sandbur, *Cenchrus incertus:* (1) whole plant; (2) modified spikelet or bur.

Figure 3.28 Stinkgrass, *Eragrostis cilianensis:* (1) whole plant; (2) spikelet; (3) seed.

Field sandbur, *Cenchrus incertus.* Field sandbur (Figure 3.27) is a warm-season annual grass found throughout the United States. It grows most readily in sandy or coarse-textured soils. The stems can be matlike, 6 inches to 2 ft in length, with smooth, twisted leaf blades. The spikelets are borne on a terminal spike and are enclosed in a sharp spiny bur containing one to three seeds. Field sandbur, like puncture vine, presents a hazard to man and animals due to the painful spikes on the bur.

Stinkgrass, *Eragrostis cilianensis.* Stinkgrass (Figure 3.28) is widely distributed throughout the United States. It has many slender, smooth stems arising from the crown. The leaves have smooth sheaths which are flat with long, tapering blades. The seedhead is a multibranched and moderately spreading panicle. Each spikelet contains 20 to 40 tightly compressed flowers. Stinkgrass has a disagreeable odor. *E. pectinacea* is smaller seeded and often occurs as a companion.

Weeds That First Germinate in Spring

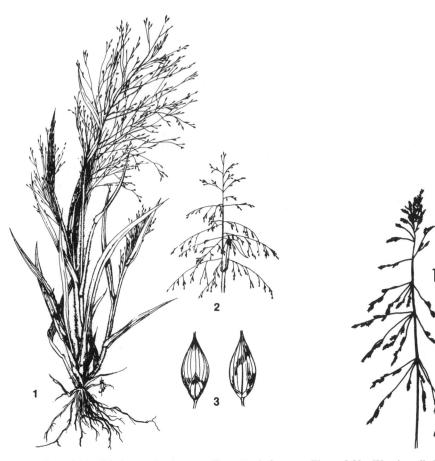

Figure 3.29 Witchgrass, *Panicum capillare:* (1) whole plant; (2) extended panicle; (3) spikelets.

Figure 3.30 Weeping alkaligrass, *Puccinellia distans:* (1) inflorescence; (2) floret.

Witchgrass, *Panicum capillare.*   Witchgrass (Figure 3.29) is widely distributed throughout the United States. The stems appear quite hairy. Leaf blades and sheaths are covered with dense, soft hairs and are medium in width. The seedhead is a many-branched panicle which is open and spreading at maturity. The spikelets are awnless and contain one flower. The entire seedhead breaks from the plant at maturity and can be blown across the ground by the wind. Witchgrass is sometimes confused with fall panicum (page 76).

Perennial Grasses

Weeping alkaligrass, *Puccinellia distans.*   Alkaligrass (Figure 3.30) is a cool-season grass species found throughout the northern United States, growing in soils with medium to high salt levels. Alkaligrass is a fine-bladed, bluish-green, bunch-type grass. The seedhead is an open panicle with four- to six-flowered spikelets. Alkaligrass is often used on roadsides where salting is carried out for the purpose of snow and ice removal.

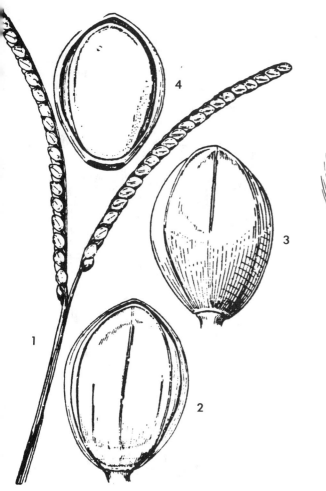

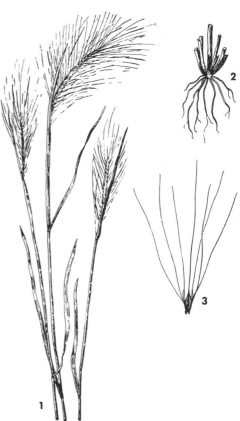

Figure 3.31 Bahiagrass, *Paspalum notatum:* (1) one-sided raceme; (2) and (3) spikelets; (4) floret.

Figure 3.32 Foxtail barley, *Hordeum jubatum:* (1) upper portion of plant with inflorescence; (2) base of plant; (3) seed with awns.

Bahiagrass, *Paspalum notatum.*   Bahiagrass (Figure 3.31) is a warm-season perennial found extensively through the warm, humid region. It is a coarse-textured, wide-bladed grass, with short, heavy stolons and rhizomes. The seedhead is a raceme with solitary spikelets. Bahiagrass is extensively grown as a low-maintenance turf through the southernmost areas of the warm, humid region (Figure 2.1). It can become a troublesome weed in finer-bladed, warm-season turfs. It is well adapted to low-fertility, coarse-textured soils.

Foxtail barley, *Hordeum jubatum.*   Foxtail barley (Figure 3.32) is a cool-season perennial grass found throughout the United States except in the southeast. It is a medium-bladed, yellow-green grass with a bunch-type growth habit. The seedhead of foxtail barley is a spike with one-flowered spikelets and extremely long awns. Foxtail barley germinates early in spring and is a persistent pest in semiarid areas.

Figure 3.33 Cogongrass, *Imperata cylindrica:* (1) whole plant with rhizome; (2) ligule and portion of sheath and blade; (3) spikelets.

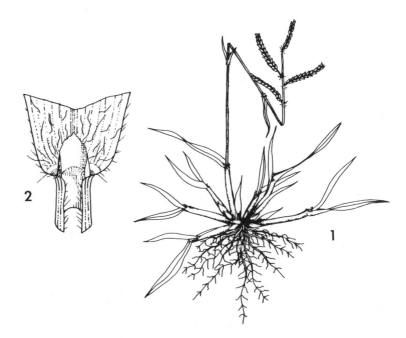

Figure 3.34 Dallisgrass, *Paspalum dilatatum:* (1) whole plant with inflorescence; (2) ligule.

Cogongrass, *Imperata cylindrica.* Cogongrass (Figure 3.33) is a warm-season perennial grass found throughout Florida and the Gulf coast. Cogongrass, which spreads by rhizomes, has medium-width leaf blades which are long and hairy. The spikelets are formed in a loosely branched panicle, with long silky hairs.

Dallisgrass, *Paspalum dilatatum.* Dallisgrass (Figure 3.34) is a warm-season perennial. It occurs extensively throughout the warm, humid region. Dallisgrass is one of the first grasses to begin growth in the spring. It is coarse-bladed and light yellow. The seeds are borne on a tightly branched raceme seedhead with rows of four tightly grouped spikelets. Dallisgrass can be an aggressive grass in medium-maintained turfs.

Johnsongrass, *Sorghum halepense.* Johnsongrass (Figure 3.35) is a warm-season perennial grass found in high-cut, low-maintenance turfs. It is a pale green, coarse-bladed rhizomatous grass, and a persistent pest in many crops. The seedheads of johnson-grass are open panicles with paired spikelets, the bottom spikelet having a long distinctive awn. Johnsongrass is a difficult-to-control weed in highway rights-of-way in the south. Its persistence can be minimized through frequent mowing at low heights.

Figure 3.35 Johnsongrass, *Sorghum halepense:* (1) main culm with rhizomes; (2) inflorescence; (3) group of spikelets; (4) leaf blade and sheath; (5) seed.

Weeds That First Germinate in Spring

Orchardgrass, *Dactylis glomerata.* Orchardgrass (Figure 3.36) is a cool-season, perennial grass found throughout the United States. It is principally used as a pasture or forage grass but can be introduced to turf as a contaminant in seed mixtures. It is a coarse-bladed, pale green bunch grass. The seedhead of orchardgrass is a short-branched panicle of four-flowered spikelets. In low-maintenance turf, orchardgrass is generally a problem only where it is introduced in establishment.

Figure 3.36 Orchardgrass, *Dactylis glomerata:* (1) whole plant with inflorescence; (2) spikelet; (3) floret.

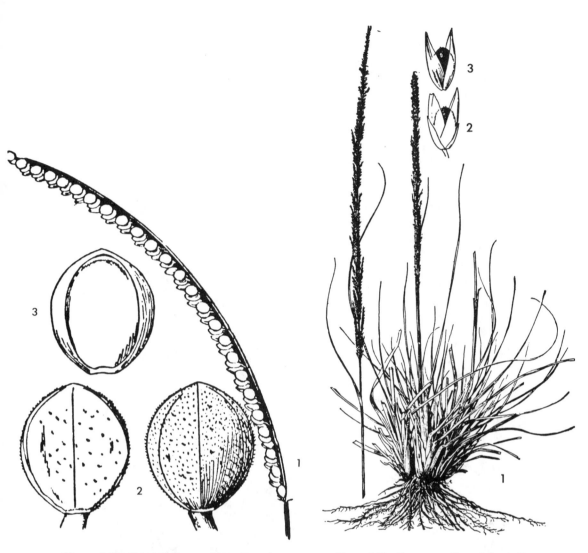

Figure 3.37 Fringeleaf paspalum, *Paspalum setaceum* var. *ciliatifolium:* (1) one-sided raceme; (2) spikelets; (3) floret.

Figure 3.38 Smutgrass, *Sporobolus indicus:* (1) whole plant with inflorescence; (2) spikelet; (3) floret.

Fringeleaf paspalum, *Paspalum setaceum* var. *ciliatifolium.*   Fringeleaf paspalum (Figure 3.37) is a warm-season perennial grass found throughout the warm, humid region. It thrives in sandy or droughty soil, is coarse-bladed, and has weak rhizomes. The seedhead of fringeleaf paspalum is a one- to three-branched raceme with two rows of spikelets on the underside. This species is extremely variable. The presence of hair or the shape of spikelets will vary even on a single plant.

Smutgrass, *Sporobolus indicus.*   Smutgrass (Figure 3.38) is a warm-season perennial distributed throughout the southeastern United States. The leaf blades are narrow, long, and pointed. The seedhead is a spikelike panicle. Smutgrass gets its name because a black fungus commonly grows on the maturing seedhead.

Weeds That First Germinate in Spring

Figure 3.39 (left) Timothy, *Phleum pratense:* (1) whole plant with inflorescence; (2) glumes; (3) floret.

Figure 3.40 (right) Torpedograss, *Panicum repens:* (1) whole plant with rhizomes; (2) spikelets; (3) floret.

Timothy, *Phleum pratense.* Timothy (Figure 3.39) is a cool-season perennial grass found throughout the northeastern United States. Timothy is commonly used as a forage or pasture grass and occurs as a weed in low-maintenance turf, where it is introduced in seed. It is bluish green and grows in coarse-bladed, bunch-type clumps. The seedhead of timothy is a single terminal spike with one-flowered, awned spikelets. It is easily recognized by the swollen or bulblike stems at the base of each shoot.

Figure 3.41 Common velvetgrass, *Holcus lanatus:* (1) whole plant; (2) *Holcus mollis,*
base of plant with rhizomes; (3) spikelet; (4) floret; (5) spikelet; (6) floret; (7) mature
fertile floret.

Torpedograss, *Panicum repens.* Torpedograss (Figure 3.40) is a warm-season
perennial found along the Gulf coast. It is strongly rhizomatous, with a bladeless sheath
at the base of all shoots. Higher up on the stem are medium-width leaf blades. The
seedhead is an extensively branched, open panicle, with two-flowered spikelets.

Velvetgrasses, *Holcus lanatus* and *H. mollis.* Velvetgrasses (Figure 3.41) are cool-
season perennials found in northern United States. *H. lanatus* is fibrous rooted and *H.
mollis* is rhizomatous. They are grayish green with fine pointed leaf blades. The seedhead
is a shortly branched panicle of two-flowered spikelets in bunches. Velvetgrass survives
close mowing and can be a persistent pest in moist soils.

Bedstraws, *Galium* spp.   Bedstraws (Figure 3.42) are annuals, multibranched, with narrow, rough leaves, in a circle of six to eight on jointed stems. The flowers are small, white, have four petals, and are borne on slender branches attached to the joints of the stem. The seeds are formed in round pods that have stiff bristles. Bedstraws can be found throughout the eastern United States and northwest coast but do not persist in closely mowed turf.

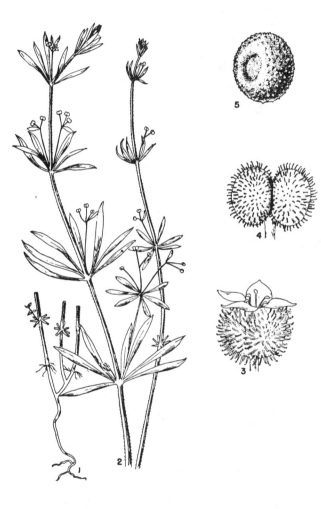

Figure 3.42 Bedstraw, *Galium aparine:* (1) lower section of plant; (2) upper portion of stem; (3) flower; (4) seedpod; (5) seed.

Buffalobur, *Solanum rostratum.*   Buffalobur (Figure 3.43) is an annual which generally occurs in low-fertility soils. The stems are multibranched, can reach heights of 24 in., and are covered with hairy, long, stiff, yellow prickles. The leaves are long, alternate on the stem, are dense and hairy, and cut into deep, rounded lobes. The flowers are yellow with five lobes and form a spike with rough burs that enclose the seeds. Buffalobur is found mostly in semiarid regions.

Figure 3.43 Buffalobur, *Solanum rostratum:* (1) whole plant; (2) and (3) seedpods; (4) flower.

Figure 3.44 Carpetweed, *Mollugo verticillata.*

Little burclover, *Medicago polymorpha* and *M. arabica.*   Little burclover (*Color plate 5*) is a winter annual weed found throughout most of the eastern and southern United States (*M. arabica*). The stems are round and smooth with a creeping growth habit. Leaves of little burclover are compound with leaflets in groups of three, resembling those of clover or black medic. Occasionally, they have white or dark red spots across the surface. The yellow-orange flowers appear in loose clusters. The seed pods appear twisted and are covered with barbed or hooked spines. These seed pods can be a nuisance in turf and can easily attach themselves to clothing or the fur of animals. Little burclover, with its prostrate growth habit, can spread even in closely mowed turfs.

Carpetweed, *Mollugo verticillata.*   Carpetweed (Figure 3.44) is an annual with smooth, tonguelike leaves. The stems branch in all directions, forming flat, circular mats. Carpetweed is slow to germinate in the spring but spreads rapidly in hot weather. Its many branches radiate from a single taproot. Single leaves are arranged like wheelspokes around the nodes. Small greenish-white flowers arise from the leaf axils. Carpetweed occurs in turfs throughout the United States.

Weeds That First Germinate in Spring

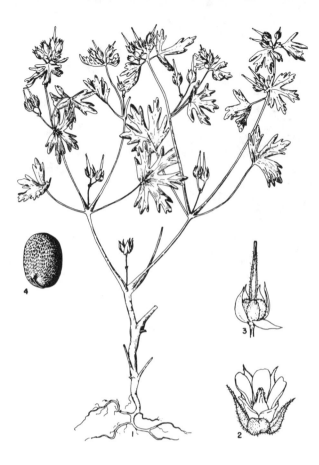

Figure 3.45 Carolina geranium, *Geranium carolinianum:* (1) whole plant; (2) flower; (3) seedpod; (4) seed.

Redstem filaree, *Erodium cicutarium.*   Redstem filaree (*Color plate 11*) is a prostrate, spreading annual that forms rosettes. It is widely distributed throughout the upper half of the warm, humid region. The deeply lobed leaves are hairy, dark green, and average about 1 in. in length. The flowers are small with five bright, rose to purple petals.

Carolina geranium, *Geranium carolinianum.*   Carolina geranium (Figure 3.45) is an annual or, sometimes, a biennial. Its root system is fibrous; stems are erect and branch at the base, reaching heights of 20 in. The leaves are 1 to 3 in. across and alternate with deeply cut, fingerlike divisions. The flowers are small, five-petaled, pale pink to lavender, and generally occur singly or in loose clusters at the tips of stems and branches. Carolina geranium can be found throughout most of the United States.

Prostrate knotweed, *Polygonum aviculare.*   Prostrate knotweed (Figure 3.46), an annual, is low-growing and appears early in spring. Its features vary depending on its maturity. Young plants have long, slender, dark green leaves that occur alternately on a tough, knotty stem. Mature plants have smaller, dull green leaves and inconspicuous white flowers. The swollen, or knotted, joints along the stem are covered with a thin, papery sheath. Knotweed persists in soil-compacted areas and is an excellent indicator of compacted soil or areas of excessive wear. It occurs throughout the United States but is particularly abundant in cool areas.

Figure 3.46 Prostrate knotweed, *Polygonum aviculare:* (1) whole plant; (2) flower on stem.

Figure 3.47 Kochia, *Kochia scoparia:* (1) whole plant; (2) flower.

Kochia, *Kochia scoparia.* Kochia (Figure 3.47) or Mexican fireweed is an annual found on dry sites. It has smooth, green, multibranched stems that grow to heights of 6 ft. The leaves are alternate, simple, hairy, 1 to 2 in. long, and attached directly to the stem. The flowers are small, greenish, without petals, and borne in the junction of the stem and upper leaves. Due to its adaptation to dry areas, it is most commonly found in semiarid places.

Weeds That First Germinate in Spring

Common lambsquarters, *Chenopodium album.*   Common lambsquarters (Figure 3.48) is an annual widely distributed throughout the United States. The stem arises from a taproot and is smooth with red or light green stripes. It can obtain heights of 3 to 4 ft. The extent of stem branching varies considerably, depending on other plant competition. The leaves are alternate, 1 to 3 in. long, with a distinct white, mealy coating on the underside. The edges are somewhat toothed. The flowers are small, green, without petals, and borne on the ends of branches and in the axils of stems. Common lambsquarters does not persist well in mowed turf but can be troublesome in newly established sites.

Common mallow, *Malva neglecta.*   Common or roundleaf mallow (Figure 3.49) is an annual or short-lived perennial. It has a long taproot and rounded leaves with five distinct lobes. The leaves are opposite on the stem and closely resemble those of ground ivy (page 126), for which it is sometimes mistaken. The flowers have five pinkish-white petals and arise from the leaf axil on the main stem. Unlike ground ivy, the spreading branches of mallow do not root at spots that touch the ground. Common mallow can be found throughout the United States but is especially persistent in cool regions.

Parsley-piert, *Alchemilla arvensis.*   Parsley-piert (*Color plate 6*) is a small, cool-season annual with small fanlike leaves that appear in clusters on the stem. The minute green flowers are in dense clusters in the leaf axils. Parsley-piert is common in dry, loamy, calcareous soils, where it appears in early (southern U.S.) or late (northern U.S.) spring and throughout the summer. Both leaves and stems are hairy with terminal growth reaching 4 to 9 in.

Birdseye pearlwort, *Sagina procumbens.*   Birdseye pearlwort is found extensively on the west coast of the United States, where it can heavily infest soils of low fertility. It is a small, fine-leafed plant which spreads into a dense circular or oval patch. Birdseye pearlwort is normally an annual but occasionally can be found surviving as a perennial. The leaves are smooth and narrow. Flower stalks are longer than the leaves and end with tiny white flowers. Although most common turf management practices have little effect, a good fertilization program can often discourage its spread. Early small infestations can be removed physically for control.

Prostrate pigweed, *Amaranthus blitoides.*   Prostrate pigweed (Figure 3.50) is an annual that is most often found in farm fields. Its prostrate growth habit can present a problem in newly established sites. Pigweed is a prolific seed producer and has good tolerance to hot, dry weather, competing well under such stress. The leaves are spear-shaped, dull green, and covered with dense, coarse hairs. Red or light green stripes run the length of the main stem. The seed develop in bushy terminal spikes and along the leaf axils. Prostrate pigweed occurs throughout the United States.

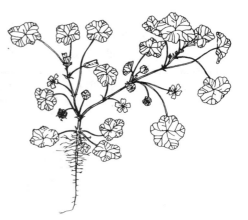

Figure 3.48 Common lambs-quarters, *Chenopodium album:* (1) taproot; (2) stem with inflorescence; (3) flowers.

Figure 3.49 Common mallow, *Malva neglecta.*

Figure 3.50 Prostrate pigweed, *Amaranthus blitoides:* (1) lower portion of plant with roots; (2) upper stem with flowers.

Weeds That First Germinate in Spring

Poorjoe, *Diodia teres.*   Poorjoe (Figure 3.51) is a creeping annual with long, narrow leaves, which makes it somewhat difficult to distinguish from coarse-textured grasses. The leaves are opposite and attached directly to long trailing stems covered with soft, inconspicuous hairs. Round, buttonlike seed capsules form at the leaf axils. The starlike, four-petaled purple flowers are conspicuous.

Figure 3.51 Poorjoe, *Diodia teres:* (1) whole plant; (2) seed capsule.

Puncturevine, *Tribulus terrestris.*   Puncturevine (Figure 3.52) is an annual found in warm, humid or arid regions. It has multibranching, hairy stems, arising from simple taproots and a prostrate growth habit. The leaves are compound, oblong, opposite, and hairy. The flowers are small, yellow, five-petaled, and produced in the leaf axils. The seeds mature in a pod containing five sharp burs stiff enough to penetrate shoes or golf-cart tires. Puncturevine therefore presents a serious problem even in low populations. It occurs throughout the southern half of the United States.

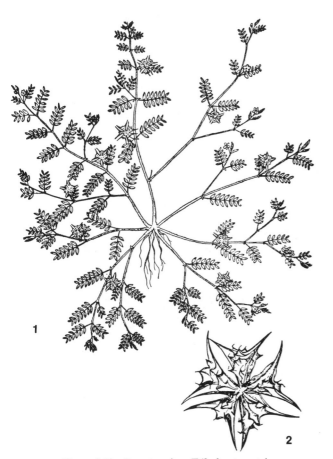

Figure 3.52 Puncturevine, *Tribulus terrestris:* (1) whole plant; (2) seedpod with burs.

Figure 3.53 Common purslane, *Portulaca oleracea.*

Common purslane, *Portulaca oleracea.* Common purslane (Figure 3.53) is an annual often found in newly established sites, where it can present a major source of competition. Common purslane has a fibrous root system with thick, succulent, often reddish stems that form dense mats 1 foot or more in diameter. It thrives well in extremely hot, dry weather due to its ability to store moisture. The leaves are alternate, or clustered, and thick and fleshy, similar to those of a jade plant. The waxy coating on the leaves not only minimizes water loss, but also makes common purslane difficult to control with herbicides. The flowers are small, yellow, and occur in the leaf axils. The seeds may be dormant in the soil for many years. Common purslane is widely distributed and occurs throughout the United States.

Figure 3.54 Annual sowthistle, *Sonchus oleraceus.*

Annual sowthistle, *Sonchus oleraceus.* Annual sowthistle (Figure 3.54) is an annual found in cool, humid regions. The stem is smooth, 1 to 6 ft tall, and has a milky juice. The erect growth habit does not allow persistence under mowing conditions. Annual sowthistle is thus a problem only in newly established sites. The leaves at the base of the stem have short petioles, while leaves at the top of the stem are directly attached. The leaves are long and deeply toothed with short spines at the margin. The flowers occur in light yellow masses, similar to a daisy, and are borne on stalks at the top of the plant. Annual sowthistle can be mistaken for dandelion (page 108).

Prostrate spurge, *Euphorbia humistrata* and *E. supina.* Prostrate spurge (Figure 3.55) is an annual appearing in late spring. The stems are prostrate, forming a mat. The leaves are opposite and frequently have a red blotch in the center. The stem, when broken, oozes a milky sap. Prostrate spurge occurs throughout the northern United States and persists well under closely mowed turf.

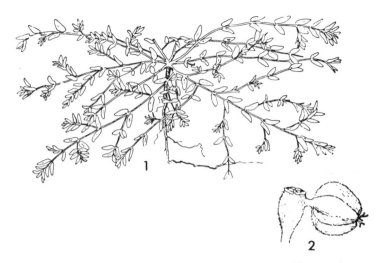

Figure 3.55 Prostrate spurge, *Euphorbia humistrata:* (1) whole plant; (2) seedpod.

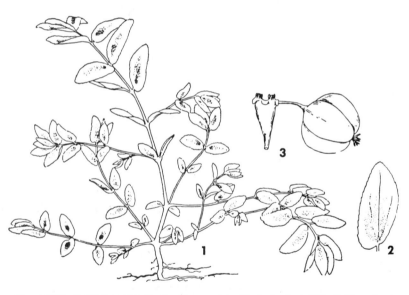

Figure 3.56 Spotted spurge, *Euphorbia maculata:* (1) whole plant; (2) leaf; (3) seedpod.

Spotted spurge, *Euphorbia maculata.* Spotted spurge (Figure 3.56) is an annual similar to prostrate spurge. It germinates in late spring or early summer and has a shallow taproot. It is more erect in its growth, however, than prostrate spurge but can spread from 6 in. to 3 ft. There are generally fewer (than prostrate spurge) but larger leaves on the stem, each leaf with a conspicuous red blotch in the center. Spotted spurge is found throughout the eastern United States, being more abundant in warmer areas.

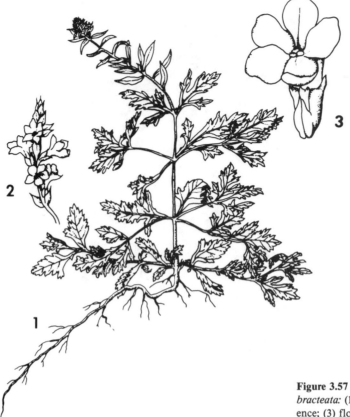

Figure 3.57 Prostrate vervain, *Verbena bracteata:* (1) whole plant; (2) inflorescence; (3) flower.

Prostrate vervain, *Verbena bracteata.* Prostrate vervain (Figure 3.57) is an annual occasionally found in turf. The hairy stems are prostrate from a few inches to more than a foot long, branching freely at the base. The numerous leaves are small, rough, opposite, and deeply lobed or toothed, with conspicuous hair. The flowers are blue or purplish, small, and in dense spikes almost hidden by the surrounding green petals. Prostrate vervain is generally found in warm, humid, or arid regions.

Waterpod, *Ellisia nyctelea.* Waterpod (Figure 3.58) is a cool-season annual found throughout the northern United States. It germinates early in spring, with flowers appearing in April or May and seeds maturing in early summer. The roots are shallow and fibrous and the stem is succulent and branching with sparse hairs. Unmowed, the plant grows from 3 to 15 in. tall. The sparingly toothed leaves are deeply divided and are either opposite and alternate with long petioles, depending on their position on the plant. The single, small white flowers develop into fruit, which generally contains four seeds. Waterpod will tolerate shade and occurs in lawns with partial to heavy shade.

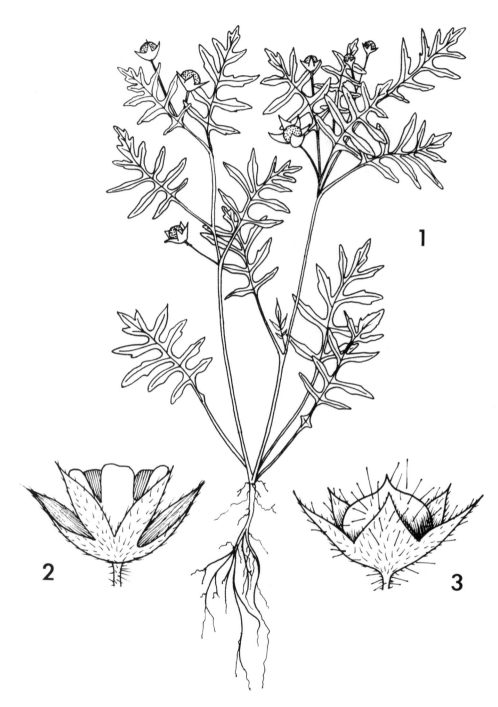

Figure 3.58 Waterpod, *Ellisia nyctelea:* (1) whole plant; (2) flower; (3) fruit.

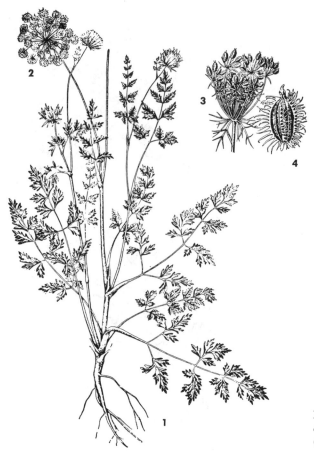

Figure 3.59 Wild carrot, *Daucus carota:* (1) whole plant; (2) inflorescence; (3) seedhead; (4) seed.

Biennial Broadleaf Weeds

Wild carrot, *Daucus carota.* Wild carrot (Figure 3.59) or Queen Anne's lace is a biennial producing rosettes with a fleshy taproot in the first year. The leaves are alternate and finely divided, hairy, with a distinctive carrotlike odor. In the second year, the floral stalks appear with small five-petal flowers, borne in groups at the ends of branches. Wild carrot can survive close mowing and produces clusters of flowers which are flat and near the ground. It is often confused with yarrow, a similar fine-leafed perennial. Wild carrot is widely distributed throughout the eastern United States.

Curly dock, *Rumex crispus.* Curly dock (Figure 3.60) is a low-growing perennial found throughout the United States. A branched taproot forms a rosette of long leaves with wrinkled margins. The flowers form in dense clusters on erect branches that develop in unmowed situations. Curly dock is competitive during summer stress, due to food reserves in the taproot.

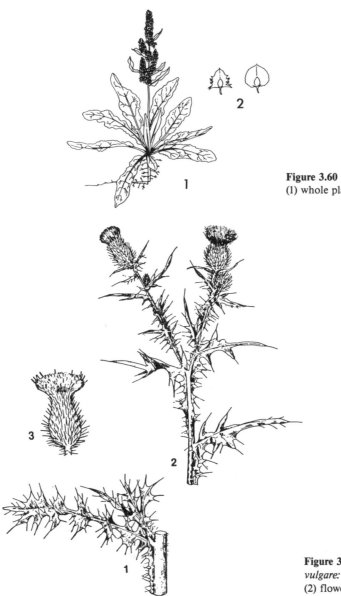

Figure 3.60 Curly dock, *Rumex crispus:* (1) whole plant; (2) flowers.

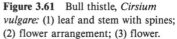

Figure 3.61 Bull thistle, *Cirsium vulgare:* (1) leaf and stem with spines; (2) flower arrangement; (3) flower.

Bull thistle, *Cirsium vulgare.* Bull thistle (Figure 3.61) produces a rosette of deeply cut, hairy, spiny green leaves. The spines are hard and can puncture the skin. In the second year, flowering stems bear reddish-purple spiny flowers. Bull thistle does not tolerate mowing and is generally a problem only in newly established turf. It has wide distribution throughout the cool, humid region.

Perennial Broadleaf Weeds

Creeping bellflower, *Campanula rapunculoides.* Creeping bellflower (Figure 3.62) is a perennial common throughout the upper cool-humid region. It spreads throughout the turf by short stolons. The stems are generally erect, reaching heights of 3 ft, and contain a milky juice. The basal leaves have a long petiole and are heart-shaped with minimal serrate margin, while the upper leaves are smaller and directly attached to the stem. The flowers are numerous and bell-shaped, approximately ¾ in. long with five purple teeth scattered along the upper portion of the stem. Creeping bellflower, sometimes used as an ornamental, can become a troublesome weed in turf.

Florida betony, *Stachys floridana.* Florida betony (Figure 3.63) is a cool-season weed found mostly in the southeastern United States. It generally appears in fall in cool, moist weather spreading through underground white tubers. The stems are square and not branched, with leaves opposite, broad at the base, and tapered to a round tip. The edges are serrated or sawtoothed. Florida betony has irregular, trumpet-shaped lavender flowers. It is generally dormant during the summer season.

Figure 3.62 Creeping bellflower, *Campanula rapunculoides:* (1) upper stem with inflorescence; (2) lower stem and roots; (3) immature plant.

Figure 3.63 Florida betony, *Stachys floridana.*

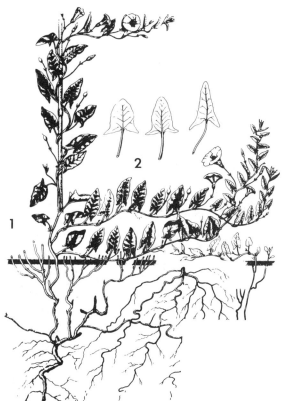

Figure 3.64 Field bindweed, *Convolvulus arvensis:* (1) whole plant with stolons and rhizomes; (2) variation in leaf shape.

Field bindweed, *Convolvulus arvensis.* Field bindweed (Figure 3.64) is a low-growing, creeping perennial found throughout most of the United States. It has a very extensive, deep, multibranched root system which ensures its survival through periods of stress. The stems are smooth and slender, 2 to 7 ft long, with a vinelike growth habit that twists and covers plant material in its path. The leaves are arrow-shaped but variable in shape and size. The white and pink flowers are funnel-shaped, approximately 1 in. across, and formed singly in the leaf axils. Field bindweed is a serious weed in agriculture and is considered a noxious weed in many states.

Weeds That First Germinate in Spring

Creeping buttercup, *Ranunculus repens.* Creeping buttercup (Figure 3.65) is a perennial introduced from Europe, found in the northern United States. It thrives in moist, rich soils and occurs in lawns and along ditches. The stems are low and hairy, and creep, rooting at the nodes. This growth habit quickly covers the ground with a network of plants. The leaves are long petioled and alternate, three-divided, and three-lobed. They are hairy, dark green, and sometimes have lighter spots. Yellow, five-petaled flowers appear between May and August, producing numerous seeds. The perfect flowers are approximately ½ in. long and borne at the end of long, terminal stalks. Improving soil drainage and lowering the mowing height aids in the control of creeping buttercup.

Figure 3.65 Creeping buttercup, *Ranunculus repens.*

Figure 3.66 Virginia buttonweed, *Diodia virgin* (1) whole plant; (2) seedpods.

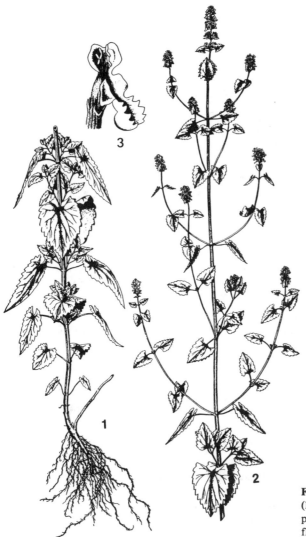

Figure 3.67 Catnip, *Nepeta cataria:* (1) lower portion of plant; (2) upper portion of plant and inflorescence; (3) flower.

Virginia buttonweed, *Diodia virginica.* Virginia buttonweed (Figure 3.66) is one of the most troublesome turf pests in the southeastern United States. It is a prostrate-growing perennial with somewhat fleshy lanceolate leaves. The white or purplish flowers resemble those of poorjoe but have two sepals instead of four. Virginia buttonweed is most severe in moist areas.

Catnip, *Nepeta cataria.* Catnip (Figure 3.67) is an erect-growing perennial found throughout the United States. The stems, which are covered with fine, short hairs, are 2 to 3 ft tall, square, and light green. The heart-shaped leaves are opposite and pointed with soft-toothed margins. The leaves are darker green on the upper surface and light green or whitish underneath. The flowers, with the petals formed into a two-lipped tube, form in dense clusters at the ends of the stems and branches. Catnip is a serious pest only in newly established turfs.

Figure 3.68 Mouseear chickweed, *Cerastium vulgatum.*

Mouseear chickweed, *Cerastium vulgatum.* Mouseear chickweed (Figure 3.68) is a low-growing perennial found throughout most of the United States. The roots of this species are shallow, branched, and fibrous. The stems are generally hairy, slender, and spread closely over the ground. The leaves are small, very hairy, opposite, and somewhat thickened or fleshy. The flowers are small, white, five-petaled, and notched at the tip. The bracts surrounding the flower are also hairy. Growth of mouseear chickweed is stimulated by close, continuous mowing. The stems of this species can root from nodes that come into contact with the soil.

Chicory, *Cichorium intybus.* Chicory (Figure 3.69) is an erect perennial found throughout the northern United States. It has a large, deep, fleshy taproot and stems that are erect, branched, and smooth with a milky sap. The basal leaves are long and deeply lobed, forming a basal rosette; leaves growing on the stems are smaller and much less lobed. Small, blue, daisylike flowers are borne on long petioles. Chicory is quite resistant to mowing and is more prevalent in low-maintenance or newly established turf.

Silvery cinquefoil, *Potentilla argentea.* Silvery cinquefoil (Figure 3.70) is an erect perennial found throughout the northern parts of the cool, humid region. The stems are long and prostrate, with leaves having five to seven sharply toothed leaflets. The lower leaf surface is densely covered with short hairs and silvery in color. The yellow-petaled flowers are about ½ in. across and borne on short stalks in the leaf axils. Silvery cinquefoil is an indicator of poor soil fertility. It is a tough wiry plant, and is often confused with wild strawberry (page 116). Unlike the three-lobed strawberry leaf, silvery cinquefoil leaves are divided into five leaflets. It is seldom a serious turf pest.

Clovers, *Trifolium* spp. Several species of clover, including bur, crimson, hop, and white clover, can often invade turf, presenting a difficult weed problem. Each species has flowers of a unique color and size (*Color plates 7 to 9*). They are generally borne on separate stems in a single, tightly bunched cluster. Clover stems are prostrate and root from nodes that touch the soil. The leaves are compound with three short, soft leaflets. The leaves of white clover, the most common turf pest, have white markings across each leaflet. Clovers are often used in low-maintenance seed mixtures but can become dominant in a turf. They are widely distributed and common throughout the United States.

English daisy, *Bellis perennis.*   English daisy (Figure 3.71) is a low-growing perennial first introduced as an ornamental. It occurs throughout the west coast. It usually grows in soil that is low in fertility. The leaves are rounded, slightly toothed, narrow at the base, and vary from nearly smooth to slightly hairy. The daisylike flowers are whitish to pink with bright yellow centers. English daisies can form extensive patches in turf in a short period of time.

Figure 3.70 (below) Silvery cinquefoil, *Potentilla argentea.*

Figure 3.69 (below) Chicory, *Cichorium intybus:* (1) basal whorl of leaves; (2) upper branch with flower.

Figure 3.71 (below) English daisy, *Bellis perennis.*

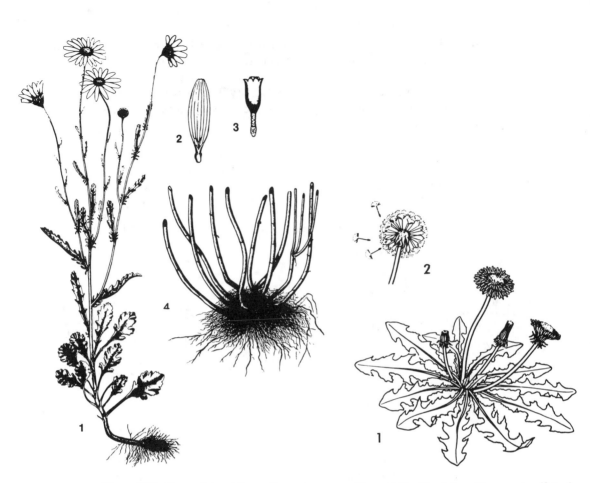

Figure 3.72 Oxeye daisy, *Chrysanthemum leucanthemum:* (1) whole plant with flowers; (2) ray flower; (3) disk flower; (4) lower stems and roots.

Figure 3.73 Dandelion, *Taraxacum officinale:* (1) whole plant; (2) mature seedhead.

Oxeye daisy, *Chrysanthemum leucanthemum.*   Oxeye daisy (Figure 3.72) is a low-growing to upright perennial that produces rhizomes. The stems are smooth, seldom branched, and 1 to 3 ft high, bearing simple, alternate leaves which are usually conspicuously low. The flowers are daisylike in appearance. Oxeye daisy is an indicator of low fertility but is seldom a problem in mowed turf. It is widely distributed throughout the cool, humid region.

Dandelion, *Taraxacum officinale.*   Dandelion (Figure 3.73) is a low-growing perennial common throughout the entire United States. Its roots are thick, fleshy, and often branched. Dandelion stems never elongate and produce a basal rosette of leaves. The leaves are simple but are deeply lobed, with the lobes pointing back toward the stem. The flowers are borne on single stalks with bright yellow flowers. Dandelions often regenerate from pieces of root or stem. When mature, dandelion seed develops a pappus and are transmitted through the air over large distances.

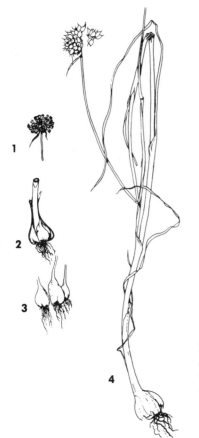

Figure 3.74 (left) Wild garlic, *Allium vineale:* (1) flower cluster; (2) old bulbs and bulblets; (3) underground bulblets; (4) whole plant.

Figure 3.75 (right) Wild onion, *Allium canadense:* (1) whole plant; (2) flower cluster; (3) old bulb.

Dichondra, *Dichondra repens.*   Dichondra (*Color plate 10*) is a low-growing perennial that is well adapted to a turf site. The stems form a low, dense mass that spreads across the ground. The leaves are kidney-shaped and pale green. The small, pale green flowers are inconspicuous. Dichondra is often used in southern California as a turf. As a weed in turf it is highly competitive, due to similar growth requirements. It occurs throughout most of the warm, humid zone.

Wild garlic, *Allium vineale,* and **wild onion,** *Allium canadense.*   Wild garlic (Figure 3.74) and wild onion (Figure 3.75) are similar species of perennial, grasslike plants. Both species have a hollow stem, 1 to 3 ft tall, which is smooth and waxy. The leaves of wild garlic are slender, hollow, nearly round, and attached to the lower half of the stem; the leaves of wild onion are flat and not hollow. These weeds have a characteristic strong odor. They are difficult to control in turf due to their waxy leaf coating which resists the penetration of most herbicides. They can reproduce in many ways, including under- and aboveground bulblets, flowers, and a central bulb. The flowers are greenish white, small, and borne on a short stem above aerial bulblets. Both species often occur together.

Mouseear hawkweed, *Hieracium pilosella.*   Mouseear hawkweed (Figure 3.76) is a perennial that varies in height from 6 in. to nearly 3 ft. The stems are covered with bristlelike hairs and spread by slender rhizomes and stolons. The spatula-shaped leaves may reach 10 in. in length and are most often found in basal rosettes. The flowers are yellow and daisylike.

Healall, *Prunella vulgaris.*   Healall (Figure 3.77) is an erect or low-growing perennial found throughout the cool, humid zone. Healall stems are long, branched, square, hairy when young, but smooth when mature. The leaves are oval, opposite, with smooth margins or very slightly notched, and 1 to 4 in. long with long petioles. The flowers are violet or purple with two-lipped tubes and form in groups at the ends of branches. Due to healall's creeping growth habit, it can form dense patches that escape close, continuous mowing. Despite its name, healall has no known medicinal value.

Common lespedeza, *Lespedeza striata.*   Common lespedeza (Figure 3.78) is a warm-season perennial found throughout the warm, humid region. It is well adapted to acidic soils of low fertility. Lespedeza is commonly grown for erosion control, soil improvement, and as a forage, but can escape and become a troublesome weed in turf. Lespedeza has small purple flowers and compound leaves with three leaflets. It is widely distributed through the southern United States and is particularly well adapted to the transition zone.

Figure 3.76   Mouseear hawkweed, *Hieracium pilosella.*

Figure 3.77 Healall, *Prunella vulgaris:* (1) whole plant; (2) rhizomatous growth habit; (3) flower.

Figure 3.78 Common lespedeza, *Lespedeza striata.* (Courtesy B. J. Johnson.)

Weeds That First Germinate in Spring

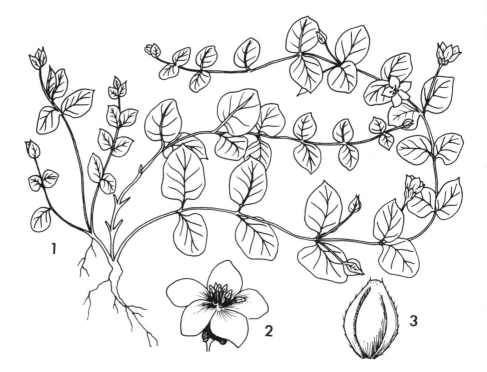

Figure 3.79 Moneywort, *Lysimachia nummularia:* (1) whole plant; (2) flower; (3) seed capsule.

Moneywort, *Lysimachia nummularia.*   Moneywort (Figure 3.79) is a prostrate perennial found throughout the eastern United States from Georgia to Canada. It is most abundant in moist, rich, shaded soils and reproduces by seed but more often through a creeping growth habit. The leaves are simple, short-petioled, nearly round, opposite, with a smooth margin, and ½ to 1 in. in diameter. Solitary, five-petaled, yellow flowers arise from leaf axils and are borne on slender pedicels. Moneywort was introduced as an ornamental from Europe and is still used as a ground cover. Moneywort blooms occur throughout summer from June to August. It is sometimes confused with ground ivy and is also called creeping jenny and creeping charlie. Its adaptation to moist, shady sites makes it more difficult to control.

Yellow nutsedge, *Cyperus esculentus,* and **purple nutsedge,** *Cyperus rotundus.* Yellow nutsedge (Figure 3.80) and purple nutsedge (Figure 3.81) are low-growing perennials that resemble grasses. They occur throughout the United States, particularly in turf under a medium to high level of irrigation. Nutsedges are light yellow-green, with triangular stems bearing three-ranked leaves, unlike the two-ranked leaves of the grass family. Yellow nutsedge has yellowish scales at the base of the stem and onionlike corms or nutlets. Purple nutsedge has reddish to purple scales, produces rhizomes, and lacks corms. The root systems are fibrous. Deep-rooted tubers or nutlets have the potential for reproducing new plants. The flowers are yellow to yellowish brown and three-ranked in a paniclelike arrangement. Sedges are often grouped with broadleaf plants because they can be selectively controlled in turf with herbicides.

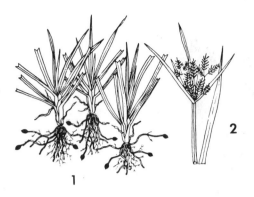

Figure 3.80 Yellow nutsedge, *Cyperus esculentus:* (1) whole plant with nutlets; (2) inflorescence.

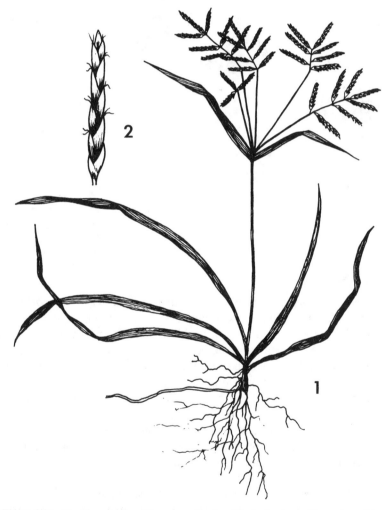

Figure 3.81 Purple nutsedge, *Cyperus rotundus:* (1) whole plant; (2) portion of inflorescence.

Weeds That First Germinate in Spring

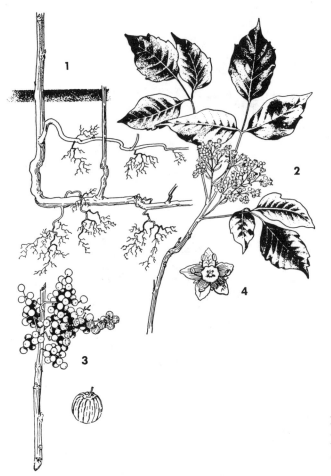

Figure 3.82 Poison-ivy, *Rhus radicans:*
(1) root and base of plant; (2) flowering
branch; (3) cluster of berries and single
berry; (4) flower.

Poison-ivy, *Rhus radicans,* and **poison-oak,** *R. toxicodendron.* Poison-ivy
(Figure 3.82) and poison-oak (Figure 3.83) are woody perennial species within the same
genus found throughout most of the United States. Poison-ivy is dominant in the eastern
half of the United States, while poison-oak is generally found in the West. The plants
may be a low-growing shrub or a vine climbing up in trees or fence rows. The leaves have
three shiny leaflets, 2 to 4 in. long, with pointed tips. The edges of leaflets may be smooth
or irregularly toothed. The flowers are small, green, five-petaled, and borne in a head
of 1 to 3 in. Each flower produces a berry which is small, white, round, and hard. All
parts of poison-oak and poison-ivy contain a material that can cause blistering of the
skin. Poison-ivy leaves often turn bright red in the fall. Both species vary in leaf shape,
rooting habit, and the amount of hair on the leaves.

Red sorrel, *Rumex acetosella.* Red sorrel (Figure 3.84) is a low-growing, creeping perennial found throughout the eastern United States. It has an extensive, shallow-
branching root system. New plants are generated along the branches. The stems are

Figure 3.83 Poison-oak, *Rhus toxicodendron*.

Figure 3.84 Red sorrel, *Rumex acetosella*.

generally short but can range up to 16 in. high if unmowed. Several stems may arise from a single crown. The leaves are arrow-shaped, somewhat thick and fleshy, and 1 to 3 in. long. Early growth consists of a rosette of basal leaves. The flowers are yellow to red and borne on branching seed stalks at the ends of stems. Male and female flowers are borne on different plants. The male flowers are yellow to yellow-green and female flowers are red to reddish brown. Red sorrel persists well in acidic, low-fertility soils and can be an indicator of a low pH. It can be difficult to control due to its thick, fleshy leaves and extensive root system.

Weeds That First Germinate in Spring

Figure 3.85 Speedwell, *Veronica officinalis:* (1) whole plant; (2) seed capsule.

Speedwells, *Veronica* spp. Speedwells (Figure 3.85) are a group of species of low-growing annual or perennial weeds that are similar in appearance. They are distributed throughout the cool-humid region. Speedwells have a fibrous root system with smooth branching stems that are seldom over 8 in. tall. The leaves are simple and narrow, with opposite leaves at the base and slightly toothed, alternate, and smooth-margined leaves on the stems. The axillary flowers are small and white to blue, giving rise to characteristic heart-shaped seed capsules. Speedwells are one of the most difficult turfgrass weeds to control.

Little starwort, *Stellaria graminea.* Little starwort (Figure 3.86) is a perennial generally found in coarse soils in the eastern United States and Canada. Its leaves are simple, opposite, narrow, and broader near the base. From May through July, white, perfect flowers appear on long-stalked, terminal, spreading cymes. The stems of little starwort are nearly prostrate, slender, and without hair. This weed is more abundant in damp, poorly drained soils.

Wild strawberry, *Fragaria vesca.* Wild strawberry (*Color plate 12*) is a perennial found throughout the United States. It generally resumes growth early in spring and blooms from May to July. The regular, small flowers have five rounded white petals. The compound leaves are in groups of three leaflets with sharply toothed margins. Both the stems and leaves are densely hairy. Wild strawberries have short, upright stems that produce numerous lateral stolons. The American Indian used strawberry juice and water to treat inflamed eyes. Root infusions were used to treat gonorrhea and mouth sores.

Canada thistle, *Cirsium arvense.* Canada thistle (Figure 3.87) is an extensively spreading, rhizomatous perennial widely distributed through the northern United States.

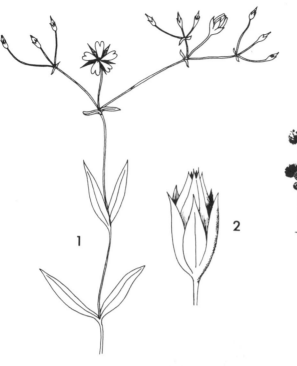

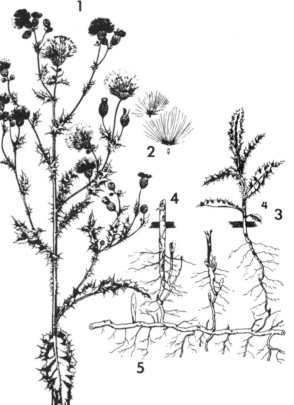

Figure 3.86 (above) Little starwort, *Stellaria graminea:* (1) whole plant; (2) seed capsule.

Figure 3.87 (right) Canada thistle, *Cirsium arvense:* (1) whole plant; (2) down with seed; (3) new shoot; (4) base of stem; (5) root system.

The multibranched roots can extend several feet deep into the soil. The stems can reach 2 to 5 ft tall, branch at the top, and are slightly hairy when young. The leaves have spiny margins and are somewhat lobed and smooth. Both the stems and leaf margins have hard, pointed spines which can easily penetrate the skin. The bright lavender flowers generally do not exist in mowed turf but are borne in apical bunches. Male and female flowers are in separate blooms and generally on separate plants. New plants can arise from broken root pieces, nullifying any potential physical control of this plant.

Hairy vetch, *Vicia villosa.* Hairy vetch (*Color plate 13*) is just one of a number of species of *Vicia* which occurs as weeds in turf. Hairy vetch is used as a cover crop or a green manure crop, sometimes escaping cultivation. It is often a component in seed mixtures. Hairy vetch occurs throughout the United States and can persist under normal mowing heights. The leaves are generally compound, alternate, narrow, and oblong with terminal climbing tendrils on the stem. Blue-and-white bicolored, ½-inch flowers form on a one-sided raceme, growing downward. They are irregular and pealike. Vetches are used extensively as a forage crop and are generally high in nitrogen due to their association with nitrogen-fixing bacteria.

Figure 3.88 (left) Violet, *Viola spp.*

Figure 3.89 (below) Common yarrow, *Achillea millefolium.*

Violets, *Viola* spp.   Violets (Figure 3.88) are a group of low-growing perennial species that produce strong rhizomes and extensive root systems. They are generally introduced from cultivated plantings. Their leaves are small, round, and borne on a long petiole. The flowers are generally white to lavender or purple. Violets are extremely difficult to control in shaded turf and are often resistant to selective herbicides.

Common yarrow, *Achillea millefolium.*   Common yarrow (Figure 3.89) is a perennial that produces rhizomes. The stems can be 1 to 2 ft tall and branch at the top. The leaves are soft, covered with hair, finely divided, and appear fernlike. The basal leaves are longer than the leaves arising from the stemless branches. The flowers are small, white, and in groups of 5 to 10. Yarrow can persist well under close mowing on poor soils but does not compete well in rich soils.

WEEDS THAT GERMINATE IN LATE SPRING AND SUMMER

Annual Grasses

Crabgrasses, *Digitaria* spp.   Large crabgrass, *Digitaria sanquinalis* (Figure 3.90), and smooth crabgrass, *Digitaria ischaemum* (Figure 3.91) are annuals which persist well under most turf conditions. They are coarse-bladed and light or apple green in color. Crabgrasses are highly competitive in turf and their spreading growth habit tends to minimize recovery by turfgrass species. Crabgrasses can germinate throughout the entire growing season after soil temperatures have warmed in the spring. Germination occurs after each irrigation or rainy period, thus requiring persistent control.

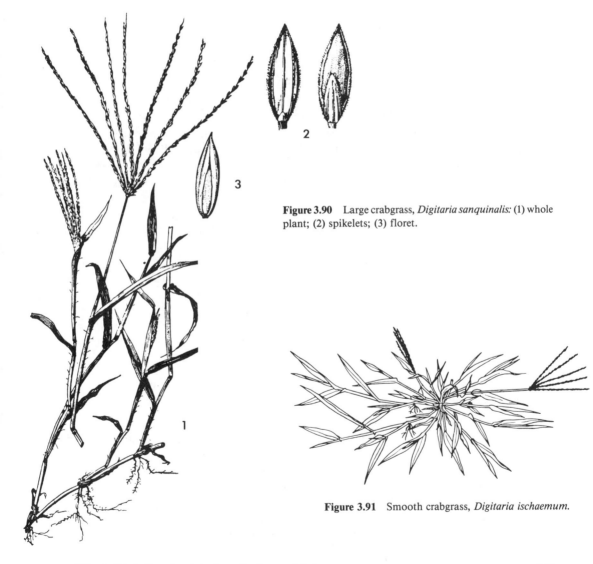

Figure 3.90   Large crabgrass, *Digitaria sanquinalis:* (1) whole plant; (2) spikelets; (3) floret.

Figure 3.91   Smooth crabgrass, *Digitaria ischaemum.*

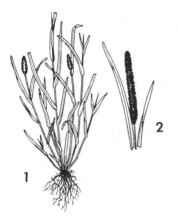

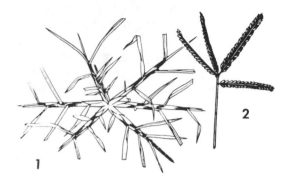

Figure 3.93 Goosegrass, *Eleusine indica:* (1) whole plant; (2) inflorescence.

Figure 3.92 Yellow foxtail, *Setaria glauca:* (1) whole plant; (2) inflorescence.

Yellow foxtail, *Setaria glauca.* Yellow foxtail (Figure 3.92) is a cool-season annual grass found throughout the United States. Introduced from Europe, it is most prevalent in thin turfs on rich soils. The stems are erect, branching, and compressed at the base. Leaf blades are flat and medium in width. The sheath is smooth and has a few long hairs at its base. Unlike most other cool-season grasses, yellow foxtail has a ring of hairs for a ligule. Young shoots have a rolled vernation. The inflorescence of yellow foxtail is a narrow spikelike panicle of one-flowered spikelets. Yellow foxtail receives its name from the yellowish appearance of the seedhead as it dries late in the season. It is generally not a serious weed in a well-established turf but can present serious competition to seedling grasses.

Goosegrass, *Eleusine indica.* Goosegrass (Figure 3.93) or silver crabgrass is a warm-season annual which generally germinates several weeks after crabgrass in the north during the spring. It can grow under extremely closely mowed conditions, such as a putting or bowling green. Under these conditions the lower portions of each stem are white or silvery. All spikelets on the seedhead are borne on one side of a branched panicle. Goosegrass grows abundantly in compacted or poorly drained soil. It is found throughout the United States, particularly in irrigated turf.

Perennial Grasses

Bermudagrass, *Cynodon dactylon.* Bermudagrass (Figure 3.94) is a warm-season perennial found throughout much of the United States. It is fine- to medium-bladed and low-growing, producing both rhizomes and stolons. Bermudagrass is extremely aggressive and one of the most rapidly growing grasses commonly found in turf. It has a deep root system that provides tolerance to drought but is particularly troublesome in moist soils. The seedhead of bermudagrass is a whorl of three or four racemes with small, one-flowered spikelets. Bermudagrass is the principal turfgrass species used in warm, humid regions but can become a troublesome pest when it invades other turfs.

Figure 3.94 Bermudagrass, *Cynodon dactylon:* (1) whole plant; (2) inflorescence.

Kikuyugrass, *Pennisetum clandestinum.* Kikuyugrass (Figure 3.95) is a warm-season perennial found in southern California and Hawaii. It is low-growing, with both rhizomes and stolons, and used somewhat as a turf species. The stems are compact and hairy with narrow leaf blades. The seedhead is a tightly compacted panicle at the tip of the flowering stem with two to four spikelets. The lemma is distinctly awned. Kikuyugrass is very difficult to control.

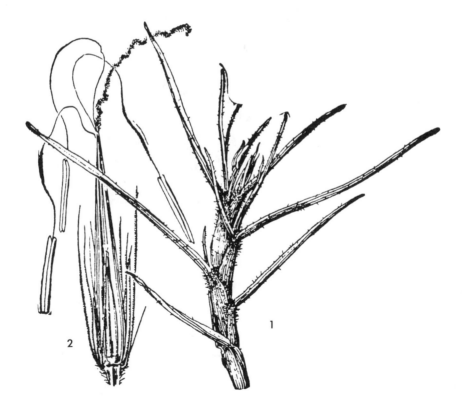

Figure 3.95 Kikuyugrass, *Pennisetum clandestinum:* (1) shoot with enclosed inflorescence; (2) spikelet.

Weeds That Germinate in Late Spring and Summer

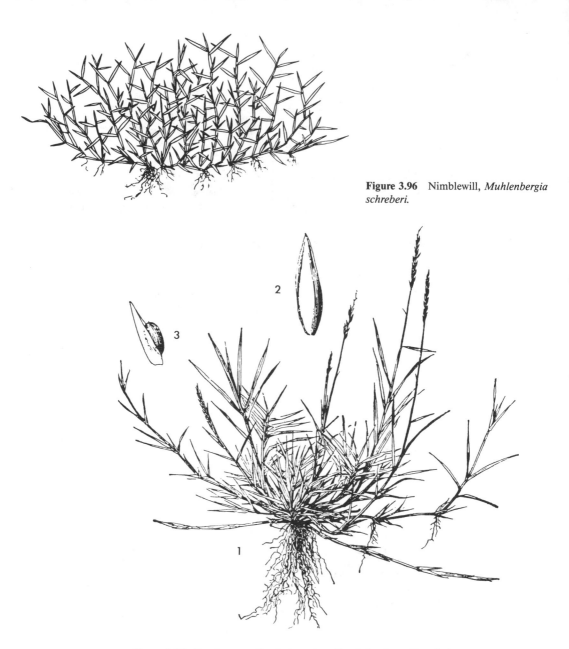

Figure 3.96 Nimblewill, *Muhlenbergia schreberi.*

Figure 3.97 Zoysiagrass, *Zoysia japonica:* (1) whole plant; (2) spikelet; (3) floret.

Nimblewill, *Muhlenbergia schreberi.* Nimblewill (Figure 3.96) is a warm-season perennial found throughout the United States with the exception of the northern border states. Nimblewill forms bluish-green patches in the turf. It has short, tapered leaf blades and stems that root at the nodes in contact with the soil. The seedhead is a spikelike panicle of single-flowered spikelets. Nimblewill is a pest in cool-season turfs, where it is generally aggressive during dry summer months, and forms brown patches during cooler periods of the year.

Figure 3.98 Spotted catsear, *Hypochoeris radicata.*

Zoysiagrasses, *Zoysia* spp.   Zoysiagrasses (Figure 3.97) are warm-season perennial grasses found throughout the southern half of the cool regions and the southern United States. Common zoysiagrass (*Z. japonica*) is a well-adapted turfgrass species for many places. It can be introduced to a nonzoysiagrass turf where it becomes a troublesome weed. Zoysiagrass is medium- to fine-bladed, and upright growing. It has both stolons and rhizomes. The seedhead is a compacted raceme with one-flowered spikelets resembling a spike. Zoysiagrass is difficult to control due to its aggressive growth habit, although its rate of spread is relatively slow. It is resistant to wear and can outcompete other turf species in high-use areas.

Perennial Broadleaf Weeds

Spotted catsear, *Hypochoeris radicata.*   Spotted catsear (Figure 3.98) is a perennial that occurs throughout the northern United States from the Pacific coast through eastern Canada. The yellow flowers of spotted catsear resemble dandelions and are generally over 1 in. in diameter, and borne on the end of a branch stalk nearly 1 ft high. The plant is often found as a basal rosette of irregular, round-lobed, hairy leaves with a thick milky taproot. The flowering stems are leafless and multibranched.

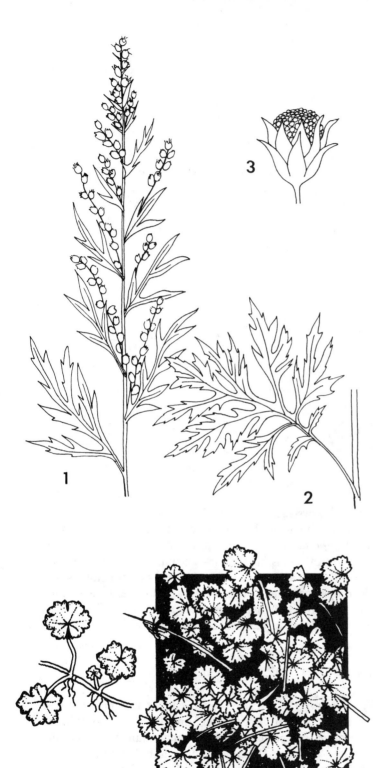

Figure 3.99 Mugwort, *Artemisia vulgaris:* (1) flowering shoot; (2) lower leaf; (3) flowerhead.

Figure 3.100 Lawn pennywort, *Hydrocotyle sibthorpioides.*

Biology and Control of Weeds in Turfgrasses   Chap. 3

Mugwort, *Artemisia vulgaris.* Mugwort (Figure 3.99) is a perennial most often found in western and northern United States. A native of the western states, it has been introduced eastward and is represented by several forms. Mugwort seed generally germinates in July. It has erect, rigid branching stems which are often reddish and can reach 1 to 3 ft when not mowed. The leaves are alternate and deeply lobed. These leaves have a woolly, white mass of hair on the underside and a long petiole. The flowers are numerous, small, and borne in spikelike clusters. Mugwort thrives well on calcareous soils and increases both by seed and short rootstocks.

Lawn pennywort, *Hydrocotyle sibthorpioides.* Lawn pennywort (Figure 3.100) is a perennial most noticeable during the summer in the Midwest and northeastern United States. Lawn pennywort was introduced from Asia and was used as a groundcover or ornamental plant. It increases by seed and stems rooting at nodes. Lawn pennywort can be found in medium-maintained turfs. The leaves are alternate and nearly rounded or shield-shaped, ½ to 1 in. in diameter, generally glossy, and with a slender petiole. The stems are prostrate and root at the nodes. The flowers are white.

WEEDS THAT GERMINATE IN SPRING AND FALL

Annual Broadleaf Weeds

Black medic, *Medicago lupulina.* Black medic (Figure 3.101) or yellow trefoil is an annual, biennial, and often a perennial found throughout the cool regions. It has a shallow taproot with slender and multibranching stems that spread from 1 to 2 ft. The leaves have three leaflets: the center one on a short petiole, similar to clover. The stems do not take root at the nodes. The flowers are bright yellow and compressed into small clusters. Black medic can be distinguished from white clover (page 106) by the lack of markings on the leaves and the distinctive yellow flowers. Black medic, a member of the legume family, is common throughout the United States.

Figure 3.101 Black medic, *Medicago lupulina.*

Yellow woodsorrel, *Oxalis stricta.*   Yellow woodsorrel (Figure 3.102) or oxalis is a perennial, with hairy stems weakly branched at the base. These may root at the nodes. It can be easily mistaken for a clover, with leaflets in groups of three. The middle leaflet, however, is not borne on a short stalk. The flowers are small with five conspicuous bright yellow petals. As the flowers mature, cucumber-shaped seedpods are formed. When dry, the seeds may scatter for several feet in all directions. Yellow woodsorrel occurs extensively throughout the United States and is a very common turf weed.

Perennial Broadleaf Weeds

Ground ivy, *Glechoma hederacea.*   Ground ivy (Figure 3.103) or creeping charlie is a low-growing perennial widely distributed throughout the United States. It forms dense patches in turf. It has shallow-rooted creeping stems. The square stems root at the nodes that come in contact with the ground. The leaves are almost round or kidney-shaped with round-toothed edges. Leaves are generally bright to dark green, somewhat hairy, opposite, and borne on long petioles. Ground ivy is well adapted to moist, shady areas, where it can easily outcompete turfgrass. The purplish-blue flowers have the typical trumpet shape found in the mint family. Due to its extensive stolons and root system, ground ivy is difficult to control.

Plantains, *Plantago* spp.   Broadleaf (*P. major*) (Figure 3.104), blackseed (*P. rugelii*), and buckhorn (*P. lanceolata*) plantains (Figure 3.105) are low-growing perennial species found throughout much of the United States. These species form basal rosettes of leaves. Buckhorn leaves are long, narrow, hairy, and 2 to 10 in. long. Broadleaf and blackseed plantain leaves are broad, simple, and egg-shaped. Blackseed plantain has a purplish petiole. The flowers of all species are borne on a leafless stem. Buckhorn plantain flowers are in a tight spike at the end of the stem, while broadleaf and blackseed plantain flowers are borne on an elongated spike on the stem. Plantains are common weeds in turf.

Annual Grasses

Annual bluegrass, *Poa annua.*   Annual bluegrass (Figure 3.106) is a winter annual or perennial that can persist in closely mowed turfs for many seasons. It is apple green in color and produces hundreds of whitish-green seedheads at all mowing heights. Seedhead production persists even at the extremely close mowing heights of a putting green. The ligule of annual bluegrass is acute, which readily distinguishes it from the truncate ligule of Kentucky bluegrass. It grows well on compacted soils under moist and shaded conditions and frequently occurs in dense patches. Seedheads are produced throughout the growing season but are particularly abundant during midspring. Closely mowed, perennial-type annual bluegrass is susceptible to winter damage and many diseases.

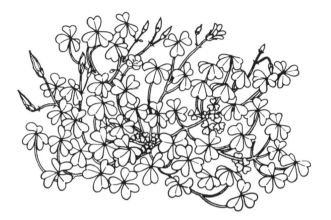

Figure 3.102 Yellow woodsorrel, *Oxalis stricta.*

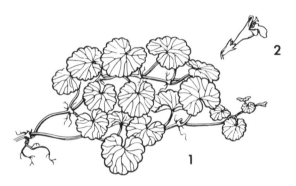

Figure 3.103 Ground ivy, *Glechoma hederacea:* (1) whole plant; (2) flower.

Figure 3.104 Broadleaf plantain, *Plantago major.*

Figure 3.105 Buckhorn plantain, *Plantago lanceolata.*

Figure 3.106 Annual bluegrass, *Poa annua.*

Weeds That Germinate in Spring and Fall

Perennial Grasses

Bentgrasses, *Agrostis* spp.   Bentgrasses (Figure 3.107) are cool-season perennial grasses found throughout the United States. They are medium to dark green, medium- to fine-leaved, prostrate, stoloniferous grasses. The seedhead is an open panicle of one-flowered spikelets with glumes longer than the flowers. Most bentgrass species are aggressive in closely mowed, moist soils of moderate to high fertility. In favorable environments bentgrass can spread rapidly and outcompete most other turfgrasses.

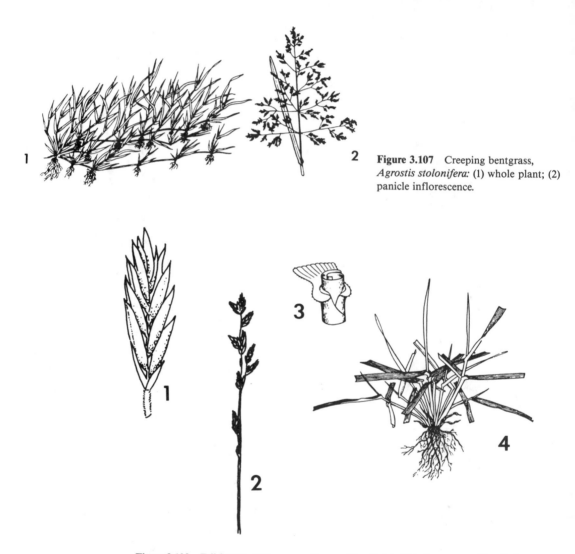

Figure 3.107   Creeping bentgrass, *Agrostis stolonifera:* (1) whole plant; (2) panicle inflorescence.

Figure 3.108   Tall fescue, *Festuca arundinacea:* (1) spikelet; (2) inflorescence; (3) rolled vernation; (4) whole plant.

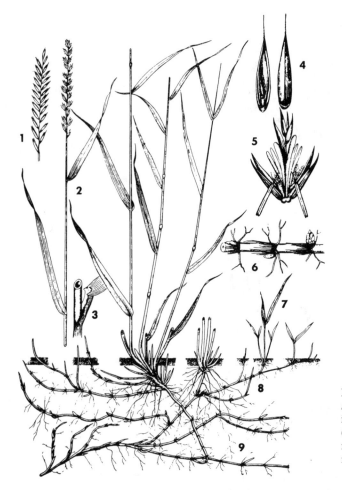

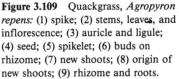

Figure 3.109 Quackgrass, *Agropyron repens:* (1) spike; (2) stems, leaves, and inflorescence; (3) auricle and ligule; (4) seed; (5) spikelet; (6) buds on rhizome; (7) new shoots; (8) origin of new shoots; (9) rhizome and roots.

Tall fescue, *Festuca arundinacea.* Tall fescue (Figure 3.108) is a coarse-bladed, cool-season perennial grass found throughout the United States. It is used widely in warmer areas, where it provides a good turf with some tolerance to shade, drought, and heat. Tall fescue is a medium-green bunch-type grass. It is often used as a single species for low- to medium-quality turfs but forms objectionable bunches or clumps of weeds in finer-bladed turfs. The seedhead of tall fescue is a slightly branched panicle of several flowered spikelets.

Quackgrass, *Agropyron repens.* Quackgrass (Figure 3.109) is a cool-season perennial found throughout the northern United States. Quackgrass is a medium-bladed, often blue-green rhizomatous grass which is persistent in cool-season turfs. The seedhead is a spike of multiflowered spikelets. Quackgrass has long, clawlike, though not very conspicuous auricles, that clasp the stem. Once established it is difficult to eradicate in turfs maintained at higher than ¾ in.

Weeds That Germinate in Spring and Fall

Figure 3.110 Redtop, *Agrostis alba:*
(1) main shoot and rhizomes; (2) ligule;
(3) inflorescence; (4) spikelet; (5) floret.

Redtop, *Agrostis alba.*   A cool-season perennial grass, redtop (Figure 3.110) is found throughout the northern United States. The leaf blades are medium to coarse in width, long, and tapered to a sharp point. The ligules are rounded to acute and tall. The inflorescence is typical of the bentgrasses. The glumes are longer than the florets in each spikelet. Redtop is very similar to bentgrass but does not have surface stolons and is sometimes bluish gray in color. It is tolerant of a wide range of soils and moisture conditions and will thrive in acidic or porous soils. Due to its coarse leaf texture, redtop is generally not used for fine turfs but is more appropriate for pasture or highway right-of-way use.

Perennial ryegrass, *Lolium perenne.*   Perennial ryegrass (Figure 3.26) is a cool-season bunchgrass found throughout the United States. It is often used as a turf. It is well adapted to medium maintenance. It is generally less tolerant to environmental extremes than Kentucky bluegrass, however, and is used principally in mixtures with other turfgrass species. As a very small percentage in a mixture, perennial ryegrass can become a serious weed. Perennial ryegrass is an excellent seedling competitor and can dominate in a mixture. While it tolerates a wide range of soil and environmental conditions, heat,

Figure 3.111 Downy brome, *Bromus tectorum:* (1) whole plant; (2) floret; (3) panicle inflorescence; (4) spikelets.

cold, and drought can take their toll on perennial ryegrass stands. The leaves are narrow to medium in width, light to dark green, and generally shiny on the underside. The auricles are short and stubby. The inflorescence is a long spike of many-flowered spikelets. Perennial ryegrass can be distinguished by the presence of short or stubby auricles, unlike the long clasping auricles of annual ryegrass. Also, perennial ryegrass is folded in the bud shoot, whereas annual ryegrass is generally rolled.

WEEDS THAT GERMINATE IN THE FALL

Annual Grasses

Downy brome, *Bromus tectorum.* Downy brome (Figure 3.111) or downy chess is widely distributed throughout the United States, with the exception of the extreme southeast. Downy brome, a cool-season grass, is often abundant in cultivated fields and sometimes in fall-seeded turf. The medium-coarse leaf blades and sheaths are pubescent. The inflorescence consists of a dense panicle, 2 to 10 in. long, with soft, drooping spikelets. Each spikelet forms 4 to 10 seeds with long conspicuous awns.

Smooth brome, *Bromus inermis.*   Smooth brome (Figure 3.112) has smooth stems and the flowers lack awns. It produces rhizomes and has a perennial growth habit. Smooth brome is a cool-season perennial grass often used for forage and erosion control. It has an open panicle seedhead with multiflowered spikelets. The sheath is not split or overlapped.

Annual Broadleaf Weeds

Hairy bittercress, *Cardamine hirsuta.*   Hairy bittercress (Figure 3.113) is a winter annual found throughout the eastern United States. In turf, it is generally found as a

Figure 3.112   Smooth brome, *Bromus inermis:* (1) base of plant with rhizomes; (2) panicle inflorescence; (3) spikelet.

Figure 3.113   Hairy bittercress, *Cardamine hirsuta.* (Courtesy B. J. Johnson.)

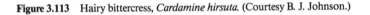

basal rosette of leaves which are deeply pinnately lobed and somewhat resemble a dandelion, with the exception of hair across the surface. Small white flowers are borne on racemes from February through May. Hairy bittercress is generally a pest in newly established turfs in moist, sandy soils.

Lawn burweed, *Soliva pterosperma.*   Lawn burweed (*Color plate 14*) is a low-growing winter annual found in warm, humid regions. The finely divided leaves are in narrow segments and appear twisted. Many conspicuous greenish flowers are attached directly to the spreading stems. The seeds produce a sharply pointed spine which can easily pierce the skin. Lawn burweed was first imported from South America as an ornamental but quickly became a troublesome weed in turf.

Mayweed chamomile, *Anthemis cotula.*   Mayweed chamomile (Figure 3.114) is a winter annual producing a short, thick taproot. It is also known as dog fennel or stinking fennel. The stems are erect, slender, much branched, nearly smooth, and reach a height of 12 to 18 in. when unmowed. Its flowers, ½ to 1 in. across, resemble those of daisies, growing singly at the ends of branches. Mayweed chamomile occurs throughout

Figure 3.114 Mayweed chamomile, *Anthemis cotula:* (1) whole plant; (2) seedling.

Weeds That Germinate in the Fall

133

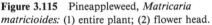

Figure 3.115 Pineappleweed, *Matricaria matricioides:* (1) entire plant; (2) flower head.

the eastern United States and closely resembles pineappleweed (Figure 3.115) found in the west. It has a strong, disagreeable odor.

Common chickweed, *Stellaria media.* Common chickweed (Figure 3.116) or starwort occurs throughout the United States. It is a winter annual, germinating in the fall and producing abundant growth in early spring. In protected areas, common chickweed may persist throughout the summer. It prefers moist, shady areas, where it spreads readily, impeding normal turf growth. Its creeping growth habit allows dense patches to form, competing well with the existing turf. In dormant, warm-season turfgrasses, common chickweed can spread extensively. The leaves are a bright shiny green, rounded and tapered to a point, borne opposite each other on hairy stems. Stem nodes touching the ground take root to form new plants. Common chickweed flowers are white with five deeply notched petals. They are extremely small but conspicuous.

Purple deadnettle, *Lamium purpureum.* Purple deadnettle (Figure 3.117) is a winter annual that occurs throughout the United States. It is generally more prevalent

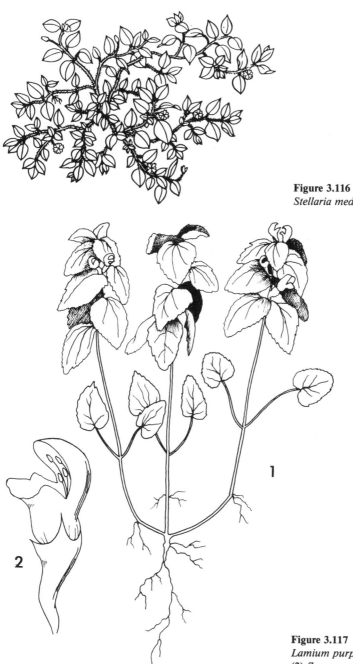

Figure 3.116 Common chickweed, *Stellaria media.*

Figure 3.117 Purple deadnettle, *Lamium purpureum:* (1) whole plant; (2) flower.

in fertile, moist soils. Purple deadnettle is more erect than henbit and can grow from 6 to 18 in. in height. It has square, purplish branched stems which can root from the nodes. The leaves are somewhat heart-shaped and hairy. The purple flowers, which can be found from April to October, are approximately ½ in. in length in whorls or bunches at the top of the stems.

Weeds That Germinate in the Fall

135

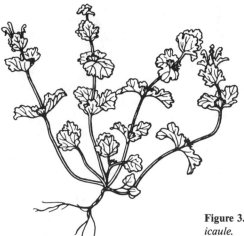

Figure 3.118 Henbit, *Lamium amplex-icaule.*

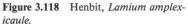

Figure 3.119 Wild mustard, *Sinapis arvensis:* (1) lower part of plant; (2) inflorescence; (3) leaf from upper part of stem; (4) flower cluster; (5) seedpod.

Henbit, *Lamium amplexicaule.*   Henbit (Figure 3.118) is typically a winter annual that usually germinates in early fall. It also germinates to a certain extent in early spring. Henbit, a member of the mint family, has a typical square stem. The leaves are rounded, coarse-toothed, hairy, deeply veined, and grow opposite each other on the main branches. The flowers are trumpet-shaped and pale purple. Henbit is primarily an upright grower but can root and vine from nodes. In warm-season turfs, henbit can be a particular early season problem.

Wild mustard, *Sinapis arvensis.*   Wild mustard (Figure 3.119) is a winter annual common in the warm, humid region and occasionally found in cool, humid zones. Its leaves are narrow and decrease in size toward the tip of the stem. They are alternate and irregularly lobed. The flowers of wild mustard are conspicuous, with four yellow petals, that appear in clusters at the ends of the branches. Wild mustard seeds live in the soil for many years.

Field pennycress, *Thlaspi arvense.*   Field pennycress (Figure 3.120) is a winter annual with an erect stem and is up to 20 in. tall in nonmowed areas. Its leaves are alternate, simple, toothed, and ½ to 2 in. long. The leaves clasp the upper stem with earlike projections. The flowers are white with four petals and are borne alternately along terminal branches. Field pennycress is generally found in cool regions.

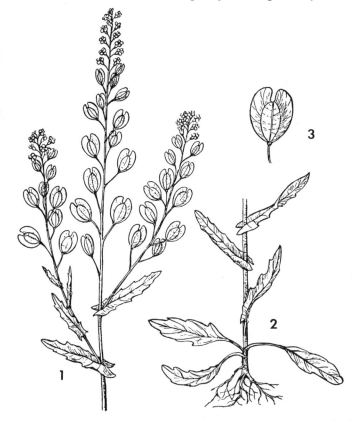

Figure 3.120   Field pennycress, *Thlaspi arvense:* (1) whole plant; (2) lower part of plant with roots; (3) seed.

Field pepperweed, *Lepidium campestre.*   Field pepperweed (Figure 3.121) is a winter annual. It resumes rapid growth in spring. Although generally a weed of open field and waste areas, it thrives well in turfs. Field pepperweed has a rosette growth habit through fall and early spring, when a single, long-flowering stem appears. As the flowering stem develops, the rosette disappears and is replaced by arrow-shaped leaves that clasp the stem. Field pepperweed is a member of the mustard family, with small, white flowers that contain four petals. The leaves are bright green with toothed margins and blunt or rounded tips. The seedpods have a distinct, strong, peppery taste typical of the mustard family. Field pepperweed is found throughout northern United States. *L. virginicum,* a similar species, is found throughout the southeastern United States.

Figure 3.121 Field pepperweed, *Lepidium campestre:* (1) upper part of plant with inflorescence; (2) leaf from basal whorl.

Figure 3.122 Yellow rocket, *Barbarea vulgaris:* (1) upper part of plant with inflorescence; (2) basal rosette of leaves with roots; (3) seedpod; (4) flower; (5) root.

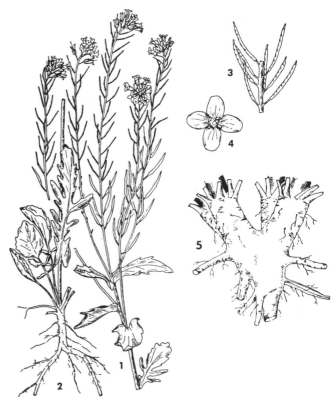

Yellow rocket, *Barbarea vulgaris.*   Yellow rocket (Figure 3.122) is a winter annual of the mustard family. It forms a rosette of leaves in early fall and generally remains in this state due to mowing of the turf. The leaves of yellow rocket are a bright, shiny green and deeply notched along the edges. They terminate in a large, rounded lobe. Its flowers are yellow, small, have four petals, and are found in clusters at the tips of the uppermost branches. Yellow rocket is found in cool regions.

Shepherdspurse, *Capsella bursa-pastoris.*   Shepherdspurse (Figure 3.123) is a winter annual that forms a basal rosette during early fall. While in the rosette stage, shepherdspurse can be misidentified as a dandelion (page 108). The leaves are coarsely lobed but generally more narrow than dandelions. As the weather warms in spring, a multiple-branched seed stalk arises from the center of the rosette. The leaves on these stems are arrow-shaped and coarsely toothed. The flowers of shepherdspurse are typical of the mustard family—small, white, and four-petaled. As the seeds mature, they form heart-shaped capsules resembling the purses used by shepherds in biblical times. Shepherdspurse can be found in cultivated areas throughout the world. It is primarily a problem in newly seeded turf.

Figure 3.123   Shepherdspurse, *Capsella bursa-pastoris:* (1) whole plant; (2) roots with basal rosettes; (3) flower; (4) seedpods.

Swinecress, *Coronopus didymus.* Swinecress (*Color plate 15*) is a winter annual found throughout the southeastern United States. It forms a basal rosette of leaves which are pinnately lobed toward the apex. Small, white flowers form in racemes on stems with opposite leaves. Swinecress produces an unpleasant pungent odor when bruised or ruptured.

CULTURAL CONTROL METHODS

Nonchemical controls for minimizing weed populations in turf are simple in concept. With few exceptions, turfgrass weeds will not flourish well under the same conditions as those optimal for turfgrass growth. Thus the turfgrass manager must provide growing conditions that enhance the rapid growth and development of turfgrasses at the expense of weeds. Many of the basic turfgrass cultural principles outlined in Chapter 2 are utilized to suppress weed populations.

Cultural and routine maintenance operations, such as mowing, irrigation, and fertilization, should proceed on schedule at the appropriate rate. Overfertilization is detrimental to turfgrass species and encourages an increase in weed populations. Underfertilization limits the competitive ability of the turf to outgrow weeds, minimizing the duration of chemical weed control practices.

The soil environment is also critical to proper turfgrass growth and the minimization of weed populations. The pH of turf soils, when feasible, should be kept between 6.0 and 7.0. In compacted fine-textured soils, core aerification should be utilized to alleviate compaction and provide more oxygen for root growth. Soil moisture should be adequate but not excessive to promote healthy turfgrass root development.

Turfgrass weeds are opportunistic and will invade damaged turf areas. It is important to ensure weed control in turf damaged from insect or disease problems (see Chapters 4 and 5). The turfgrass must be encouraged to regrow in damaged areas to gain a competitive edge on potential weeds. Many weeds can be excluded from turfgrass sites by frequent, regular mowing.

CHEMICAL CONTROLS

Herbicides are pesticides that kill one or more plant species. Only a small number of currently available herbicides are used in turfgrass weed control. They can be classified into one of three categories depending on the nature of their activity.

1. *Contact herbicides.* Contact herbicides kill plant parts that come in contact with the chemical. They are absorbed by living tissues of a plant to a small degree but do not move throughout the plant tissues. Since only the tissue contacted is killed, surfactants are often added to improve the coverage of the foliage. Contact herbicides have a very rapid effect and are used to quickly remove annual weeds. The injury symptoms of a plant treated with a contact herbicide are usually visible within hours. Temperature may affect the control. Cool weather may slow down the effectiveness of the contact herb-

icide. Many contact herbicides used have little or no soil activity. For example, paraquat is a contact herbicide often used to renovate or clean up dormant, warm-season turf. Contact herbicides do not provide effective control of perennial species, which may regrow from underground storage organs or roots.

2. *Systemic herbicides.* Systemic herbicides are absorbed by external tissue of plants (leaves, stems, and roots) and transported throughout the plant to provide killing action to the entire plant. Most herbicides used on turf are systemic in nature. They may be selective or nonselective. A selective herbicide is one that has a greater degree of activity on one group of plants while not injuring others. Nonselective herbicides provide the same amount of control for most species. For example, 2,4-D is a selective systemic herbicide which has high activity on most broadleaf weeds while showing little effect on most grasses. Glyphosate (Roundup or Kleenup) is an example of a nonselective systemic herbicide that kills most species of plants found in a turf landscape, including the turf itself.

3. *Soil sterilants.* Soil sterilants are chemicals that render the soil toxic to higher plant life. The difference between a soil sterilant and a nonselective herbicide is that the chemical remaining in the soil kills seeds that germinate for extended periods of time, thereby preventing regrowth of plants. The length of time soil remains void of plants depends on the material used, rate of application, and the environmental conditions, such as light, temperature, moisture, and soil properties, which affect the rate of decomposition of the herbicide. Soil sterilants are not generally used in turfgrass management. They are used, however, in preventing plant growth under fences, near curbing, or other areas where mowing is difficult or impossible. Some soil-sterilant herbicides move laterally in the soil solution and affect areas not initially treated with the sterilant. Prudent use around the edges of turf is necessary to ensure an attractive appearance and to prevent injury to landscaping materials which have roots extending into treated areas.

Control Strategy

The first step in the selection of an appropriate control strategy is in the correct identification of the weed. Most herbicides will control a broad spectrum of weeds.

Turfgrass weeds can be divided into three convenient groups, based on their most effective mode of control. Annual grasses and many broadleaf weeds are controlled with the use of herbicides applied prior to germination of the targeted weed species. These are called preemergence herbicides. Perennial grasses, due to their growth habits, which closely resemble those of the turf, provide a difficult problem as to selective control. For the most part, they are controlled with a nonselective herbicide and require renovation of the affected areas as a second step. Most broadleaf weeds and many grasslike weeds can be controlled selectively with a group of herbicides that have varying degrees of plant safety for different turfgrass species. These herbicides are usually applied to the actively growing weed and are absorbed through the foliage. They are called postemergence herbicides.

Although these broad classifications of weed control cover most weeds found in turf, there are many exceptions, particularly in different areas throughout the country. Information on local weed control methods and selection of herbicides should be obtained from the state extension turfgrass specialist. This information will generally contain specific control methods for common weeds in your area.

Environmental conditions both at the time of application and during the period of herbicide absorption and translocation will greatly influence the ability of the herbicide to control the weeds. The greatest absorption of herbicide will take place in weeds that are actively growing. Cool, dry soil conditions will minimize the effectiveness of a herbicide application. Under dry conditions, it is advantageous to irrigate prior to a herbicide application or to wait for a rainfall.

The relative stage of growth of weeds can also be an important factor in their control. Young, rapidly expanding weeds are more sensitive to injury and control from herbicides than are older, maturing plants. Applications of herbicides after plant emergence are most effective when the plants are young and actively growing.

Preemergence Herbicides

Most annual grasses can be controlled with a wide spectrum of materials used as preemergence herbicides (Table 3.1). These chemicals have a wide degree of safety and can be used on most turfs. However, most limit the versatility that a turfgrass manager might have in reseeding or overseeding a thin turf to provide additional plant density. With the exception of siduron and ethofumesate, preemergence herbicides are injurious to turfgrass seedlings. Siduron has selective activity on warm-season annual grasses and can be used in a cool-season turf seedbed. It can control a broad spectrum of weeds when applied at the time of seeding of perennial ryegrass turf. Application of ethofumesate should be made directly to the soil surface prior to any mulching. The period of active control of a preemergence herbicide depends on the material used, rate of application, soil temperature and moisture, and soil texture in general. Most preemergence herbicides are degraded in the environment through their gradual breakdown by microbial organisms. Losses through leaching, runoff, or chemical decomposition are generally minimal. The breakdown rate of a preemergence herbicide is therefore accelerated when conditions enhance the growth and development of microorganisms. Warm moist soil, with adequate aeration, will provide the best environment for breakdown, while cool, dry, or compacted soils will slow down the degradation process. An additional important consideration in the effectiveness of the preemergent herbicide is the degree of adsorption of the materials to clay particles in the soil. The greater the clay content in the soil, the greater the adsorption, leaving less herbicide available for absorption into emerging plants. Herbicide labels often instruct the user to apply more material in heavier clay soils to compensate for this process. In lighter, sandy soils, it is necessary to reduce the rate of application to minimize the possibility of injury to the turf. Second applications, often at reduced rates, are sometimes necessary to provide season-long weed control. Providing control of annual grasses is the primary use of preemergence herbicides. A secondary benefit is often realized in the control of annual broadleaf species. This minimizes the need for postemergent control of broadleaf annuals.

Postemergence Herbicides

Postemergence herbicides are utilized to selectively control many broadleaf and grass weeds in turf. These materials are systemic, absorbed through leaf and stem or root tissue,

TABLE 3.1 PREEMERGENCE HERBICIDES USED TO CONTROL WEEDS IN TURF

Herbicide: common name (trade name)	Weeds controlled	Tolerant turfgrasses	Rate (lb AI/acre)[a]
Benefin (Balan)	Crabgrasses, barnyardgrass, fall panicum, yellow foxtail, goosegrass, junglerice, seedling johnsongrass, Italian ryegrass, field sandbur, carpetweed, prostrate knotweed, lambsquarters, prostrate pigweed, purslane, annual bluegrass, chickweed	Kentucky bluegrass, perennial ryegrass, centipedegrass, tall fescue, fine fescues, zoysiagrass, bermudagrass, St. Augustinegrass, bahiagrass	2 to 3
Bensulide (Betasan)	Crabgrasses, yellow foxtail, barnyardgrass, annual bluegrass, lambsquarters, shepherdspurse, henbit	Kentucky bluegrass, zoysiagrass, rough bluegrass, creeping bentgrass, perennial ryegrass, St. Augustinegrass, tall fescue, fine fescues, redtop, bermudagrass, bahiagrass, dichondra, centipedegrass	7.5 to 10
DCPA (Dacthal)	Crabgrasses, annual bluegrass, spotted spurge, prostrate spurge, yellow foxtail, barnyardgrass, goosegrass	All turfgrasses except when grown at putting green height	10 to 15
Diphenamid (Enide)	Most grasses	Dichondra turfs only	10
Ethofumesate (Prograss)	Annual bluegrass, large crabgrass, barnyardgrass, yellow foxtail, common chickweed, common purslane	Perennial ryegrass, dormant bermudagrass	.75 to 1.5
Monuron (Cooke Oxalis Control)	Annual grasses, chickweed, woodsorrel	Dichondra turfs only	1
Oxadiazon (Ronstar)	Goosegrass, crabgrasses, annual bluegrass, barnyardgrass, fall panicum, hairy bittercress, carpetweed, common purslane, lambsquarters, speedwell, spotted catsear, swinecress, yellow woodsorrel	Perennial ryegrass, Kentucky bluegrass, bermudagrass, St. Augustinegrass, tall fescue, zoysiagrass	2 to 4

143

TABLE 3.1 PREEMERGENCE HERBICIDES USED TO CONTROL WEEDS IN TURF (continued)

Herbicide: common name (trade name)	Weeds controlled	Tolerant turfgrasses	Rate (lb AI/acre)[a]
Pendimethalin (Scotts Weedgrass Control 60WDG, Pre M) Light Rate	Crabgrasses, foxtails, barnyardgrass, fall panicum, annual bluegrass	Kentucky bluegrass, perennial ryegrass, fescues, bermudagrass, St. Augustinegrass, centipedegrass, bahiagrass, zoysiagrass	1.5
Pendimethalin (Scotts Weedgrass Control 60WDG, Pre M) Heavy Rate	Crabgrasses, foxtails, barnyardgrass, fall panicum, annual bluegrass, prostrate spurge, yellow woodsorrel, hop clover, cudweed, evening primrose, chickweed, henbit	Bermudagrass, bahiagrass, St. Augustinegrass, centipedegrass, zoysiagrass, tall fescue	3.0
Siduron (Tupersan)	Crabgrasses, foxtails, barnyardgrass	Kentucky bluegrass, tall fescue, fine fescues, smooth brome, perennial ryegrass, orchardgrass, Seaside, Highland, Astoria, and C-7 creeping bentgrasses	6 to 12
Simazine (Princep)	Annual bluegrass, little burclover, crabgrasses, lawn burweed, chickweed, speedwell, henbit, hop clover, yellow foxtail, barnyardgrass	Bermudagrass, St. Augustinegrass, zoysiagrass, buffalograss, centipedegrass	1 to 2

[a]AI, active ingredient.

and transported throughout the plant to affect all parts. Table 3.2 lists the selective postemergence materials for broadleaf weed control for use on turf. Bromoxynil, 2,4-D, MCPP, and dicamba are often available in varying combinations. They may also be tank mixed. When applied in combination, these materials exhibit a synergistic property. This enhanced activity may also cause injury to the turf. The user is cautioned to seek advice on the relative concentration of materials to be used in combinations. Optimum application conditions require moist, warm soil conditions for active weed growth. Postemergence herbicides must remain on leaf and stem surfaces for a period of time after application for thorough absorption. They should not, therefore, be applied prior to an anticipated rain. Cool weather and/or dry conditions after application can minimize the effectiveness of postemergence herbicide applications.

TABLE 3.2 POSTEMERGENCE HERBICIDES USED FOR SELECTIVE CONTROL OF BROADLEAF WEEDS IN TURF

Herbicide: Common name (trade name)	Rate (lb AI/acre)	Remarks
Bentazon (Basagran)	1	Use to selectively control yellow nutsedge in turf; repeat applications are sometimes necessary for total control
Bromoxynil (Brominal, Chipco Buctril, etc.)	0.375 to 2	May be used for broadleaf seedling control in newly seeded turf or in combination with 2,4-D, MCPP, or dicamba for use on established turfs except bentgrass
2,4-D (many trade names)	1	See Table 3.3 for spectrum of weeds controlled
MCPP (many trade names)	0.5 to 1	See Table 3.3 for spectrum of weeds controlled
Dicamba (Banvel)	0.25 to 1	See Table 3.3 for spectrum of weeds controlled
2,4-D + MCPP + Dicamba (Trimec, Trex-san, etc.)	1 to 1.5	See Table 3.3 for spectrum of weeds controlled
Triclopyr + 2,4-D (Turflon D)	0.75 to 1	Will control most weeds listed in Table 3.3; provides partial control of violets

Table 3.3 lists the relative sensitivity of broadleaf weed species to different postemergence herbicides. Sensitivity of each weed to the listed herbicide or herbicide combination is given in a scale of sensitive to resistant. Response ratings indicate control possibilities under ideal conditions. Poorer control is generally found under less than optimal conditions. Lack of a rating for a herbicide–weed combination indicates that information

TABLE 3.3 SUSCEPTIBILITY OF BROADLEAF WEEDS IN TURF TO POSTEMERGENCE HERBICIDES[a]

Broadleaf weed	2,4-D	MCPP	Dicamba	Combination of the three
Bedstraw	I	I	S	
Betony, Florida	I	I	S	
Bindweed, field	S-I	I	S	
Bittercress, hairy	S-I	I	S	
Burweed, lawn			S	
Buttercup, creeping	S-I	I	S	

Chemical Controls

TABLE 3.3 SUSCEPTIBILITY OF BROADLEAF WEEDS IN TURF TO POSTEMERGENCE HERBICIDES[a] (Continued)

Broadleaf weed	2,4-D	MCPP	Dicamba	Combination of the three
Carpetweed	S	I	S	S
Carrot, wild	S	S-I	S	S
Catnip	S			
Catsear, spotted	S	S	S	
Chamomile, mayweed	I			
Chickweed				
Common	R	S-I	S	S
Mouseear	R	S-I	S	S
Chicory	S	S	S	S
Cinquefoil, silvery	S-I	S-I	S-I	
Clover				
Crimson	S	S	S	
Hop	I	S	S	
White	I	S	S	S
Daisy				
English	R	I	S	
Oxeye	R	I	I	I
Dandelion	S	S-I	S	S
Deadnettle, red	I	I	S	
Dichondra	S-I	I	S-I	
Dock, curly	I	I-R	S	S
Filaree, redstem	S-I	I	S	
Garlic, wild	I	R	S-I	
Geranium, Carolina	S-I	S-I		
Hawkweed, yellow	S-I	R	S-I	S
Healall	S	S-I	S	
Henbit	I	I	S	S
Ivy				
Ground	I-R	I	S-I	S
Poison-	I			
Knotweed, prostrate	R	I	S	S
Kochia	S	S	S	
Lambsquarters	S	S	S	S
Lespedeza, common	I-R	S	S	
Mallow, roundleaf	I-R	I	S-I	S
Medic, black	R	I	S	S
Moneywort	S	S	S	
Mugwort	S-I	S-I	S	
Mustard, wild	S	I	S	
Onion, wild	I	R	S-I	S
Parsley-piert	R	S	S	
Pennycress, field	S	I	S	
Pennywort, lawn	S-I	S-I		
Pepperweed, field	S	S-I	S	
Pigweed, prostrate	S	S	S	

TABLE 3.3 SUSCEPTIBILITY OF BROADLEAF WEEDS IN TURF TO POSTEMERGENCE
HERBICIDES[a] (Continued)

Broadleaf weed	2,4-D	MCPP	Dicamba	Combination of the three
Plantain				
Broadleaf	S	I-R	R	S
Buckhorn	S	I-R	R	S
Poorjoe	S	S	S	
Puncturevine	S			
Purslane, common	I	R	S	S
Shepherdspurse	I	S-I	S	
Sorrel, red	R	R	S	S
Sowthistle, annual	S			
Speedwell				
Creeping	R	R	R	I
Purslane	I	I	I	S
Spurge, prostrate	I-R	I	S-I	S
Starwort, little	I	I	S	
Strawberry, wild	R	R	S-I	
Thistles				
Bull	S	I	S	
Canada	I	I	S	
Vervain, prostrate	S-I	I	S-I	
Violets	R	R	R	
Woodsorrel, yellow	I	I	I	S
Yarrow, common	I	I-R	S	S

[a]Indication of relative sensitivity of weed species under optimum conditions (warm, moist soil for rapid growth); cool, dry conditions will generally reduce susceptibility: S, susceptible; I, intermedially susceptible; R, resistant.

was not available at the time of publication. This sensitivity can be altered by the combination of materials, which often provides a synergistic degree of control. Most postemergence herbicides remain active long enough to prevent early reseeding or renovation of a turfgrass site. Very few postemergence herbicides have minimal soil activity and can be used in seedbeds to help control broadleaf weeds competing with turfgrass seedlings.

Annual grass weeds occasionally escape preemergence control. A group of postemergence herbicides is available for their control (Table 3.4). These herbicides should be applied in sequential applications to provide consistent, thorough control. Once the annual grass plant reaches a state of maturity, rates of herbicides required for consistent control are injurious to the turf.

Chemical Controls

TABLE 3.4 POSTEMERGENCE HERBICIDES USED FOR SELECTIVE CONTROL OF ANNUAL GRASS WEEDS IN TURF

Herbicide: common name (trade name)	Rate (lb AI/acre)	Tolerant turfgrasses	Weeds controlled	Remarks
DSMA (Weedone Crabgrass Killer, Scott's Summer Crabgrass Control, DSMA Liquid, etc.)	4 to 6	Consult label for formulation; do not use on St. Augustinegrass, bentgrasses, or fine fescues	Crabgrasses, dallisgrass, yellow nutsedge	High rates are needed for mature crabgrass; requires two to three resprays at 5- to 10-day intervals; apply when temperatures are below 85°F; will often result in yellow, discolored turf for a short period
MSMA (Acme Crabgrass and Nutgrass Killer, Bueno 6, etc.)	4 to 6	Consult label for formulation; do not use on bentgrass, St. Augustinegrass, red fescue, dichondra, or zoysiagrass	Crabgrasses, dallisgrass, yellow nutsedge	Air temperature and turf type determines degree of sensitivity; apply when air temperatures are below 85°F; most turfs are generally more sensitive to MSMA than to DSMA
CSMA (Weedone Crabgrass Killer)	2 to 5	Consult label for formulation; use low rate in bentgrass, dichondra, or fine fescue turf; may injure St. Augustinegrass, fescue, and some bentgrass species	Crabgrasses, dallisgrass, yellow nutsedge	Do not use when temperatures exceed 85°F; mature weeds may require repeat applications at 5- to 10-day intervals; may temporarily discolor or yellow turf
Pronamide (Kerb)	1	Bermudagrass	Annual bluegrass	Can be applied both pre- and postemergence for control of annual bluegrass
Fenoxaprop (Acclaim)	0.117 to 0.250	Kentucky bluegrass, perennial ryegrass, fine fescues, tall fescue, annual bluegrass	Crabgrasses, goosegrass, barnyardgrass, foxtail spp., panicum spp., johnsongrass	Apply prior to 2nd tiller, do not apply to Kentucky bluegrass less than 1 year old; do not tank mix with other herbicides

Nonselective Herbicides

Nonselective herbicides are most often used to control perennial grasses in turf (Table 3.5). For small weed populations a spot or localized application is generally appropriate. For large populations, broadscale applications are made with a follow-up reestablishment of the turf. Nonselective herbicides are generally chosen on the basis of the time they remain active in the soil and the possibility of their causing injury to turfgrass seedlings or sod. Herbicides such as glyphosate or paraquat, which have limited activity in the soil, are often chosen to minimize the interval between weed control and reestablishment of the turf. It is imperative that the application of nonselective herbicides precede a period in the year optimal for turfgrass establishment. Poor timing of nonselective weed control is generally not successful, due to reinvasion of the turf with similar weeds.

TABLE 3.5 NONSELECTIVE POSTEMERGENCE HERBICIDES USED TO CONTROL WEEDS IN TURF

Herbicide: common name (trade name)	Rate (lb AI/acre)	Remarks
Amitrole (Amitrole T)	5	Repeated treatments may be necessary for complete control of some weeds
Cacodylic acid (Phytar 560)	6 to 8	Apply as a preplant for control of principally annual weeds
Dalapon (Dowpon M)	10	Repeated treatments may be necessary for complete control of some weeds; used primarily in grass control
Glyphosate (Roundup, Kleenup)	1 to 2	Glyphosate has no residual activity in the soil; repeated treatments may be necessary for complete control of some weeds
Paraquat (Ortho Paraquat)	0.5	Contact herbicide; will not control established perennial weeds; surfactant will enhance coverage; no soil residue; may seed after treatment

Other nonselective herbicides (atrazine, bromacil, diuron, etc.), which act as soil sterilants, are sometimes used to maintain weed-free areas near established turfs. Their high degree of soil activity, however, limits their use in turf. They can often cause problems to turf and desirable ornamental plants if soil movement (i.e., erosion) occurs.

SELECTED REFERENCES

ANDERSON, W. P. 1977. *Weed Science Principles.* St. Paul, MN: West Publishing Co. 598 pages.

Anonymous. 1981. *Weeds of the North Central States.* College of Agriculture Bulletin 772, Agricultural Experiment Station, University of Illinois at Urbana-Champaign. 303 pages.

Anonymous. 1983. *Herbicide Handbook of the Weed Science Society of America,* 5th ed. Champaign, IL: Weed Science Society of America. 515 pages.

ASHTON, F. M., and A. S. CRAFTS. 1981. *Mode of Action of Herbicides.* New York: John Wiley & Sons, Inc. 525 pages.

FERNALD, M. L. 1950. *Gray's Manual of Botany,* 8th ed. New York: American Book Company. 1632 pages.

GLEASON, H. A., and A. CRONQUIST. 1963. *Manual of Vascular Plants of Northeastern United States and Adjacent Canada.* Princeton, NJ: D. Van Nostrand Company. 810 pages.

GOULD, F. W. 1968. *Grass Systematics.* New York: McGraw-Hill Book Company. 382 pages.

HITCHCOCK, A. S. (revised by Agnes Chase). 1950. *Manual of the Grasses of the United States.* United States Department of Agriculture Miscellaneous Publication 200, Washington, DC. 1051 pages.

KING, L. J. 1966. *Weeds of the World: Biology and Control.* Plant Science Monograph, N. Poulnin, ed. New York: Wiley-Interscience. 526 pages.

Biology and Control of Insects and Related Pests in Turfgrasses

INTRODUCTION

Insects are animals. Many people do not associate insects, such as beetles, with being relatives of other members of the animal kingdom. Of the over 800,000 species of insects in the world, less than 1% are considered pests. In the United States there are about 100,000 insect species, with less than 1% a pest of crops or people. In the area of turf-grass management the number of pest insect species is fewer than 100.

Not all insectlike animals are classed as insects; they are only relatives. Insects have three pairs of legs and three distinct body parts—head, thorax, and abdomen—as adults. Spiders and mites are close relatives but have four pairs of legs as adults. Many adult insects have two pairs of wings; others have one pair and some have none.

Centipedes, with long antennae and a pair of legs on each of many body segments, are a relative of the insect world; so are millipedes, with two pairs of legs on each body segment. Sowbugs and pillbugs are also close relatives of insects; other relatives include land snails and slugs.

Insects are shaped differently than most other groups of animals. The body form is somewhat cylindrical and divided into segments. The outer covering or body wall of the insect acts as the skeleton, entirely supporting the internal muscles and organs.

Insects use a respiratory system to breathe. Air is taken in through openings along the sides of the body wall. The nervous system consists of a brain located in the head, a nerve cord running the length of the body, and a system of connecting nerve cells. Sensory nerves are found in the antennae, eyes, mouth, and sometimes on the feet or tarsi of some insect species.

The method by which insects feed varies from group to group. Certain species devour grass roots by chewing on them, while others suck plant sap from the plants. There are a variety of feeding methods and mouth parts in the broad spectrum of insects. There are those with chewing mouth parts fitted with mandibles or toothlike structures to aid in tearing off pieces of plant material. Beetles and caterpillars commonly have chewing mouth parts. The opposite type consists of sucking mouth parts with an elongated beak or syringe to insert into plant or animal material to extract food. Aphids, leafhoppers, and mosquitoes are examples of insects equipped with sucking mouth parts. There are many variations of these two basic types. One type is siphoning, found in most moths and butterflies. There is no piercing of plant tissue but sucking or siphoning of liquids, such as dew from foliage. Other mouth-part variations include rasping in thrips, sponging, and many other modifications.

Insect growth and development vary from one species to another but again is quite different from those of other animals. Many species of insects emerge from eggs laid by adults. The emerging young or immature insect may appear similar in appearance to the adult form except for being smaller and without wings. Examples of this kind of development are found in aphids, leafhoppers, and chinch bugs. This growth or development is often called gradual or simple metamorphosis. Immature insects with a simple development are commonly referred to as nymphs. Some newly hatched young may be completely different from adults of the species. The young or immature stages are called larvae and the development or metamorphosis is said to be complete. The life stages of these insects passes from egg to larva to pupa and then is transformed into an adult. Butterflies, moths, beetles, and flies grow from egg to adult through complete metamorphosis. Caterpillars, grubs, and maggots are examples of immature or larval stages in this complete development.

Another unique characteristic of insect growth is that it is accomplished not by a gradual increase in size but by shedding of the external skin. Throughout its immature life there are commonly four or five stages or instars of increasing size before transformation into a pupa or resting stage prior to emergence as an adult. Adult insects usually do not change in appearance, size, or form. Some adults change color. For example, black turfgrass ataenius beetles change from a reddish color to shiny black after emergence from the soil.

Reproduction is quite variable among insect species. Length of development from egg to adult can vary greatly. For example, certain species of wireworms require 3 or more years to complete immature growth. At the other extreme, certain aphids complete more than 10 generations per year. Fruit or pomace flies may pass through 20 or more generations annually.

Not all stages of insects attack plants, annoy people, destroy stored products, or cause other economic damage. In many instances it is the immature stage of an insect that is the cause of plant damage. Grubs, the immature stage of beetles, are generally the damaging stage. Cutworms, armyworms, and webworms are the immature stages of moths. The adult moths do not feed on plants. The feeding of beetles, the adult stage of grubs, is usually on foliage other than the grass attacked by grubs. The Japanese beetle feeds heavily on many plant species, but the adult southern masked chafer, also called the annual white grub adult, is unable to feed.

Larval stages vary in the degree of food consumption which can translate into plant damage. Full-size or last-instar larvae of caterpillars, armyworms, cutworms, and sod webworms probably consume more plant material than their previous three or four instars combined.

In summary, it is important to have detailed knowledge about the biology of the pest insect you are attempting to control.

The key to identifying turfgrass insects and related pests that follows is a quick reference for identifying insects. Later in this chapter appear specific details concerning the biology, description, life history, habits, and potential for damage to turfgrasses or the people occupying these areas.

The final portion of this chapter deals with control. You must view this discussion and the enclosed table as alternative methods to reducing a pest insect population. Insect populations are reduced or suppressed, not eradicated. In fact, no insect pest has ever been eradicated from the world.

KEY TO IDENTIFYING INSECTS AND RELATED PESTS OF TURFGRASSES

There is more than one method of dividing the insect pests of turfgrass. This division is as follows: two major groups are those that damage plants below the soil surface and those that feed above ground on the turfgrass. The aboveground feeders can be further divided into those insects which chew on foliage and those which suck plant juices from the leaves and stems.

Another group indirectly damages grass areas by burrowing, nesting in, or building mounds. Still another large group of insects, sometimes found in and around turfgrass areas, are nuisance insects—a nuisance to people and/or pets occupying these areas. This group can be subdivided into those insects which sting or bite as opposed to those nuisance insects which are simply present and in moderate or high numbers.

Main Key

A. *Insects that feed on roots of turfgrasses; turf dies in irregular areas*
Light to severe grass-root pruning, with C-shaped worms present in the root area. Roots often pruned so severely that sod can be lifted from soil . . . . . *White grubs,* page 155

Dead or wilting grass blades and stems can be lifted out of sod. Grass roots chewed off by small, legless grubs . . . . *Billbugs,* page 162

Roots fed on or burrowed into by hard-shelled, yellowish, or rust-colored worms . . . . *Wireworms,* page 163

Brown to grayish-brown, winged burrowing crickets; front feet spadelike for digging . . . . *Mole crickets,* page 164

Tiny (⅛ in.-diameter), pearl-like scales attached to the roots of bermudagrass . . . . *Ground pearls,* page 164

B. *Insects that chew on the leaves and stems of grasses; irregular brown or dead areas in turf*
Spotted worms chew on grass and live in silken-lined burrows. Adult moths appear as white "millers" as they fly in a zigzag pattern over grass area in evening. . . . . *Sod webworms or lawn moths,* page 166

Numerous dark-colored, striped caterpillars are visible crawling in grass, chewing on leaves and stems . . . . *Armyworms,* page 169

Light-to-dark, more- or less-striped, thick-bodied caterpillars feed on grass leaves. When not feeding in daytime, they curl up on or near soil surface . . . . *Cutworms,* page 168

Variously sized, winged or wingless, brownish or green hoppers that feed on grass foliage, sometimes in great numbers. In late summer may be up to
1½ in. long . . . . *Grasshoppers,* page 170

Slender, spotted caterpillars which, when disturbed, become very active; feed on grass leaves . . . . *Lucerne moth,* page 170

Caterpillars with large black and white spots plus stripes along the length of the body. These worms "loop or measure" as they move . . . . . *Striped grass loopers,* page 171

Tiny maggots tunnel into stems of grasses, especially bentgrasses; plants may die. The adults are tiny black flies that hover over the turf at midmorning . . . . *Frit flies,* page 171

C. *Insects that suck juices from the leaves and stems of grasses*
Small, winged or wingless bugs, up to ⅛ in. long; black with white wings, or black with white stripe across body. Small nymphs are often red. Very numerous in thatch or at the soil surface in sunny areas . . . . *Chinch bugs,* page 172

Small, green, soft-bodied plant lice suck juices from grass leaves. Often in shady area of a tree . . . . *Aphids or greenbug,* page 174

Small globular, scalelike insects attached to the leaves of bermudagrass . . . . *Scale insects,* page 177

Masses of spittle on grass blades with a pale-colored insect inside the mass . . . . *Spittlebug,* page 177

Microscopic, eight-legged, insectlike animals feed on grass leaves, causing them to be blotched or white. Severe feeding may kill the plants . . . . *Mites,* page 178

D. *Insects that produce mounds or holes in turf*
Small mounds or hills of granular soil scattered about the turfgrass area. Numerous dark-colored active insects in and around mounds . . . . *Ants,* page 179

Robust yellow and black wasps enter turf and leave holes in soil. There is usually a small mound of soil by the entrance hole . . . . *Cicada-killer wasp,* page 181

Many holes in the soil, especially under trees. Shed skins of insects attached to nearby tree trunk, fences, or plant stems . . . . *Cicadas,* page 182

Small bees and wasps that burrow into the soil . . . . *Ground-nesting bees and wasps,* page 183

E. *Insects that often infest turf but do little or no feeding damage to grass*
Oval, gray, insectlike animals, up to ½ in. long, with several pairs of legs . . . . *Sowbugs and pillbugs,* page 183

Many-legged segmented worms often very numerous in damp areas or present after heavy rains. Usually dark brown with a hard, shell-like body covering . . . . *Millipedes and centipedes,* page 184

Beetlelike insects, about ¾ in. long, with a pair of "forceps" at the rear of the body . . . . *Earwigs,* page 185

Large, dark brown or black, jumping, chirping insects; usually near buildings in late summer . . . . *Crickets,* page 186

F. *Insects often found in turf which, rather than feed on grass, annoy, bite, or sting people*
Small, flat-sided, wingless insects that jump when disturbed. Most common where cats or dogs are kept . . . . *Fleas,* page 186

Small, tough, spiderlike animals that attach their mouth parts to skin of human beings and pets. Most common in wooded areas .... *Ticks,* page 187

Tiny, microscopic mites that irritate skin of human beings. Often cause a severe rash where clothes fit tightly to the body. Mites come from grassy areas, especially in or near woods .... *Chiggers,* page 188

Swarms of tiny, soft-bodied, hairy-winged, biting flies; active in the evening and remain in shady areas during the day. Often numerous near ponds, lakes, or other bodies of standing water .... *No-see-ums or punkies,* page 188

Individuals or swarms of soft-bodied flies most active in the evening; their blood-sucking bite is annoying to people .... *Mosquitoes,* page 188

Tiny brush-winged, fast-moving black insects that may bite a person working about the turf... *Thrips,* page 189

Variously shaped, eight-legged creatures; often with webbing on or about the grass area .... *Spiders,* page 190

Long-legged insects with two large, leathery-appearing wings. Usually most common near water, such as a stream, creek, or poorly drained areas .... *Crane flies or leather jackets,* page 190

BIOLOGY OF TURFGRASS INSECTS AND RELATED PESTS

White Grubs

Several species of beetles have an immature or larval stage called grub, white grub, or simply grubworm. White grubs, when fully grown, are robust, white or cream-colored, with three pairs of legs, a brown head, and a dark area at the posterior end of the body (*Color plate 16*). These larvae are usually in a C-shaped position when discovered damaging turfgrass. The size of larvae can vary between species as well as their age, but most grubs range in length from ¼ to ¾ in. (Figure 4.1).

Figure 4.1 White grubs under rolled-back sod.

White grubs as a group include the immature stages of the Japanese beetle (*Color plate 17*), European chafer, northern masked chafer, southern masked chafer (also called annual white grub) (*Color plate 18*), Oriental beetle, and Asiatic garden beetle or green June beetle (Figure 4.2). In general, these species complete their life cycle in 1 year. Adults emerge from the soil, eggs are laid on or beneath the soil surface, hatch, and the larvae feed on the roots of turfgrass during its growing season (*Color plate 19*), causing extensive damage.

Another group of white grub species complete their life cycle in 2 or 3 years and are the immature stage of beetles referred to as May beetles or "June bugs" (Figure 4.3). In the United States there are over 100 species of May beetles, with over 40 being identified in Illinois alone. Not all May beetle larvae attack the roots of turfgrass, but there are an adequate number of species to supply at least one for each of the many turfgrass areas across the country. White grubs of May beetles (*Phyllophaga species*) have more than a 1-year life cycle. Some species require 2 years to complete their development; others require 3 years (Figure 4.4). The length of time varies for a species depending on the latitude in which it occurs.

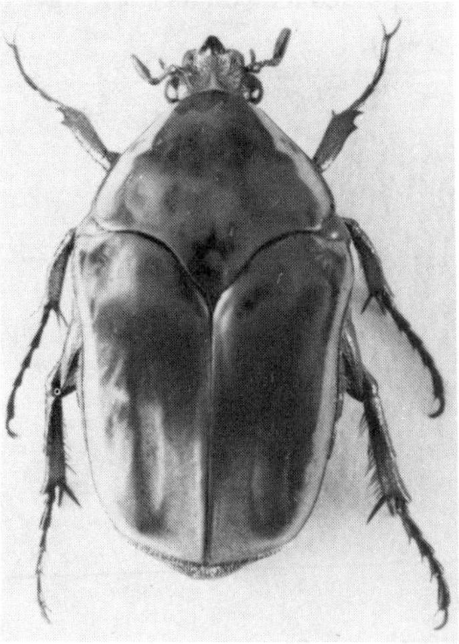

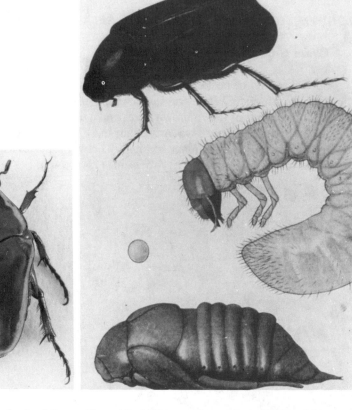

Figure 4.2 Green June beetle adult.

Figure 4.3 Life stages of true white grub; left to right—pupa, egg, larva or grub, and adult.

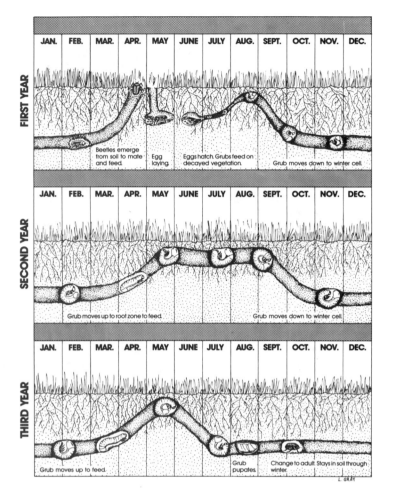

Figure 4.4 Life cycle of the May beetle.

Another white grub species that has become an important pest of golf courses is the black turfgrass ataenius. It is not a new insect pest but has caused root-pruning damage to fairways and greens in the past 10 years. In most areas of the United States where they have been observed, there are two generations per year. Some northern states, such as Minnesota, have one generation per year.

Japanese beetle (*Popilla japonica*) adults are ½ in. long, metallic bronze and green in color, with a row of five white spots along each side of the body and a pair of white spots at the tip of the rear end of the body (*Color plate 17*). These adults fly only during the daytime. Eggs are laid in the soil of turfgrass. As adults these beetles feed heavily on more than 200 different plants. Field crops, flowers, and small fruits are favorite host plants for adults.

Japanese beetles complete a life cycle similar to other annual grubs. Eggs are laid in midsummer; the eggs hatch and the larvae feed on the roots of turfgrass, hibernate

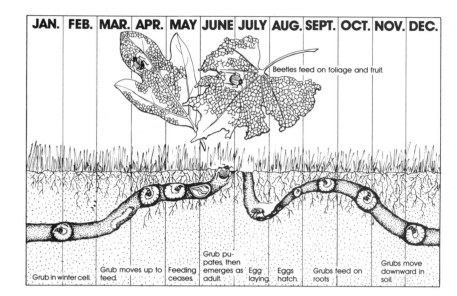

| JAN. | FEB. | MAR. | APR. | MAY | JUNE | JULY | AUG. | SEPT. | OCT. | NOV. | DEC. |

Beetles feed on foliage and fruit.

| Grub in winter cell. | Grub moves up to feed. | Feeding ceases. | Grub pupates, then emerges as adult. | Egg laying. | Eggs hatch. | Grubs feed on roots. | Grubs move downward in soil. |

Figure 4.5 Life cycle of the Japanese beetle.

deep in the soil during the winter, and return to feed on grass roots in the spring. The adult beetles emerge in time to feed, mate, and begin the cycle over again (Figure 4.5).

Infestations of Japanese beetles are common in the northeastern United States, with scattered infestations in the midwest and as far south as Georgia. In many areas the adults are noticeable, but little or no damage to turf is observed.

The northern masked chafer (*Cyclocephala borealis*) extends as far south as Alabama and westward to California, but is most prevalent and damaging to lawns and other turfgrass areas in the northeastern United States. Eggs of the northern masked chafer are laid 4 to 6 in. below the soil surface during midsummer. Damage by the larvae increases throughout the summer and fall months. The grubs hibernate below the frostline in the soil and return to feed the following spring. Chestnut brown, ½-in.-long adults emerge in early summer. They remain in the soil during the day and become active at about dusk. The adults are attracted to lights and are unable to feed on foliage.

The southern masked chafer (*Cyclocephala immaculata*) is common in the southeastern United States but is becoming more of a pest of turf in the midwest. In many areas this grub species is called the annual white grub. The adult beetles cannot feed or "chafe" on the foliage; they emerge from the soil, mate, lay eggs, and starve.

The life cycle of the southern masked chafer is very similar to that of the Japanese beetle and northern masked chafer. Adult, ½-in.-long tan beetles (*Color plate 18*) emerge from the soil in midsummer and mate. The eggs are laid in the soil after dark. The eggs hatch and grubs begin to feed on grass roots (*Color plate 19*). They overwinter deep in the soil and return to feed a short time in the spring months (Figure 4.6).

The European chafer (*Rhizotrogus majalis*) was first observed as a pest problem in New York in the early 1940s. It is believed that this insect entered the United States in the 1920s, but it is now present in many of the northeastern states and westward into Michigan. The eggs are laid in midsummer, 2 to 6 in. deep in the soil, just before the adults die. The eggs hatch and larvae feed until winter, then move below the frostline. After a short period of feeding by the grubs in the spring, the adults emerge in large

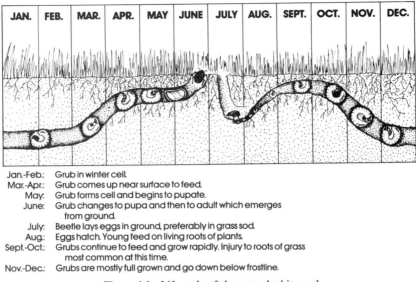

| JAN. | FEB. | MAR. | APR. | MAY | JUNE | JULY | AUG. | SEPT. | OCT. | NOV. | DEC. |

Jan.-Feb.:   Grub in winter cell.
Mar.-Apr.:   Grub comes up near surface to feed.
May: Grub forms cell and begins to pupate.
June: Grub changes to pupa and then to adult which emerges
      from ground.
July: Beetle lays eggs in ground, preferably in grass sod.
Aug.:   Eggs hatch. Young feed on living roots of plants.
Sept.-Oct.:   Grubs continue to feed and grow rapidly. Injury to roots of grass
      most common at this time.
Nov.-Dec.:   Grubs are mostly full grown and go down below frostline.

Figure 4.6   Life cycle of the annual white grub.

numbers and swarm with a buzzing sound around trees and shrubs at sunset. The adults are oval, about ½ in. long, and light brown or tan. Shallow grooves run lengthwise on their shell-like wing covers. Every European chafer grub does not change to and emerge as an adult beetle at the end of its first year. Some larvae spend a second summer as a grub and mature in early summer of the second year.

The Oriental beetle (*Anomala orientalis*) is a pest grub in New York, Connecticut, Massachusetts, and New Jersey. The adults are about ⅓ to ½ in. long, straw-colored to brown, with black markings on the wing covers and just behind the head. The adult beetles feed on flowers. The immature or grub stage emerge from eggs laid 6 in. deep in the soil. Grub damage occurs in late summer and fall. The grubs overwinter in the soil and return to the turf root zone in the spring.

The Asiatic garden beetle (*Maladera castanea*) is found in scattered areas along the Atlantic coast, from Massachusetts to South Carolina. The adult is a ¼-in.-long, chestnut brown beetle. Its ventral or underside is covered with short yellow hairs. The grub stage hatches from eggs to early summer and feeds only on the small roots, causing very little serious damage to turfgrass. Adults emerging in early summer are active only after dark and feed on various kinds of plants.

The green June beetle (*Cotinus nitida*) as an adult is sometimes called the fig eater. This insect is present in the southeastern states northward to central Illinois and Long Island. The larvae emerge from eggs laid in July. The eggs are often laid in high-organic-matter soils, tobacco beds, or rotting compost in the soil. The grubs grow quite large, up to 2 in. long. They burrow through the soil humus, drying it out, and in periods of heavy rains will come to the surface. The grubs have a habit of always crawling on their back. The adults emerge in June and July. They are almost an inch long and are metallic green with brownish-yellow wing covers. The ventral side of the body is a shiny greenish yellow-orange.

The group of white grubs called May beetles belong to a genus called *Phyllophaga*. This is a large group of species, but only a few in each geographic region are serious pests of turfgrass areas. Many species attack the roots of corn, small grains, and soybeans. All the adults are similar in size and appearance, and are brown to blackish brown. Some species feed heavily on tree foliage, whereas other species feed very little. Oak, willow, apple, poplar, birch, hickory, and other trees have been observed with May beetles feeding on the foliage.

Most species of May beetles that attack turfgrass require 2, 3, or even 4 years to complete their life cycle from egg to adult. Species with a 3-year life cycle emerge as adults in April and May, feed on tree foliage, mate, and lay eggs in the soil beneath the sod. Young grubs emerge, feed, and grow during the summer and fall months. Winter is spent below the frost zone. The grubs return to the root zone to feed during the spring, summer, and fall months, then return below the frost-free area. In the third spring the full-grown grub feeds and then pupates about 1 ft or more below the soil surface. It then emerges the following spring to mate, lay eggs, and initiate the next generation. Damage is observed only in the second and third years of the grub's life cycle, but there can be overlapping generations (Figure 4.4).

The black turfgrass ataenius (*Ataenius spretulus*) is a relatively new insect pest to many golf course personnel. This species, although occasionally observed and written about for the past 60 years, was first observed damaging golf course turf near Minneapolis in 1932. In 1973, the grubs were found near Cincinnati, Ohio, feeding on and pruning the roots of annual bluegrass and bentgrass in fairways. Since 1973 it has been found damaging golf course fairways in at least 25 of the northern states.

Black turfgrass ataenius grubs are very similar to all other grubs—C-shaped and white with a brown head. When full grown, however, they are only one-fourth or less the size of the common May beetle or chafer grubs.

Adult ataenius beetles hibernate beneath the soil surface in the woods, usually bordering or near a damaged golf course. In the spring these ¼-in.-long, shiny black beetles migrate to the golf course and can be observed flying about over greens and fairways, often sitting on the leaves of closely mowed bentgrass greens (*Color plate 20*). They are most active during the warmest period of the day, from noon until 3 P.M. The eggs are laid beneath the soil surface in late May and June. Newly hatched grubs soon begin to feed on the roots. Annual bluegrass seems to be their favorite host plant. Although the ataenius grubs are small compared to other soil-infesting grubs, their numbers can range from a harmless few up to 500 or more per square foot. Adults mate in July and lay eggs for a second generation. During the early fall period, the adults can be observed flying to hibernation sites on the border of wooded areas (Figure 4.7). There is usually only one generation per year in northern regions of the United States.

Summary. White grubs can be the immature stage of many adult beetles. Although similar in appearance, the grubs can be identified with some close observation. The major difference between all grubs species is the setal or stiff hairy pattern on the underside of the rear end of the body. This pattern, also called raster (Figure 4.8), can be seen with a magnifying glass or hand lens.

There are very few natural enemies of white grubs. Sometimes they are attacked by large parasitic wasps. Sometimes diseases reduce their numbers. A bacterial agent, a species of *Bacillus,* is sometimes found infecting grubs in the soil. This disease is commonly called "milky disease." It is specific to each grub species in which it is found and

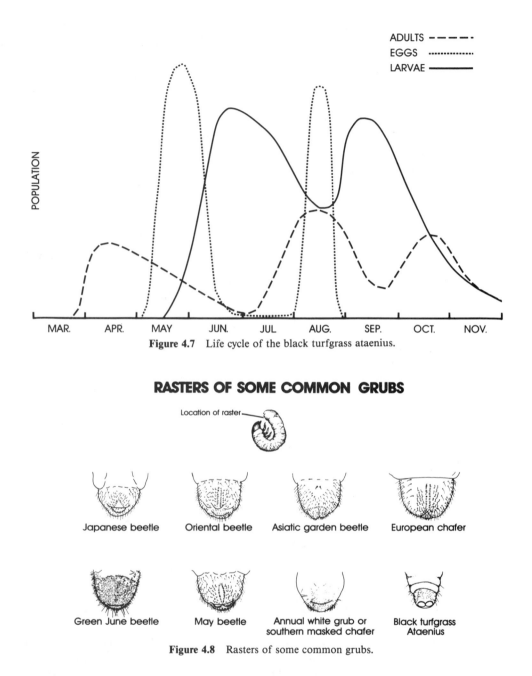

Figure 4.7 Life cycle of the black turfgrass ataenius.

RASTERS OF SOME COMMON GRUBS

Location of raster

Japanese beetle   Oriental beetle   Asiatic garden beetle   European chafer

Green June beetle   May beetle   Annual white grub or southern masked chafer   Black turfgrass Ataenius

Figure 4.8 Rasters of some common grubs.

has been observed on *Phyllophaga, Cyclocephala,* and *Ataenius* species, plus Japanese beetle grubs.

The milky disease has been packaged and is available to home and commercial users for controlling Japanese beetle larvae only. This commercially prepared material is not effective against other white grub species.

Biology of Turfgrass Insects and Related Pests

Trapping has been attempted to reduce or suppress populations of adult beetles or grubs. The only one to exhibit promise is a trap containing a combination of a sex or pheromone lure plus a food attractant. These traps are marketed for reducing numbers of Japanese beetles and have reduced populations and eventually the egglaying and hatching of grubs. These traps are put out when the adults emerge in midsummer.

Warm-blooded animals such as moles, skunks, and sometimes birds damage high-quality turfgrass that is grub-infested. The tunnels or runs of moles, the plowing and turning over of sod by skunks, and the pecking and scratching by birds cause much more physical damage to the turf than the infestation of grubs. These animals acting as a grub-control agent often cause more damage to turfgrass than the grubs themselves.

Grub control consists of (1) applying a preventative treatment to the turf area prior to the appearance of damage, or (2) when grubs are detected, and (3) treating the grub-damaged turfgrass after damage is visible. Prior to the mid-1970s, many of the applied materials for white grub control were residual (lasting up to 5 years), water insoluble, and broad spectrum. Emergency control or treatment of an existing damaging grub population provided less than satisfactory results. Most controls were applied to the turf, watered into the thatch and soil, but control was maintained for 3 to 5 years.

Today, shorter residual, more water soluble, and more specific materials have replaced the chlorinated hydrocarbon insecticides of the period 1950 through the early 1970s. They are applied annually if there has been a history of grub infestation. Some are applied near to the period of egg hatch and the chemical irrigated or watered into the soil surface, the site of the damaging grubs.

Specific chemical control suggestions are given in Table 4.1 at the end of the chapter.

Billbugs

Billbugs are a group of weevils or beetles with bills or snouts. The snouts are used for burrowing and are capable of chewing off plants using a pair of jaws at the end of the snout. Various species are pests of turfgrass. The Phoenix billbug (*Sphenophorus phoeniciensis*) attacks bermudagrass in the southwestern United States. The hunting billbug (*Sphenophorus venatus vestitus*) is a pest insect of zoysiagrass. The bluegrass billbug (*Sphenophorus parvulus*) is primarily a pest of Kentucky bluegrass in regions where this grass is grown in home lawns or other turf areas, but can also infest other species of turfgrass.

The adult beetles (Figure 4.9) range from ¼ to ¾ in. long and the color varies between species from black or brown to a dull yellow. Adult bluegrass billbugs spend the winter in or near turfs infested the previous year. In the spring they can be seen crawling on sidewalks and driveways. Eggs are laid in stems above the crown of bluegrass plants. White, legless larvae with brown heads feed and tunnel into the stems, eventually migrating into the root zone (*Color plate 21*). Peak feeding activity occurs in July as they continue to feed on the roots. There is one generation per year. New, ⅜-in.-long, brown or black adults emerge in early fall and are visible again on walks and driveways before hibernating for the winter.

Billbug damage can be distinguished from white grub feeding. Billbug-damaged plants pull loose from the crown. The stem is chewed on, leaving sawdustlike material

Figure 4.9 Bluegrass billbug adult.

(frass) present in the chewed area. Late in the season dead areas appear in the grass. The sod *cannot* be easily rolled back as with grub feeding, but the legless grubs will be present if the sod is removed. Detection of bluegrass billbug adults can be made in the spring or fall of the year. Adults crawling about on driveways, patios, sidewalks, and other paved areas are an indicator of the potential for future larval damage during the summer.

Chemical control of billbugs is suggested where there has been a past history of damage. Control of adult beetles is achieved by placing the insecticide on grass foliage and thatch in the spring when adults are moving about. Larval or grub control is similar to white grub control. The insecticide is drenched or irrigated into the soil site where the billbug larvae are during midsummer. For specific control suggestions, refer to Table 4.1.

Wireworms

Wireworms (*Elateridae*) are the larval or immature stages of insects commonly called click-beetles, snapping beetles, or skipjacks. These ½-in.-long, narrow-bodied, hard-shelled beetles have the ability to flip themselves into the air when placed on their backs. The beetles commonly live for almost a year, laying eggs on the roots of grasses. Wireworm larvae (Figure 4.10) usually spend the next 2 to 6 years in the soil, depending on the species. The brownish or rust-colored worms are about 1½ in. long when full grown.

Figure 4.10 Wireworm.

Biology of Turfgrass Insects and Related Pests

Wireworms occasionally damage turf by eating or boring into the roots of grasses. Wireworm-damaged turf has irregular areas of wilting or dead grass due to the roots being eaten away. Wireworms can be found in the soil near the surface in the spring but farther down as the soil temperature rises. For current insecticide suggestions, refer to Table 4.1.

Ground Pearls

Ground pearls (*Margarodes* spp.) are tiny scale insects that attack the roots of bermudagrass and centipedegrass primarily in the southern and southwestern states. Infested turf turns brown and eventually dies in late summer, leaving irregular brown patches (Figure 4.11).

Figure 4.11 Ground pearls injury to a bermudagrass lawn. (Courtesy Milwaukee Sewerage Commission.)

The eggs are laid in a group enclosed in a waxy sac. The tiny scale nymphs hatch, move out, and attach themselves to the grass roots (Figure 4.12). At the same time they secrete a shell or covering about themselves. Feeding damage to the roots causes the plants to turn yellow and then brown. Ground pearls may require more than a year to complete a life cycle.

Irrigation and fertilization to maintain good grass vigor is a practical method of control. Some of the newer soil insecticides (Table 4.1) have given routine results when drenched into infested soil.

Mole Crickets

Mole crickets (*Scapteriscus* and *Gryllotalpa* spp.) may be found burrowing in the soil of turfgrass. They often burrow 6 to 8 in. or more below the soil surface in burrows ½ in. in diameter. They are most common in the south Atlantic and Gulf coast states, but are observed in areas farther northward.

There are at least three species of mole crickets: the northern mole cricket, the southern mole cricket, and the tawny mole cricket.

Figure 4.12 Close-up of ground pearls. (Courtesy Milwaukee Sewerage Commission.)

Mole crickets are light brown with a front pair of spadelike feet developed for digging, which act as a pair of scissors in cutting small roots as they move through the soil (Figure 4.13). All stages of immature and adult crickets feed and move through the soil. Mole crickets damage turf areas in two ways: they feed on the roots and physically lift up the soil when burrowing near the soil surface. The uplifted turf feels soft or fluffy when walking across it. The burrowing and root pruning dry out grass areas, causing wilting and death. Mole crickets can be very destructive to new turfgrass seedings.

Adult mole crickets emerge to the soil surface in the spring to mate. Eggs are deposited in newly constructed burrows in the soil. Nymphs or young mole crickets with

Figure 4.13 Mole cricket.

Biology of Turfgrass Insects and Related Pests

short wings remain in the soil and increase in size throughout the summer and fall. There is only one generation per year.

Mole crickets spend much of their time in burrows below the soil surface, thus complicating control. The residual insecticides of the 1950s and 1960s provided fair to good control. The insecticides being used on turf today provide erratic results. The best control is achieved using isofenphos (Oftanol), a residual insecticide. June applications, drenched in after the young mole crickets hatch, seem to be the best control. For specific insecticide suggestions, see Table 4.1.

Sod Webworms

Sod webworms are the larvae of several species of moths. Important species include the vagabond webworm (*Crambus vulgivagellus*); silver-striped webworm (*Crambus praefectellus*); bluegrass webworm (*Parapediasia teterrella*); tropical sod webworm (*Herpetogramma phaeopteralis*); and the lawn or large sod webworm (*Pediasia trisectus*). Sod webworms do extensive damage to turf areas (*Color plate 22*).

The majority of adult webworm moths listed above wrap their wings around the body when at rest (*Color plate 24*). The buff-colored adults of the large sod webworm, vagabond, and silver-striped webworms all have a wing span of about 1 in. The moths are easily flushed from their hiding places when grass is being mowed or shrubbery is disturbed. They fly in a jerky fashion for a few feet, then dive down to rest on a grass blade. The moths are readily attracted to lights at night. The oval eggs, dropped among the grass blades by the female moths as they fly above the turf, are tiny, dry, and nearly impossible to find.

Larvae of the large sod webworm are about 1 in. long when fully grown, and are gray to dusky green with a brown head and brown spots over the body (Figure 4.14). The larvae often hide during the day in silk-lined burrows in the thatch layer or on the soil surface. Larval excrement appears as a cluster of small, pale to dark green pellets, some the size of a pinhead (*Color plate 23*). The resting stage between the larva and adult is a dark brown, torpedo-shaped pupa about ½ in. long.

The large sod webworm and some of the other species pass the winter as larvae, tightly coiled in a closely woven silk case covered with particles of soil. In the spring, the larvae resume feeding, grow rapidly, and pupate in cells in the soil. The adult moths emerge in about 2 weeks. About 1 day after emerging, the female moths begin to lay eggs as they fly in a zigzag pattern a few inches above the turf, usually in the early evening. Each female lays about 500 eggs. In hot weather the eggs hatch in about 6 days. The larvae or webworms require 4 to 5 weeks to complete their full growth. The entire life cycle from adult to adult usually requires 6 to 8 weeks. Thus, under normal conditions, there are two or three generations a year, with additional ones in the south.

Sod webworm larvae feed on more than one species of grass. They clip off the blades of grass just above the crown. Irregular brown spots appear in the turf area where the larvae are numerous (*Color plate 22*).

Microsporidia diseases, predator insects, and birds help to reduce sod webworm populations. After the second year of peak webworm populations as many as 90% of the adult moths have been found to be infected. They continue to lay eggs, and the eggs hatch, but many of the diseased larvae do not survive the winter. A well-kept turf, fer-

Figure 4.14 Sod webworm in burrow.

Figure 4.15 Two burrow linings of the burrowing webworm.

tilized and watered, supports more webworm feeding than one with poor management. Four or more webworms per square foot will do severe damage to any turf area.

The bluegrass webworm is a pest of Kentucky bluegrass in the eastern United States. It is especially numerous in the bluegrass regions of Kentucky and Tennessee. On golf courses, the larvae have damaged bentgrass roots in greens, similar to grub feeding. The pupae are located vertically through the thatch layer, with the small moths emerging from the upper end of the pupal case. They can be found resting on the closely mowed turf (*Color plate 25*). Damaged bentgrass sod can be rolled back to expose the larvae.

An insect similar in appearance to webworms, which also feeds on the roots of Kentucky bluegrass, is the cranberry girdler (*Chrysoteuchia topiaria*). It has been reported in grass production fields in the west and midwest. Feeding by this insect severs the roots, allowing the infested, wilted sod to be rolled back. The larvae are found in the remaining roots at the soil surface. The cranberry girdler overwinters in the soil similar to sod webworms, but produces injury to turf like grubs. Control measures applied for grubs also control this insect.

The burrowing webworm (*Acrolophus popeanuellus*) occasionally infests lawns and golf course fairways in the northeastern and north-central states. This insect lives in a 2-in.-long vertical burrow in the soil lined with a paperlike white sac (Figure 4.15). The larvae feed at night on the grass blades surrounding their burrow. Control is commonly accomplished by the feeding of birds. Birds pull out the burrow lining, eat the webworm, and leave the paperlike sac laying on the grass. This insect is not a severe pest, but the scene of many white paper tubes scattered across the lawn can be dramatic to the homeowner.

Biology of Turfgrass Insects and Related Pests

Figure 4.16 Sod webworm flushed to the surface by pyrethrin solution; note the bird feeding holes.

Early detection of webworms in turf areas is important in preventing serious feeding damage. Large numbers of moths flying over the lawn at dusk, collecting on doors and windows and around outside lights, mean that the caution sign is out. Egglaying time in midsummer for the second generation usually results in the most moths. Additional moth flights continue into September, with overlapping generations in some areas. The presence of unusual numbers of birds, especially robins, blackbirds, flickers, and other species, feeding on the lawn may indicate a webworm infestation. You can detect webworms simply by carefully digging through the sod searching for silken burrows, frass, grass clippings, or the webworms themselves. A simple, quick survey method is to mix 1 tablespoon of 2% pyrethrin in a gallon of water. Sprinkle this mixture over 1 sq ft, then count the number of webworms leaving the crown area to climb up onto the grass blades (Figure 4.16). The pyrethrin is very irritating to the worms and other insects hiding in the turf. Armyworms and cutworms also crawl out when the solution is applied. The mixture can be made of the same dilution with other concentrations of pyrethrin (e.g., using 2 tablespoons of 1%, or 1 teaspoon of 6%). A liquid concentrate of pyrethrin may be difficult to purchase by a homeowner. This chemical is sometimes sold in agricultural pesticide outlets and sold as a fly spray or as a vegetable garden spray.

Insecticides for sod webworm control are listed in Table 4.1 at the end of the chapter. The insecticide can be applied as a granular formulation or as a spray using 2.5 to 3 gal of mixed spray per 1000 sq ft of infested turf.

Cutworms

Cutworms are a group of thick-bodied caterpillars. They hatch from eggs laid by robust, dark, night-flying moths. Cutworm damage is similar to that of other leaf-eating worms— chewing off the grass blades above the crown.

The black cutworm (*Agrotis ipsilon*) overwinters in the southern states and migrates northward each spring. The eggs are laid by the sooty black moths especially on winter annual weeds such as chickweed and yellow rocket, and bentgrass sod in golf course greens and tees. The young gray to black worms that hatch from the eggs curl up in the grass during the day and feed at night. Full-grown worms are 2 in. long (*Color plate 26*). The

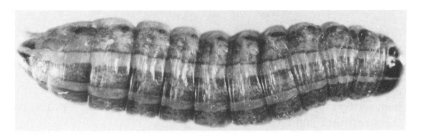

Figure 4.17 Bronzed cutworm.

feeding and scratching of the turf by birds in their search for the cutworms can cause as much or more damage than the cutworms alone.

The life cycle of black cutworms is completed about every 30 to 40 days. Control treatments are usually applied at the first symptom of bird damage, and as needed thereafter throughout the growing season.

The bronzed cutworm (*Nephelodes minians*) is dark brown or almost black across the top and lighter on the underside (Figure 4.17). Both the larvae and adult moths have a distinct copperlike or bronze appearance. This cutworm infests bluegrass turfs in numbers, leaving large straw-colored or dead areas in early summer.

Other species, such as the variegated cutworm (*Peridroma saucia*), may simply hide in the grass during the day and feed only at night on adjoining plants in flower beds. Bedding plants that are cut off indicate the presence of this cutworm.

Cutworms can be controlled by sprays containing one of the insecticides listed in Table 4.1. Repeat applications are often necessary to control black cutworms, as there are multiple generations.

Armyworms

Two species of armyworm sometimes infest turf areas. The true armyworm or simply, armyworm (*Pseudaletia unipuncta*), feeds on agricultural crops such as small grains and corn. Sometimes a large number of larvae may suddenly appear moving across a lawn area like an "army." The adult, night-flying moth is about 1 in. long, tan to grayish brown, with a tiny white dot in the center of each forewing. The female deposits her eggs, which are small, white globules, in rows or groups on the leaves of grasses and then rolls the blade around the egg mass. Full-grown larvae are about 1½ in. long with two orange stripes on each side of the mostly brown or black body (Figure 4.18). Another pale orange stripe passes down the back of the insect. Within this stripe is a fine, light-colored, broken line. Small armyworms, less than half grown, appear dark or almost black with small stripes.

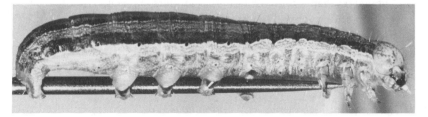

Figure 4.18 Armyworm.

Biology of Turfgrass Insects and Related Pests

Armyworms overwinter in the southern United States. The moths migrate northward during the spring to most states east of the Rocky Mountains. There are three generations in the south and commonly two farther north. In humid regions, armyworm populations are sometimes greatly reduced by a fungus disease that prevents further generations. A parasitic fly may attach its egg by the armyworm's head. The hatching maggot feeds inside the armyworm and kills it.

The fall armyworm (*Spodoptera frugiperda*) attacks a more diversified group of plants than the true armyworm, feeding on corn, alfalfa, clover, tobacco, and various grasses. The adults resemble cutworm moths, with dark forewings mottled with light and dark spots. They are also active only at night. The eggs are deposited on grasses in groups of 100 or more which are covered with fuzz from the adult moth's body. The eggs hatch into young worms in 2 to 10 days. Newly hatched larvae are white with black heads. Their bodies become darker as they feed. During growth, they may curl up in leaf sheaths, suspend themselves from plants by threads, or crawl about on the ground. Fall armyworms become full grown in 2 to 3 weeks. In the south the armyworm is one of the most destructive turf insects in certain years, particularly to bermudagrass. Most high populations and their resulting damage occur after a cold, wet spring. Young larvae feed on the lower surfaces of leaves. Later, as they mature, entire leaves are eaten, leaving only the stem. The full-grown larvae attain a size similar to that of the true armyworm, 1½ in. long. The larval body is dull black with several stripes alongside the body. There is a distinct inverted light-colored "Y" on the front of the head. Fall armyworms overwinter in the southern United States. They migrate northward in late summer to northern states from Montana to the northeast. There are as many as six generations in the south but only one in its northern limits.

Night feeding by this insect causes the grass to appear ragged, uneven, and often bare. High populations of full-grown fall armyworms can eat grass down to the crown. Specific chemical controls are listed in Table 4.1.

Grasshoppers

Grasshoppers (*Melanoplus* spp.) are not a common pest of turfgrass. Grasshoppers may migrate to well-kept turfs located in a new subdivision or near rural areas where pasture or hay crops are growing, rather than remain in a nearby dried-up or dormant crop. Adult hoppers may be yellow with brown or black markings, are winged, and can fly as well as hop to turf areas (Figure 4.19). The immature hoppers, called nymphs, are wingless but otherwise resemble the larger adult. The eggs are laid in uncultivated areas in the fall, overwinter in the soil, and hatch in early summer. There is one generation a year. Applied or chemical control of grasshoppers (Table 4.1) is necessary only if adult grass-hoppers have migrated to a turf to feed on grass leaves and stems. For insecticides that effectively control grasshoppers, see Table 4.1.

Lucerne Moth

Larvae of the lucerne moth (*Nomophilia noctuella*) commonly feed on clovers and similar legumes, and occasionally on turfgrasses. The caterpillars are larger than sod webworm

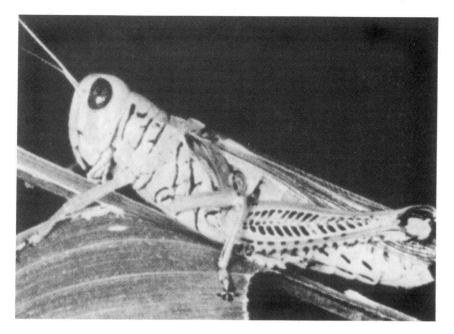

Figure 4.19 Grasshopper.

larvae, but their bodies are similarly spotted. They wriggle actively when disturbed. The webwormlike larvae construct small horizontal silken tubes near the base of clover plants.

Adult moths are a mottled gray-brown with two pairs of dark spots on the front wings, which span about ½ in. The eggs are laid on clovers and sometimes on grasses. Newly hatched caterpillars feed on the clover or grass on which the eggs were laid. There are two to four generations through the growing season. If damage appears, it is usually in late summer.

Control is usually not necessary (Table 4.1), but the larvae may be mistaken for sod webworms.

Striped Grass Loopers

Several species of striped grass loopers (*Mocis* species) feed on grass areas. When numerous they may invade home lawns. The loopers, "measuring" worms, or "inch" worms are about 2½ in. long when full grown. They range in color from cream to blue-gray, brown, black, or orange, depending on the species. The loopers have large black and white spots, and stripes that extend the length of the body.

Control measures are rarely needed, and then only if the caterpillars are doing visible damage. See Table 4.1 for specific insecticides.

Frit Fly

The frit fly (*Oscinella frit*) is probably more of a turfgrass nuisance than a damaging insect on golf courses. The larvae or maggots infest the stems of wheat, rye, and other grains, causing the seedheads to be white and empty. Other species of *Oscinella* infest the seedheads of Kentucky bluegrass, causing silver top, a general term used to describe a condition in which the seedhead is pale or white, with few or no viable seeds. In a Kentucky study, nine species were found in sweeping bluegrass fields. The frit fly has long been a pest of grains and grasses in Europe.

The adult frit fly is a minute black fly with yellow on its legs, about $\frac{1}{16}$ in. long. The flies often hover over golf tees or an area of the fairway. They may be found in collected clippings of the greens mowers along with ataenius beetle adults (page 160). Both insects frequent high-quality bentgrass greens—ataenius beetles in the early afternoon and frit flies in the midmorning. Frit flies are also attracted to white objects such as golf balls, towels, and golf carts. The adult flies do no damage to grass but are a nuisance, laying eggs on the leaves and leaf sheaths. Yellow-white, legless maggots hatch and burrow into grass stems to feed. There are about four generations per year during the summer months.

Damage may appear as scattered yellow or dead leaves throughout the turf. Close examination reveals a central dead leaf, or possibly the entire shoot will be dead. Frit fly maggots may be found feeding at the base of the dead leaf on the dead shoot. The yellow-white, legless worms move about when disturbed.

Control of frit flies is sometimes justified to keep the adult flies from bothering people on the golf course or elsewhere. As with most insects, large numbers of adults may indicate a damaging infestation of larvae in a few days or a week or two. Chemical controls applied to golf greens and collars will reduce the population of this fly (Table 4.1).

Chinch Bugs

Chinch bugs, like many turf insects, are often common pests of field crops. The common chinch bug (*Blissus leucopterus*) has long been a serious pest of corn, wheat, rye, oats, and barley; it also feeds on some forage grasses but is rarely a serious problem. It is occasionally a pest of bermudagrass in the southern United States.

There are two other chinch bug species and at least one is a major turf insect pest in the eastern half of the country. The southern chinch bug (*Blissus insularis*) is a common turfgrass pest in Florida and Louisiana on St. Augustinegrass. Southern chinch bugs are often found damaging zoysiagrass turf as far north as Indiana, Illinois, and Missouri.

The hairy chinch bug (*Blissus leucopterus hirtus*) has long been a pest of turf in the northeastern states. It feeds on bentgrasses, fescues, and Kentucky bluegrass and has damaged lawns in the upper midwest as well as the northeast.

The life cycles of all species of chinch bugs are similar. Adult bugs are $\frac{1}{5}$ in. long and black with white wings overlapped over the back (Figure 4.20). The wings usually cover the tip of the abdomen, but some adults have shorter wings, one-half the length of normal wings.

The adults lay eggs over a period of time with the egg hatch varying from 10 to 25 days depending on the temperature. Hatching bugs, called nymphs, are tiny, red with a white band across the body, and wingless. There are usually five immature stages before the winged adults emerge (Figure 4.21). Hairy chinch bug nymphs change from red and white, to orange, to brown, to black and white as they become adults. There are usually

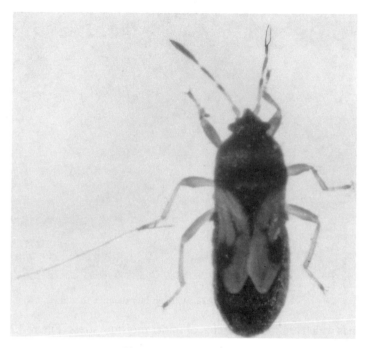

Figure 4.20 Chinch bug adult.

L. GRAY

EGGS   IMMATURE OR NYMPHS   ADULT

Figure 4.21 Life stages of a chinch bug.

two generations per year in the midwest and one in more northern states. Adults hibernate during the winter in clumps of grass and under debris.

Southern chinch bugs can complete five or six generations annually in Florida. Overlapping generations are common after early summer. Farther north, the adults hibernate and pass through two to three generations. Adults pass the winter in dead grass, leaves, and other debris.

Chinch bugs, both the adults and all sizes of nymphs, damage grass by injecting salivary fluids into the plants as they suck sap from them. Many bugs mass on one plant, then leave to attack adjoining plants. This type of feeding produces scattered patches in a turf area rather than a uniformly damaged one. Favorite feeding sites of chinch bugs

Biology of Turfgrass Insects and Related Pests

Figure 4.22 Chinch bug damage to a lawn.

are turfs which are sunny, sloping, or under moisture stress (Figure 4.22). Damaged plants change from green to pale yellow and eventually brown. A very light population of chinch bugs may be present with no visible damage, but 100 to 300 bugs of all sizes in a droughty area can severely damage or kill the turf.

Detection of chinch bugs involves more than walking over the turf. Bugs may be crawling about on a driveway or sidewalk when high numbers are present and the grass is dead or almost dead. Vigorous scratching in the damaged area will often cause the bugs present to scatter. Forcing a strong stream of water from a garden hose into the crown area of the grass plants will usually float out the bugs. Another effective method is to drive an open can or metal ring into the soil surface and fill the ring with water. (Remove both ends of a coffee or shortening can and drive one end through the turf into the soil and fill it with water.) If chinch bugs are present, they will float to the top in 5 to 10 minutes.

Predators of chinch bugs quite often run about in the turf area damaged by chinch bugs. One such insect is called the big-eyed bug (*Geocoris* spp.) and more than one species may be present. Big-eyed bugs are about the same size as chinch bugs, except that their body is oval in shape rather than narrow. Their eyes are also very large; hence the common name. This predator, along with lady beetles, earwigs, and ants, can reduce chinch bug populations. A fungus disease (*Beauveria bassiana*) is sometimes an enemy of chinch bugs. High humidity plus a population of the bugs are necessary before the fungus can increase, spread among the population, and reduce the numbers of bugs. Specific insecticide suggestions are given in Table 4.1.

Aphids

Aphids, or plant lice as they are called, attack many agronomic and horticultural crops. Rose aphids suck the sap from rose foliage and stems. Tomato aphids can increase rapidly on tomatoes, and corn leaf aphids may dry up the tops of corn plants. There are aphids that infest stands of grain, including the English grain aphid, apple grain aphid (also a pest of apples), oat-bird cherry aphid, and the greenbug.

The oat-bird cherry aphid (*Rhopalosiphum padi*) has been observed feeding on stands of bluegrass. The only other aphid recognized as a turf pest is the greenbug (Figure 4.23). The greenbug (*Schizaphis graminum*), sometimes called the spring grain aphid, is the most destructive aphid, attacking grain crops, damaging barley, oats, and wheat from Texas to Nebraska. Aphids such as the greenbug have a rather unusual life cycle. Adult females give birth to young during the grain-growing season or the summer months. Continuous generations are produced in the south. Farther north, both winged males and females are produced in the fall, and black, shiny overwintering eggs are laid.

In 1970, the greenbug was observed and identified as the cause of rust-colored grass areas beneath trees across central Illinois. This was the first reported widespread appearance of a strain or biotype of the greenbug feeding on Kentucky bluegrass. The oval areas were easily observed while driving along highways or down streets in cities and towns (*Color plate 27*).

The relationship of greenbug damage and trees is not clearly understood. One can speculate that migrating winged adults (Figure 4.24) strike objects and end up in the shade, giving birth to living young. Greenbugs have been found under trees, next to buildings, and even around the base of utility poles along highways. The greenbug is one of many species of grain aphids which migrate into the midwest on the southerly or southwesterly prevailing winds. In a midwestern study of migrating grain aphids during the 1960s, the greenbug was the most common species trapped in water pans and wind socks.

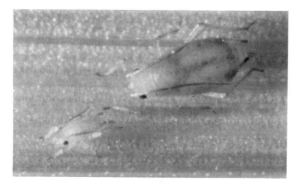

Figure 4.23   Greenbug adult and young.

Figure 4.24   Adult winged greenbug.

Since 1970, greenbugs have been reported feeding on turfgrass in the upper Mississippi and Ohio valleys. Infestations sometimes reappear in the same turf in successive years. In some communities the number of infested lawns increased from year to year, up to one-half of all lawns, then disappeared completely.

At present, greenbug infestations vary greatly from year to year. Greenbugs are often resistant to the insecticides commonly used for aphid control. This is not surprising since much of the grain acreage infested with greenbugs is treated on a regular basis, and resistance to more than one insecticide has been verified.

Greenbug damage commonly first appears in early July. The rust-colored areas expand as the numbers of the aphids increase (*Color plate 28*). The females give birth to three to five young per day, which reach maturity in about a week and are then capable of producing young. No males or eggs are present during the increase in numbers during the summer. The adult females and young aphids mass around the border or rim of the damaged area (*Color plate 27*). Greenbug eggs have been found which survived the winter to produce young the following spring. But in most instances greenbugs appear in July and August.

It is common to find predators and parasites in the greenbug population. Lady beetles, syrphid fly larvae, and parasitic wasps attack the pest insects. With a rapid population growth, greenbugs often increase in numbers in spite of the beneficial insects. In humid periods fungus diseases can reduce the populations of greenbugs. New outbreaks appearing in an area may be resistant to the insecticide used for other foliage-feeding insects. If treatments are ineffective, other labeled insecticides listed in Table 4.1 will control greenbugs.

Leafhoppers

Adult leafhoppers are tiny, wedge-shaped, pale green and yellow-gray or mottled in color. The young or nymphs resemble the adults except that they are wingless. Both adults and young can hop and crawl about on foliage. Leafhoppers feed on plant juices with their sucking mouthparts.

The most common species associated with turfgrass damage is the potato leafhopper (*Empoasca fabae*) (Figure 4.25). It is a serious pest of alfalfa in the eastern United States but also feeds on over 100 kinds of plants, including potatoes, beans, young shade trees in nurseries, and turf areas. Adult potato leafhoppers are about ⅛ in. long and pale green. This species has a tendency to swarm in large numbers, moving about from area to area. They are strongly attracted to lights at night.

Large numbers of leafhoppers can cause the turf to be mottled or whitened in areas. Sucking of the plant sap causes drying out of the grass leaves and stems and can be mistaken for drought or disease. A close examination of hopper-damaged leaves reveals tiny, white feeding punctures which cause the entire leaf to appear mottled. Potato leafhoppers feeding on potatoes cause curling, browning, and dwarfing of the foliage. Bean leaves infested with leafhoppers are crinkled and curled. Turfgrasses are not affected as severely, with only mottled, pale foliage.

Detection of leafhopper injury to grass may have to be made without the presence of the insect. A swarm of potato leafhoppers will often feed heavily on an area for a few days, then move as a group to a more favorable food source. Control treatments (Table 4.1) are usually impractical unless the leafhoppers persist in an area for a con-

Figure 4.26 Rhodesgrass scale injury to bermudagrass turf. (Courtesy Milwaukee Sewerage Commission.)

Figure 4.25 Potato leafhopper.

siderable time and damage is evident. New seedings are sometimes severely damaged, necessitating a control treatment.

Scale Insects

Adult scales are legless, small immobile insects with an armored or waxy, shell-like protective cover. The tiny, globular or oval insects are easily overlooked when damaged grass areas are examined. Very young or immature scale insects are mobile. They settle on a grass leaf blade or stem, insert their needlelike mouth parts, suck plant juices, lose their legs, and begin to secrete the waxy covering.

Several species of scales infest turf, but the life cycles are almost alike. The Rhodesgrass scale (*Antonina graminis*) is found in the Gulf states and other states, including California, as a pest on rhodesgrass. It infests pasture grasses and also occurs in turf areas. This scale attacks plant crowns, causing infested plants to wither and die (Figure 4.26). The adults are globular, ⅛ in. across, and dark purplish brown. All adults are female and give birth to living young. The life cycle takes about 50 days to complete and there are usually five generations annually.

Bermudagrass scales (*Odonaspis ruthae*) attach themselves to the nodes of bermudagrass stems. They are white when mature and 1/16 in. long. Infested bermudagrass crowns have a "moldy" appearance.

Ground pearls, a scale insect attacking the roots of centipedegrass, bermudagrass, and St. Augustinegrass was discussed earlier (page 164) in the section on root-feeding insects. Control suggestions for scales are given in Table 4.1.

Spittlebugs

The spittlebug is a tiny, wedge-shaped insect which resembles a leafhopper. The adults are heavy-bodied and about ¼ in. long. They are usually mottled brown and cream-colored but vary from cream to almost black. They jump readily, making an audible thump. The small, yellow-to-white eggs are laid in rows on plant leaves and stems.

Two species are found on turfgrass. The meadow spittlebug (*Philaenus spumarius*) often makes its presence known by its spittle masses on clover in turf (*Color plate 29*). The nymphs or young cause the damage, if any. They are found behind leaf sheaths, in folded leaves, and on stems in masses of froth or spittle during the summer months. There is one generation each year. The meadow spittlebug overwinters in the egg stage. Feeding damage to clover and occasionally weeds in the lawn is not an economic loss, but the unsightly spittle masses can be a nuisance.

Whereas the meadow spittlebug is present in the northeast and midwest, another species is found in the southeast. This species, the two-lined spittlebug (*Prosapia bicincta*), is dark brown to black as an adult and ⅜ in. long. The nymphs feed on bermudagrass, St. Augustinegrass, and centipedegrass. Spittle masses are more of a concern than damage from the insect's feeding. Chemical control is probably rarely justified, but if necessary select one of the insecticides suggested in Table 4.1.

Mites

Mites are tiny, microscopic, eight-legged relatives of insects. In a thorough examination of a piece of turf, several mite species may be present. Some are beneficial or predator mites that feed on pest mites. Mite pests open leaf cells and consume the sap causing severe chlorosis and browning of the leaves.

Bermudagrass mites (*Eriophyes cynodoniensis*) can cause considerable damage to bermudagrass lawns. These cigar-shaped mites are white rather than reddish or green as are some other mite species. They are not visible to the unaided eye, but can be observed with a microscope. Bermudagrass mites, as with most mite species, multiply rapidly and cause severe damage in a short period. The females lay eggs under the leaf sheaths. Immature mites that hatch from eggs are six-legged rather than eight-legged as are the adults. The life cycle of the bermudagrass mite, from egg to adult laying eggs, is about 1 week. The eggs hatch quickly and many mites may soon be feeding on the stems and in protected areas of the leaf sheaths.

Bermudagrass mites suck juice from plants, causing them to turn yellow or brown. Stem feeding causes shortening of internodes and a rosetted or tufted growth. Heavily infested plants turn brown and die. When mite damage is severe, the grass is thinned and soon invaded by weeds.

The clover mite (*Bryobia praetiosa*) (Figure 4.27) is more a nuisance pest inside and on the outside of homes rather than of turf. (This mite has been known to cause significant injury to turf in home lawns.) It feeds mainly on clovers and some other plants, but large populations build up that may invade homes. This migration occurs mostly in late winter or spring but sometimes in the fall. There are several generations each year.

Clover mites resemble reddish-brown specks of dust crawling about on walls, windows, curtains, and so on. Under a hand lens they appear oval, eight-legged, and the front pair of legs are more than twice the length of the other legs. When crushed on walls or curtains inside a home, clover mites leave a red stain. As a house pest, they are only a nuisance, but large numbers can build up on and around windows.

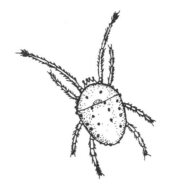

Figure 4.27 Clover mite.

Keeping a zone of bare soil or nongrass about 18 to 24 in. wide around the house foundation usually prevents clover mites from migrating into the home. This strip can be planted to flowers that do not attract clover mites.

Another mite species, the winter grain mite (*Penthaleus major*), is a pest of small grains and some grasses. It is known as a pest of grass seed fields in Oregon. Recently, it was observed on Kentucky bluegrass and red fescue. In the past 5 to 10 years it has caused damage to bentgrass fairways in Ohio and Pennsylvania, and to Kentucky bluegrass and fine fescue turfs in Ohio. Damage due to winter grain mites has been reported in other states east of the Mississippi River.

This mite is unique in that it is most numerous and damaging during the winter and early spring months. The eggs hatch in October. Young mites are reddish orange but become darker brown or black as they grow. The olive-black adults with eight reddish-orange legs emerge in November. The adults are small but can be easily observed with the naked eye.

On close inspection of damaged turf on winter days, winter grain mites can be seen in the thatch or on the damaged crowns. The mites increase to great numbers in late winter. Several thousand per square foot is not unusual. They feed on cloudy days and at night and their damage may be incorrectly diagnosed as winterkill or desiccation. Heavy mite populations diminish in April as eggs are laid on dead grass plants. The eggs do not hatch until late fall.

Applied control measures are very effective if the problem is correctly diagnosed. Suggested insecticides are listed in Table 4.1.

Ants

Several species of ants can be a nuisance in turf areas. They are also often a nuisance inside the home, especially the kitchen area. Most species of ants in the United States are social insects that live in colonies or nests, in which remain the egg-laying queens, the young or larvae, pupae, and many worker ants. The workers, all sterile females, care for the colony as well as search for food and bring it to the nest. In the spring or fall ant colonies may produce winged males and females which fly about, mate, and have the ability to start a new colony.

Biology of Turfgrass Insects and Related Pests

Figure 4.28 Little black ant.

Ants construct mounds or small hills of granulated soil which may smother out the surrounding grass. Grass may also be killed as the soil around the grass roots dries out from the effects of the digging and burrowing.

Some species of ants which frequent turfgrass areas, and eventually construct ant-hills, include the little black ant (*Monomorium minimum*) (Figure 4.28), the pavement ant (*Tetramorium caespitum*), and the thief ant (*Solenopsis molesta*). These ants all live in the soil and construct small hills. The worker ants can be observed constantly in search of food to bring back to the colony.

Other ant species may be in or near grass areas. The black carpenter ant (*Camponotus pennsylvanicus*) nests in dead trees, logs, and even structural wood in houses. These large, winged, black ants often exceed ½ in. in length. Winged males and females may swarm occasionally but do not nest in turfgrass soil.

Swarming winged ants are often mistaken for winged male and female termites. The two insects are easily distinguished. The bodies of winged termites are black; the ants may be black, red, yellow, tan, or almost red. Termites have bodies that are a *uniform* width throughout. The bodies of ants are narrow or constricted just behind the wing-bearing area of the body. The wings of termites are of equal size and shape, while the front pair of ants' wings are much larger than the hind pair.

The red imported fire ant (*Solenopsis invicta*) is an important turf pest, especially in the southeast from the Carolinas along the Gulf coast to Texas and Arkansas. Since the 1920s this insect has spread out from its original entry into this country in Alabama. The red imported fire ant has become a "political insect problem" as well as a mound builder in lawns and an important pest of people. This ant has received considerable publicity concerning its potential for spread throughout other regions of the United States, its damaging mound-building activities in both agricultural and urban areas, and its ability to sting people. Federal and state funds have been allocated to eradicate this insect, but it seems firmly established across much of the south.

Entomologists in the Gulf states have studied the habits, biology, and damage of the red imported fire ant. The colony constructs honeycomb mounds containing up to half a million worker ants. These mounds are found in pastures, roadsides, field borders, and forests. In urban areas they occur on playgrounds, golf courses, cemeteries, and in home lawns. The ants build mounds in many areas but prefer sunny sites and clay soils over sandy soils. In home lawns and other managed turfgrass areas, the mounds usually reach only the height of the grass. In unmowed situations, the mounds may be up to 1½ to 2 ft tall.

The strategy for controlling the red imported fire ant is not its eradication but to reduce the population in the existing mounds. Fire ants increase their mound size in wet seasons to move above the moist area. Applied controls (Table 4.1) are made to the mounds without disturbing the structure. Baits are also being used to kill the producing queen.

Imported fire ant stings are painful. When a person is stung, venom is injected. The site of a sting may only turn red, or a lesion may develop which can lead to infection and scarring. Because of the potential for being stung, fewer people use parks and other turfgrass areas infested with fire ant mounds.

Cicada Killer

Cicadas, including the dog-day species and the many broods of periodical cicadas, have a very active insect predator. This predator is a black-and-yellow-marked wasp about $1\frac{1}{2}$ in. long called the cicada killer (*Sphecus speciosus speciosus*) (Figure 4.29). It is commonly seen buzzing and darting about lawns or gardens in late summer. As they fly about you can hear their rapid wing beat. There may be a few or a dozen or more, depending on how well they prefer an area for nesting. These bright-colored wasps begin to appear in July and remain through September.

Female cicada killers search for cicadas, struggle with, and sting them. The cicada is much larger than the wasp. The paralyzed cicada is carried, partially in flight, by the female wasp to previously prepared burrows in the soil. It is dragged into the burrow and placed in an enlarged cell at the bottom of the hole. The wasp lays an egg on the paralyzed cicada. The egg hatches in a few days into a larva that feeds on the cicada. It remains in the soil overwinter. The adults emerge in early to midsummer.

These wasps are expert and energetic diggers, throwing up a mound of soil near each burrow. These mounds may suddenly appear in the morning from digging performed the previous evening. The wasp prefers sandy soil on a slope or terrace in which to dig. Often their burrows are under spreading shrubs in the foundation planting. The holes are about ¾ in. in diameter, extend 6 in. or more into the soil, and then branch out several times and extend another 6 to 8 in. into the soil. Although formidable-appearing, these wasps are not vicious, but can inflict a severe sting, if disturbed or annoyed.

Figure 4.29 Cicada-killer wasp.

The cicada killer is a predator insect, but its digging and the soil mounds it creates can be a nuisance to high-quality turf. Soil insecticide drenches on infested areas will control these wasps, if needed (Table 4.1).

Cicadas

Cicadas are large, robust, winged insects which announce their presence with the day-long shrill "singing" of the males. The common dog-day, or annual cicada (*Tibicen* species), is a nuisance with its loud singing every year but causes very little, if any, damage.

The periodical cicada (*Magicicada* species) is smaller than the annual cicada and the body is darker (*Color plate 30*). The wings contain orange veins and the eyes are red. There are six distinct species, but all are similar in appearance. Three species are usually present in broods occurring every 13 years and the other species in broods that emerge every 17 years. There are some 18 different broods, most in the eastern half of the United States. Large numbers of cicada nymphs emerge from the soil at one time and change into adults after living in the soil as young for almost 13 or 17 years. Adult cicadas begin emerging in late May.

In moist soil the nymphs, before emerging, construct mud tubes or "chimneys" that extend up to 3 in. above the ground level (Figure 4.30). Great numbers of nymphs emerge at the same time. They crawl up tree trunks, posts, or other objects. A few hours later the adults emerge, leaving their many grayish-brown shed skins on posts, trees, and so on. Cicada males announce their presence to the noiseless females by making a continuous, high-pitched sound. This sound is produced by vibrating membranes on the underside of the first abdominal segment.

After mating, the females lay eggs in rows in pockets that they cut in small branches and twigs of trees with their long, knifelike egg layer. The eggs hatch in 6 or 7 weeks; the newly hatched nymphs fall to the soil surface and burrow until they find tree roots to feed on. With their sucking mouth parts, they immediately begin to suck sap from the root.

Primary damage to turfs by periodical cicadas occurs when the full-grown nymphs dig themselves out of the ground at the end of their 13- or 17-year cycle. If the number

Figure 4.30 Periodical cicada nymph emergence holes or "chimneys."

of nymphs that burrow into the soil and survive is large, the number of chimneys, burrows, or holes that suddenly appear under a tree may be quite striking—one for every square inch.

The nymphs of periodical cicadas are impossible to control, as they live at least a foot deep in the soil before emerging. The adults can be controlled (Table 4.1) to prevent egg-laying damage to trees as well as to reduce the population of a generation 13 or 17 years later.

Ground-Nesting Bees and Wasps

Ground-nesting bees (*Andrenidae* species) and wasps (*Sphecidae* species), other than the cicada killer described previously, may nest in burrows in the soil. The bees are also called mining or solitary bees. Ground-nesting wasps provision their soil nests with adult flies; some use crickets and grasshoppers for food. A social wasp, the eastern yellow jacket (*Vespula maculifrons*), lives as a colony in an aerial nest in shrubs, on buildings, or in soil. Worker yellow jackets forage in late summer for insects to feed their young, as well as feeding on ripening and overripe fruit.

Ground-nesting bees and wasps in a turf area may continually be constructing new burrows or are simply a nuisance to turf owners or people using a public area such as a park or golf course.

Soil drenches, if needed, will reduce these pest insects (Table 4.1). Avoid being stung by making control applications at dusk when this insect's activity is low.

Sowbugs and Pillbugs

Sowbugs (*Omiscus* spp.) and pillbugs (*Cylisticus* spp.) are not insects but are more closely related to crayfish. They are small, hard-shelled, tubular-bodied, segmented animals about ½ in. long, and slate gray. The adults have seven pairs of legs.

Pillbugs (*Color plate 31*) are similar in appearance to sowbugs (Figure 4.31) but also have the ability to roll themselves into tight little balls when disturbed. Both animals live in damp areas, such as under boards, stones, leaves, and other debris. They feed

Figure 4.31 Sowbugs.

Biology of Turfgrass Insects and Related Pests

primarily on decaying vegetable matter. Occasionally, they feed on healthy plant tissue, including grasses. Sowbugs and pillbugs may invade structures in large numbers. They cannot remain in dry areas away from damp vegetation, litter, and stones or they will desiccate and die.

The development of sowbugs and pillbugs is very similar. The eggs of both species develop in brood pouches. An average of two generations or broods are produced each year. Adult sowbugs and pillbugs live for about 2 years.

The numbers of these animals can be reduced by removing their hiding places—leaves, rocks, boards, and other debris around the foundations of buildings. Chemical treatments are also available (Table 4.1).

Millipedes and Centipedes

Millipedes (*Diploda* spp.), often called thousand-legged worms, are not insects but are elongate, wormlike animals with 30 or more pairs of legs. Centipedes (*Chilopoda* spp.) are elongated, flattened wormlike animals with 15 or more pairs of legs; often referred to as hundred-legged worms.

Millipedes curl up when disturbed (Figure 4.32). The adults are 1 to 2 in. long and brown, tan, or gray. They have two pairs of legs on each body segment except the three segments behind the head.

Centipedes are 1 in. or more in length with numerous body segments (Figure 4.33). There is one pair of long legs for each body segment. In females, the last pair of legs is more than double the body length. A pair of long antennae project forward from the head.

Most millipedes are found in damp areas, such as under leaves, stones, boards, compost piles, or in the soil. They feed on decaying plant material. Sometimes they damage

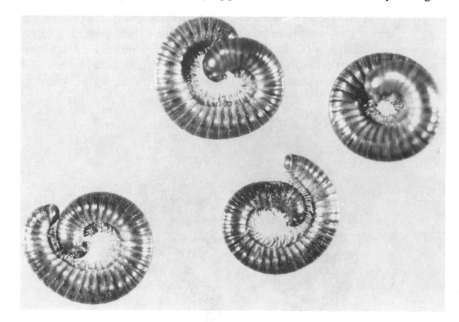

Figure 4.32 Millipedes.

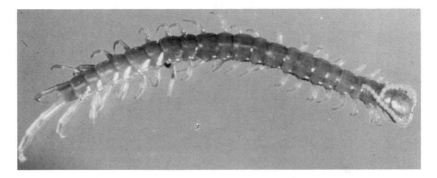

Figure 4.33 Centipede.

young plants as they feed on the roots. These animals may invade structures, causing considerable annoyance. Some species of millipedes eject a foul-smelling fluid through openings along the sides of their bodies.

Centipedes are predators that feed on small insects and spiders. If threatened, some centipedes may bite, producing swelling and some pain.

Both millipedes and centipedes overwinter as adults in protected areas. Millipedes lay their eggs during the summer, often in nests in the soil or in damp areas without constructing a nest. Newly hatched young have three pairs of legs; more are added as the animal increases in size. Adult millipedes may live about 7 years.

Centipedes lay eggs during the summer. The eggs and hatching young are protected by the adults. Centipedes live approximately 6 years under favorable conditions.

Some reduction in the population of millipedes and centipedes can be accomplished by changing the environment near turfgrass areas. Elimination of piles of organic matter, such as compost, grass clippings, and other damp debris, reduces their feeding and egglaying sites. Removal of stones, boards, leaves, and other debris, together with the elimination of damp locations, also discourages a population buildup of both millipedes and centipedes. The decaying organic matter or the damp areas that they prefer may be on adjoining properties. Many new subdivisions are plagued by millipedes, due to vacant or poorly managed areas near new homes and lawns.

If large populations of these animals are present and are a nuisance, they can be controlled on the turf, in waste areas, or near buildings. Chemical controls are listed in Table 4.1.

Earwigs

Earwigs are slender, beetlelike insects with short wings and a large pair of "forceps" on the rear of the body. They are a dark reddish-brown and about ¾ in. long. The most common species is the European earwig (*Forficula auricularia*), found in the northeastern and some western states (*Color plate 32*). Other species (*Euborellia annulipes* and *Labidura riparia*) are commonly found around homes in the southeastern United States.

The name "earwig" is derived from an old superstition that has these insects entering people's ears at night while they are asleep. This belief is totally untrue, as earwigs are completely harmless to human beings.

Biology of Turfgrass Insects and Related Pests

Figure 4.34 Field cricket.

Earwigs are active primarily at night, hiding during the day in cracks and under boards, rocks, and similar dark places. Most are scavengers but they occasionally feed on ornamental plants, fruits, and vegetables. Large populations have been observed in piles of grass clippings. One species, *Labidura,* is an important predator of chinch bugs in south Florida. Earwigs overwinter as adults. The eggs are laid in clusters within burrows beneath the soil surface. Young earwigs somewhat resemble the adult.

Control is rarely, if ever, necessary. An earwig population may build up over a 1- to 2-year period and then decrease dramatically. There are effective controls when their numbers are a nuisance. These are listed in Table 4.1.

Crickets

Crickets are often a nuisance to homeowners. Field crickets (*Gryllus* spp.) are brownish to black, ¾-in.-long, short-winged, hopping insects (Figure 4.34). The chirping of male field crickets is a common sound to many people. Field crickets feed on some agricultural crops and when numerous also damage ripening garden vegetables. They spend the winter in the egg stage. Egg hatch occurs in early summer and young nymphs increase in size throughout the summer. Large adult crickets begin to be observed in August and are most noticeable with the cooler temperatures of autumn as they migrate and seek out sheltered areas, including homes. A single generation is completed each year in the northern United States. Sometimes great numbers of these black, jumping, chirping crickets can be found along the foundation of a house, garage, or other building.

Applied control of crickets in turfgrass areas is unneeded, as they do not damage the grass, but the homeowner often desires to control them around the building foundation. There are effective chemical controls (Table 4.1).

Fleas

Adult fleas (*Ctenocephalides* spp.) are small, ⅛-in., dark brown to nearly black insects that move swiftly among the hairs on animals (Figure 4.35). They are capable of jumping as much as a foot when off an animal. Their eggs are tiny, oval, and white. The hatching larvae are slender, whitish worms with light brown heads.

Fleas attack a wide variety of animals, including people. Female fleas lay eggs wherever they happen to be at the time. The eggs are laid among the hairs of the host animal but soon drop to the ground. The hatching larvae are scavengers and feed on a wide range of debris. This stage is harmless, but when the fleas become adults they search for a host animal.

In turfgrass areas frequented by pets, both immature and adult fleas can build up in numbers to constantly reinfest pets running across the lawn. Occasionally, people who walk across an infested turf are bitten by fleas.

Control of fleas is commonly directed at the infested pet or its bedding by the use of flea collars, dusts, or sprays applied to the body of the animal. Dogs and cats are "walking bait stations" for fleas. As long as the animal is around, people are seldom attacked. If needed, there are effective controls (Table 4.1) to apply to infested grass areas.

Ticks

Ticks are close relatives of insects. Their primary food is the blood of warm-blooded animals. There are various species, but the one commonly associated with turfgrass areas is the American dog or wood tick (*Dermacentor variabilis*) (Figure 4.36). This tick is hard-bodied, about ¼ in. long and flattened, with a shield containing silver markings on its back. After feeding on one of several wild animal hosts, the female expands to about ½ in. long and is only slightly flattened. Only the adult stage attacks larger animals, including people and dogs; the immature stages feed on smaller animals. After hatching, there are three stages: a small six-legged larva, an intermediate eight-legged nymph that resembles the adult, and the adult.

Adult American dog or wood ticks are most active in early summer. They are especially numerous in brush or tall grass areas, waiting to attach themselves to passing animals as they pass by. Ticks do not do well in short vegetation such as mowed lawns. Sites of tick infestations are adjoining roadsides, fence rows, woods, brush, and other unmowed areas.

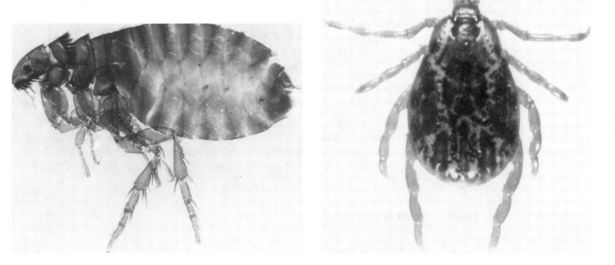

Figure 4.35 Flea.   **Figure 4.36** Tick.

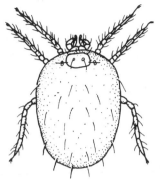

Figure 4.37 Chigger.

Avoiding tick-infested areas during early summer is the best prevention of ticks attaching themselves to the skin. Protective clothing such as long pants and boots help prevent tick attacks. Mosquito repellents on exposed parts of the body also discourage them. Tick-infested areas can be sprayed with an insecticide to control them (Table 4.1).

Chiggers

Chiggers (*Eutrombicula* spp.), also called redbugs, are mites that occur throughout the United States. There is more than one species, but their activities are similar. Chiggers pass the winter as adults near or below the soil surface. Eggs are laid in the spring and the newly hatched nymphs are six-legged. Later they change to eight-legged nymphs and eventually to eight-legged adults.

The stage of chiggers that is a pest of people is the six-legged immature stage (Figure 4.37). They are almost invisible to the naked eye, being less than $\frac{1}{150}$ of an inch in diameter, oval, a bright orange-yellow, and move about quickly. Chiggers insert their mouthparts into the skin of human beings, usually in a skin pore or hair follicle. They are found especially in regions of the body with tight-fitting clothes. When fully-fed, young mites drop off the host. Later they enter the soil to pass the winter. There is one generation each year. Anyone who has been bitten by chiggers may not feel their bites for several hours after exposure.

Chiggers are found where vegetation is abundant, such as shaded areas, high grass or weeds, or fruit plantings. However, they may become serious pests of lawns, golf courses, and parks.

To check a suspected chigger-infested area, place a piece of black cardboard edgewise on the ground where chiggers may be. If present, tiny yellow or pink mites will soon move rapidly over the cardboard and gather along the upper edge.

Controlling chiggers around the home should be directed at reducing nearby egg-laying sites. Wooded or grassy areas may be mowed to reduce the cover. Good repellents applied to the body are available which prevent or repel chiggers from feeding. Chigger-infested areas can also be treated with a chemical (Table 4.1).

No-See-Ums and Mosquitoes

No-see-ums, punkies, or sand flies are names given to a group of tiny, blood-sucking midges or flies (*Ceratopogonidae* spp.) that can be a nuisance to lawn owners and turfgrass managers. The young, immature maggots develop in moist vegetation or in water, such as creeks and ponds. The flies generally hide during the day and are active in the evening and early morning hours. The tiny size of the biting flies and their painful bite is out of proportion to each; hence the name "no-see-ums."

Mosquitoes (*Culicidae* spp.) have habits similar to no-see-ums. They are larger flies, with the females doing the blood-sucking (*Color plate 33*). The larvae or wrigglers need to live in standing water for about a week prior to becoming adults. In addition to their irritating bite, mosquitoes transmit several important diseases to human beings, including encephalitis, malaria, and yellow fever.

Control of no-see-ums and mosquitoes can be partially or completely achieved by elimination of standing water in such places as eave troughs, old tires, tin cans, rain barrels, storm sewers, open garbage cans, and other water-holding containers. Spraying shrubbery where the adults hide during the day reduces their numbers (Table 4.1).

Aerosols or "flying insect" sprays in pressurized cans give a quick temporary knockdown of these pests at outdoor cookouts or parties. There are also effective insect repellents for use on exposed skin.

Thrips

Thrips are tiny, black or yellow, brushy-winged insects up to ⅛ inch long (Figure 4.38). "Oat-bugs" or "oat-lice" are common names people use to refer to these nuisance pests. These minute insects move about quickly on grass blades or other plants.

They feed on many species of plants. One species, the grass thrips (*Anaphothrips obscurus*), is almost specific to bluegrasses, but has been found on other plants. Injury

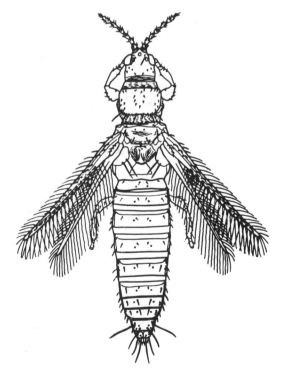

Figure 4.38 Line drawing of a thrips.

Biology of Turfgrass Insects and Related Pests

Figure 4.39 Black widow spider.

by thrips is done by their rasping mouthparts, which scratch the green tissue from the upper leaf surface. A damaged plant or turf area has a silver-top or whitish appearance.

Occasionally, thrips may crawl on a person and may even bite the skin surface. If numerous, thrips can be controlled in turf areas (Table 4.1).

Spiders

Spiders (*Aranae*) can often be found near tall grass, flowers, shrubbery, and on or by buildings. All spiders are predaceous, feeding mostly on insects and other small animals. Some species spin webs to trap their prey; others pounce on prey; still others lie in wait, hidden on plants and other sites.

Young spiders hatch from eggs and resemble their parents. They gradually undergo development to adults. Unusually high numbers of spiders often indicate the presence of other insects that provide their food.

Spiders are disliked by many people, especially if inside the home or on flowers. It is true that many species do bite, but only a few species are poisonous. These include the black widow (*Latrodectus mactans*) (Figure 4.39) and brown recluse (*Loxosceles reclusus*) spiders. Many spiders, however, are beneficial, playing an important role in keeping down populations of pest insects.

If spiders are numerous in and around the home or apartment building, they can be prevented from entering by using an insecticide treatment on the foundation. Specific insecticide suggestions are given in Table 4.1.

Crane Flies

Crane flies, often called leather jackets, resemble overgrown mosquitoes with extremely long legs. They occur primarily in damp locations where vegetation is abundant.

Young crane flies are worms that live in bodies of water and feed on decaying vegetation. Some species feed on living plants, including turfgrasses. No damage is done to turfgrass by crane fly adults, but some larvae mature in the soil surface and feed on living plants, including grass roots. This results in small, irregular brown patches in the turf. The size of crane flies and their similarity to oversized mosquitoes probably gives them an inflated nuisance rating. The European crane fly (*Tipula paludosa*) can quickly damage lawns, putting greens, and so on when maggot numbers are over 20 per sq ft.

Other Insects

Night-flying insects are often attracted to lights in turfgrass areas. Certain moths and beetles often hide in the grass area during the day and fly to lights at night. Not all the insects found in turf are pests.

Some insects are predators of pest insects. For example, lady beetles, both adults and their young (*Color plate 34*), feed on greenbugs and other small insects. Syrphid fly larvae are small, legless larvae which also feed on aphids. The identification of an insect population found in a grass area and determining its potential for damage is the first step to insect pest management. Insect predators need to be correctly identified and their value to control pests recognized.

Slugs and Snails

Slugs and snails are mollusks, not insects, being more closely related to such aquatic animals as clams and oysters. Garden slugs (*Color plate 35*) are more common than snails and a greater nuisance. Slugs are described as "snails without their shells." They are typically gray or spotted, and range from ½ in. to more than 2 in. long. They secrete a characteristic slimy mucous residue on plants or other objects over which they crawl. This slimy trail is often the only visible evidence of their past activity.

Slug eggs are laid in clusters in hidden, moist locations. Most species overwinter in the egg stage. Slugs may live a year or more after hatching. Sometimes, in warmer regions, there is more than one generation each year.

Slugs are pests of flower beds, ornamentals, and seedling vegetable plants. They feed at night, eating holes in the foliage or crowns of plants. They can be especially numerous where the plants are heavily mulched. Slugs and snails are not feeders on turfgrasses.

The numbers of slugs and snails can be reduced by removing their hiding places and egg-laying sites. In the fall, clean up flower beds and vegetable gardens by picking up all debris, such as boards, dead leaves and stems, and other material. There is no effective insecticide which can be applied that will control slugs or snails. Attractant bait formulations are available for use in and around flower and ornamental plantings and vegetable gardens. Metaldehyde has long been used as a chemical attractant and a stomach poison for slugs and snails. It is marketed as a pelleted bait. Mesurol is a new chemical, now formulated into slug baits. Shallow containers of stale beer are also attractive to slugs. The aldehyde odor attracts the slugs, causing them to crawl into the shallow dish of beer and drown.

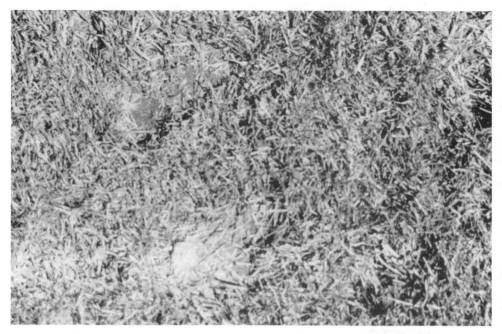

Figure 4.40 Earthworm casts that have been rolled down. (Courtesy Milwaukee Sewerage Commission.)

Earthworms

Earthworms live all year in the soil of many turfgrass areas. They are most evident in the spring and fall by their burrowing and feeding activity and the mounds, called casts or castings (Figure 4.40), they leave behind. High populations of earthworms are usually associated with a moist, cool soil high in organic matter. They move to the soil surface during cool periods to pull leaves, stems, and other undecomposed debris from the soil surface. This feeding activity is a primary remover of thatch that accumulates on the soil surface. Large amounts of undecomposed material passes through earthworms and is left in the soil. The small mounds or castings left by earthworms can be objectionable, if numerous, especially on a golf or bowling green or other fine turf area. The benefits of earthworms have to be weighed against the objectionable uneven soil surface caused by their castings. Most insecticides labeled for use on turf insects have no effect on the feeding activity of earthworms, but some do. The arsenicals, especially calcium arsenate, discourage earthworms from coming to the soil surface.

Crayfish

These aquatic animals often infest turf, leaving holes about 1 in. in diameter at the soil surface. Soil castings are mounded up around the holes. Unusually wet soil conditions are conducive for crayfish activity. They are most prevalent, when present, during an unusually wet spring or early summer.

Figure 4.41 Eastern mole.

Probably the easiest method to eliminate crayfish activity is to improve the drainage of infested areas by installing drain tile below the soil surface.

Moles

Moles (Figure 4.41) can be a serious pest of home lawns, golf courses, and other highly managed turfgrass areas. These small mammals spend most of their lives in underground burrows. They are similar in appearance and size to meadow mice and shrews. Their legs are strong, the neck short, and the head elongated. The most noticeable features are the enlarged paddlelike forefeet and prominent toenails, which allow the mole to move easily through the soil.

Moles may be found in forests, wetlands, grasslands, and cultivated grass areas. They construct extensive underground passageways. These tunnels are shallow in the spring, summer, and fall (Figure 4.42), and deeper in the winter months. Their nests are connected to the deep tunnels.

Figure 4.42 Mole runs or burrows. (Courtesy Milwaukee Sewerage Commission.)

Biology of Turfgrass Insects and Related Pests

Moles feed actively day and night the year around. Their food is usually insects, snails, spiders, small vertebrates, earthworms, and sometimes a small amount of vegetation. Moles rarely eat flower bulbs, shrub roots, or other plant material. They prefer loose, sandy soils to heavy clay areas. In a natural environment moles cause little damage. They are seldom noticed until their tunneling is observed in mowed areas. The upheaved ridges of mole tunnels make mowing difficult. Since roots are disturbed, the grass may be uneven in color or turn brown. Plant baits such as poison peanuts are mostly ineffective in controlling moles. Baits are being tested that contain animal products as the attractant, and these show some promise. At present, trapping is the most effective control. The traps are set over fresh tunnels or runs. Control of soil insects will decrease the food supply of moles (see Table 4.1).

Skunks

Skunks feed on soil insects as well as fruits and berries. In search of grubs, they often dig cone-shaped holes in lawns, cemeteries, golf course fairways, and other turf areas. Grub-infested turf may be overturned in large patches.

Skunk damage to turf areas can be reduced or prevented by the use of a soil insecticide to control root-feeding insects, especially grubs (see Table 4.1).

Rodents

Pocket gophers, ground squirrels (Figure 4.43), and meadow mice often frequent the edges of cultivated turf areas.

Pocket gophers tunnel into the sod, creating burrows and mounds of piled-up loose soil. They eat vegetation bordering the holes in the sod, as well as cutting off and destroying the roots, crowns, and stems of plants. They also gnaw on and girdle tree roots.

Ground squirrels are capable of climbing. They may feed on nuts and fruit, but their primary food is seeds and vegetation. Ground squirrels dig extensive burrows

Figure 4.43 Ground squirrel. (Courtesy U.S. Fish and Wildlife Service.)

Figure 4.44 Ground squirrel burrows. (Courtesy U.S. Fish and Wildlife Service.)

(Figure 4.44) that remain open even when the squirrels are hibernating. Plant material and seeds are stored in the burrows. Most burrows are about 4 in. in diameter.

Meadow mice dig burrows 1 to 2 in. in diameter that open straight down into the soil. They will tunnel under a snow cover in the turf, leaving numerous runways when the snow melts. They often girdle and kill young trees or other woody vegetation.

All of these rodents can be reduced by trapping. Various types of traps are sold in garden supply stores. Specific poison baits prepared for these ground-nesting animals are also available.

Birds

Birds, such as robins, starlings, and grackles (Figure 4.45), frequently visit turf areas to feed on leaf-eating caterpillars and other insects. The birds often provide valuable assistance in the early detection of potential damage from sod webworms, cutworms, and similar caterpillars.

Figure 4.45 Grackle. (Courtesy U.S. Fish and Wildlife Service.)

In fine turf, such as golf greens, the feeding of birds on cutworms results in physically damaged areas more serious than that caused by the feeding of the insects.

Direct control of birds is unnecessary. Chemical control of foliage feeding caterpillars (Table 4.1) reduces or eliminates bird activity and will not harm the birds.

CONTROL OF TURFGRASS INSECTS

Insect control is an important part of turfgrass management. To be successful, the identification and some biological information about the pest insect is essential. The preceding text covered much of this information on each turf insect.

One insect specimen in a turf never causes damage to that area. Pest insects occur as populations of specimens of varying numbers, often including adults, young, and eggs. Low populations probably do not exhibit damage to the grass.

The aim of insect control is not to eradicate a pest population from a region, community, or turf area. It is the suppression of the existing damaging or potentially damaging population of a turf insect pest. Population suppression reduces the numbers below an "economic threshold" level capable of damaging the turf. *This control can be applied (application of insecticide) or natural control (climatic or biological factors) can occur.* Applied control is by far the most common, but natural control plays a greater role than is realized. Many insects can successfully overwinter only in the southern states. Species of cutworms, armyworms, leafhoppers, and some aphids must migrate northward each year to be found in the north-central and northeastern regions of the United States. Predators, parasites, and diseases have a distinct limiting effect on populations of insects, especially aphids, caterpillars, and mites.

Applied control or suppression of a pest insect population with insecticides is often termed management of the insect, pest management, or insect pest management. The principles are not new, just the name. Insect pest management is a series of decision-making steps to insect control rather than treating for turfgrass insects on a regular basis. The five basic steps are:

1. Identifying the insect and its population
2. Determining the potential for damage
3. Deciding what tactics to use to suppress the population, if needed
4. Taking action against the insect, if possible
5. Evaluation of the results of the action

These steps are well known to many experienced turf managers.

There are more insecticides available to the turfgrass manager now than ever before. Arsenicals were used as stomach poisons on chewing insects more than 40 years ago. Chlordane, aldrin, dieldrin, and DDT were used in 1950s and into the early 1970s. These persistent chlorinated hydrocarbons have now been replaced by the following organic phosphates and carbamates currently labeled for use on turfgrass.

Diazinon: broad-spectrum, moderately toxic organic phosphate. It is nonsystemic and moderately residual in the soil and on foliage. It is effective against a broad spectrum of insects. Diazinon is formulated both as a spray and as granules.

Chlorpyrifos (Dursban): broad-spectrum, moderately toxic organic phosphate. It is nonsystemic, moderately residual on foliage, and moderately residual and effective against certain soil insects. Dursban gives fair control of white grubs and excellent control of black cutworms. It is formulated both as a spray and as granules.

Malathion: very short residual, low-toxicity organic phosphate for use against nuisance insects on or near turf areas.

Aspon: moderately residual, low-toxicity organic phosphate used for control of chinch bugs and sod webworms.

Trichlorfon (Proxol, Dylox): moderately residual, moderately toxic, nonsystemic insecticide for control of grubs and leaf-feeding caterpillars. It is formulated as a soluble powder to be applied as a spray.

Isofenphos (Oftanol): long residual organic phosphate of moderately high toxicity that is effective against soil insects, including white grubs and billbug larvae. It is also effective against chinch bugs and billbug adults. Both spray and granular formulations are available.

Acephate (Orthene): systemic, low-toxicity, moderately residual insecticide labeled on turf to control greenbug. It may control other insect pests but is very effective on the greenbug. Orthene is applied as a spray.

Carbaryl (Sevin): low-toxicity, moderately residual carbamate. It controls bees, wasps, and some leaf-eating caterpillars. It is formulated as a spray.

Bendiocarb (Turcam, Dycarb): moderately residual, moderately toxic carbamate for control of white grubs and certain leaf-feeding caterpillars. A recently labeled product, it will be suggested for control of additional insects in the future.

Undoubtedly, some insecticides presently in use will be discontinued by the manufacturer or in usage by turfgrass managers. Others will be labeled and used for turfgrass insect control. Triumph is an organic phosphate shown to be highly effective against both turfgrass soil insects and foliage feeders. It is not labeled but could receive label clearance any time in the future. Other insecticides will be added to the arsenal in the years ahead.

Read the insecticide label as to safety precautions, amount to use, timing of applications, and directions on how to apply the chemical. Table 4.1 lists the common turfgrass insect pests and the suggested insecticides which are effective in reducing their populations. For further information on applying pesticides and precautions for their safe use, read Chapter 6.

TABLE 4.1 CHEMICAL CONTROL OF TURFGRASS INSECTS

Insect	Suggested insecticide	Remarks
White grubs	Diazinon, isofenphos (Oftanol), trichlorfon (Proxol, Dylox), bendiocarb (Turcam)	Treat when grubs are small or at egg hatch; Oftanol provides control throughout the growing season; drench with ½ to 1 in. water (300 to 600 gal per 1000 sq ft)
Billbugs	Chlorpyrifos (Dursban), isofenphos (Oftanol), diazinon	Apply in spring for adult control; for larval control, drench into the soil in June or July with ½ to 1 in. of water
Wireworms	Diazinon	Drench into the soil with ½ to 1 in. of water when worms are present
Ground pearls	No effective chemical control	Irrigate and fertilize the infested area to stimulate vigorous growth (see Chapter 2)
Mole crickets	Isofenphos (Oftanol), diazinon, chlorpyrifos (Dursban), bendiocarb (Turcam)	Apply in early summer and repeat when damage appears later; drench into the soil with ½ to 1 in. of water (300 to 600 gal per 1000 sq ft)
Sod webworms	Diazinon, chlorpyrifos (Dursban), Aspon, trichlorfon (Proxol, Dylox), carbaryl (Sevin)	Apply as a spray or as granules when webworm adults are present; use 3 gal of spray per 1000 sq ft of turf; repeat if necessary
Cutworms	Chlorpyrifos (Dursban), trichlorfon (Proxol, Dylox)	Apply as a spray using 3 gal per 1000 sq ft; repeat when damage reappears
Armyworms	Carbaryl (Sevin), chlorpyrifos (Dursban), trichlorfon (Proxol, Dylox)	Apply as a spray using 3 gal per 1000 sq ft if many worms are present and feeding on the grass
Grasshoppers	Chlorpyrifos (Dursban), carbaryl (Sevin)	Applied control is seldom necessary; if "hoppers" have migrated into turf areas and are feeding, apply as a spray using 3 gal of spray per 1000 sq ft
Lucerne moth	Carbaryl (Sevin)	Apply if damage is being done and larvae are present
Striped grass looper	Carbaryl (Sevin)	Apply if damage is being done and larvae are present; use 3 gal of spray per 1000 sq ft
Frit flies	Diazinon, chlorpyrifos (Dursban)	Treat damaged area using 3 gal of spray per 1000 sq ft
Chinch bugs	Chlorpyrifos (Dursban), isofenphos (Oftanol)	Apply as a spray using 25 to 30 gal of water per 1000 sq ft; treatment may need repeating in 2 weeks
Aphids— greenbugs	Acephate (Orthene), chlorpyrifos (Dursban)	Treat the infested area plus a 2- to 3-ft green border around the damaged area; apply 3 to 4 gal per 1000 sq ft
Leafhoppers	Diazinon, carbaryl (Sevin)	Control is unnecessary unless many leaf-hoppers are present and damage is observed; apply as a spray if needed
Scale insects	Diazinon, chlorpyrifos (Dursban), malathion	Apply as a spray and drench into the crowns using 25 to 40 gal per 1000 sq ft

TABLE 4.1 CHEMICAL CONTROL OF TURFGRASS INSECTS (continued)

Insect	Suggested insecticide	Remarks
Spittlebugs	Carbaryl (Sevin), diazinon	Control is not needed unless spittle masses are objectionable; apply as a spray if needed
Mites	Diazinon, malathion, chlorpyrifos (Dursban)	Treat in the spring for the bermudagrass mite; may need to be repeated; treat for the winter grain mite, if needed, in late winter; apply the miticide as a spray, using 3 to 4 gal of spray per 1000 sq ft
Ants	Diazinon, chlorpyrifos (Dursban)	Treat anthills or mounds by drenching insecticide into the nest in the soil
Cicada killer, ground-nesting wasps and bees	Diazinon, carbaryl (Sevin)	Chemical control is needed only if wasps and bees are a nuisance; drench the chemical into open holes in the soil at dusk or early evening
Periodical cicada	Carbaryl (Sevin)	Soil treatment is not effective; spray nearby shrubs and young trees if damage is occurring
Sowbugs and pillbugs	Diazinon, chlorpyrifos (Dursban)	Chemical control is seldom necessary; if necessary, treat the foundation of buildings
Millipedes and centipedes	Carbaryl (Sevin), diazinon	Spray the turf area bordering the home or other buildings plus the foundation
Earwigs	Diazinon, chlorpyrifos (Dursban)	Spray areas where the earwigs are congregating plus a border area around the home; apply treatment only if earwigs are a problem
Crickets	Diazinon, chlorpyrifos (Dursban)	Spray the foundation plus a narrow area of grass around the home
Fleas	Chlorpyrifos (Dursban), carbaryl (Sevin), malathion	Apply to turf as a supplement to dusting the pet and bedding or using a treated collar
Ticks	Malathion, carbaryl (Sevin), diazinon, chlorpyrifos (Dursban)	Spray tick-infested border areas of unmowed grass and shrubbery
Chiggers	Malathion, diazinon	Spray turf and border areas which are the source of chiggers; insect repellents can be used by persons entering infested areas
No-see-ums and mosquitoes	Malathion	Spray shrubbery for temporary control of adult insects; repeat as needed
Thrips	Diazinon, carbaryl (Sevin)	Chemical control is rarely necessary; spray if thrips are numerous and damage is observed
Spiders	Chlorpyrifos (Dursban), diazinon	Apply as a foundation spray to prevent entry of spiders; repeat in 4 weeks if needed
Crane flies	Chlorpyrifos (Dursban)	No control is usually necessary

SELECTED REFERENCES

BEARD, J. B. 1973. *Turfgrass: Science and Culture.* Englewood Cliffs, NJ: Prentice-Hall, Inc. 658 pp.

HANSON, A. A., and F. V. JUSKA, eds. 1969. *Turfgrass Science.* Agronomy Monograph 14. Madison, WI: American Society of Agronomy, Inc. 713 pp.

METCALF, R. L., C. L. METCALF, and W. P. FLINT. 1962. *Destructive and Useful Insects.* New York: McGraw-Hill Book Company. 1087 pp.

NIEMCZYK, H. D. 1981. *Destructive Turf Insects.* Wooster, OH: H.D.N. Book Sales. 48 pp.

SHETLAR, D. J., P. R. HELLER, and P. D. IRISH. 1983. *Turfgrass Insect and Mite Manual.* University Park, PA: Pennsylvania Turfgrass Council, Inc. 83 pp.

SWAN, L. A., and C. S. PAPP. 1972. *The Common Insects of North America.* New York: Harper & Row Publishers, Inc. 750 pp.

TURGEON, A. J. 1980. *Turfgrass Management.* Englewood Cliffs, NJ: Prentice-Hall, Inc. 432 pp.

Biology and Control
of Diseases in Turfgrasses

WHAT IS A PLANT DISEASE?

When a plant is more or less continuously injured or subjected to stress over a long period by some factor in the environment that interferes with its normal appearance, structure, growth, or functional activities, it is generally considered to be diseased. The disease that results is expressed by characteristic symptoms and/or signs. Diseases such as a wilt or viral infection affects the entire plant; others, such as leaf spots and powdery mildews, affect only part of a plant. Considerable knowledge of a plant's normal growth habits, cultivar characteristics, and normal variability within a species, as related to the environmental conditions under which the plant is growing, is required for recognizing disease.

Plant injury, in contrast, usually results from *momentary or discontinous* damage. No one quarrels that lightning, mechanical damage by a lawn mower, or a chemical spill results in injury. Rodent, insect, and mite feeding are generally considered as injuries. But how about a toxin secreted by an aphid or chinch bug when it feeds on a grass plant over a period of several hours or days that results in a slow and progressive scorching, wilting, or dieback of leaves? Is this disease or injury? There is no sharp distinction between disease and injury.

CAUSES OF GRASS DISEASES

Diseases of turfgrasses are conveniently divided into two principal groups: those caused by unfavorable growing conditions (sometimes called disorders, noninfectious or abiotic diseases); and those caused by parasites or pathogens (biotic, infectious, or transmissible).

Unfavorable Growing Conditions

These noninfectious disorders are *not* contagious. Included here are an excess, deficiency, or unavailability of water, light, air movement, about 20 essential elements, oxygen for normal root development, extreme soil acidity or alkalinity (a soil pH below 5.0 to 5.5 or above about 7.5), leaf and crown bruises, mower shredding of leaf blades, and scalping. Other noninfectious disorders include animal urine or salts, pesticide and fertilizer injury, chemical spills, extremely high or low temperatures, shallow soil and soil compaction, buried debris causing shallow roots, excessive thatch, shading or root competition, and other injurious impurities in the air or soil. Turfgrass plants in poor health due to unfavorable growing conditions probably far outnumber plants significantly injured by disease-causing fungi.

Suspect a noninfectious problem when a large turf area suddenly deteriorates, especially when other nongrass plants in the area are similarly affected. Although noninfectious agents are capable of inducing disease, they commonly cause plants to become more susceptible to attack by infectious agents (fungi, bacteria, viruses, and nematodes). More commonly, two or more noninfectious disorders and several infectious agents act together to produce a complex or poorly defined disease. Here it is necessary to eliminate the unfavorable growing conditions before, or simultaneously, with controls aimed at checking the growth and spread of infectious agents.

Parasites or Pathogens

Parasitic organisms obtain their food from living plants. If these organisms cause injury or disease, they are called pathogens. An obligate parasite (such as a rust or powdery mildew fungus, plant-parasitic nematode, or virus) requires living plant tissue as food, while a facultative parasite (which includes most turfgrass fungi) may obtain its nutrition from either a living or a dead plant.

Diseases to be discussed in detail are those caused by infectious fungi, bacteria, viruses, and nematodes. The size relationships of various pathogens are shown in Figure 5.1. These pathogens get their nourishment from grass plants, and cause roots, stems (crowns, tillers, rhizomes, and stolons), or leaves to grow abnormally.

Fungi. Most pathogenic turf diseases are caused by fungi. These largely microscopic organisms lack chlorophyll and hence cannot produce their own food by the process of photosynthesis. Most fungi are multicellular, usually threadlike or filamentous (Figure 5.2), and most have well-developed cell walls and nuclei. Some fungi are almost as small as bacteria (see below); others, such as mushrooms, are clearly visible both above and below ground. Fungi are transported over long distances by air currents, splashing or flowing water, insects and other animals, turfgrass equipment, seed, sprigs, plugs, and sod; many are capable of growing short distances on plants or through soil. Nourishment is obtained from dead or living plants. Most of the fungi that can be found in turf—1 lb of topsoil contains 4½ to 225 million fungi—feed on dead and decaying organic matter, such as dead roots, stems, and leaves either in the soil or in the thatch. These fungi are generally considered to be beneficial since they aid in thatch decomposition. Approximately 200 fungi attack living turfgrass plants under favorable conditions of

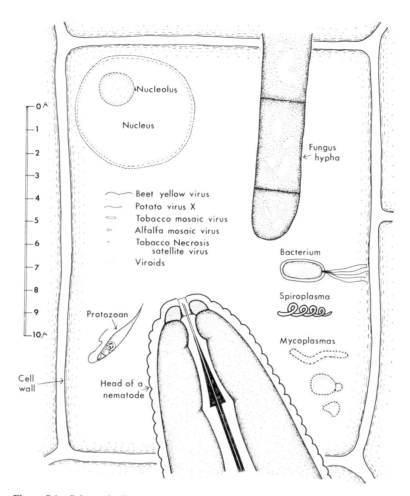

Figure 5.1 Schematic diagram showing the relative sizes of certain plant pathogens in relation to a plant cell. Viroids, spiroplasmas, and protozoa are not known to infect turfgrasses. Modified from Agrios, *Plant Pathology, 2nd ed.* Academic Press, 1978.

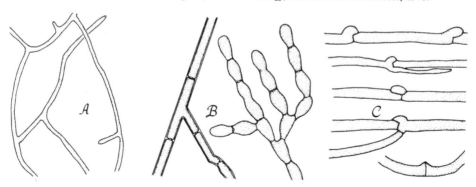

Figure 5.2 Fungus hyphae. A, Delicate nonseptate hyphae of *Pythium;* B, young (left) and mature (right) hyphae of *Rhizoctonia solani;* C, hyphae typical of *Typhula, Coprinus, Limonomyces,* and *Sclerotium,* showing various types of clamp connections.

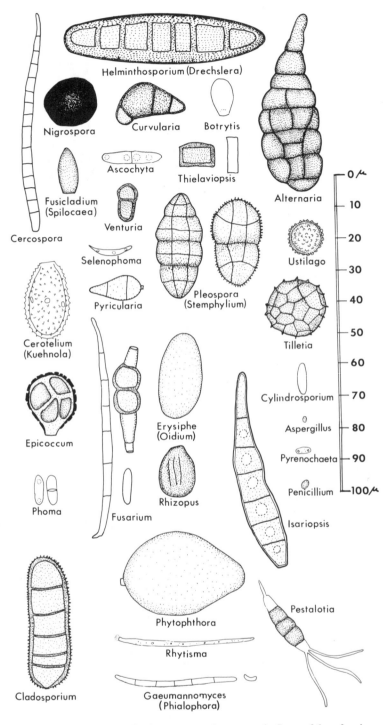

Figure 5.3 Representative fungus spores drawn to scale. Some of these fungi do not infect turfgrasses.

temperature and moisture. Disease-causing fungi can be found in large numbers on dead and decaying leaves and stems where grass plants are growing poorly under stress conditions. Weakened or injured plants often lose much of their natural resistance to fungi and exhibit more damage from disease than do vigorous plants. But some fungi can also cause disease on vigorously growing turf.

Fungal hyphae enter grass plants through mowed leaf tips and other wounds, through natural openings (stomates), and by direct penetration through a plant's epidermis. After growing for several days or weeks at the expense of a grass plant, many disease-causing fungi produce spores or spore-producing bodies that cause more infection or to complete their life cycle. The microscopic spores are of many different shapes, sizes, and colors (Figure 5.3) and are borne in a variety of ways. Some appear as mold growth on the surface of leaves [gray and Cercospora leaf spots of St. Augustinegrass, red thread and pink patch, Pythium blight, "Helminthosporium" (*Bipolaris, Drechslera, Exserohilum*) leaf spots, snow molds, copper spot, leaf smuts, rusts, powdery mildew, and slime molds]; others are borne in speck-sized, dark fungus fruiting bodies embedded in diseased plant tissue (*Septoria, Ascochyta, Leptosphaerulina,* and *Gaeumannomyces*).

Fungal spores and other parts are easily transported by air currents, splashing or flowing water, insects, mites, other animals, mowers or other turf equipment, shoes, and grass parts, including seed, sod, sprigs, plugs, and clippings. Most fungus spores and hyphae are easily killed by adverse conditions. Thick-walled resting spores allow certain turfgrass fungi (such as *Pythium, Sclerophthora,* and *Fusarium*) to withstand unfavorable growing conditions, such as extreme heat or cold, drying, and flooding. Resting spores may lie dormant for several years or more before germinating. Still other fungi, including species of *Rhizoctonia, Sclerotium,* and *Typhula,* produce hard, compact masses of hyphae, called bulbils or sclerotia, that can withstand even more unfavorable conditions than can resting spores. These structures may also lie dormant in the thatch or upper ½ in. of soil for several years before germinating and initiating disease.

Fungi are often more common and damaging to plants in moist or overly fertilized turf than in dry or moderately nourished grass. Examples include snow molds, take-all patch, gray leaf spot, brown patch, and Pythium blight. Free moisture is essential to rapid reproduction, spread, and infection of grass plants by all fungi except powdery mildew. Rusts, dollar spot, red thread, and pink patch are examples of diseases that injure slow-growing, nitrogen-deficient turf when light rains or morning dews persist.

Fungal diseases are controlled through the cultural practices outlined on pages 212 to 214, growing resistant species and cultivars, and by the timely application of fungicides to the seed, foliage, and soil (Table 5.4).

Bacteria.   Only a few turfgrass diseases are caused by bacteria. The only widespread and important one is bacterial wilt of Toronto (C-15) creeping bentgrass.

Bermudagrass stunting disease in southern Florida is believed to be caused by a small bacterium, *Clavibacter xyli* sub. sp. *cynodontis.* This disease is predominantly a problem in bermudagrass golf greens where unsightly circular, chlorotic patches of dying grass are seen. Stunting disease is worst under such environmental stresses as low light intensity.

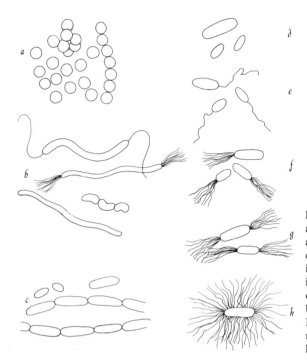

Figure 5.4 Bacteria. Different shapes and arrangements as you might see them under a powerful laboratory microscope. A, Coccus forms occurring singly, in a chain and an irregular cluster; B, spirillum forms, single and in a short chain; C, rodlike or bacillus forms, occurring singly and in chains. D–H, Rodlike bacteria showing various types of flagella: D, none; E, monotrichous; F, polar, multitrichous; G, bipolar flagella, lophotrichous; H, peritrichous.

Bacteria exhibit three fundamental shapes: spherical, spiral or curved rods, and rods (Figure 5.4). Bacteria that cause plant disease are microscopic, one-celled organisms that are rod-shaped and measure about 0.5×2 μm (up to about 1/12,000 of an inch long). They can be seen only with a good compound light microscope at about 400 to 600 magnification. Some species have whiplike flagella that may aid them to move in water.

Bacteria, like fungi, lack chlorophyll and hence cannot manufacture their own food. Most bacteria feed on dead organic matter (saprophytes), but a few are pathogenic. They do not require a living grass plant for replication and growth.

Bacteria enter plants through natural openings, such as stomates, or through wounds, principally those produced by insects, nematodes, or human activities (such as turfgrass equipment and shoes). Water-soaked and succulent tissues often predispose plants to invasion by bacteria. Free moisture and moderate-to-warm temperatures (68 to 86°F) are general requirements for reproduction and disease development. The bacteria that infect plants are usually favored by a near-neutral (pH 6.5 to 7.5) growth medium.

Bacteria are spread through planting, cultivation, mowing, and transporting diseased plant material. Animals (including insects, mites, and nematodes), splashing or flowing water, and windblown rain or dust are other common disseminating agents.

Bacteria reproduce by simple fission where a mother cell divides in half to produce two identical daughter cells. Under favorable conditions bacteria can reproduce at an astonishing rate. If a single bacterial cell divided in half and all its descendants did likewise every 20 minutes for just 12 hours, nearly 70 billion bacteria would be produced. Due to lack of food, the accumulation of toxic wastes, and other limiting factors, reproduction soon slows down and finally stops.

Infected grass plants display a wide range of symptoms. Most bacterial diseases are controlled by preventing the injuries that allow bacteria to enter plants, by starting with disease-free planting material, or by growing resistant grass species and cultivars.

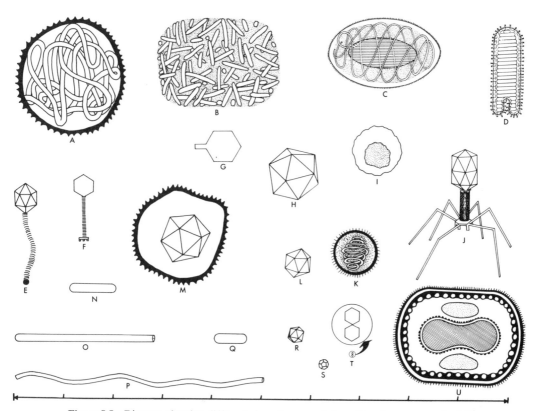

Figure 5.5 Diagram showing different virus shapes and sizes. Key: A, paramyxovirus; B, poxvirus (vaccinia); C, poxvirus (Orf); D, rhabdovirus; E, flexuous-tailed phage (lambda); F, contractile bacteriophage; G, coliphage T-3; H, adenovirus; I, enveloped herpes simplex virus; J, T-even phage; K, influenza virus; L, polymer/papilloma virus; M, herpesvirus; N, barley stripe mosaic virus; O, rodlike virus (tobacco mosaic virus); P, flexuous filamentous virus (potato virus Y): Q, component of alfalfa mosaic virus; R, polio/coxsackie virus; S, ΦX174 phage; T, geminivirus (more recent research has shown that the two hexagons are side by side instead of end to end); U, thin section of vaccinia virion. The line across the bottom of the figure equals 1 micrometer or micron. (Adapted from R. W. Horne; revised from *Scientific American,* 1963.)

Viruses.   Only a handful of turfgrass diseases are caused by viruses. The only widespread and serious disease is St. Augustinegrass decline or SAD.

Viruses are infectious agents that can be seen only with the aid of an electron microscope. They are macromolecules composed of either ribonucleic acid (RNA) or deoxyribonucleic acid (DNA) surrounded by a protective protein or lipoprotein coat. Virus particles, or virions, can multiply (replicate) *only* within specific living cells and thus are obligate parasites. Some viruses have been isolated from infected organisms and crystallized in the laboratory. Outside a host cell, they are like chemical substances; yet inside a living host cell they function like living organisms.

The virions can be filamentous (long rigid or flexous rods), roughly spherical (polyhedral or isometric), or bacilliform in shape. They are much smaller than bacteria (perhaps 1/200,000 of an inch long; see Figure 5.5). They range in diameter from 10 to 70 nm [a nanometer (nm) is one-thousandth of a micron or micrometer], and rod lengths can exceed 3 μm.

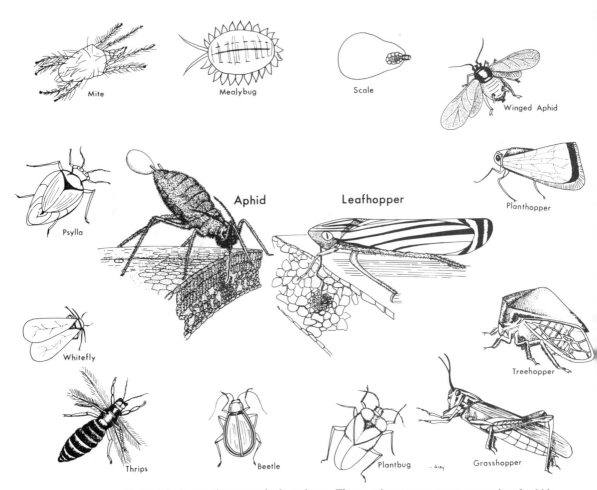

Figure 5.6 Insects that transmit plant viruses. The most important vectors are species of aphids and leafhoppers.

Viruses produce disease by upsetting the normal growth processes of plant cells, causing the cells to produce abnormal and injurious substances, including more virus particles. The more obvious symptoms of virus infection are yellowing, stunting, and loss of vigor due to destruction of chlorophyll. Because of their weakened state, virus-infected plants may be more susceptible to other diseases. Virus diseases are often confused with nutrient deficiencies or genetic abnormalities, insect-induced toxemias, pesticide or fertilizer injury, mite feeding, or other injuries.

Viruses are transmitted from plant to plant by the feeding activities of insects, primarily specific species of leafhoppers and aphids (Figure 5.6). Some circulative viruses persist for weeks or months and replicate in their insect vectors; other nonpersistent or stylet-borne viruses are carried for only a few minutes to an hour. Viruses are usually systemic within their hosts and thus are commonly spread by vegetative propagation (e.g., infected sod, plugs, and sprigs). Viruses may also be disseminated by the transfer of infected plant sap into healthy plants, by infected seed, and a few by pollen, mites, slugs and snails, birds, mammals, primitive soilborne fungi, nematodes, or possibly other minute fauna.

Viruses often overwinter in biennial and perennial crops and weeds, in the bodies of insects, but not in dead plant parts. Plants, once infected, normally remain so for life. Most, if not all, plant-infecting viruses persist in a number of different plant hosts; many of these, however, may be symptomless. The latter plants are latent carriers and are often a major source of infection to other plants.

Viruses are identified by: (1) host specificity, (2) particle morphology, (3) mode(s) of transmission, and (4) their physical, biochemical, and serological properties.

Virus diseases are controlled principally by limiting their transmission in vegetative plant parts, by controlling their vectors, and by growing resistant species or cultivars.

Nematodes. Nematodes are important agents of disease in turf. They are probably the most numerous multicellular animals on earth. They are usually microscopic (most species range from $\frac{1}{10}$ to $\frac{1}{75}$ of an inch long; the largest being 3 mm long), slender, largely transparent, unsegmented roundworms—sometimes called eelworms or nemas (Figure 5.7). Exceptions are several rather sluggish types that feed on root surfaces and the adult females of certain genera (e.g., root knot and cyst) whose bodies become swollen and saclike.

Nematodes can be found almost everywhere on earth from ocean waters to the tops of mountains, the bodies of animals and human beings, and the tissues of higher plants. It is likely that every form of plant and animal life is fed upon by at least one type of nematode. Most plant-infecting species live in soil and attack small roots. Many genera and species are present in turf. As many as 20,000 individuals of 10 species can be found in 1 pint of soil. Only a few of the 60 genera and 2200 species of plant-parasitic nematodes feed on the roots of grass plants and cause disease. About 3 billion nematodes are estimated to live in an average acre of soil, most of them in the top 6 in. Even when parasitic nematodes are found associated with the roots of grass plants, fairly high populations of most species must be present for damage to occur. Nematodes seldom kill grass plants by themselves; however, they are capable of greatly curtailing the growth of plants by reducing their root systems.

Nematodes have bodies differentiated for feeding, digestion, locomotion, and reproduction (Figure 5.8). Some of the anatomical features used for identification include the size and shape of the adult female, the size and shape of the stylet and tail, the shape of the esophagus and reproductive organs, and cuticular patterns.

Nematodes feed by penetrating the root cells with a hollow stylet that resembles a minute hypodermic needle, injecting enzymes into the cells and then ingesting the partially digested contents. Root-rotting fungi and bacteria commonly enter through these wounds. Fortunately, most nematode species are harmless, feeding on decaying organic material and other soil organisms. Several hundred species are beneficial to people (and turfgrass) since they are parasitic on plant-feeding types, fungi, bacteria, insects, protozoa, or other pests.

Passive movement of nematodes occurs in water, soil, and infected plant parts. Nematodes are disseminated by the wind, animals, tools, vehicles, and machinery carrying infested soil. Active movement of nematodes through soil is very limited, considered rarely to exceed 12 to 30 in. per year.

Nematodes are extracted from soil by various flotation, sieving, and centrifugation procedures and from roots by incubation techniques. Normally, mixtures of parasitic

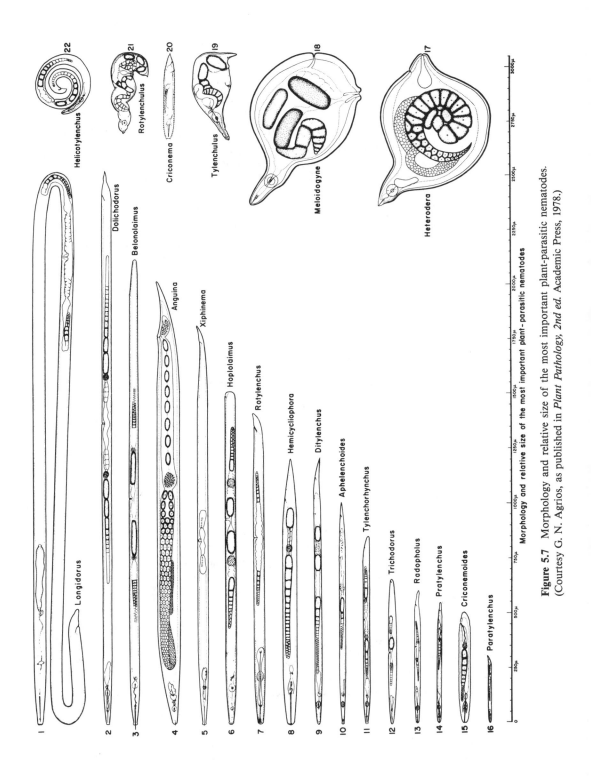

Figure 5.7 Morphology and relative size of the most important plant-parasitic nematodes. (Courtesy G. N. Agrios, as published in *Plant Pathology, 2nd ed.* Academic Press, 1978.)

Morphology and relative size of the most important plant-parasitic nematodes

Helicotylenchus 22
Rotylenchulus 21
Criconema 20
Tylenchulus 19
Meloidogyne 18
Heterodera 17

Longidorus 1
Dolichodorus 2
Belonolaimus 3
Anguina 4
Xiphinema 5
Hoplolaimus 6
Rotylenchus 7
Hemicycliophora 8
Ditylenchus 9
Aphelenchoides 10
Tylenchorhynchus 11
Trichodorus 12
Radopholus 13
Pratylenchus 14
Criconemoides 15
Paratylenchus 16

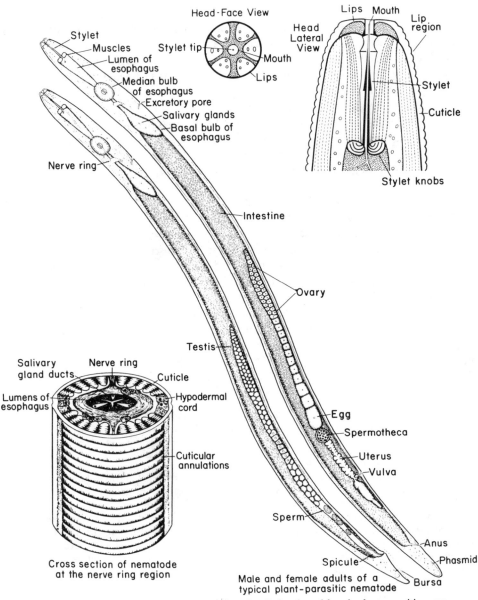

Figure 5.8 Morphology and main characteristics of typical male and female plant-parasitic nematodes. (Courtesy G. N. Agrios, as published in *Plant Pathology, 2nd ed.* Academic Press, 1978.)

and nonparasitic nematodes occur in, on, or about plant roots. Inferences about the pathological importance of each plant-parasitic species are drawn from knowledge of their feeding habits, relationship of above- and below-ground symptoms to numbers present, and frequency of occurrence. Inoculation of plants with individual species is usually necessary to demonstrate parasitism and the degree of pathogenicity.

Diagnosis of nematodes should *never* be made solely on plant symptoms. Symptoms of nematode damage often mimic those induced by other factors, such as low or unbalanced fertility, sunscald or frost, poor drainage, drought, insect or mite injury, wilt or root-rot fungi, and herbicide damage. Accurate diagnosis of a nematode problem requires proper sample collection and handling of soil and roots, and laboratory analysis by a competent nematologist (Chapter 1).

Nematodes are controlled by starting with disease-free planting material and following the best cultural practices to ensure steady vigorous growth. If the results of a nematode analysis indicate potentially serious population levels, a soil fumigant can be applied before planting or a nematicide can be applied to established turf.

Other infectious agents. Viroids, spiroplasmas, and protozoa are known to cause diseases of plants; none, however, are known to occur in turfgrasses.

Turfgrass diseases vary in severity from year to year and from one locale to another, depending on the environment (principally soil and air moisture conditions, temperature, humidity, and grass nutrition), the relative resistance or susceptibility of the grass plant, and the pathogen or pathogens involved. Good cultural practices help maintain healthy turf despite the presence of disease-causing organisms. Vigorous turf better withstands wear and recovers more quickly from injury or disease.

Table 5.1 lists a number of cultural management practices that aid in controlling turfgrass diseases and includes a listing of diseases that are at least partially controlled by each practice.

TABLE 5.1 CULTURAL MANAGEMENT PRACTICES THAT AID IN CONTROLLING TURFGRASS DISEASES

Cultural management practices	Diseases partially controlled
Provide good surface and subsurface drainage when establishing a new turf area. Fill in low spots, where water may stand. Before establishment remove stumps, large roots, construction lumber, bricks, concrete, plaster, tin cans, and other debris. Uniformly mix all soil amendments (e.g., peat moss, calcined clay, etc.) into the soil. Test the soil reaction (pH) and follow the recommendation in the soil report. A pH between 6 and 7 is best for practically all turfgrasses (5.5 is best for reducing pink snow mold or Fusarium patch and take-all patch).	"Helminthosporium" diseases, brown patch, dollar spot, red thread and pink patch, summer patch and necrotic ring spot, snow molds, Pythium blight, fairy rings, take-all patch, downy mildew or yellow tuft, Physoderma brown spot, spring dead spot, seed rot, seedling blight, nematodes, algae, moss, chlorosis, wet wilt.
Grow locally adapted, disease-resistant grasses in blends or mixtures, or substitute grass species. Check with your local county extension office or extension turf specialist for suggested grass species and cultivars to grow and for available disease resistance in turfgrass cultivars. In shaded areas, grow shade-tolerant cultivars or species.	"Helminthosporium" diseases, rusts, leaf smuts, summer patch and necrotic ring spot, snow molds, dollar spot, powdery mildew, anthracnose, take-all patch, Pythium blight in overseeded turf, nematodes, gray and Septoria leaf spots, red thread, St. Augustinegrass decline, salt tolerance, traffic, spring dead spot, bacterial wilt, winter injury, wet wilt.

TABLE 5.1 CULTURAL MANAGEMENT PRACTICES THAT AID IN CONTROLLING TURFGRASS DISEASES

Cultural management practices	Diseases partially controlled
Buy only top-quality certified sod, sprigs, plugs, or pathogen-free seed from a reputable dealer. Whenever possible, plant at suggested rates when the weather is cool and dry. The seedbed should be well prepared and fertile. Avoid overwatering, especially from planting to seedling emergence or plant establishment.	"Helminthosporium" diseases, Pythium blight, seed rot, seedling blights, leaf smuts, rusts, dollar spot, summer patch and necrotic ring spot, snow molds, yellow patch, yellow ring, nematodes, bacterial wilt.
Fertilize (supply nitrogen, potash, and phosphorus) according to local recommendations and soil tests. Recommendations will vary with the grasses grown and their use. In hot weather, avoid overstimulation with fertilizer, especially with a water-soluble nitrogen material. A high level of potassium (potash) may help suppress disease development. Reduce winter injury and snow-mold damage by avoiding nitrogen fertilization after about 6 weeks prior to winter dormancy. Slowly released forms of nitrogen fertilizers are recommended. (Attacks of red thread, pink patch, and dollar spot are lessened by applications of fertilizer; the opposite is true of diseases such as Pythium blight and brown patch.)	"Helminthosporium" diseases, powdery mildew, rusts, brown patch, dollar spot, fairy rings, snow molds, Pythium blight, summer patch and necrotic ring spot, leaf smuts, red thread and pink patch, anthracnose, Nigrospora blight, take-all patch, seed rot, seedling blights, Ascochyta, gray, and Septoria leaf spots, downy mildew or yellow tuft, copper spot, Leptosphaerulina leaf blight, southern blight, spring dead spot, nematodes, algae, chlorosis, moss, slime molds, bacterial wilt, wet wilt, winter injury.
Mow frequently at the height recommended for the area, season, and grasses grown. Essentially all diseases are increased by scalping. Remove no more than one-third of the leaf height at one cutting. Keep the turf cut in late fall until growth stops. Keep the mower blades sharp.	"Helminthosporium" diseases, powdery mildew, brown patch, snow molds, dollar spot, rusts, slime molds, summer patch and necrotic ring spot, red thread and pink patch, nematodes, Septoria and Ascochyta leaf spots, bacterial wilt, wet wilt, winter injury, scalping.
Water established turf thoroughly during droughts. Moisten the soil to a depth of at least 6 in. at each irrigation. Repeat every 7 to 10 days if the weather remains dry. Water as infrequently as possible to allow gaseous exchange between soil and atmospheric air. Avoid frequent light sprinklings, especially in late afternoon or evening. Daily watering may be needed in certain cases to prevent wilt and symptoms of summer patch and necrotic leaf spot, Nigrospora blight, and where plant parasitic nematode populations are high.	"Helminthosporium" diseases, brown patch, rusts, dollar spot, red thread and pink patch, powdery mildew, Pythium blight, summer patch and necrotic ring spot, leaf smuts, fairy rings, Nigrospora blight, nematodes, seed rot, seedling blights, Physoderma brown spot, take-all patch, anthracnose, Ascochyta, Cercospora, gray, and Septoria leaf spots, Leptosphaerulina leaf blight, Curvularia blight or fading-out, southern blight, algae, moss, slime molds, wilt, winter injury.
Increase light penetration and air movement to the turfgrass area and speed drying of the grass surface by selectively pruning or removing dense trees, shrubs, and hedges bordering the turf area. When landscaping, space plantings and other barriers properly to avoid too much shade and increase air movement across the grass.	"Helminthosporium" diseases, brown patch, snow molds, dollar spot, rusts, red thread and pink patch, powdery mildew, seed rot, seedling blights, Pythium blight, gray, Cercospora, Septoria, and Ascochyta leaf spots, tar spot, algae, moss, slime molds.

Causes of Grass Diseases

TABLE 5.1 CULTURAL MANAGEMENT PRACTICES THAT AID IN CONTROLLING TURFGRASS DISEASES

Cultural management practices	Diseases partially controlled
Remove excess thatch in early spring or fall when it accumulates to ½ in. for higher-cut grasses, ⅛ in. for fine turf. Thatch control will reduce essentially all diseases. Use a vertical mower, power rake, or similar dethatching equipment. These machines may be rented at most large garden supply stores or purchased from turf equipment suppliers.	"Helminthosporium" diseases, brown patch, dollar spot, red thread and pink patch, rusts, snow molds, anthracnose, fairy rings, summer patch and necrotic ring spot, Pythium blight, leaf smuts, yellow ring, yellow patch, southern blight, white patch, Curvularia blight or fading-out, spring dead spot, slime molds, nematodes, algae, moss, take-all patch, wilt, winter injury.
Core (aerify) compacted turf areas one or more times each year, using a hand aerifier or power machine. Eliminate foot and vehicle traffic by putting in walks, fences, shrubbery, patios, parking areas, etc.	"Helminthosporium" diseases, Pythium blight, rusts, summer patch and necrotic ring spot, snow molds, dollar spot, gray leaf spot, brown patch, rusts, anthracnose, southern blight, compaction, algae, moss, spring dead spot, wilt, winter injury.
Follow suggested insect and weed control programs for the area and grasses being grown. Some insects transmit disease-causing fungi; weeds may harbor them.	Practically all diseases. This area has not been studied extensively by plant pathologists. See Chapters 3 and 4 for suggestions on controlling weeds and insects.

KEY TO INFECTIOUS TURFGRASS DISEASES

Below is a key to most of the infectious turfgrass diseases that appear in the United States, plus a number of noninfectious diseases or disorders (see also Chapter 2) that are often confused with true diseases. The key is organized according to the air-temperature ranges at which the disease is *first visible* (temperature ranges are given in degrees Fahrenheit). For conversion of Fahrenheit to Celsius or centigrade, see page 378 in Appendix A.

    I. *Cold-weather* (32 TO 45°F) *diseases;* usually visible after the winter period or a prolonged snow cover

        A. Irregular patterns or streaks in turf

            1. Bleached or dead grass, especially in wind-swept areas free of snow with deeply frozen soil . . . . *Winter desiccation,* page 44

            2. New leaves killed back (often in yellow to white patches) following freezing temperatures . . . . *Spring frost,* page 45

        B. Turf killed (rotted or straw-colored) in *wettest* areas

            1. May follow drainage patterns . . . . *Water and ice damage,* page 44

            2. Circular patches of dead grass from 1 in. to 3 ft across

                a. Wet grass is often covered with white to bright pink mold; *no sclerotia* present. Mycelium lacks clamp connections . . . . *Pink snow mold or Fusarium patch,* page 295

                b. Wet grass covered with white to gray or bluish-gray mold; minute, yellow to dark brown or reddish *sclerotia* often present in or on grass leaves

(1) Mycelium *with* clamp connections

.... *Gray snow mold or Typhula blight,* page 293

(2) Mycelium *without* clamp connections

.... *Sclerotinia snow mold or snow scald,* page 298

II. *Cool-weather* (45 TO 60°F) *diseases;* occur in early spring and late fall

A. Circular patches or rings in turf after grass greens up in spring

1. Yellow patches or "tufts" usually less than 1 in. across

.... *Downy mildew or yellow tuft,* page 232

2. Sunken, straw-colored patches, 1 to 6 in. across. Grass leaves matted

.... *Pythium blight,* page 265

3. Patches from 1 in. to about 3 ft across

a. A prolonged cool rain commonly following melting snow or a prolonged cool rain. Wet grass is often covered with white to bright pink mold

.... *Pink snow mold or Fusarium patch,* page 295

b. White patches or rings. Wet grass at margins is often covered with whitish mold. Dense white mycelium in thatch .... *White patch,* page 309

c. White to yellow or straw colored sunken rings with green centers. Wet grass not covered with mold .... *Winter brown patch or yellow patch,* page 277

d. Initially yellow, then reddish brown or bronzed, and finally sunken, tan rings. Centers invaded by weeds. Most commonly found in cool, moist, coastal climates .... *Take-all patch,* page 306

e. Sunken, straw-colored dead areas in well-maintained *bermudagrass* as turf breaks dormancy in spring. Centers may survive; become invaded by weeds

.... *Spring dead spot,* page 301

f. Patches of dead grass up to 15 ft or more across appear in zoysiagrass as turf breaks dormancy in spring .... *Zoysia patch,* page 312

4. Rings up to 15 ft or more across; often with outer ring of dark green grass

.... *Fairy rings,* page 234

B. Irregular patterns (usually) in turf

1. *Powdery mold* on leaf surfaces; leaf spots not usually evident

a. Milky white to gray mold; found mostly in shade and easily wiped off; turf thins out .... *Powdery mildew,* page 264

b. Gray to black streaks in leaves; leaves split into ribbons and curl. Grass may later die in irregular patches or causes a general thinning .... *Leaf smuts,* page 249

c. Pink to reddish mycelium on leaves and sheaths; or red threadlike growths extend beyond the leaf tips. Appears tan in patches

.... *Red thread/pink patch,* pages 270 and 258

2. Seedling turf is thin or bare in spots; seedlings wilt and collapse

.... *Seed decay, damping-off, and seedling blights,* page 287

3. Leaves distinctly spotted or striped; wither, and die back.

a. Black leaf spots often with a yellowish "halo" .... *Tar spot or blister smut,* pages 309 and 225

b. Tan to brown leaf spots (rare)................. *Tan leaf spot,* page 309

c. Yellow to yellowish-brown stripes in leaves

.... *Cephalosporium stripe or blister smut,* page 225

d. Oval to eye-shaped, dark-bordered spots

  (1) Dark specks (*pycnidia*) *present* in older spots
    . . . . *Selenophoma leaf spot,* page 289

  (2) *Pycnidia absent* in older spots
    "Helminthosporium" diseases or Spermospora blast, pages 242 and 300

4. Irregular blotches in leaves; leaves often die back from the tip

  a. Dark specks (*pycnidia* or perithecia) present in older leaves

    (1) Yellow to gray-green or brown spots; mostly at or near leaf tips
    . . . . *Septoria leaf spot,* page 290

    (2) Purplish to chocolate-brown spots that enlarge, become tan to straw-colored . . . . *Ascochyta leaf spot or blight,* page 222

    (3) Yellow or brown leaf spots that turn a bleached white. Leaves die back from the tip . . . . *Leptosphaerulina leaf blight,* page 252

  b. *Pycnidia absent.* Grayish-green to brown or gray blotches with dark brown margins . . . . *Rhynchosporium leaf blotch,* page 279

5. Toronto (C-15) creeping bent leaves wilt, shrivel, turn reddish brown, and die
  . . . . *Bacterial wilt,* page 224

III. *Warm-weather* (60 TO 75°F) *diseases;* occur in late spring to late summer or early fall

  A. Round patches in turf *1 to 7 in.* across; often follows heavy dews or rainy weather

    1. Straw-colored, somewhat sunken patches. May be covered with dense white mold in damp weather

      a. Whitish leaf spots *with* brown, reddish brown, or purplish borders
      . . . . *Dollar spot,* page 228

      b. Tan leaf spots *without* reddish-brown borders . . *Pythium blight,* page 265

    2. Coppery red to salmon-pink . . . . *Copper spot,* page 227

    3. Yellow and bunchy; plants easily pulled from turf
    . . . . *Downy mildew or yellow tuft,* page 232

  B. Patches or rings up to *2 or 3 ft* across; usually with green centers

    1. Dull yellow to straw-colored rings . . . . *Yellow patch,* page 277

    2. Lemon- to bright yellow rings; dense white mold in thatch beneath yellowed leaves
    . . . . *Yellow ring,* page 312

    3. Bronzed to reddish-brown rings with blackened stem bases and roots. Usually found in *cool, moist, coastal climates* . . . . *Take-all patch,* page 306

    4. Tan to reddish-brown patches or rings with blackened stem bases and roots
    . . . . *Necrotic ring spot,* page 303

  C. Rings or arcs up to 15 or more feet across; often with zone of dark green grass. Mushrooms may pop up in ring . . . . *Fairy rings,* page 234

  D. Mostly irregular patterns in turf.

    1. *Powdery mold* on leaf surfaces; leaf spots usually absent

      a. Milky-white to gray mold, found mostly in shade and easily wiped off. Grass thins out . . . . *Powdery mildew,* page 264

      b. Bright yellow, orange, or reddish-brown pustules. Occurs during dry periods
      . . . . *Rusts,* page 280

c. Turf is first slimy or "greasy"; then superficial blue-gray, ash-gray, creamy yellow, or black powdery structures on leaves; easily wiped off .... *Slime molds,* page 291

2. Tan or blighted irregular patches; usually 2 to 15 in. across but may be larger

    a. Coral-pink to blood-red "threads," cottony flocks, or sheaths bind leaves together .... *Red thread/pink patch,* pages 270 and 258

    b. Leaves die back from tips. Tan lesions, often with purple to reddish-brown borders, form in some cultivars .... *Nigrospora blight,* page 254

3. Leaves spotted; turf is thinned and weakened

    a. Distinct round to oval leaf spots

        (1) Blue-gray to brown spots with darker brown or purple to reddish-brown margins .... *Gray leaf spot,* page 241

        (2) Tan to ash-gray leaf spots with distinct dark-brown to purple-black margins .... *"Helminthosporium" diseases,* page 242

    b. Leaves with irregular blotches or mottling; tips of leaves often die back

        (1) Spots or blotches in leaves usually *without* dark borders

            (a) Dark specks (*pycnidia*) *present* in older lesions

                • Purplish to chocolate-brown lesions that enlarge, become tan, then straw-colored .... *Ascochyta leaf spot or blight,* page 222

                • Yellow to gray-green or brown spots; mostly at or near leaf tips .... *Septoria leaf spot,* page 290

            (b) *Pycnidia absent*
            Irregular dull tan spots with brown border; pink fungus masses on stem bases when wet .... *Fusarium leaf spot,* page 238

4. St. Augustinegrass becomes progressively more yellowed. Leaves have pale green to yellow spots, blotches, and stippling .... *St. Augustinegrass decline,* page 286

5. Mushrooms (toadstools) or puffballs suddenly appear in turf but not in rings .... *Mushrooms and puffballs,* page 254

IV. *Hot-Weather* (over 75°F) *diseases;* occur from late spring to late summer

  A. Round patterns in turf

    1. Sunken patches usually *1 to 6 in.* across; appear in wet weather.

        a. Dead grass blades matted, slimy, and straw-colored. Patches may occur in streaks. A cottony mold grows over wet grass .. *Pythium blight,* page 265

        b. Coppery-red to salmon-pink leaves in patches..... *Copper spot,* page 227

        c. Straw-colored, somewhat sunken patches. Tan leaf spots with reddish-brown borders; wet grass may be covered with a cottony mold .... *Dollar spot,* page 228

        d. White patches or rings up to 15 in. across with white mold in the thatch .... *White patch,* page 309

    2. Patches up to *2 to 3 ft across*

        a. Straw colored; centers often remain green. Appear during droughts .... *Summer patch and necrotic ring spot (Fusarium blight),* page 303

        b. Light brown; grass blades usually not matted. Patches appear during wet periods .... *Brown patch,* page 274

c. Yellow to white patches that enlarge; outer ring turns reddish brown and dies. Fluffy white mold and numerous small round sclerotia in dying grass (found only in southern states) . . . . *Southern blight,* page 299

d. Yellow rings with dense white mold in thatch beneath yellowed leaves . . . . *Yellow ring,* page 312

   3. Rings or arcs of brown and/or stimulated grass up to 15 ft or more across. Mushrooms may suddenly appear in ring . . . . *Fairy rings,* page 234

B. Irregular patterns of weak, thin, dormant, or dead grass

   1. Large areas appear dry, then wilt, and turn brown

      a. Turf is yellowish, then reddish brown. Leaves spotted to blighted. Black spiny "cushions" evident on older leaves with a hand lens . . . . *Anthracnose,* page 219

      b. Irregular dry, "patchy" turf areas that enlarge, turn yellow to brown

         (1) Some oval or eye-shaped spots with dark margins
            "Helminthosporium" diseases or Curvularia blight, pages 242 and 228

            Crowns and roots often rotted and reddish brown to black
            . . . . *Plant-parasitic nematodes,* page 259

         (2) Irregular, dull tan leaf spots; pink fungal masses on crowns when wet
            . . . . *Fusarium leaf spot,* page 238

         (3) Leaves spotted or streaked, yellowish or tan, then bleached.

            (a) Roundish, dark brown to purple spots with tan to gray centers
               . . . . *Cercospora leaf spot,* page 226

            (b) Blue-gray to brown spots with darker brown or purple to reddish-purple margins . . . . *Gray leaf spot,* page 241

            (c) Yellow or brown leaf spots that turn a bleached white. Leaves die back from the tip . . . . *Leptosphaerulina leaf blight,* page 252

            (d) Yellowish spots or stripes that turn brown, then ash gray. May appear in bands across leaf . . . . *Physoderma brown spot,* page 256

C. *Powdery mold* on leaf surfaces

   1. Bright yellow, orange, red, or brown pustules. Occurs during dry periods
     . . . . *Rusts,* page 280

   2. Turf covered with slimy or "greasy" mold; then bluish-gray, creamy-yellow, or black powdery structures appear; are easily wiped off. . . . . *Slime molds,* page 291

D. St. Augustinegrass becomes progressively more yellowed. Leaves have pale green to yellow spots, blotches, and stippling . . . *St. Augustinegrass decline,* page 286

E. Seedling turf is thin or bare in spots; seedlings wilt and collapse
   . . . . *Seed decay, damping-off and seedling blights,* page 287

V. *Other causes of poor turf* (usually independent of temperature)

A. Turf *gradually* becomes pale green to golden yellow, grows slowly; often becomes thinned

   1. Definite leaf lesions or mottling present . . . . *Air or soil pollution,* page 45

   2. Yellow streaks may form parallel to the leaf veins
     . . . . *Chlorosis; iron or nitrogen deficiency, etc.,* page 39

B. Turf *suddenly* appears scorched

1. Usually in patches, bands, or streaks
    . . . . *Chemical burn or mower burn,* pages 39 and 21
2. Bands, streaks, or irregular patterns; grass is stimulated at margins
    . . . . *Fertilizer burn,* page 39
3. Ring of dark green grass at margins; patches up to about 1 ft across
    . . . . *Dog injury,* page 41
4. Entire turf area or patches over slight elevations or mowing corners are yellow
    to brown . . . . *Scalping injury,* page 20
5. Leaf tips are shredded; appear gray, then tan . . . . *Dull mower injury,* page 21
- C. Round to irregular patches of dead or dormant grass; often follows dry periods
    . . . . *Buried debris, insect injury, or thick thatch,* pages 41, 153, and 34
- D. Turf bare or thinned; often in traffic areas, dense shade, waterlogged soil, etc.
    1. Greenish to brown scum that later forms a black crust . . . . . . *Algae,* page 41
    2. Small green plants that grow on soil in slight mounds . . . . *Moss,* page 41
    3. Soil hard in heavily tracked paths, under swings, etc.
        . . . . *Compaction,* page 36
- E. Turf dry, bluish green (easily tracked), wilts, may later turn brown
    . . . . *Drought, wilt, or improper watering,* pages 42 and 26

Anthracnose

Anthracnose, caused by the fungus *Colletotrichum graminicola* [*Microdochium* or *Gloeosporium bolleyi*] is very widely distributed and probably infects all turfgrasses in hot (optimum 80 to 85°F), prolonged moist weather. The fungus is also apparently pathogenic in cool weather. Annual bluegrass, fine-leaved fescues, perennial ryegrass, and centipedegrass are the most commonly found infected turfgrasses. Anthracnose usually occurs where the turfgrass is weakened by other causes (such as "Helminthosporium" diseases, page 242), low or unbalanced fertility, a thick thatch, drought stress, insect damage, compacted soil, and so on. The fungus commonly colonizes dead or naturally dying (senescing) leaves and stems.

Symptoms. During warm to hot weather, the lesions on individual leaves are round to elongate, reddish-brown to brown blotches often surrounded by a yellow halo, that may merge to blight entire leaves (*Color plate 36*). The leaves turn yellow, then light tan to brown. Numerous, minute, raised, black-spined fruiting bodies (acervuli) can often be seen on the senescing and dead leaves with the aid of a magnifying lens (Figure 5.9).

Figure 5.9 An acervulus of *Colletotrichum graminicola* (the anthracnose fungus) with a cluster of black, hairlike setae, as seen with the aid of a hand lens. (Courtesy J. M. Vargas, Jr.)

Key to Infectious Turfgrass Diseases

Figure 5.10 Anthracnose on a golf course fairway. (Courtesy J. M. Vargas, Jr.)

The fruiting bodies are also evident on young leaves when the disease is active. Tiller infections result in stem girdling and the later appearance of yellow-bronze patches varying in size from a few inches followed by a slow deterioration of large areas 10 to 20 ft. in diameter with an irregular outline (Figure 5.10). Diseased turf is reddish brown at first, fading to yellow, then tan to brown. The stem bases, crowns, and root systems of severely infected plants may be shallow and brown or black.

Disease Cycle.   The anthracnose fungus produces large numbers of microscopic, bean- or crescent-shaped spores (conidia) in the acervuli on the leaf and stem lesions (Figure 5.11). The conidia are distributed by water, air currents, and turf maintenance equipment. The fungus survives the winter as dormant mycelium in dead grass debris in the thatch layer. Under prolonged, warm, moist weather the fungus hyphae actively infect living grass plants that are under stress from temperature extremes, compaction, drought, and have unbalanced fertility.

Control.   Follow the suggested cultural control measures outlined on pages 212 to 214. Maintain an adequate level of nitrogen fertilization.

Where feasible, cool the turf one or more times at midday during hot weather by syringing for a few minutes. A preventive fungicide program (Table 5.4), aimed at controlling "Helminthosporium" diseases and dollar spot (pages 242 and 228), may be beneficial. There are a number of systemic fungicides that have been shown to control anthracnose effectively (Table 5.4).

Strains of creeping bentgrass and annual bluegrass are highly resistant or immune. Resistant hard fescues include Aurora, Reliant, Spartan, and Waldina.

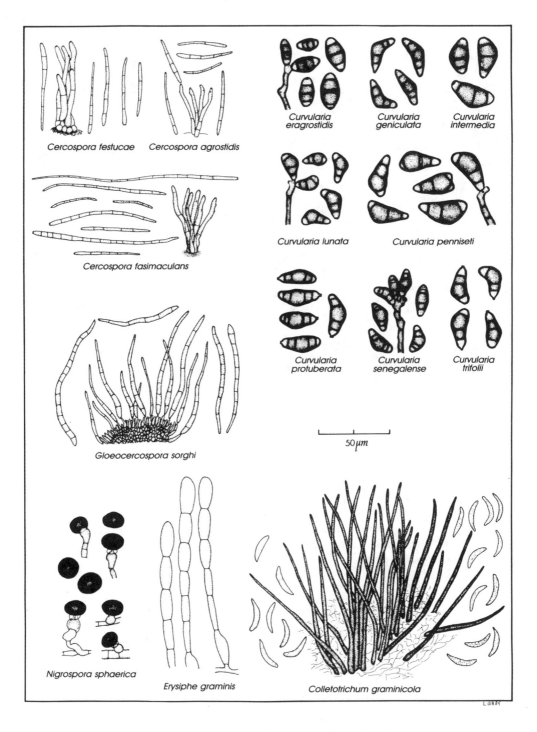

Curvularia
eragrostidis

Curvularia
geniculata

Curvularia
intermedia

Curvularia lunata

Curvularia penniseti

Curvularia
protuberata

Curvularia
senegalense

Curvularia
trifolii

Cercospora festucae

Cercospora agrostidis

Cercospora fasimaculans

Gloeocercospora sorghi

50 μm

Nigrospora sphaerica

Erysiphe graminis

Colletotrichum graminicola

L GRAY

Figure 5.11   Species of fungi that cause disease in turfgrasses.

Figure 5.12   Ascochyta leaf blight. (Courtesy R. W. Smiley.)

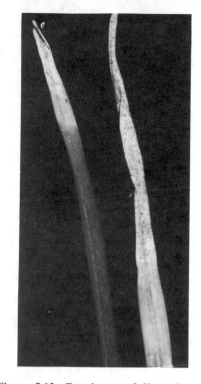

Figure 5.13   Two leaves of Kentucky bluegrass infected with Ascochyta leaf blight. Note the dark pycnidia embedded in the dead leaf tissue. (Courtesy R. W. Smiley.)

Ascochyta Leaf Spot or Blight

Ascochyta leaf blight or spot, caused by more than 20 species of the fungus genus *Ascochyta*, are common but minor diseases of Kentucky bluegrass, Italian and perennial ryegrasses, fescues (red, meadow, sheep, tall), bentgrasses, wheatgrasses, redtop, tall oatgrass, velvetgrass, quackgrass, and numerous other forage, wild, and weed grasses. The *Ascochyta* fungi seldom cause extensive damage.

Symptoms.   Large turf areas may appear uniformly blighted, or localized pockets of infection may have a patchy appearance with healthy and infected leaves growing interspersed. Individual leaves often die back from the tip and uniform lesions may extend down to the leaf sheath (Figure 5.12). Individual leaf spots are small and purplish to chocolate-brown. The spots enlarge, become tan, and finally straw-colored. Speck-sized, yellow-brown, rust-brown, brick-red, or black fungus fruiting bodies (pycnidia) form in the centers of older spots (Figure 5.13). The disease may closely resemble that of Septoria leaf spot or tip blight (page 290).

Disease Cycle.   *Ascochyta* fungi have the same general disease cycle as the *Septoria* fungi (page 290). Both produce pycnidia in older leaf spots. The spores or conidia (Figure 5.14) formed in the pycnidia ooze out in tendrils in wet weather and are carried

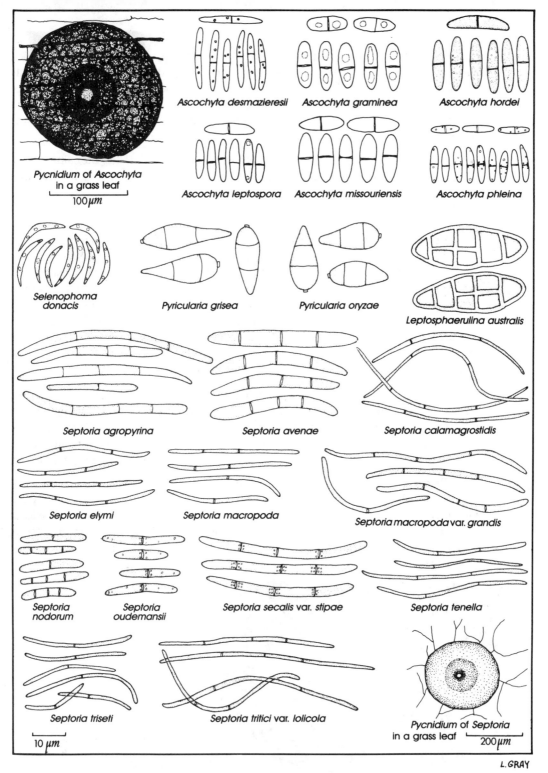

Pycnidium of *Ascochyta*
in a grass leaf
100 μm

Ascochyta desmazieresii *Ascochyta graminea* *Ascochyta hordei*

Ascochyta leptospora *Ascochyta missouriensis* *Ascochyta phleina*

Selenophoma donacis *Pyricularia grisea* *Pyricularia oryzae* *Leptosphaerulina australis*

Septoria agropyrina *Septoria avenae* *Septoria calamagrostidis*

Septoria elymi *Septoria macropoda* *Septoria macropoda* var. *grandis*

Septoria nodorum *Septoria oudemansii* *Septoria secalis* var. *stipae* *Septoria tenella*

Septoria triseti *Septoria tritici* var. *lolicola* Pycnidium of *Septoria* in a grass leaf 200 μm

10 μm

L. GRAY

Figure 5.14 Species of leaf-spotting fungi that cause diseases of turfgrasses.

to new leaves by splashing or running water, mowers and other turf equipment, and shoes. The fungus usually enters grass leaves soon after mowing and later grows from the freshly cut end toward the leaf base. The pycnidia form after the leaf dies. Ascochyta leaf spot or blight occurs throughout the growing season. Periods of damp weather or frequent irrigations favor the disease during the summer months. Frequent mowing favors the disease by creating potential infection sites.

Control. Control measures are rarely necessary. If needed, follow the cultural practices outlined on pages 212 to 214. Information about cultivar resistance is not available.

Bacterial Wilt

This disease, which affects Toronto or C-15, Seaside, and Nimisilia creeping bentgrasses and annual bluegrass in the United States, is caused by a bacterium, *Xanthomonas campestris* pv. *graminis.* The disease occurs during warm, sunny weather following wet, cool to warm weather from spring through autumn. Strains of the same bacterium in Europe and New Zealand, based on antigen-antibody reactions, are reported to infect certain cultivars of perennial and Italian ryegrasses, bluegrasses, and tall and meadow fescues, as well as orchardgrass and timothy. Preliminary evidence in the United States indicates that the bacterium may be adapting itself to other grasses, such as bluegrasses. Diagnosis of bacterial wilt can be extremely difficult.

Symptoms. The leaves on individual plants very rapidly wilt, appear blue-green, twisted, shrivel, and turn reddish brown within 48 hours, resulting in irregular patterns of withered and dead grass (*Color plate 37*). The roots on diseased plants initially appear white and healthy but quickly decompose with the rest of the plant. Diseased turf areas often show an uneven, mottled effect with resistant grass cultivars or species remaining unaffected.

Disease Cycle. The bacterium overwinters in diseased plants and thatch, but is spread from plant to plant and from one area to another by mowers and other turfgrass equipment, shoes, and by planting infected sprigs, plugs, or sod. The bacterium is believed to enter a grass plant through mowing or other physical wounds and is concentrated in the water-conducting vessels (xylem) of the roots, crown, and leaves. The water-conducting vessels become plugged, causing the plants to wilt and die (Figure 5.15).

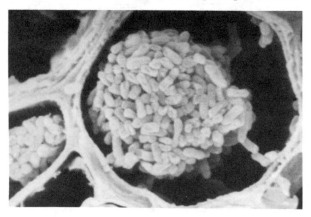

Figure 5.15 Scanning electron micrograph of a Toronto creeping bentgrass xylem vessel filled with bacterial cells of *Xanthomonas campestris* pv. *graminis.* (Courtesy D. L. Roberts.)

Control.   The antibiotic oxytetracycline (Mycoshield, C. Pfizer Corp.) may be used to manage the disease by suppressing symptoms during the current growing season if it occurs early. This treatment is both tedious and expensive. Applications are needed at 3- or 4-week intervals, and the antibiotic must be drenched in (at least 50 gal of water per 1000 sq ft), which makes the job time consuming. In late summer or early fall, the greens should be reseeded or resodded with a resistant creeping bentgrass cultivar such as Penncross or Penneagle.

Blister or Spot Smut

Blister or spot smut, caused by two widespread species of the fungus *Entyloma,* produce variable symptoms on individual grass blades, mostly of bluegrasses. These minor smut fungi do *not* rupture the leaf epidermis as do the leaf (stripe and flag) smut fungi (page 249). Instead, they induce "blisters" or spots to develop on the leaves. Mature smut-infected leaves do not become shredded or dusty with smut spores, as is the case with stripe and flag smuts (page 249).

Symptoms.   The leaf blisters (or sori) are small (up to 2 mm long), oval, and black to lead gray, evident only on the lower leaf surface, and are usually surrounded by a yellowish zone or "halo" (*Entyloma dactylidis*), or as short brown stripes in the leaves up to 1 mm long (*E. spragueanum*). Infected leaves may later become yellow or whitened. Turf severely infected with a blister or spot smut fungus may take on an overall yellowish appearance when viewed from a distance.

Disease Cycle.   Apparently these smut fungi are *not* systemic in plants. Most infections are believed to result from smut spores (teliospores) in the soil, thatch, or infected foliage. The spores germinate to produce minute spores (sporidia) that are blown, splashed, tracked, or carried on maintenance equipment to grass leaves, where they germinate and produce the characteristic dark, oval to elongated blisters (sori).

Control.   No specific measures have been devised to control blister smuts. The cultural practices outlined on pages 212 to 214 should keep these very minor diseases in check.

Cephalosporium Stripe

Cephalosporium stripe is caused by the soilborne fungus *Cephalosporium gramineum.* This pathogen may infect the vascular systems of ryegrasses and bluegrasses when grown as turfgrasses. This fungus has also been associated with dying bentgrass leaves. The fungus, however, is much more common and serious as a vascular wilt of cereals and many wild and forage grasses. The fungus is most active during cool to cold wet weather from late fall into spring.

Symptoms.   Stunted leaves with one or two narrow, yellow to yellowish-brown stripes that extend the length of the leaf are uniformly and widely scattered in affected turf (*Color plate 38*). The disease often is most prevalent in relatively wet areas. Infected leaves soon become yellow, then turn brown. Diseased turf appears green but unthrifty.

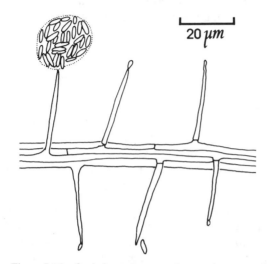

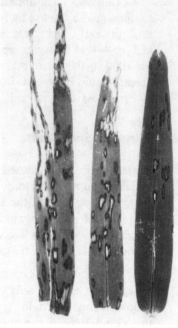

Figure 5.16 *Cephalosporium gramineum,* the cause of Cephalosporium stripe, as seen in culture under a high-power microscope.

Figure 5.17 Cercospora leaf spot of St. Augustinegrass. (Courtesy T. E. Freeman.)

Areas with many infected tillers grow slowly and respond poorly to applications of nitrogen fertilizer and water.

Disease Cycle. The fungus probably survives warm and dry periods as mycelium in infected grass tissues, and as minute spores or conidia (Figure 5.16) in the soil. Infection occurs through secondary roots or root wounds caused by nematodes, insects, coring, thatch removal, and frost heaving.

Control. No special measures have been developed because of its infrequent appearance in severe form.

Cercospora Leaf Spot

Cercospora leaf spot is caused by four species of the fungus *Cercospora.* The leaf spot–causing species of *Cercospora* and the turfgrasses that each infects are: *C. agrostidis* (bentgrasses), *C. fasimaculans* (St. Augustinegrass), *C. festucae* (fescues), and *C. seminalis* (bermudagrass and buffalograss). The disease is most damaging to yellow-green or common selections of St. Augustinegrass in the southeastern United States when it occurs. Because of similar symptoms, Cercospora leaf spot of St. Augustinegrass is often confused with the much more common and damaging gray leaf spot disease (page 241). Both diseases occur during prolonged periods of warm, very humid weather.

Symptoms. Small (0.5 to 1×1 to 4 mm), uniformly dark brown to purple, oval to round or oblong spots form on the leaves and leaf sheaths. The enlarging, elongated lesions develop tan to gray centers and conspicuous dark margins (Figure 5.17). In damp weather the spots are covered with a whitish to gray sheen containing large numbers of spores or conidia (Figure 5.11). Severely affected leaves turn yellow to brown, wither, and die, leading to a thinned and weak turf.

Disease Cycle. The *Cercospora* fungi overseason as free conidia and as dormant mycelium in infected leaves and grass debris. During warm, damp weather the spores germinate and penetrate the leaves. Visible leaf spots appear a few days later. Disease activity is favored by prolonged, warm and rainy or foggy weather, and heavy dews.

Control. Follow the cultural suggestions outlined on pages 212 to 214. Where cultural practices are not checking Cercospora leaf spot, apply a fungicide as suggested for gray leaf spot (Table 5.4). Blue-green (Bitter-Blue) selections of St. Augustinegrass are not damaged as severely as the yellow-green (common) types.

Copper Spot

Copper spot, called zonate leaf spot on bermudagrass and zoysiagrass, is caused by the fungus *Gloeocercospora sorghi*. The disease is most common in turfs grown in acid soils in humid coastal regions during warm (65 to 85 °F), moist weather. Copper spot frequently occurs together with dollar spot (page 228) in the same turf area. Velvet, colonial, and creeping bentgrasses and redtop are most severely attacked in infertile soils when the soil reaction (pH) is quite acid, pH 4.5 to 5.5. Velvet bentgrass is perhaps the most susceptible turfgrass to this disease.

Symptoms. The disease appears as scattered, distinct, more or less circular patches from 1 to 3 in. across. Affected patches are coppery red to salmon-pink in color (*Color plate 39*). In warm, moist weather the grass blades are covered with gelatinous, salmon-pink, slimy spore masses. Upon close examination, infected leaves have small reddish lesions, which become darker red as they enlarge. Several lesions may merge, blighting an entire leaf. In severe attacks, a number of spots may merge to form irregular, copper-colored areas.

Disease Cycle. The fungus overwinters as minute, black sclerotia in grass debris. The sclerotia germinate when air temperatures reach 65 to 70 °F. The resulting hyphae rapidly penetrate grass leaves in warm (70 to 85 °F), moist weather. New leaf lesions appear within 1 to 2 days, with large numbers of microscopic spores (Figure 5.11) being produced on the surface of the lesions. The spores (conidia) are spread by splashing or flowing water, animals, people, as well as by mowing and other turf equipment when the grass is wet.

Control. Apply a nitrogen fertilizer and lime according to a soil test report. Follow local cultural recommendations for the grass or grasses grown. The soil pH should be between 6 and 7. When needed, apply a fungicide as suggested for dollar spot (Table

5.4). Spray at about 10-day intervals in warm, moist weather starting when the mean air temperatures remain in the range 68 to 75 °F (and daytime temperatures are 85 to 90 °F).

Curvularia Blight

Curvularia blight or fading-out, caused by five or more species of *Curvularia* (Figure 5.11), is similar to diseases caused by species of *Bipolaris* (see "Helminthosporium" Leaf, Crown, and Root Diseases, page 242). *Curvularia* fungi can infect all turfgrasses with isolates differing greatly in their virulence. Most damage occurs during hot weather (temperatures of 86 °F or above) when grass plants are growing under stress or are in an advanced state of senescence. For this reason, species of *Curvularia* are generally thought to be weak, secondary pathogens.

Symptoms. Turfgrass areas show a general decline and thinning. Irregular patches or streaks of thinned grass may develop which often merge to form large irregular areas (Figure 5.18). Bluegrass and fescue leaves develop indefinite, yellow and green dappled patterns that extend downward from the leaf tip. The affected tissue turns brown and finally gray as it withers and dies. A reddish-brown margin may separate diseased from healthy tissue. Bluegrass and fescue leaves may also develop tan lesions with red or brown margins. Bentgrasses are similarly affected except that the tip dieback is first yellow, then tan, instead of brown or gray; no leaf lesions have been observed. A dark brown decay of leaf sheath and crown tissues may occur on all turfgrasses. During high temperature stress, *Curvularia* fungi are occasionally associated with decline of *Poa annua* in transition zone regions.

Species of *Curvularia* sporulate profusely, causing affected and dead leaves to be blackened with dark spores (conidia) and conidiophores (Figure 5.11).

Disease Cycle. Same as for "Helminthosporium" leaf, crown, and root-infecting fungi; see Figure 5.33. *Curvularia* fungi grow well on dead grass debris at or above the soil surface. Survival during unfavorable weather occurs as dormant mycelium and conidia on or in living and dead plants. When the weather is hot and wet, infection proceeds rapidly. Penetration of leaves occurs only through cut leaf tips or already existing diseased leaf tissue.

Control. Same as for "Helminthosporium" leaf, crown, and root diseases (page 242). Where feasible, cool the turf one or more times at midday in hot weather by syringing the turf for a few minutes.

Dollar Spot

Dollar spot, believed to be caused by species of the fungi *Lanzia* and *Moellerodiscus* (formerly known as *Sclerotinia homoeocarpa*), has been reported from most areas of the United States. The disease is widespread during warm, moist weather and may be serious on closely mowed bentgrasses (especially creeping bent), bluegrasses, fine-leaved fescues, redtop, ryegrasses, bermudagrass, and zoysiagrass. Dollar spot is seldom found on bahiagrass, centipedegrass, and St. Augustinegrass. Disease attacks occur in warm (60 to 85 °F), wet and humid weather, particularly on turf deficient in nitrogen. The

Figure 5.18 Curvularia blight or fading-out in a Kentucky bluegrass lawn. (Courtesy O. M. Scott & Sons.)

Figure 5.19 Dollar spot in Kentucky bluegrass.

incidence of the disease is often higher in low-rainfall seasons, presumably from the adverse effect of low moisture on the growth of grass plants.

Symptoms. The disease appears as more or less round, straw-colored, and somewhat sunken spots (about the size of a silver dollar) in closely cut bentgrass and bermudagrass putting greens, hence the descriptive name "dollar spot" (*Color plate 40*). On coarse, taller, lawn-type grasses (e.g., bluegrasses, fescues, and ryegrasses), the spots may reach 4 to 6 or more inches in diameter (Figure 5.19). Dollar spot is distinguished

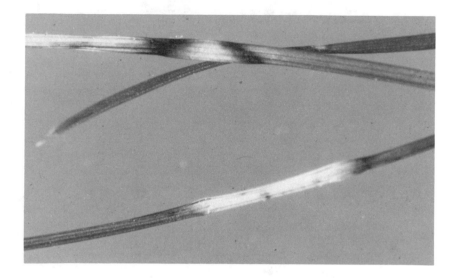

Figure 5.20 Dollar spot (*Lanzia* and *Moellerodiscus* spp.) infecting Kentucky bluegrass leaf blades. (Courtesy D. H. Scott.)

from most other turfgrass diseases by the characteristic, bleached-white to tan girdling lesions with a brown, reddish-brown, or purplish border on the leaf blades of live plants at the margin of the affected area. These lesions may be up to 1 in. long (Figure 5.20), and resemble those formed by the Nigrospora blight fungus (page 254). The lesions usually extend across the blades of fine-leaved grasses. On coarser grasses, such as tall fescue, the lesions tend to occur along the leaf margins.

Under close mowing (as on putting or bowling greens), the spots rarely enlarge beyond 2 to 2½ in. in diameter. If fungicides are not applied, the spots may become so numerous that they merge and produce large, irregular, sunken areas of straw-colored dead turf (*Color plate 40*). When dew is present on the grass blades on overcast days or early in the morning and the dollar-spot fungi are active, a grayish-white cobwebby or cottony growth (mycelium) of the causal fungi may be seen on the diseased turf (Figure 5.21). Guttation fluid ("dew") increases the infection process. Some mycelium

Figure 5.21 Dollar spot. Mycelium of the dollar spot fungi (*Lanzia* and *Moellerodiscus* spp.) growing out from Kentucky bluegrass leaves.

may persist under the leaf sheaths, but most disappears as it is dried by wind and sun. The mycelium of the dollar spot fungi is often confused with spider webs. Spider webs, however, are in a single plane while dollar spot is three dimensional.

When turf is maintained at a higher cut of 1 to 2½ in., the diseased areas are noticeably more irregular in outline and larger, with some spots 4 to 8 in. in diameter. The spots may coalesce to give diseased turf a drought-stricken appearance. The rhizomes and roots are not invaded by these fungi. A fungus-produced toxin, however, affects water and nutrient uptake, which causes the roots to thicken, stop growing, and turn brown. The replacement roots soon are similarly affected. This is why dollar spot is most severe in dry soils.

Disease Cycle. The dollar spot fungi survive unfavorable growing periods as black, paper-thin flakes (stromata) on foliage surfaces and in soil, and as dormant mycelium in living or dead turfgrass tissues. In spring or early summer, when the temperature reaches 50 to 60°F, the mycelia and stromata resume mycelial growth. The fungi enter plants through cut leaf tips and natural openings (stomates) when plant surfaces are wet. Maximum disease development usually occurs between 70 and 80°F in dry soils where there is a buildup of thatch and soil nitrogen and potassium levels are low. Infected tissue first appears water-soaked and dark, becoming light tan when dry. If the nights are cool and dry soon after infection has occurred, or if cultural and chemical control measures are applied promptly, damage is limited to the leaf blades and diseased turf usually recovers quickly (especially if it is growing rapidly). If nights are warm and damp and heavy dews persist after infection, and if fungicides are *not* applied, the dollar-spot fungi rapidly kill plant tissues, and diseased areas may require weeks or months to recover. When turf-grasses are maintained with adequate nitrogen, potash, and water, less dollar spot occurs and recovery is more rapid.

Dollar spot "infection periods" consist of two consecutive wet days with an average temperature of 72°F or more or at least three consecutive wet days when the average temperature is 60°F or more. The dollar spot fungi spread to new areas mostly by transport of infected sod or clippings, on mowers, other turf equipment, hoses, golf carts, animals, water, wind, and shoes.

Control. Follow the cultural control practices outlined on pages 212 to 214. On golf and bowling greens, remove guttation water (dew) in early morning by dragging a hose or long bamboo pole over the wet grass or by hosing down the turf lightly with water. Maintain adequate nitrogen and potassium fertility during the growing season.

Grow or overseed with cultivars that are resistant to various strains of the dollar spot fungi. Bentgrasses differ in resistance.

Kentucky bluegrass cultivars generally considered to be tolerant or at least moderately resistant to dollar spot include A-20 and A-34 (Bensun), Adelphi, America, Aquila, Banff, Bonnieblue, Bristol, Brunswick, Campina, Challenger, Classic, Columbia, Delft, Eclipse, Enita, Entoper, Galaxy, Georgetown, Haga, Majestic, Merit, Midnight, Nassau, Parade, Park, Plush, Princeton 104, Sodco, Trenton, Vantage, and Windsor. Moderately susceptible to very susceptible Kentucky bluegrass cultivars include Argyle, Baron, Birka, Cello, Cheri, Dormie, Enmundi, Fylking, Geronimo, Glade, Kenblue, Kimono, Merion, Monopoly, Mystic, Newport, Nugget, Ram I, Rugby, Shasta, South Dakota Common, Sydsport, Touchdown, Victa, and Wabash.

Fine-leaved fescues considered tolerant or resistant to dollar spot include Aurora, Banner, Bighorn, Biljart, Center, Checker, Epsom, Flyer, Fortress, Highlight, Jade, Jamestown, Longfellow, Magenta, Mary, Pennlawn, Reliant, Scaldis, Shadow, Spartan, Tamara, Valda, Waldina, and Wilma. Susceptible fine-leaved fescues include Beauty, Dawson, Enjoy, Ensylva, Estica, Golfrood, Lovisa, Oasis, Robot, Ruby, Waldorf, Weekend, and Wintergreen.

Perennial ryegrasses tolerant or resistant to some strains of the dollar spot fungi include All-Star, Birdie, Birdie II, Blazer, Cigil, Delray, Elka, Fiesta, Gator, NK-200, Omega, Palmer, Pennant, Prelude, Premier, Regal, Tara, and Yorktown II. Manhattan, Linn, and Pippin are very susceptible. Ormond, Sunturf, and Tifway bermudagrasses, Pensacola bahiagrass, and Emerald zoysiagrass are very susceptible to dollar spot.

Start fungicide applications when the disease is *first* evident. Apply a protective fungicide (Table 5.4) at 7- to 21-day intervals during moist weather in the spring, summer, and fall when day temperatures average between 60 and 85 °F. Apply the fungicide in 3 to 5 gal of water per 1000 sq ft of turf area, and avoid continuous use of chemically related fungicides (page 320).

Downy Mildew or Yellow Tuft

Downy mildew or yellow tuft is caused by the water mold fungus *Sclerophthora macrospora.* This disease occurs on most cultivated turfgrass species but is generally considered to be a minor problem except on turfs maintained at shorter mowing heights, such as a golf green. The disease is mostly associated with seedling or immature turfs grown on poorly drained and heavily watered areas. Downy mildew may weaken creeping bentgrass to such an extent that additional stress, such as excess traffic, drought, or extreme cold or heat, will kill infected plants. Voids left by the dead plants are later filled by weeds such as *Poa annua.*

Symptoms. In cool, humid regions, such as the northeastern United States, small clumps of slightly stunted grass appear with somewhat thickened or wider leaf blades. When severe, small yellow patches, ¼ to 4 in. in diameter, appear in the turf (yellow tuft). Each patch is composed of a dense cluster of excessively tillered, stunted, and yellowed shoots with stunted roots (*Color plate 41*). These plants can be easily pulled from the turf and infected plants commonly die from heat and drought stress or attacks of secondary fungi such as those causing leaf smuts or "Helminthosporium" diseases. Affected turf appears unsightly, being spotted or mottled with an uneven surface. During cool, wet periods a white, downy growth (sporangiophores bearing lemon-shaped sporangia) may appear on the leaves. Symptoms of the disease are most prominent during late spring and autumn, especially in poorly drained soils. Large turfgrass areas in wet soils may turn yellow, wither, and die during hot, dry weather. More commonly, many infected plants survive such stress periods and mask the thinning of turf caused by this fungus.

Infected plants of St. Augustinegrass do not appear to be seriously affected; white raised streaks appear in the leaves (parallel to the midrib) which also become wrinkled or rippled. Leaf streaks appear in the spring and remain throughout the summer, giving the leaves a yellow appearance with some tip dieback. The length and width of leaves and internodes may be reduced. Growth and vigor may also be suppressed.

If left unmowed, the heads of infected turfgrass plants assume grotesque shapes, as if injured by a phenoxy herbicide (Figure 5.22).

Figure 5.22 Heads of K-31 tall fescue affected by the downy mildew or yellow tuft fungus, *Sclerophthora macrospora.* (Courtesy J. L. Dale.)

Disease Cycle. This downy mildew fungus survives as systemic mycelium and thick-walled oospores in infected leaves, stems, and crowns (Figure 5.23). In wet weather from late spring to autumn, stalklike structures (sporangiophores) grow out through the stomates on both leaf surfaces and on leaf sheaths and bear pearly white, spore-bearing

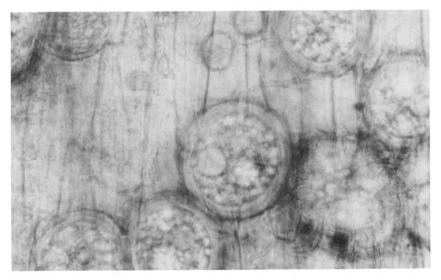

Figure 5.23 Oospores of the downy mildew fungus, *Sclerophthora macrospora,* in creeping bentgrass leaves. (Courtesy Noel Jackson.)

structures (sporangia) at the tips of their branches (Figure 5.24). The sporangia germinate in water by releasing 50 or more microscopic motile spores (zoospores) that swim actively about for 1 to 24 hours before settling down (encysting) on the grass host and later germinating to produce a hyphal strand which infects young meristematic tissue of healthy plants. Very young seedlings are most likely to become infected, whereas mature plants usually escape infection. Numerous round oospores are produced in infected leaves and are evident with a microscope. The oospores overseason in dead tissues and may germinate in the presence of moisture to produce a sporangium. Spores of the downy mildew fungus spread in splashing or flowing water, on turfgrass equipment and shoes, and in infected sod, sprigs, and plugs.

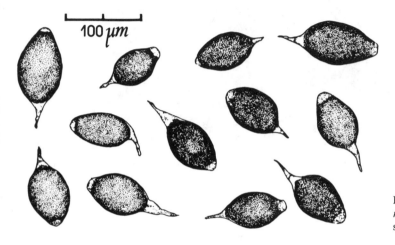

Figure 5.24 Sporangia of *Sclerophthora macrospora* from Kentucky bluegrass, as seen under a microscope.

Control. Provide adequate surface and subsurface drainage when preparing a seedbed. Avoid overwatering. Follow other cultural practices (pages 212–214) that promote active but not lush growth. Mow only when the grass is dry. Preventive fungicides that are active against Pythium blight (see Table 5.4), such as Subdue, should also control downy mildew or yellow tuft. The fungicide must be applied *before* infection occurs; infected plants cannot be cured.

Kentucky bluegrass, and creeping bentgrass cultivars are not known to differ in their resistance to downy mildew or yellow tuft, while a number of St. Augustinegrass cultivars are highly susceptible.

Fairy Rings

Fairy rings may be produced in all cultivated turfgrasses by the growth of any one of about 50 species of soil-inhabiting fungi [mushrooms (toadstools) and puffballs]. Three of these include the common field mushroom, *Psalliota* (*Agaricus*) *campestris* (or *A. bisporus*), that is sold in grocery stores; the small, tan, mushroom, fairy ring fungus, *Marasmius oreades;* and the large, white, poisonous mushroom *Chlorophyllum molybdites* (*Lepiota morgani*); see Figure 5.25. (*Warning:* Do *not* eat any mushrooms appearing in turf without first having them identified by a competent authority.)

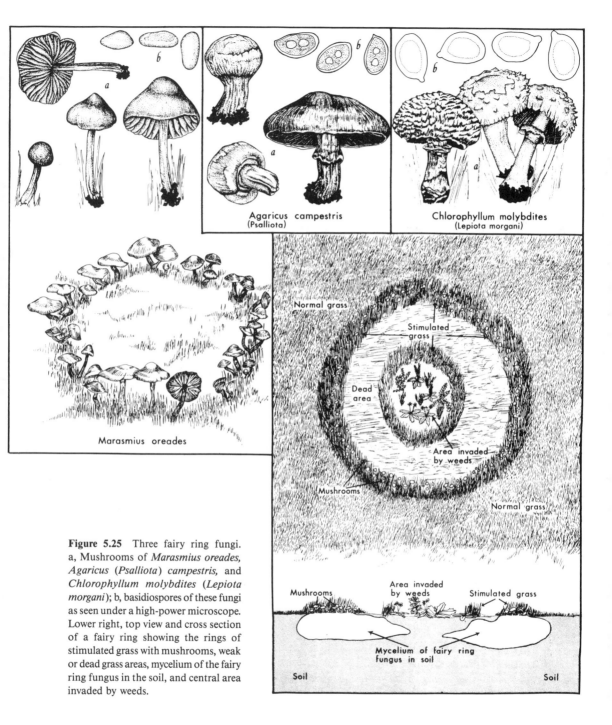

Figure 5.25 Three fairy ring fungi. a, Mushrooms of *Marasmius oreades, Agaricus* (*Psalliota*) *campestris,* and *Chlorophyllum molybdites* (*Lepiota morgani*); b, basidiospores of these fungi as seen under a high-power microscope. Lower right, top view and cross section of a fairy ring showing the rings of stimulated grass with mushrooms, weak or dead grass areas, mycelium of the fairy ring fungus in the soil, and central area invaded by weeds.

Agaricus campestris (Psalliota)

Chlorophyllum molybdites (Lepiota morgani)

Marasmius oreades

Normal grass

Stimulated grass

Dead area

Area invaded by weeds

Mushrooms

Normal grass

Mushrooms

Area invaded by weeds

Stimulated grass

Mycelium of fairy ring fungus in soil

Soil

Soil

Symptoms. Fairy rings usually appear as circles, arcs, or ribbons of darker green, fast-growing grass during the spring, summer, and early autumn. Zones of thin, dead, or dormant grass may develop both inside and outside this circle. During dry weather, especially in late summer and autumn, the dead ring is normally outside the inner or between the inner and outer dark green zones. Fairy rings are very variable in size. In mild weather, after rains or heavy sprinkling, large numbers of mushrooms or puffballs (the fruiting bodies of the fairy ring fungi) may suddenly pop up in the circle that outlines the fairy ring (Figure 5.25).

Commonly, several distinct rings or arcs develop in the same general area. In the case of some of the fungi, where the rings meet, the rings die out and take on a scalloped outline (Figure 5.26).

Generally, fairy rings are first seen as a cluster of mushrooms or as a tuft of stimulated turf. The rings enlarge each year from 5 in. to 2 ft or more. Some rings disappear unexpectedly for a year or more and then reappear, usually larger in diameter.

Disease Cycle. Fairy rings are initiated by the germination of a spore or pieces of fungus-infested soil, and mycelial growth continues radially in all directions. The fungus grows throughout the soil, sometimes to a depth of 8 in. or more. In some species (e.g., *Marasmius oreades*) it forms an extensive, dense, white, mycelial network which has a strong moldy smell. The fungus uses organic matter (e.g., thatch and plant debris), which it decomposes, as a food supply.

The lush, dark green grass of the fairy ring is due partly to the increased amount of nitrogen made available to the grass roots by the fungus as it breaks down organic matter in the thatch and soil. The ring of brown, dormant grass is caused by the dense layer of mushroom spawn, which impedes water movement into the soil, depletes nutrients essential for plant growth, and may produce toxic levels of hydrogen cyanide, as is suspected for *Marasmius oreades.* The grass in this area may become so weakened that it succumbs to environmental stresses or is killed by other diseases and invaded by weeds. As the fungus grows outward, its older parts in the interior of the ring die, releasing nitrogen and other nutrients for use by the grass plants, initiating the formation of the inner ring of lush grass.

Fairy rings are usually most severe in light-textured, low-fertility soils that are low in moisture. Turf with a thick thatch growing in a sandy soil is very vulnerable to damage.

Control. Controlling fairy rings and other mushrooms or puffballs is difficult because the soil becomes almost impervious to water. Before planting a new turf area, remove tree stumps and large roots, construction lumber, and other large pieces of organic matter from which these fungi obtain nutrients. Keep the new planting well fertilized and watered. It is best to moisten the soil to a depth of 6 in. or more. Shallow watering probably encourages the germination of many fairy ring fungi. In established turf, fairy rings can be effectively controlled but the methods are laborious and time consuming. Fairy rings can be combated in one of three ways: suppression, eradication, and antagonism.

A. *Suppression.* To suppress ring formation, water the turf thoroughly and fertilize well.

1. The symptoms are easily "masked" by pumping large quantities of water 10 to 24 in. deep into the soil at 1-ft intervals, for a distance of 18 to 24 in. on either side of the stimulated zone of dark green grass. Maintain the soil in a water-soaked condition

Figure 5.26 Fairy rings in Kentucky bluegrass turf. Three rings have met, fungus activity has ceased, and the rings now have a scalloped effect. (Courtesy D. H. Scott.)

for 4 to 6 weeks by watering every 2 to 3 days. Use a tree-feeding lance or root-feeder attachment on a garden hose. Repeat the treatment several months to a year or more later when the rings begin to wilt.

2. Since there are fewer rings and they are much less conspicuous on adequately watered and fertilized turf, apply nitrogen fertilizer to the turf several times during the year. Follow local recommendations based on a soil test and the cultivar or blend of grass being grown. Avoid excessive applications of nitrogen and organic matter (manure or mulches), as they tend to stimulate the development of fairy rings and encourage other turf diseases.

B. *Eradication.* Fairy rings can be eradicated by soil fumigation or excavation. Drenching with fungicides, such as carboxin and benodanil, has met with only moderate success, and the risk of chemical injury (phytotoxicity) is often high. To fumigate the soil:

1. Carefully strip and dispose of the sod in an area 2 ft inside and 2 ft outside the outer green ring of grass. *Be careful not to spill any of the infested soil or sod on the healthy turf.* A better but more expensive method is to apply glyphosate (Roundup, Kleenup) to the area. This will kill the grass in about a week, with little or no chemical residue remaining to affect the new planting. You still have to dispose of the dead turf after using glyphosate since it may still contain mycelium of the fairy ring fungus. Loosen the soil underneath to a depth of 6 to 9 in. with a spading fork or by rototilling, to improve the results. Be careful not to spread the fungus with the tiller. Equipment used to cultivate the soil should be sterilized with formaldehyde solution or household liquid

bleach. Fumigate the soil with methyl bromide, chloropicrin, formaldehyde, Vorlex, or Stauffer Vapam Soil Fumigant. Carefully follow the manufacturer's directions when using any fumigant.

If using formaldehyde, prepare a 2 to 3% solution by mixing 4 to 6 pints of commercial (40%) formaldehyde and ½ pint of liquid wetting agent or household detergent to 10 gal of water. This amount will treat 90 sq ft. Pour the formaldehyde solution uniformly on the loosened soil with a sprinkling can. Do *not* drip the solution on healthy grass since it will scorch and kill the leaves.

The soil temperature should be 60°F or above for fumigation. The vapors of the fumigant are kept in the soil by covering the stripped areas with a gas-proof plastic cover for 7 to 10 days, depending on the fumigant used. The plastic cover is removed after the fumigation period. After removing the cover, the soil should be stirred and left exposed to the air for 2 weeks or until all odor of the chemical has disappeared. Fresh soil should be added to the area as needed, followed by seeding or sodding. Soil fumigation should *only* be done by a certified golf course superintendent or turfgrass specialist who is licensed to handle and apply restricted pesticides.

2. *Excavation.* Carefully dig out and discard all infested soil in the ring (12 in. or more deep and extending 2 ft on either side of the outer stimulated zone, including all mushroom spawn) and replace soil in the trench with fresh, clean soil that is free of fairy ring fungi. The area is then sodded or reseeded.

C. *Antagonism.* Antagonism is most effective when a turf area is heavily infested with fairy rings. The biology of these fungi, for example, *Marasmius oreades,* will ensure that two or more strains will eliminate each other when occupying the same site. Figure 5.26 shows how antagonism has stopped disease development where two fairy rings meet. This method of control, while requiring the same initial steps that are used for eradication, is much cheaper because the costs for chemical fumigants and for a licensed applicator are eliminated. Also, there is no danger of injury from contact or inhaling chemical fumes.

1. After killing the infested area with glyphosate and stripping the sod, rototill the entire area covered by the fairy rings. Mix the mycelium-infested soil by multiple cultivations with a rotary cultivator to a depth of 6 to 8 in. in several directions to effectively mix the spawn of the fungi.

2. Wet the soil to a depth of 8 in. or more using a wetting agent to increase water infiltration into the deeper layers. Sod or reseed the area and keep it well watered and fertilized.

Fusarium Leaf Spot, Crown and Root Rot

Fusarium leaf spot is caused by at least six species of *Fusarium* fungi (*F. acuminatum, F. crookwellense, F. culmorum, F. graminearum, F. heterosporum,* and *F. poae* or *F. tricinctum*). The disease may occur uniformly over large areas of turf in warm to hot, moist weather (Figure 5.27). Typically, Fusarium leaf spot occurs mostly on older, senescing leaves and on tillers weakened by drought stress or root and crown rot (see melting-out, page 245, and summer patch and necrotic ring spot, page 303). Fusarium crown and root rots are most serious in drought-prone regions.

Figure 5.27 Fusarium leaf spot (caused by *Fusarium acuminatum*) in a Kentucky bluegrass lawn. (Courtesy R. W. Smiley.)

Symptoms. Irregular spots that are first dark green and water-soaked, then fading to dull tan, usually with a light brown to reddish-brown border, occur mostly on older leaves (*Color plate 42*). Lesions originate at the cut tips or on the leaf surface. Infected leaves may turn yellow and die back from the cut leaf tip to the base. This disease can be confused with dollar spot (page 228) or leaf spot (page 242). Fusarium crown and root rots (Figure 5.28) produce symptoms that resemble the melting-out caused by

Figure 5.28 Fusarium crown and root rot of Kentucky bluegrass. (Courtesy R. W.. Smiley.)

Key to Infectious Turfgrass Diseases

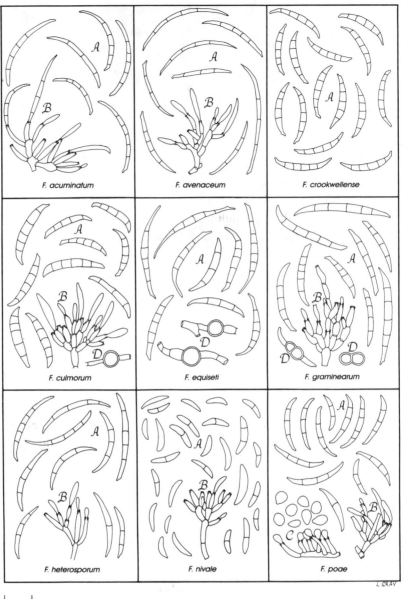

Figure 5.29 Nine species of *Fusarium* that cause disease in turfgrasses as seen under a high-power microscope. A, Macroconidia; B, conidiophores some bearing young to mature macroconidia; C, microconidia; D, chlamydospores.

Drechslera and *Bipolaris* (page 245). The species primarily responsible are *F. culmorum* (*F. roseum* f. sp. *cerealis* 'Culmorum') and *F. poae* (*F. tricinctum*).

Disease Cycle. Species of *Fusarium* overseason as dormant mycelium in or on infected plants and grass debris or as thick-walled resistant spores (chlamydospores; see Figure 5.29) in the thatch or upper soil. When favorable conditions (proper temperature,

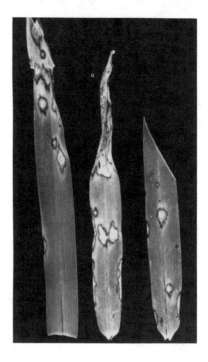

Figure 5.30 Gray leaf spot of St. Augustinegrass. (Courtesy L. T. Lucas.)

moisture, and nutrition) return, the mycelium resumes rapid growth and the spores (largely conidia and chlamydospores) germinate to produce additional mycelium that infects the grass leaves or other parts of the turfgrass plant. *Fusarium* fungi produce large numbers of spores (crescent-shaped macroconidia and smaller oval or round microconidia) in hot weather (80 to 95 °F), especially in dry thatch when it is rewetted (see Figure 5.29). Entire tillers or plants may die when the crowns, roots, rhizomes, and stolons die in hot, dry weather.

Control. Same as for summer patch and necrotic ring spot (page 303). Chemical controls (see Table 5.4) are not usually required. If applying a fungicide, use Tersan 1991, Fungo 50, or Cleary's 3336. Do *not* use Chipco 26019, Bayleton, Banner, or Rubigan.

Gray Leaf Spot

Gray leaf spot, caused by the fungi *Pyricularia grisea* and *P. oryzae,* is a common and serious disease of St. Augustinegrass in the southern and southeastern United States. Other cultivated turfgrasses attacked include centipedegrass, bermudagrass, perennial ryegrass, fescues, and bahiagrass. St. Augustinegrass is most susceptible, particularly the blue-green (Bitter-Blue) selections. Disease attacks occur in warm to hot, humid, rainy weather and is more severe in newly sprigged plantings than in well-established ones. Shady locations with poor air movement favor disease development. Prolonged wet foliage that is high in nitrogen tends to increase both the severity and spread of gray leaf spot.

Symptoms. Spots start as small, round, water-soaked, olive green to brown lesions that enlarge rapidly, become oval to elongate, and blue gray, dirty yellow, or brown to gray with definite darker brown or purple to reddish-brown margins. The lesions form on the leaves, leaf sheaths, stems, and spikes (Figure 5.30). In warm, moist weather, the enlarging spots become covered with the grayish velvety mycelium of *Pyricularia* containing large numbers of spores (conidia). Where spots are numerous, severely diseased leaves turn yellow to brown, wither, and die early, causing thinning of the grass. Large turf areas may thus have a rather unthrifty, "scorched" or brownish appearance from death or spotting of leaf blades and are more susceptible to drought and other damage. Gray leaf spot can cause extensive foliar damage but seldom kills the grass.

Disease Cycle. The *Pyricularia* fungi overwinter as free spores or conidia (Figure 5.14), as dormant mycelium in older infected leaves and grass debris, and possibly in or on seed. The spores are spread about by wind, water, mowers or other turf equipment, animals, and shoes. During warm weather, when the air is moisture saturated, the conidia germinate and penetrate young leaves directly and through stomates. Visible leaf spots appear 5 to 7 days after infection. Disease activity is favored by prolonged rainy or foggy weather, heavy dews, or frequent shallow irrigations, and a temperature between 70 and 90 °F.

Control. Follow the cultural control suggestions outlined on pages 212 to 214. Avoid stresses such as soil compaction, drought, a thick thatch, and excessive rates of herbicides. Fertilize lightly in warm humid weather with high-nitrogen materials. Follow local recommendations based on a soil test. Do *not* fertilize with water-soluble fertilizers. Use very low rates of nitrogen where gray leaf spot is a problem. If a darker green turf color is desirable, use an iron-containing fertilizer.

Where cultural practices are not checking gray leaf spot, apply a suggested fungicide (Table 5.4). Repeated applications at 10- to 14-day intervals may be needed during prolonged rainy periods.

Yellow-green or common types of St. Augustinegrass (e.g., Roselawn and Floratam) are more resistant than the blue-green types, such as Bitter-Blue and Floratine, which are very susceptible. Selections of perennial ryegrass also have some resistance.

"Helminthosporium" Leaf, Crown, and Root Diseases

"Helminthosporium" leaf, crown, and root rots are the most common and serious group of diseases that attack cool-season grasses in the United States. One or more of the causal fungi attack essentially all turfgrasses (Table 5.2) as well as numerous forage, wild and weed grasses, and cereals.

These diseases reduce vigor and can be very destructive during wet, humid weather, where the turf is sprinkled frequently, especially in late afternoon and early evening, in poorly drained areas, and where it is shady.

These diseases are favored by dry periods alternating with prolonged, cloudy, moist weather and moderate temperatures; the use of susceptible cultivars; letting clippings drop in place; close mowing; slow growth of grass; low fertility, or excessive shade and nitrogen fertilization; thatch buildup; frequent light sprinklings; compaction from excessive traffic; nematode damage; and applications of certain postemergence herbicides such as 2,4-D, mecoprop (MCPP), and dicamba.

Helminthosporium fungi (now generally referred to species within the genera *Bipolaris, Drechslera,* and *Exserohilum;* see Table 5.2) may be responsible for the gradual

TABLE 5.2 PRINCIPAL "HELMINTHOSPORIUM" LEAF, CROWN, AND ROOT DISEASES, THE FUNGI THAT CAUSE THEM, AND THE GRASSES ATTACKED

Common name of disease	Old name(s) (*Helminthosporium*)	New name(s) (*Bipolaris, Drechslera, Exserohilum*)	Turfgrasses attacked
Leaf spot, melting-out; leaf, crown, and rhizome rot	*H. vagans (H. poae)*	*D. poae (D. vagans)*	Bluegrasses, ryegrasses, fescues
Leaf spot; leaf, crown, and root rot	*H. sorokinianum (H. sativum)*	*B. sorokiniana (D. sorokiniana)*	Bluegrasses, bentgrasses, ryegrasses, fescues, wheatgrasses, turf timothy
Net-blotch; crown and root rot	*H. dictyoides, H. dictyoides* var. *phlei*	*D. dictyoides* f. sp. *dictyoides, D. dictyoides* f. sp. *perenne*	Fescues, ryegrasses
Zonate leaf spot or eyespot	*H. giganteum*	*D. gigantea*	Bermudagrass, bentgrasses, bluegrasses, wheatgrasses, turf timothy
Brown blight; leaf, crown, and root rot	*H. siccans*	*D. siccans*	Ryegrasses, tall fescue
Leaf blotch; crown and root rot	*H. cynodontis*	*B. cynodontis*	Bermudagrass
Red leaf spot	*H. erythrospilum*	*D. erythrospila*	Bentgrasses, redtop
Leaf spot	*H. rostratum*	*E. rostrata*	Bermudagrass, St. Augustinegrass
Leaf blight and crown rot	*H. catenarium*	*D. catenaria*	Bentgrasses, redtop
Stem, crown, and root necrosis	*H. tetramera (H. spiciferum)*	*B. tetramera (D. spicifer)*	Bermudagrass, zoysiagrasses
Other leaf diseases of bermudagrass	*H. stenospilum* *H. triseptatum*	*B. stenospila* *D. triseptata*	Bermudagrass Bermudagrass
Minor diseases	*H. buchloës* *H. micropus*	*B. buchloës* *B. micropa* *D. nobleae*	Buffalograss Bahiagrass Ryegrasses

browning and thinning (melting-out) of susceptible Kentucky bluegrass cultivars. As the disease progresses, large, irregular turf areas may be yellow, then brown to straw-colored, and killed (*Color plate 43*). In some instances, the entire turf is lost. Bermudagrass may be severely attacked by a number of these fungi (Table 5.2), causing leaf, crown, and root rots. The turf may be thinned, or diseased plants commonly appear in irregular patches. Fescues, ryegrasses, and bentgrasses may be similarly affected especially under high levels of nitrogen. Once one or more of these fungi become established in a turfgrass stand, they remain an ever-present problem. It is not unusual to find two or more species of these fungi infecting a single plant or even a single leaf.

Figure 5.31 Leaf blotch of bermudagrass caused by *Bipolaris cynodontis*. (Courtesy USDA and Clemson University.)

Symptoms. This group of diseases produces a variety of symptoms, depending on the cultivar and kinds of grass, culture, season (primarily day length and temperature), weather conditions, and the fungus or fungi that are present.

1. *Leaf spots or blights.* Small dark brown, reddish-brown, brownish-green to black, purplish, or purplish-black spots (lesions) appear on the leaves from early spring to late autumn. The lesions may increase rapidly in size and become round to oblong, elongate, or irregular. Their centers often fade to an ash white to pale tan or straw color. The spots are commonly surrounded by narrow, dark reddish-brown to purplish-black borders (*Color plate 44* and Figure 5.31), often described as eyespots. Under moist conditions, one or more lesions may merge and girdle a leaf blade, causing it to turn yellow, tan, or reddish brown and die back from the tip. When leaf spots are numerous, leaves may be completely blighted, wither, and die. Lesions may or may not occur on the leaf sheaths and stems, depending on the species of fungus. A diseased leaf sheath turns reddish to purple or brown. Leaf sheath infection is often so severe that the entire leaf or tiller is girdled

Figure 5.32 Severe crown and root rot in a Kentucky bluegrass lawn caused by *Bipolaris sorokiniana.*

and drops prematurely. If the moisture continues, the diseases progresses from leaf sheath to leaf sheath on a single plant until the plant is killed above ground. The disease may then involve the crown, rhizomes, stolons, and roots, killing the entire plant. In severe cases, nearly all the leaves and tillers may die, resulting in a severe thinning of turf.

In hot, humid weather closely clipped bentgrass leaves may turn reddish brown or dark gray, giving a smoky-blue cast to infected, irregularly shaped areas in golf or bowling greens. Such turf appears drought-stressed.

2. *Crown (foot) and root rots (melting-out).* This phase of the disease usually appears in warm to hot, dry weather as a reddish-brown or purplish-black decay of the stem, crown, rhizome, stolon, and root tissues, which sometimes turn reddish-brown to chocolate-brown or black when invaded by secondary bacteria and fungi. The feeding roots on diseased plants are shallow, few in number, or even absent. Such plants lack vigor and often wilt during midday, even when soil moisture is abundant. Diseased turf may have a yellow, then brown or drought-injured appearance (Figure 5.32). The damaged areas may be small and circular to large and irregular. Entire stands of bluegrasses, fescues, ryegrasses, bermudagrass, or bentgrasses may be thinned out or completely destroyed by severe crown and root rot. This phase occurs most readily when plant vigor is suppressed by one cause or another, particularly during hot weather.

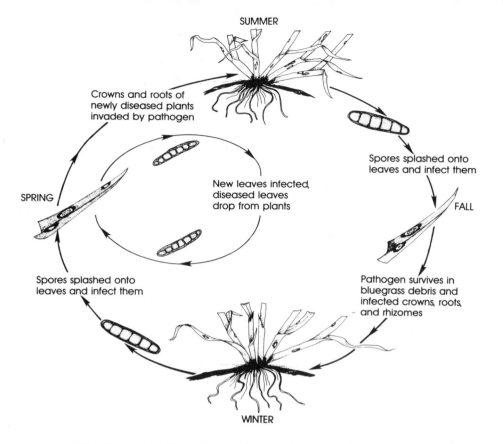

SUMMER

Crowns and roots of
newly diseased plants
invaded by pathogen

Spores splashed onto
leaves and infect them

SPRING

New leaves infected,
diseased leaves
drop from plants

FALL

Spores splashed onto
leaves and infect them

Pathogen survives in
bluegrass debris and
infected crowns, roots,
and rhizomes

WINTER

Figure 5.33 Disease cycle of *Drechslera poae* that causes leaf spot and leaf, crown, and rhizome rot or melting-out of Kentucky bluegrass and other turfgrasses.

Disease Cycle. The disease cycle for all species is essentially the same (Figure 5.33). The fungi survive from year to year (and periods of very hot or cold weather) as spores called conidia (Figure 5.34) and as dormant mycelium in dead grass tissues or in infected leaves, crowns, roots, and rhizomes. During periods of cool, moist weather, tremendous numbers of conidia are produced on debris, mostly at temperatures from 38 to 82°F (optimum 60 to 66°F), and are carried to healthy leaves and leaf sheaths by air currents, mowers and other turf equipment, flowing or splashing water, foot traffic, dragging hoses, animals, and infected grass clippings. The conidia germinate in a film of moisture and infect the leaves either directly or through stomates. Germination and infection of leaves can take place within 2 hours if the weather is favorable. These fungi are also capable of saprophytically colonizing plant debris at or above the soil surface. The fungi sporulate profusely when dry grass debris is repeatedly rewetted. The conidia, along with mycelial fragments, spread to new leaf parts and neighboring plants. Thus the cycle is repeated. New leaf and leaf sheath infections may occur as long as the weather remains moist and temperatures are favorable. The peak of disease development varies from early or mid-spring to late September or October, depending on the area of the country and the species of fungus. Some species (e.g., *Drechslera poae, D. dictyoides, D. siccans,* and *Bipolaris cynodontis*) are favored by the cool temperatures of early spring, while other species, such as *Bipolaris sorokiniana D. erythrospila,* and *D. gigantea,* are destructive only in

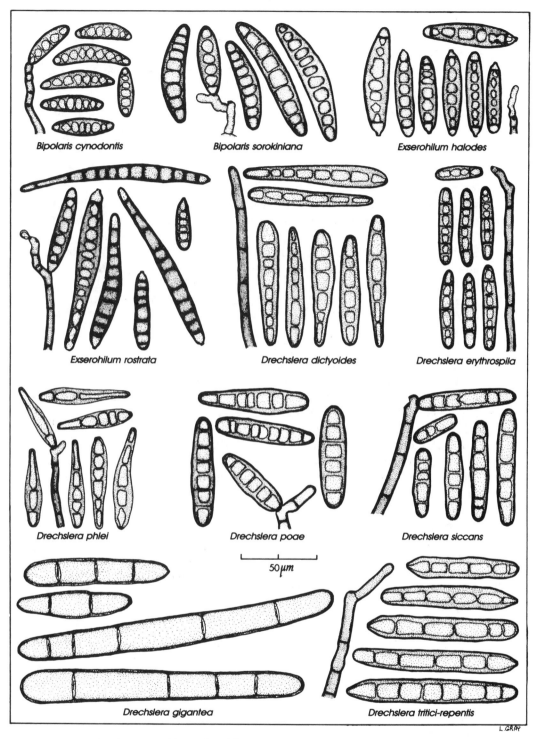

Figure 5.34 Spores (conidia) and conidiophores of eleven species of *Bipolaris, Drechslera,* and *Exserohilum* that cause "Helminthosporium" diseases.

Key to Infectious Turfgrass Diseases

warm and wet summer overcast weather. *Bipolaris sorokiniana* is also very active on old leaves during cool, wet weather in the fall and early winter.

During warm, dry weather, the leaf lesion phase decreases (except for *D. erythrospila* and *D. gigantea*) and fungal activity may be restricted to crowns, roots, rhizomes, and stolons of diseased plants, killing round to irregular turf areas (melting-out or crown and root rot). With the return of cooler, moist weather, leaf infection again becomes a problem. These fungi may also be seed-borne and cause seedling blights on new turf-grass areas (page 287).

Control. Follow the cultural practices outlined on pages 212 to 214. Buy only top-quality seed, sod, sprigs, or plugs from a reputable dealer. Grow locally adapted, leaf-spot-resistant grasses or combinations (blends and mixtures) whenever possible. Very susceptible Kentucky bluegrasses to leaf spot include Arboretum, Argyle, Bayside, Campina, Cougar, Delft, Delta, Enita, Garfield, Geary, Glade, Kenblue, Mystic, Newport, Palouse, Park, Piedmont, Prato, Sodco, South Dakota common or certified, Troy, Vantage, Victa, and Wabash. Some modern Kentucky bluegrass cultivars that are resistant to one or more of these diseases include A–20 and A–34 (Bensun), Able 1, Adelphi, Admiral, America, Aquila, Aspen, Banff, Barblue, Bonnieblue, Bono, Bristol, Brunswick, Cello, Challenger, Charlotte, Cheri, Classic, Columbia, Eclipse, Enmundi, Enoble, Escort, Farblue, Fylking, Galaxy, Georgetown, Haga, Holiday, Kimono, Majestic, Merion, Merit, Midnight, Mona, Monopoly, Mosa, Nassau, Nugget, Parade, Plush, Princeton 104, Ram II, Rugby, Shasta, Somerset, Sydsport, Touchdown, Trenton, and Windsor. Perennial ryegrasses rated as resistant to leaf spot to brown blight include Belle, Birdie II, Blazer, CBS II, Citation II, Cupido, Delray, Dasher, Derby, Diplomat, Gator, Manhattan II, Omega II, Palmer, Prelude, Ranger, Repell, Tara, and Yorktown II. Susceptible ryegrasses include Citation, Eton, Game, Linn, NK–100, Paramount, Pennfine, and Pippin. Somewhat resistant fine-leaved fescues include Atlanta, Aurora, Beauty, Bighorn, Biljart, Center, Enjoy, Lovisa, Mary, Reliant, Scaldis, Spartan, Valda, and Waldina. Tall fescues with some leaf spot resistance include Adventure, Apache, Bonanza, Galway, Houndog, Jaguar, and Olympic. The resistance to these diseases breaks down somewhat when turfgrass is subject to stress. Check with your local country cooperative extension office or the extension turf specialist for suggested grass species and cultivars to grow.

If the various "Helminthosporium" diseases cannot be controlled adequately by cultural practices, fungicide sprays may need to be applied on a *preventive* schedule (Table 5.4). For the cool, wet-weather group, begin applications in *early* spring shortly after the first new leaves are formed, and continue at 7- to 21-day intervals until warm, dry weather develops. For the warm- to hot-weather group, begin treatment following local recommendations and continue at 7- to 21-day intervals during moist weather. Such spray programs are time consuming, expensive, and often not practical for the average homeowner. When only a few sprays can be applied to a turf area, it is best to apply them in the spring. Apply the first one as the grass begins to green up, the second 2 to 3 weeks later, and the third 2 to 3 weeks after the second. Check label directions. If a turf area is not sprayed until late spring or summer—when leaf blight and melting-out (sheath and crown rot) are obvious—it is practically impossible to achieve control since the fungus or fungi are generally well established and inaccessible in the crowns, roots, rhizomes, and stolons. Granular applications of PCNB, or sprays of zineb or maneb, in the fall or early spring are reasonably effective in reducing pathogen inoculum on turf debris.

Figure 5.35 Stripe smut (*Ustilago striiformis*) infecting a Kentucky bluegrass lawn.

Best results are obtained when the fungicides are applied under pressure (25 lb per sq in. or higher) (see pages 333 to 339). The addition of a small amount of commercial spreader-sticker or surfactant to the spray solution will ensure better coverage. Ask your pesticide dealer about these materials.

The fungicides in Table 5.4 for use against "Helminthosporium" diseases primarily are protective in action and will not control satisfactorily unless the grass plants are thoroughly coated *before* infection occurs. Apply the fungicide in 3 to 5 gal or more of water, sprayed evenly over 1000 sq ft of turf. Carefully follow the manufacturer's directions regarding dosage, timing of applications, safety, and other factors. Where feasible, spray at dusk or in the early evening. None of the fungicides listed in Table 5.4 will completely control these diseases. Sprays applied at weekly intervals give better control than those sprayed at 2- or 3-week intervals. At low rates of application, certain fungicides (e.g., zineb) may actually increase damage from these fungi.

Leaf Smuts

Stripe smut, caused by the fungus *Ustilago striiformis,* and flag smut, caused by *Urocystis agropyri* are two leaf or foliar smuts widely distributed and destructive to many turfgrass species that are 3 or more years old. Smut fungi weaken the grass host making the plant easy to kill when under severe stress. Plants infected with flag smut are killed more readily than are plants infected with stripe smut. Flag smut is often more prevalent in early spring, while stripe smut generally predominates in late spring and early autumn. These smut fungi grow systemically throughout a grass plant, and both smut fungi may infect the same grass plant at the same time and even the same leaf. Once infected, a plant remains so for life. Infected plants are often weakened and invaded by other organisms. For example, smut-infected plants are more susceptible to "Helminthosporium" diseases.

Leaf smut, together with high temperatures and drought, cause grass plants to exhibit stunted growth, a brown to blackish-brown appearance, a general decline, and early death. Dead patches of grass often appear in heavily infected turf during midsummer; weed invasion soon follows (Figure 5.35).

Key to Infectious Turfgrass Diseases

The stripe and flag smut fungi infect almost 100 species of turf and forage grasses, both cultivated and wild. A number of highly specialized varieties and pathogenic races of these fungi are restricted to certain cultivars and grasses. The diseases occur most commonly on annual bluegrass and Kentucky bluegrass (especially on the cultivars Arboretum, Cougar, Delta, Galaxy, Geronimo, Merion, Newport, Park, Prato, Rugby, Troy, and Windsor). Creeping bentgrass (especially Pennlu and Toronto), colonial bentgrass, redtop, fescues, common timothy, several wildryes and wheatgrasses, orchardgrass, perennial or English ryegrass, and quackgrass are also commonly infected.

Leaf smuts are favored in locations having excess thatch, frequent irrigations or rains during spring and summer, turf that is 3 years or more old, a pH below 6.0, and where susceptible grass cultivars are grown.

Symptoms.   From a distance infected turf appears clumpy and patchy, due to the killing of individual plants and the more upright growth of infected plants. Smutted plants are most noticeable during cool weather in the spring and autumn, when they appear pale green to slightly yellow or brown, stunted, and more upright than healthy plants. Single plants may be affected, or irregular patches up to 1 ft or more in diameter may occur.

Short to long, narrow, and yellow-green streaks develop in infected leaves and leaf sheaths. These streaks soon become silvery to dull gray and extend the entire length of the leaf blade and sheath. The grass epidermis covering the streaks soon ruptures, exposing blackish-brown, dusty masses of smut spores (teliospores). After dispersal of the spores, the leaves soon split and shred into ribbons, turn brown, curl from the tip downward, turn light brown, and die (Figure 5.36). In addition, leaves of infected bluegrass and bentgrass plants tend to remain stiff and erect, rather than lax and spreading. The symptoms

Figure 5.36 Stripe smut (*Ustilago striiformis*) infecting leaves of Kentucky bluegrass. (Courtesy of D. H. Scott.)

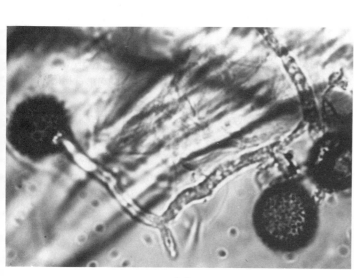

(a)

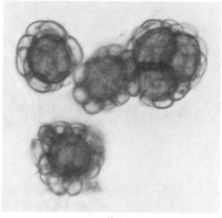

(b)

Figure 5.37 (a) Teliospores of the stripe smut fungus (*Ustilago striiformis*) germinating in a drop of water; (b) spore balls of the flag smut fungus, *Urocystis agropyri*, as you would see them under a high-power microscope. (Courtesy C. F. Hodges.)

are usually most evident in middle to late spring and autumn, when temperatures average 50 to 65 °F. Affected plants do not tiller as profusely or produce as many rhizomes as healthy plants, nor do they develop as extensive a root system.

Smutted plants are often difficult to find during hot, dry weather because a large percentage of such plants often die during summer droughts (Figure 5.35). Both smut fungi decrease leaf turgor and water potentials of infected plants under drought stress. Once infected, grass plants will rarely, if ever, recover, unless properly treated with a *systemic* fungicide.

Under close mowing, both smut fungi produce identical symptoms. Positive diagnosis can be made only through a microscopic examination of the teliospores produced by the smut fungus. The spores of *Ustilago striiformis* are single cells, round to elliptical in shape, and covered with prominent spines (Figure 5.37A). The spores of *Urocystis agropyri* are smooth and roundish and are composed of one to four, dark reddish-brown, fertile cells (teliospores) surrounded by several, smaller, empty, or sterile cells (Figure 5.37B) forming a spore ball.

Disease Cycle. The stripe and flag smut fungi overwinter and oversummer as dormant mycelium in the meristematic tissue of crowns and nodes of infected plants and as dormant teliospores in grass debris, living plants, and soil. The teliospores are carried by many agents, including wind, rain, shoes, mowing, watering, raking, dethatching, coring, and other turf maintenance practices. Spores are also transported on the seed. These teliospores may lie dormant up to 3 years (4 years in stored seed) before they germinate.

When suitable conditions occur in the spring and autumn, a teliospore germinates to produce mycelium on which minute spores (sporidia) may be borne, although this is apparently rare on certain grasses, such as Kentucky bluegrass and creeping bentgrass. Each sporidium then germinates and forms a germ tube. When the germ tubes of opposite mating types fuse (conjugate), an infection hypha forms that penetrates susceptible host tissue directly. Infection may occur through the coleoptile of seedling plants and actively growing (meristematic) tissues produced by the lateral or axillary buds on the crowns and rhizomes of older plants that come into contact with germinating spores. Once inside the grass plant, smut hyphae develop systemically in the direction of plant growth, with new leaves, tillers, and rhizomes becoming infected as they form. The mycelium continues to grow within developing tissues.

Teliospore formation begins with tangled mats of mycelium within infected grass tissues. The mycelium then breaks up to form masses of blackish-brown teliospores that are released when the host tissues rupture, shred, and die.

Smutted plants in new turfgrass areas are uncommon, indicating limited infection of seedling plants from soil- or seed borne teliospores. The large number of diseased grass plants in turf areas more than 3 years old is probably caused by the infection of lateral buds and the growth of smut fungi from perennially infected crowns. Once infected, watering and high fertility, which stimulate plant growth during droughts, create conditions that favor the buildup of leaf smuts. Such practices keep the systemically infected grass plants from dying during hot, dry weather.

Control. Grow a blend of several cultivars that generally show resistance to leaf smuts and other major diseases. Bluegrass and bentgrass cultivars apparently differ greatly in their resistance to leaf smuts. Because numerous races of the two smut fungi exist, it is difficult to predict the relative resistance or susceptibility of a cultivar in any given location. Kentucky bluegrass cultivars showing good resistance to one or both leaf smuts include A-20 and A-34 (Bensun), Able 1, Adelphi, America, Aquila, Banff, Baron, Birka, Bonnieblue, Bristol, Brunswick, Campina, Challenger, Champaign, Cheri, Classic, Columbia, Delft, Eclipse, Enita, Enmundi, Entoper, Fylking, Georgetown, Glade, Majestic, Merit, Midnight, Monopoly, Mystic, Nassau, Nugget, Parade, Plush, Princeton 104, Ram I and II, Sodco, Sydsport, Touchdown, Vantage, Victa, and Wabash.

Stripe smut has been reported to infect the following creeping bentgrass (*Agrostis palustris*) cultivars: Arlington, Cohansey, Congressional, Evansville, Old Orchard, Penncross, Pennlu, Seaside, Toronto, and Washington. The races of the stripe smut fungus that attack Kentucky bluegrass do *not* infect creeping bentgrass.

Sow *only* seed that is not surface contaminated with teliospores and is treated with a captan- or thiram-containing fungicide, or start with disease-free sod, sprigs, or plugs of a resistant cultivar. During hot weather, the smut fungi become dormant in bentgrass stolons and the healthy-appearing stolons continue to grow. When cooler weather returns in the autumn, the smut fungus resumes growth and symptoms reappear in the stolons. Renovate and overseed infected turf with a blend or mixture of relatively resistant cultivars.

Follow the suggested cultural control practices outlined on pages 212 to 214. Where practical, remove the clippings when smutted leaves are evident. Yearly treatment with a systemic fungicide is expensive, but it checks the pathogen(s); see Table 5.4.

Leptosphaerulina Leaf Blight

Leptosphaerulina leaf blight, caused by the fungus *Leptosphaerulina australis,* is a minor, warm- to hot-humid-weather disease of perennial ryegrass, Kentucky bluegrass, and creep-

Figure 5.38 Leptosphaerulina leaf blight on Kentucky bluegrass leaves. Note the dark perithecia embedded in the dead leaf tissue. (Courtesy R. W. Smiley.)

ing bentgrass in the northern United States. The disease is easily confused with Nigrospora leaf blight (page 254), Ascochyta leaf blight (page 222), Pythium blight (page 265), dollar spot (page 228), and Septoria leaf spot (page 290).

Symptoms. Large areas of turf may become uniformly blighted or appear patchy with individual leaves dying back from the tip (Figure 5.38). Uniform yellow or brown lesions may extend down to the leaf sheath. Water-soaked lesions which quickly fade to a bleached white may also occur on the leaf blades. Such lesions closely resemble the bleaching due to high temperatures, frost, or a dull mower.

Disease Cycle. The weakly pathogenic fungus overseasons as tiny, pale brown fruiting bodies (perithecia) and mycelium in dead grass tissue (Figure 5.38). Microscopic spores, the ascospores (Figure 5.14), are produced in warm, wet weather and are blown or splashed and carried on turfgrass equipment and shoes to healthy grass leaves. Disease outbreaks are most common during warm, humid weather when the turf is stressed by close mowing, drought, herbicides, and excessive rates of nitrogen fertilizer, or on newly laid sod that lacks good root contact with the underlying soil.

Control. Follow the suggested cultural control practices outlined on pages 212 to 214. Do not lay new sod before or during hot, humid weather.

Minor Viral and Mycoplasmal Diseases

A number of viruses and the aster yellows mycoplasma commonly infect grasses grown for nonturf purposes but are *not* generally considered to cause significant damage to turf. However, the susceptibility of several turfgrasses to viral agents has been confirmed in greenhouse inoculation studies. Perhaps the mycoplasma and these viruses, by reducing root growth and restricting photosynthesis, are making grass plants more susceptible to leaf, crown, and root-infecting pathogens and various environmental stresses. This area needs additional research.

The viruses reported to infect one or more turfgrass genera in North America include agropyron mosaic, barley stripe mosaic, barley yellow dwarf, brome mosaic, cynosurus mottle, lucerne dwarf, maize chlorotic dwarf, oat necrotic mottle, panicum mosaic, poa semilatent, ryegrass mosaic, sugarcane or maize dwarf mosaic, western ryegrass mosaic, wheat soilborne mosaic, wheat spindle streak mosaic, wheat streak mosaic, and wheat striate mosaic. Most of these viruses are unknown or rare on turfgrasses, but the potential for infection is always present.

The viruses are transmitted from plant to plant by highly virus-specific means. The methods of transmission and animal vectors include specific species of mites, aphids, and leafhoppers (Figure 5.6); mechanical transfer of infected sap or pollen; dagger (*Xiphinema*) nematodes (page 259); and a primitive, root-inhabiting fungus *Polymyxa graminis*. More turfgrass-infecting viruses and means of transmission will probably be discovered in the future as we learn more about double infections (e.g., a latent virus and a leaf- or root-infecting fungus or other pathogen).

Mushrooms and Puffballs

A large number of species of fungi that produce mushrooms (toadstools) and puffballs feed on decaying organic matter in the soil. These fungi, including those that produce fairy rings (page 234), are most common around dead and buried stumps, roots, boards, or excess thatch. The spore-producing mushrooms and puffballs, which are 1 to 12 in. in diameter, appear after heavy rains or watering (Figure 5.39). Some mushrooms and puffballs are foul-smelling, and a few are poisonous. These nuisance fungi overwinter as mycelial spawn in the soil and in decaying organic matter. The fruiting bodies produce tremendous numbers of microscopic spores (basidiospores) which are spread by air currents, water, turfgrass equipment, and tools of all kinds.

The control for mushrooms and puffballs, where practical, is to carefully dig up and destroy rotting stumps, roots, or other underground sources of organic debris. If you suspect the fungi of being poisonous to children or pets, break or mow off the fruiting bodies when first seen. Mushrooms and puffballs will disappear naturally only when the food base in the soil is exhausted. This process may take 10 years or more for a large stump or root.

Nigrospora Blight

Nigrospora blight, caused by the common fungus *Nigrospora sphaerica,* has been observed in the northern United States during midsummer droughts on Kentucky bluegrass, peren-

Figure 5.39 Mushrooms of *Coprinus lagopus* growing in a lawn. (Courtesy B. J. Jacobsen.)

nial ryegrass, and creeping red and chewings fescues. In the south it occurs on St. Augustinegrass in spring and early summer. The disease is easily confused with Ascochyta leaf blight (page 222), dollar spot (page 228), Pythium blight (page 265), and Leptosphaerulina leaf blight (page 252) unless you use a microscope. The *Nigrospora* fungus infects a wide range of plants besides turfgrasses.

Symptoms. Large areas of cool-season grasses (bluegrasses, ryegrasses, and fescues) become uniformly blighted or irregular patches, 4 to 8 in. in diameter, are evident (*Color plate 45*). Individual leaves die back from the tip, often with uniform lesions that extend down to the leaf sheath. Less commonly, water-soaked spots form on the leaf blade or sheath which quickly fade to tan (Figure 5.40). On some cultivars the tan lesions have a purple to reddish-brown border. The lesions may girdle the leaf blade, causing the part beyond to be tan and twisted. On other Kentucky bluegrass cultivars, the dying leaves turn a deep purple.

Figure 5.40 *Nigrospora* lesions on leaves of Kentucky bluegrass. (Courtesy R. W. Smiley.)

Key to Infectious Turfgrass Diseases

255

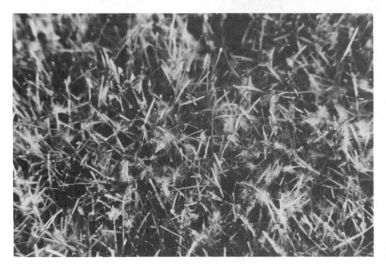

Figure 5.41 Close-up of Nigrospora blight. (Courtesy R. W. Smiley.)

In warm, very damp weather a fluffy white mycelium forms over the blighted leaf blades (Figure 5.41). This symptom is easily confused with dollar spot and Pythium blight.

Dark, often elongated and girdling lesions form on the stolons of St. Augustinegrass under close mowing. The lesions cause the shoots at the end of the stolons to wilt, turn yellow, and die resulting in a general thinning or patchiness of diseased turf.

Disease Cycle. The fungus is believed to survive unfavorable growing periods as round, black, shiny spores (conidia), and mycelium in grass debris (Figure 5.11). The spores germinate in warm, moist weather and are believed to be splashed, blown, or carried to stressed and weakened but otherwise healthy grass plants on turfgrass equipment and shoes. New infections occur where the fluffy, white aerial mycelium contacts healthy leaf tissue and also colonizes the leaf tips (probably after growing in the guttated fluid or dew). The conidia are produced in or on infected leaf tissue.

On St. Augustinegrass the disease is commonly associated with hot, dry growing conditions during the summer. Nigrospora blight also appears to be more severe on turfgrass affected by St. Augustinegrass decline (page 286).

Control. Follow suggested cultural practices (page 212 to 214) to keep the turfgrass growing steadily. Avoid severe moisture, nutritional, and other stresses. Apply adequate amounts of a balanced (N-P-K) fertilizer. Irrigate thoroughly (soil moist 2 to 3 in. deep) at 3- to 4-day intervals during prolonged hot, dry periods. Water turf in the morning so that it will be dry by evening. Avoid applications of herbicide or laying new sod during or just before prolonged periods of hot, damp weather. On St. Augustinegrass raise the cutting height in hot weather to cover the exposed stolons. Cultivars of perennial ryegrass, Kentucky bluegrass, and fescues differ in their resistance.

Where Nigrospora blight is severe and a recurring problem, apply a fungicide such as Chipco 26019, Acti-dione RZ, or Daconil 2787 following the manufacturer's directions.

Physoderma Brown Spot

Physoderma brown spot, caused by the fungi *Physoderma maydis, P. paspali,* and *P. graminis,* is a relatively rare disease of bentgrasses, bermudagrass, fescues, bahiagrass, turf timothy, and wheatgrasses.

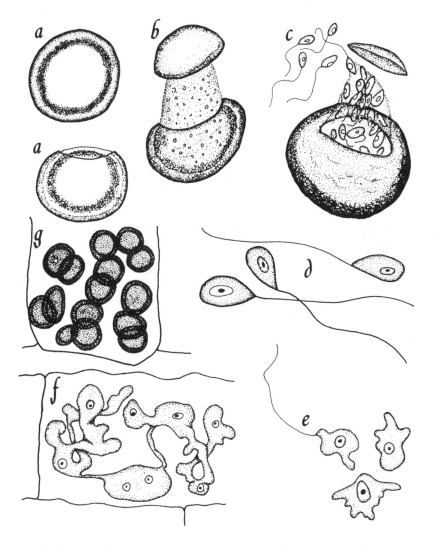

Figure 5.42 Physoderma brown spot. Stages in the life cycle of *Physoderma maydis* as seen through a high-power microscope. a, Two sporangia or resting spores, top and side views; b, opening of a sporangium showing an early stage of zoospore formation with the operculum (lid) being carried up by the enlarging sporangium; c, mature zoospores escaping through the top of the resting spore; d, zoospores with a single flagellum; e, germinating zoospores, amoeboid stage; f, *Physoderma* mycelium within a leaf cell beginning to form sporangia; g, a cell filled with mature resting sporangia.

Symptoms.   Small yellowish spots or stripes, which gradually turn brown and finally ash gray, form in the leaves. The lesions may be oval to somewhat elongated and may merge to form bands across the leaf blade. When severe, the crown may rot and a wilting and shredding of the leaves can occur. Diseased plants are dwarfed with yellow, stiff, upright leaves that may be confused with yellow tuft or downy mildew (page 232).

Disease Cycle.   The fungi overseason as microscopic, round, golden-brown sporangia in infected leaves (Figure 5.42) or in soil. In warm (73 to 86°F), wet weather

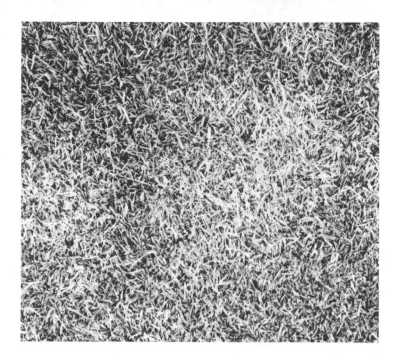

Figure 5.43 Pink patch infecting Penncross creeping bentgrass. (Courtesy P. H. Dernoeden.)

swimming spores (zoospores) are released from the sporangia and move in water to infect the lower leaves and crown. The disease cycle may be repeated at 2- or 3-week intervals as long as prolonged, warm, moist weather continues.

Control. Provide for good surface and subsurface drainage when preparing a new turf area. Water during the morning hours so that the grass surface will be dry before evening. The fungicides suggested to control Pythium blight (Table 5.4), especially Subdue, should be effective in checking Physoderma brown spot.

Pink Patch

Pink patch, formerly thought to be a form of red thread (page 270), and caused by the fungus *Limonomyces roseipellis,* is a minor disease of frequently mowed grass. The disease is apparently restricted to perennial ryegrass, Kentucky bluegrass, creeping red and chewings fescues, creeping bentgrass, bermudagrass, and zoysiagrass. Pink patch is much more severe on unmowed or infrequently mowed grasses grown under low-nitrogen fertilization than on highly maintained turfgrasses.

Symptoms. Although patches generally remain green, diseased turf may have a tannish cast. Affected areas are irregularly shaped in coarse-textured turf, but distinct pinkish patches, 2 to 6 in. across, occur in creeping bentgrass (Figure 5.43). The disease occurs in spring and autumn when air temperatures are 60 to 75 °F coupled with prolonged periods of heavy dews, light rains, and fog on turf with inadequate nitrogen fertility. Small, irregularly shaped areas of turf become covered with a pink to reddish film of mycelium that tends to form first along the leaf margins bordered by light green to yellow bands of leaf tissue; later, the entire width of the leaf blade develops a pinkish cast. Only leaves and sheaths are infected, and diseased leaves die (turn light brown to tan) from the tip downward. There are three key diagnostic characteristics used to separate pink patch and red thread: the red threads (i.e., sclerotia) and arthroconidia are *not* produced by the pink patch fungus; and hyphae of the *Limonomyces* fungus have clamp connections (Figure 5.2); whereas the hyphae of the red thread fungus do not.

Disease Cycle. Similar to red thread (page 270) except for the absence of arthroconidia.

Control. Mow frequently at the recommended height of cut for the grass or grasses grown. Fertilize based on soil test recommendations.

Plant-Parasitic Nematodes

Some of the more important types of nematodes that reduce turfgrass vigor and result in yellowing and stunting of grass plants include: lance (*Hoplolaimus* spp.), sting (*Belonolaimus* spp.), ring (*Criconemella, Criconemoides* spp.), root-knot (*Meloidogyne* spp.), lesion (*Pratylenchus* spp.), stubby-root (*Paratrichodorus* and *Trichodorus* spp.), stunt or stylet (*Tylenchorhynchus* and *Merlinus* spp.), dagger (*Xiphinema* spp.), needle (*Longidorus* spp.), sheath (*Hemicycliophora* spp.), burrowing (*Radopholus similus*), spiral (*Helicotylenchus* spp.), awl (*Dolichodorus* spp.), pin (*Paratylenchus* spp.), false root-knot (*Hypsoperine* spp.), cyst (*Heterodera* spp., *Punctodera* spp.), and *Anguina radicicola* (Figure 5.7).

All plant-parasitic nematodes are obligate parasites and must feed on living plants to complete their life cycle. Almost all feed on plant root cells by puncturing walls with a hollow stylet that resembles a minute hypodermic needle, injecting enzymes into cells, and then ingesting the partially digested contents.

Plant-parasitic nematodes are divided into two major groups according to their parasitic behavior: *Ectoparasitic nematodes* spend their life cycles outside the host and feed by inserting their stylets to varying depths within the root tissues (Figure 5.44). *Endo-*

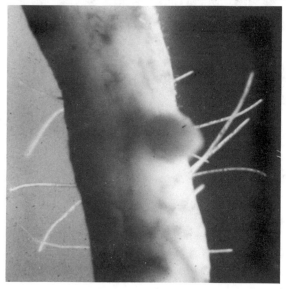

Figure 5.44 Lance (*Hoplolaimus*) nematodes feeding on a root of St. Augustinegrass.

Figure 5.45 Severe stunt nematode damage to centipedegrass; right, close-up of affected roots. (Courtesy W. M. Powell.)

parasites feed both externally on and internally within plant roots, often becoming only partially embedded in roots (semi-endoparasites). Most forms remain motile throughout their life cycles and "browse" on roots. A few (e.g., root-knot and cyst) become immotile, assuming a sedentary parasitic habit (*Color plate 46*).

Symptoms. Heavily nematode-infested turf lacks vigor and declines in growth, often appearing off-color, yellow, bunchy, and stunted. Grass blades dying back from the tips are often interspersed with apparently healthy leaves. In hot, dry weather such nematode-injured turf may thin out, wilt, and possibly die, usually in scattered, round to irregular patches during the summer (Figures 5.45 and 5.46). Hybrid bermudagrass golf greens are severely damaged by sting nematodes in the south (*Color plate 47*). Such

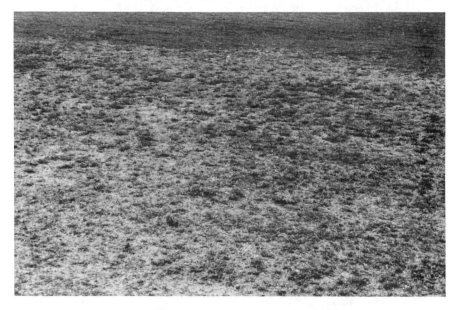

Figure 5.46 Severe nematode injury; turf in the background is treated with a nematicide. (Courtesy G. C. Smart.)

turf is also more susceptible to winterkill, serious insect injury, and other diseases. The severity of symptoms varies with soil moisture, texture and fertility, the population of plant-parasitic nematodes, and the particular species feeding on and in the roots. Symptoms are easily confused with fertilizer or pesticide burn, malnutrition, poor soil aeration and compaction, drought or excessive soil moisture, insects, diseases, and other types of injury. Heavily infested grass does not respond normally to applications of water, fertilizer, fungicides, or to increased aeration (coring) and thatch removal. Feeder root systems are greatly reduced, shallow, and may be coarse, swollen, stubby, excessively branched, show swellings or galls, and are dark in color (Figure 5.45).

Nematodes damage roots in two major ways. Root cells are injured or killed mechanically or chemically (apparently through the secretion or injection of enzymes). Such damage renders the roots less efficient in absorbing and transporting water and nutrients. In many cases root growth ceases. Nematodes also interact with fungal or bacterial pathogens to cause disease complexes that often damage roots more severely than when either the nematode or other pathogen is present alone. Nematode damage is often difficult to separate from injury due to insects or other pests.

In more severe cases, the primary symptoms of nematode damage may include various combinations of the following:

1. *Stunting:* suppressed plant growth. Plants are often somewhat uneven in height, usually in irregular areas, giving the turf a ragged overall appearance (Figure 5.46).
2. *Chlorosis or other discoloration:* loss of green color and yellowing similar to nitrogen, iron, magnesium, manganese, or zinc deficiency (*Color plate 47*).
3. *Wilting:* enhanced by wind and bright sunlight. Plants often slowly recover at night.
4. *Dieback of leaves:* plants often show a slow general decline in growth and vigor. Such plants do not respond normally to water, fertilizer, or fungicides.
5. *Root lesions:* dark brown or black, often sunken discolored areas in roots result from continued nematode feeding and invasion by other soil microorganisms. Lesion size increases from pinpoint spots to large necrotic areas. Root-rotting fungi often invade tissues damaged by root-lesion nematodes, accelerating lesion enlargement.
6. *Root swellings:* indistinct swellings, primarily of the root tips, to knotlike galls throughout the root system often are accompanied by excessive production of branch roots ("hairy-root") above the swelling (Figure 5.47).
7. *Injured or devitalized root tips:* cessation of root growth caused by feeding at or near the root tips. Tissues may retain a normal white color or turn brown and die. Devitalization frequently causes excessive production of roots near the soil surface.
   a. *Stubby roots:* root system composed of numerous short, stubby branches often arranged in clusters (Figure 5.45).
   b. *Coarse roots:* root system with few or no branch roots or feeder roots.
8. *Reduced and discolored root system:* overall reduction in the normal size of the root system accompanied by light to dark browning or blackening.
9. *Growth reduction:* growth as measured by yields of clippings is greatly reduced.

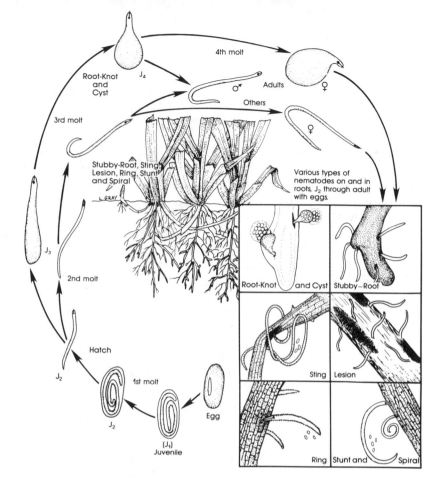

Figure 5.47 Life cycles of common parasitic nematodes that attack turfgrasses.

Disease Cycle.   The life cycle of most plant-parasitic nematodes, although varying in details, is simple and direct (Figure 5.47). Plant-parasitic nematodes in turf must have living grass tissue in order to feed, survive, and reproduce. They overwinter in the soil, grass debris, or within living roots as eggs, cysts, or juveniles (larvae). Juveniles hatch from eggs deposited by the female in the soil or within root tissue and usually resemble adults in structure and appearance. Nematodes develop through three or four stages (instars) after hatching, each completed by a molt, and become adults after the final molt. Adult nematodes, which reproduce either sexually or parthenogenetically, lay eggs to start the next generation. Under optimum conditions, most plant-parasitic species complete their life cycle in 20 to 60 days, although some, such as the dagger nematode (*Xiphinema americanum*), may require 9 months or longer to complete a cycle.

Mobility in soil, feeding and reproduction require water films. Damage is most common in sandy or sandy loam soils low in nutrients where water is deficient or abundant.

The optimum temperature for most nematodes is 60 to 85 °F. Nematode activity is stimulated by soil moisture in the range that is readily available to grass roots; their activity is restricted in dry soils and in saturated soils deficient in oxygen. Highly compacted and heavy-textured soils are less favorable than coarse-textured and sandy soils for nematode activity. Nematodes are generally most active and numerous on cool-season grasses in middle to late spring and in autumn. On warm-season grasses activity is greatest during the summer and autumn. Heavily infested turf usually becomes apparent only when the grass is under moisture, heat, and nutritional stresses, or other conditions unfavorable for growth of the grass.

Nematodes move very slowly in soil under their own power—perhaps a foot or two per year. People, however, easily spread them from one area to another in infested plant material or the accompanying soil by cultivation and watering practices, and so on.

The presence and identity of plant-parasitic nematodes can be determined *only* by taking plugs of suspected turf with underlying soil, and having this examined by a competent nematologist in a well-equipped laboratory. Most land-grant universities (see the list on page 397) provide a nematode assay service and make suggestions for their control. There may be a charge for this service.

To determine if nematodes are the cause of a decline in turfgrass vigor, first examine the turf carefully to eliminate other likely causes. Check for injury by insects and other animal life (Chapter 4), diseases, possible soil deficiencies, fertilizer or pesticide damage, frost or high-temperature injury, too much or too little water, and so on (Chapter 2). After examination, if nematodes are still suspected, contact your local county cooperative extension office for further information regarding identification of parasitic types. Soil from around the feeder roots of turfgrass plants in an *early* stage of decline is likely to contain many more nematodes than soil from around the roots of badly diseased or dead plants. Information on how to collect and mail turfgrass specimens for a nematode assay is given in Chapter 1.

Control.   Keep grass growing vigorously through proper watering, fertilizing, thatch removal, aerification, and other recommended cultural practices (see Chapter 2 and the beginning of this chapter). Applications of activated sewage sludge as a fertilizer enhances biological control of nematodes.

If not starting from seed, buy only top-quality, nematode-free sod, sprigs, and plugs from a reputable nurseryman who realizes the necessity of producing nematode-free turf. Before planting, take soil samples and have them assayed by a competent nematologist. Follow the suggestions in the report.

If plant-parasitic nematodes are found in large numbers, treat the soil *before* planting, using a nematicide or a general-purpose soil fumigant (Table 5.4) that controls fungi, insects, and weed seeds as well as nematodes. These chemicals should be applied only by an experienced and licensed pesticide applicator who has the proper application equipment and training in handling restricted use chemicals.

On existing turf, take samples from suspect areas and have them assayed to see if a nematode problem exists. It may be suggested that a nematicide (Table 5.4) be drenched into the soil when the weather is cool. Again, this is usually a job for an experienced commercial applicator. *Never* apply a nematicide without first having a nematode analysis.

Proper site preparation and the use of nematode-free planting and topdressing materials is much more satisfactory than trying to eliminate high populations after the turfgrass is established. No turfgrass species or cultivars are resistant to all nematode species.

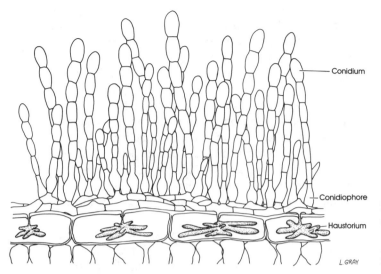

Conidium

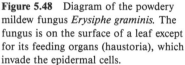

Conidiophore

Haustorium

L GRAY

Figure 5.48 Diagram of the powdery mildew fungus *Erysiphe graminis*. The fungus is on the surface of a leaf except for its feeding organs (haustoria), which invade the epidermal cells.

Powdery Mildew

Powdery mildew is caused by the fungus *Erysiphe graminis* which attacks a wide range of grasses including cereals. The disease occurs most commonly on Kentucky bluegrass, bermudagrass, redtop, fine-leaved fescues, and zoysiagrass. Highly specialized physiologic races of the fungus occur that only attack certain cultivars of one or a few turfgrass species.

Powdery mildew has become an increasingly important disease of Baron, Cheri, Fylking, Kenblue, Merion, Windsor, and other Kentucky bluegrasses in recent years. High-nitrogen fertilizers cause a dense growth of grass that creates an ideal environment for the mildew fungus. Resistance to powdery mildew is known to exist in several cultivars of Kentucky bluegrass, bermudagrass, and in several species of bluegrass and fescues.

Powdery mildew is much more severe where air circulation is reduced and the grass is growing in shaded areas (on north and east sides of buildings, under dense trees and shrubs) than in full sun. Attacks occur chiefly in the spring, late summer, and autumn when days are mild and cloudy, and nights are cool and damp. Powdery mildew is an important cause of deterioration of shady bluegrass and zoysiagrass lawns, as it significantly reduces the growth of leaves, roots, and rhizomes. A severe attack may weaken and kill the plants, especially in crowded, newly planted areas. The surviving plants are more susceptible to winterkill, drought, and attack by other disease-causing fungi.

Powdery mildew fungi live chiefly on the outer surface of the host plant. They obtain food and water by means of small, branched, rootlike organs (haustoria) that penetrate the grass leaf or sheath and enter the surface layer of cells (epidermis) (Figure 5.48).

Symptoms.   Powdery mildew appears first as superficial patches of white to light gray, dusty growth (mycelium) on the leaves and leaf sheaths (*Color plate 48*). These patches enlarge rapidly and merge, becoming more dense. The lower leaves are often completely covered. The leaf tissue under the mildew becomes yellowed soon after infection and later turns tan or brown. Heavily infected leaves gradually dry up and die. In severe outbreaks, large areas or entire grass stands are dull white, as if dusted with flour or lime.

Disease Cycle. The powdery appearance of mildew is due to the production of tremendous numbers of microscopic spores (conidia) in chains (Figures 5.11 and 5.48). The conidia are easily carried by air currents and cause new infections within 2 hours after landing on a leaf during cool (55 to 70°F; optimum 65°F), humid, cloudy weather. With a favorable temperature and high atmospheric humidity, spores are continuously produced for 7 to 14 days until the host tissue dies. The conidia are easily carried to other grass plants in the same or neighboring turf areas, where they produce new infections and start the cycle once again. New conidia may be produced within a week after infection occurs.

As the fungus matures, the mycelium forms dense mats. Occasionally, speck-sized, black, fungus-fruiting bodies (cleistothecia) develop in the mycelial mats during autumn. These bodies are especially evident on dead grass leaves. Sexual or overwintering spores (ascospores) are sometimes produced in the cleistothecia. Cleistothecia, however, are not common in turfgrasses. The powdery mildew fungus survives the winter as cleistothecia on dead plant tissues and as mycelial mats on living grass plants. The ascospores and/or conidia are released in early spring and produce the initial infections.

Control. Increase light penetration, air movement, and drying of the grass surface by pruning or selectively removing dense trees and shrubs that shade or border turf areas. Space landscape plants properly to allow adequate air movement and to avoid excessive shade. Certain shade-tolerant cultivars of Kentucky bluegrass (e.g., America, A-34 (Bensun), Bristol, Dormie, Eclipse, Enmundi, Glade, Mystic, Nugget, and Sydsport), the fine-leaved fescues (especially Houndog), Rebel tall fescue, and roughstalk bluegrass (*Poa trivialis*) do relatively well in open shady areas. Where shade is dense, it may be necessary to grow a shade-tolerant ground cover such as Japanese spurge (*Pachysandra*) and myrtle or periwinkle (*Vinca*).

Keep the turf vigorous and growing steadily by fertilizing on the basis of local recommendations for the grass(es) grown and a soil test. Recommendations will vary with the cultivar or blend grown and its use. Avoid overfeeding, especially with fertilizers containing large amounts of soluble nitrogen. Follow the other cultural practices outlined on pages 212 to 214.

On high-value turfs, where powdery mildew consistently reoccurs, a fungicide program is economically practical. When powdery mildew is *first* evident in the spring or early autumn, two or more applications of a suggested fungicide (Table 5.4) at 7- to 21-day intervals should control the disease. For effective control of powdery mildew, spray 1000 sq ft uniformly with 1 to 3 gal of water containing a small amount of surfactant or commercial spreader-sticker (about ½ to 1 teaspoonful per gallon or 1 pint to 1 quart per 100 gal). Follow the manufacturer's directions. Thorough coverage of the grass leaves with each spray is essential for good control.

Pythium Blight

Pythium blight, also known as grease spot, spot blight, and cottony blight, is caused by 14 or more species of soilborne fungi in the genus *Pythium,* especially *P. aphanidermatum* (*P. butleri*) and *P. graminicola*. All cultivated turfgrasses, especially bentgrasses, annual bluegrass, and ryegrasses, are susceptible to attack. Minor attacks of Pythium blight can occur at cool temperatures in winter, spring, and autumn during prolonged wet weather when temperatures are 50 to 65 °F (Figure 5.49). Pythium blight can be devastating during hot (80 to 95 °F), wet, or very humid weather when the grass is dense and lush and there is little air movement. During hot (90 to 95 °F), humid weather an outbreak of Pythium blight may develop and spread very rapidly, killing large areas of seedling or established turf overnight. The disease is serious in the south on overseeded bermudagrass greens.

Symptoms. Small, distinct, round to irregularly shaped, sunken spots, up to 4 to 6 in. in diameter (sometimes as large as 12 in.) suddenly appear during hot or cool, very wet, calm weather. The grass leaves at first are water-soaked, slimy to the touch, and dark in color during the early morning. They quickly fade from reddish brown to a light tan as the grass blades dry out and shrivel (Figure 5.50). When the air is moisture saturated, especially at night or in the early morning, the water-soaked grass leaves collapse and appear matted together by a fluffy, white to purplish gray, cobwebby mass of fungus mycelium; hence the name "cottony blight" (*Color plate 49*). Clusters of blighted plants may form long streaks up to 1 ft or more wide. These patterns apparently develop because spores and mycelium of the *Pythium* fungus (or fungi) are easily spread by surface drainage water, foot traffic, and by mowing when the grass is wet.

If the growth of the *Pythium* fungus is checked by a sudden drop in temperature or humidity before entire leaf blades are blighted, distinct straw-colored spots or patches develop. These spots resemble those of dollar spot (page 228) and Nigrospora blight (page 254), except they do not have brown or reddish-brown borders. Pythium-infected grass blades commonly twist, collapse, and die (Figure 5.50).

Grass seedlings affected with Pythium blight develop a watery rot, or they may wilt, collapse, and die (damp-off) in irregular patches. This condition is very common in a seedbed that is overly wet and where surface drainage is poor (see Seed Decay, Damping-off, and Seedling Blights, page 287).

Species of *Pythium* cause more root rot and damage to the crowns of grass plants in cool (60 °F), warm, and hot wet weather than is generally recognized. *Pythium aristosporum* and *P. arrhenomanes* colonize the secondary roots of creeping bentgrass in golf greens with a high sand content. Infection results in slower growth, an off color, stunted white roots, and a thinning out of grass plants. Infected plants are killed very rapidly during hot periods. Pythium blight is often followed by other organisms, including blue and green algae (page 41) and *Curvularia, Bipolaris, Drechslera,* and *Exserohilum* fungi (pages 228 to 242). There is also some evidence of a close association between species of *Pythium* and certain plant-parasitic nematodes (page 259).

Disease Cycle. Species of *Pythium* are water-mold fungi that are common in the grass thatch or mat and are widely distributed in many soils. Other species of *Pythium* that may kill or blight turfgrasses (besides *Pythium aphanidermatum,* and *P. graminicola*) include *P. afertile, P. aristosporum, P. arrhenomanes, P. catenulatum, P. debaryanum, P. dissoticum, P. irregulare, P. iwayamai, P. myriotylum, P. rostratum, P. torulosum, P. ultimum, P. vanterpoolii,* and *P. vexans.* (Some researchers feel that *Pythium arrhenomanes* is the same as *P. graminicola.*) Only an expert with a good compound light microscope and the right

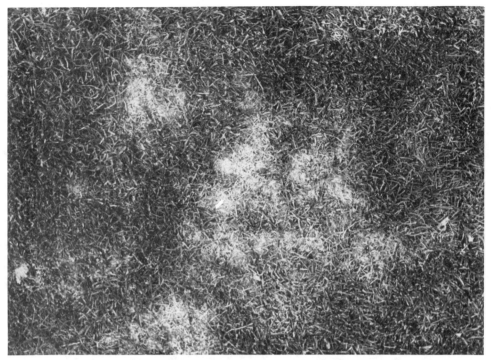

Figure 5.49 Pythium blight spots in Kentucky bluegrass turf.

Figure 5.50 Pythium blight has caused the collapse of Kentucky bluegrass leaves in this patch.

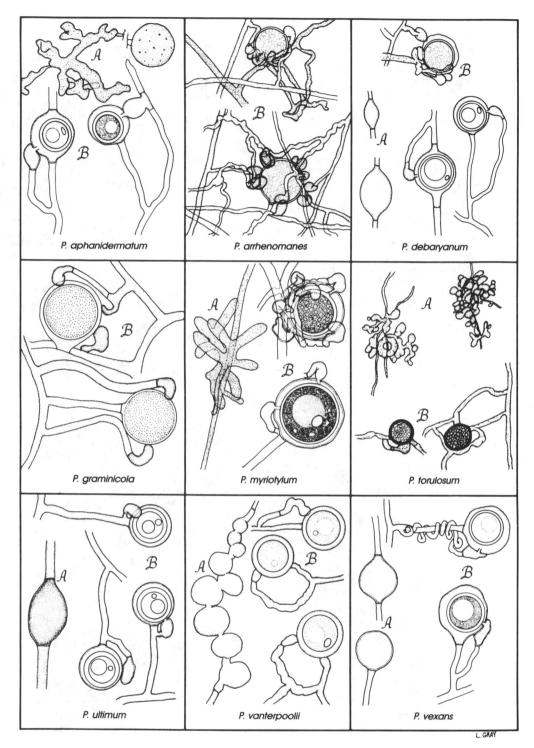

L. GRAY

Figure 5.51 Nine species of *Pythium* that cause diseases of turfgrasses. A, Various types of sporangia; B, types of sex organs (oogonia with oospores and antheridia).

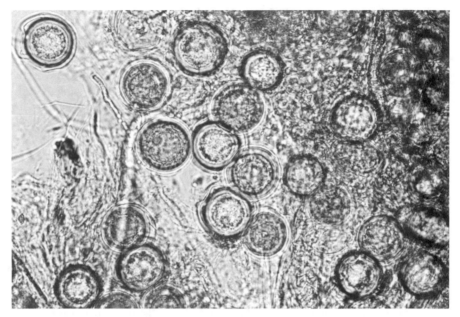

Figure 5.52 Oospores of *Pythium* sp. as seen under a high-power microscope. (Courtesy R. C. Avenius.)

stage of fungal development can identify species of *Pythium* (Figure 5.51). Commonly, two or more species may be present and killing turf at any one time.

Pythium fungi are commonly present in diseased turfgrass, thatch debris, and soil in the form of delicate, nonseptate mycelium (Figure 5.2) and round, thick-walled resting spores (oospores) embedded in dead grass tissue (Figure 5.52).

When favorable temperature and moisture conditions occur, the mycelium resumes rapid growth, while the oospores germinate to produce sporangia (bearing spores) or hyphae. The sporangia, in turn, may germinate to produce either motile zoospores or hyphae. All spores can germinate and produce hyphae capable of infecting grass plants within an hour or two.

Living and dead grass plants that were invaded earlier in the season or during the previous season commonly serve as infection centers. Disease develops rapidly from these centers by means of a cobweblike, hyphal growth of the fungus from leaf to leaf and plant to plant. Spreading of the disease occurs by very rapid growth or when oospores and zoospores, diseased plant parts, or *Pythium*-infested soil is moved by mowers, other maintenance equipment, shoes, feet of people and animals, or surface water.

The blighting of grass and the growth of *Pythium* species are most rapid and severe in moisture saturated air when air temperatures are 85 to 95 °F, with a minimum of 68 °F at night. At temperatures of 90 to 95 °F a much shorter time is required to destroy a stand of grass completely. Pythium blight is especially severe in dense lush grass in low-lying areas that have poor soil drainage and where air movement is poor. Algae (page 41) often invade diseased patches and may cause a hard dark crust.

Disease development is greater with a thick thatch and with high-nitrogen fertility or a high level of balanced fertility than with a low-fertility level.

Key to Infectious Turfgrass Diseases

Control. Follow the suggested cultural practices outlined on pages 212 to 214. Good air movement over the turf is very important.

Buy top-quality seed, sod, sprigs, or plugs from a reputable dealer. Sow seed treated with a fungicide (Table 5.4) and seed at the suggested rate. If possible, plant when the weather is cool and dry. The seedbed should be well prepared and fertile. Avoid overwatering, especially from the time of seeding, plugging, or sprigging to seedling emergence or plant establishment. Water early in the day so the grass can dry before night.

Avoid mowing when the grass is wet and avoid watering during periods of intense disease activity.

There are *no* known resistant cultivars of any turfgrass species except bermudagrass. Most of the improved cultivars of the latter grass (e.g., Everglades, Florida 50, Texas 22, Texturf, Tiffine, Tiflawn, and Tifway) are highly tolerant to Pythium blight when mature.

In southern states, delay overseeding bermudagrass and other warm-season grasses with cool-season grasses until the onset of cool weather. If winter grasses must be established in early fall, applications of a fungicide (Table 5.4) at seeding time and again at 5- to 21-day intervals during warm, moist periods will largely eliminate disease damage. Annual bluegrass is more seriously damaged on overseeded greens than is perennial ryegrass.

During extended periods of hot, wet weather, a *preventative* fungicide spray program (Table 5.4) will be needed when cultural practices do not check the development of Pythium blight. The first spray application should be made as soon as night temperatures are expected to remain at 68 °F or above, when daytime air temperatures are 80 °F or higher, and when the forecast is for continued wet or very humid weather. Depending on the fungicide used, repeat applications are needed at 5- to 21-day intervals as long as the weather stays hot and humid. For the most effective control of Pythium blight on established turf, uniformly spray 1000 sq ft of turf with the proper fungicide mixture in 10 gal of water.

To control Pythium blight on new seedlings, apply a fungicide (Table 5.4) at the suggested rate immediately after seeding. [Do *not* use chloroneb (Terraneb-SP, Teremec SP), which may affect seed germination.] Repeat within 5 to 7 days if the soil is wet and environmental conditions remain favorable for disease development. When mixing or applying any fungicide, carefully follow the manufacturer's directions and precautions.

Red Thread

Red thread is caused by the fungus *Laetisaria fuciformis* (formerly called *Corticium fuciforme*). It is an important disease, especially of slow-growing, nitrogen-deficient turf, in cooler, and more humid areas during cool (65 to 75 °F), prolonged damp weather in the spring and autumn. It has even been found growing under the snow. Susceptible turfgrasses include Kentucky and annual bluegrasses, several fine-leaved fescues (red, chewings, sheep), tall fescue, bermudagrass, perennial ryegrass, colonial, creeping and velvet bentgrasses, zoysiagrass, velvetgrass, quackgrass, and redtop. Fine-leaved fescues, Kentucky bluegrass, and especially perennial ryegrass are very susceptible. Of the bentgrasses, velvet bentgrass cultivars are more susceptible than colonial and creeping bentgrasses. Although the disease rarely kills plants outright, it does weaken turfgrasses and contributes to the decline and death of grass plants from subsequent stresses or diseases.

Figure 5.53 (left) Close-up of red thread. (Courtesy R. W. Smiley.)

Figure 5.54 (below) Red thread in red fescue turf. (Courtesy D. H. Scott.)

Symptoms. The *Laetisaria* fungus forms conspicuous, coral-pink, orange, or red mycelial masses on the leaves and sheaths. During prolonged periods of overcast, moisture-saturated air, the gelatinous mycelial masses may completely cover the leaves. The faintly pink web of mycelium may also mat the leaves and leaf sheaths together (Figure 5.53). The gelatinous masses, usually ¹⁄₁₆ to over ¼ in. long, are formed by strands of branched hyphae. They often protrude from the tips of leaves and leaf sheaths as pointed and sometimes as branched, antlerlike appendages (*Color plate 50*). The bright coral-pink to blood-red mycelial mats harden, become threadlike (red threads) when they dry, and function as sclerotia.

Small patches of infected leaves and sheaths appear water-soaked at first. They shrivel and die rapidly, fading to a bleached tan when dry. Death usually progresses from the leaf tip downward. Where infection is severe, diseased turf is yellowed or "scorched" in circular to irregular patches, which are usually 2 to 6 in. in diameter. Dead leaves are generally interspersed with apparently healthy leaves, giving diseased turf a scorched and ragged appearance (Figure 5.54). The spots may be scattered within a turf area or a number of patches may merge to form large, irregular areas of blighted turfgrass having a reddish-brown or tan cast. Only the leaves and sheaths are infected.

Disease Cycle. The *Laetisaria* fungus survives from season to season as threads of dried, dormant mycelium on the leaves and in the debris of previously infected plants. The fungus is disseminated to healthy turf areas by bits of red threads, arthroconidia, basidiospores, and as dormant mycelium in infected leaf tissue. Spreading may occur mechanically on mowers and other turf equipment, shoes, and by wind and splashing or flowing water. The fungus can infect healthy leaves through the stomates, but commonly invades the cut leaf tips.

Infection and disease development are favored by air temperatures of 60 to 75 °F, coupled with prolonged periods of overcast weather, light rains, fog, heavy dews, and moisture-saturated air. Slow-growing and poorly nourished turfs are most severely attacked. Growth of the fungus and disease development ceases below 33 °F and above 86 °F. (Optimum growth of the fungus in culture is between 60 and 70 °F). However, the pathogen remains alive and continues its activity when conditions again become suitable for disease development.

Control. Follow the cultural control suggestions outlined on pages 212 to 214. Maintain adequate and *balanced* fertility, based on soil tests and the recommended turfgrass fertilization program for your area and the turfgrasses grown. Red thread is *most* severe where potassium, phosphorus, calcium, and especially nitrogen are deficient. Avoid overstimulation with fertilizer, particularly with a quickly available, high-nitrogen product.

Where red thread has been a problem in the past, maintain a soil reaction (pH) between 6.5 and 7.0. Test the soil pH, and treat the soil accordingly, if practical.

Collecting grass clippings during periods when the grass is growing slowly and the disease is active may reduce the number of red threads that eventually fall back into the turf.

Where red thread has been particularly devastating, apply one of the suggested fungicides (Table 5.4) at 10- to 14-day intervals during prolonged, moist weather in the spring and autumn when daytime temperatures average between 65 and 75 °F. Start applications when the disease is *first* evident. Apply the fungicide in 5 to 10 gal of water per 1000 sq ft of turfgrass to ensure proper wetting.

Somewhat resistant ryegrasses include Citation II, Delray, Prelude, Premier, Regal, and Tara; Caprice, Caravelle, Elka, Pippin, and NK–200 are very susceptible. Acclaim, All-Star, Barry, Birdie, Citation, Cockade, Cowboy, Cupido, Dasher, Derby, Diplomat, Eaton, Elka, Ensporta, Epic, Fiesta, Game, Manhattan II, Omega, Palmer, Pelo, Pennfine, Ranger, Repell, and Yorktown perennial ryegrasses lie somewhere in between. Fine-leaved resistant fescues to red thread include Atlanta, Aurora, Banner, Beauty, Bighorn, Biljart, Center, Dawson, Epsom, Golfrood, Highlight, Jamestown, Koket, Longfellow, Magenta, Mary, Pennlawn, Reliant, Robot, Scaldis, Shadow, Spartan, Valda, Waldina, Waldorf, Weekend, and Wintergreen. Susceptible fine-leaved fescues are Boreal, Ceres, Commodore, Ensylva, and Ruby. Hard fescues are often overseeded where red thread is a serious problem. Somewhat resistant Kentucky bluegrasses include Adelphi, Admiral, Aspen, A-20, Banff, Barblue, Baron, Bonnieblue, Bono, Bristol, Classic, Dormie, Eclipse, Enmundi, Geronimo, Haga, Harmony, Holiday, Majestic, Merit, Midnight, Mona, Monopoly, Mosa, Nassau, Nugget, Plush, Ram I, Touchdown, Trenton, Victa, and Welcome. Susceptible Kentucky bluegrasses include Apart, Argyle, A-34 (Bensun), Glade, Kenblue, Mystic, South Dakota common, and Sydsport.

Rhizoctonia Diseases

Rhizoctonia diseases (Rhizoctonia brown patch or Rhizoctonia blight, Rhizoctonia leaf and sheath blight, and yellow patch or winter brown patch) of turfgrasses are caused by the common soilborne fungi *Rhizoctonia solani, R. cerealis, R. zeae,* and *R. oryzae.* One or more of these fungi are present in practically all soils throughout the world. The fungi are composed of a large number of strains or races that attack a wide range of different plants, including most vegetables, flowers, and field crops.

Symptoms of turfgrasses infected by species of *Rhizoctonia* vary widely and are easily confused with the symptoms of diseases produced by other pathogens. The symptoms vary with the specific combinations of turfgrass cultivar, soil and air environmental conditions, and the specific species and strains (or races) of *Rhizoctonia.* One or more species of *Rhizoctonia* infect all turfgrasses, causing foliar blights as well as seedling blights.

Species of *Rhizoctonia* produce several forms of hyphae that vary with the age of the hyphae. Diagnosticians, with access to a good compound light microscope, distinguish species of *Rhizoctonia* by the mature hyphae, which usually branch at right angles. The hyphal branch is somewhat constricted where it originates and a septum separates the hyphal branch from the parent hypha close to its point of origin (Figure 5.2).

Trying to distinguish between the species of *Rhizoctonia* is difficult and requires special staining procedures to assess the nuclear condition of hyphal cells. The mycelial cells of *R. solani* and *R. zeae* contain an indefinite number of nuclei (multinucleate), those of *R. oryzae* contain four nuclei per cell, and mycelial cells of *R. cerealis* have two nuclei. When grown in the dark on laboratory media, cultures of *R. solani* are usually some shade of brown, *R. cerealis* is buff-colored to white, and the cultures of *R. zeae* are white to salmon or pink. The hyphae of *R. cerealis* are smaller in diameter (2.4 to 6 μm) than the other three species (5 to 11 μm).

Rhizoctonia species usually produce bulbils (sclerotialike structures) in laboratory media and on and in grass plants (Figure 5.55). The bulbils of each species of *Rhizoctonia,* which function as survival structures, vary in color (from white to buff, salmon, brown, red-brown, or black) and size (from ⅟₁₀ to 10 mm in diameter).

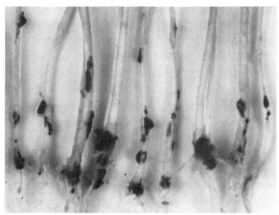

Figure 5.55 Bulbils of *Rhizoctonia solani* on seedlings of Seaside creeping bentgrass.

Brown patch (also known as Rhizoctonia brown patch, Rhizoctonia blight, and Rhizoctonia leaf and sheath blight). *Rhizoctonia solani* is by far the dominant brown patch fungus in the United States. *R. zeae,* which grows best at a higher temperature than *R. solani,* is often associated with brown patch disease in the southern United States, while *R. oryzae* is restricted to subtropical regions.

Brown patch is common in dense, highly fertilized turfgrass during extended periods of hot, moist, overcast weather when the temperature at night is above 60°F and the leaf surfaces are covered with water. *R. solani* will grow at any soil pH, temperature, and moisture level that will support the growth of turfgrasses. Bentgrasses, bluegrasses, St. Augustine-grass, centipedegrass, zoysiagrass, and hybrid bermudagrass are damaged more than other grasses. Colonial bentgrasses are more susceptible than creeping bentgrasses. Bentgrasses that are cut at golf-green height (⅛ to ¼ in.) and grown under a high level of maintenance are particularly susceptible to brown patch. Tall fescue and St. Augustinegrass lawns are most seriously damaged. St. Augustinegrass recovers much more quickly than tall fescue which lacks the stolons needed for recovery.

Symptoms. *On closely clipped bentgrass turf,* such as golf and bowling greens, the disease appears as roughly circular light brown patches that vary in size from a few inches to 2 to 3 ft in diameter (*Color plate 51*). Infected grass blades first appear water-soaked and dark purplish-green, but they soon dry, wither, and turn light brown. The dead leaves remain upright. A dark, purplish to grayish-black "smoke ring," ½ to 2 in. wide and composed of wilted, recently infected grass blades, often marks the advancing margin. This ring, which contains webbed, water-soaked grass, is most noticeable when the air is moisture saturated or during the early morning; it disappears as the grass dries. Usually, only the leaf blades are killed. After several mowings, new but thinned-out grass appears in the affected areas. Algae (page 41) often invade diseased patches and may cause a hard dark crust.

On higher-cut turf, such as home and industrial lawns, parks, athletic fields, and golf course fairways, diseased patches also are usually roughly circular, light brown, matted down, and up to about 2 ft in diameter (Figure 5.56). The patches sometimes develop green centers and may closely resemble the "frogeyes" of summer patch and necrotic ring spot (page 303). Affected areas in St. Augustinegrass are usually straw-colored and up to 50 ft across (Figure 5.57). Diseased patches of grass, however, often appear to be sunken. Grass in the centers of such patches may appear healthy or recover more rapidly, leading to the formation of ring- or doughnut-shaped areas, sometimes called "frogeyes." Symptoms of brown patch in St. Augustinegrass may be confused with chinch bug damage (page 172). Chinch bug–damaged areas are not as well defined as those of brown patch and occur mostly in sunny turf areas. Brown patches up to 20 ft in diameter may develop on hybrid bermudagrasses during cool, wet weather and green-up in the spring. The appearance of the purplish to grayish-black smoke ring borders is rare in St. Augustinegrass and other higher-cut turf. In some cases, a ring pattern is not seen. On St. Augustinegrass, when moisture is excessive, rot occurs in the leaf sheath area, causing the leaf blades to detach. Large areas of higher-cut turfgrasses may be thinned and eventually killed due to root and stem rot. This symptom is especially common on St. Augustinegrass growing in shady, wet areas. An aerial blight is common on centipedegrass, causing light tan lesions on the leaves.

Figure 5.56 Brown patch infecting seedlings of tall fescue. (Courtesy L. T. Lucas.)

Figure 5.57 Brown patch (*Rhizoctonia solani*) seriously affecting St. Augustinegrass turf. (Courtesy O. M. Scott & Sons.)

Key to Infectious Turfgrass Diseases

In light infections of brown patch, the affected turf generally recovers in 2 or 3 weeks. When the attack is severe, however, the crown, rhizomes, stolons, and roots may turn brown and rot. Such turf is thinned or killed out in large areas.

Leaf lesions (called Rhizoctonia leaf and sheath blight) may also result from infection by *Rhizoctonia solani, R. cerealis,* and *R. zeae.* Irregular water-soaked spots appear first. The center turns a straw or ash-brown color and is often surrounded by a dark border (*Color plate 52*). The size of the lesion varies with the turfgrass species, ranging from a large spot (up to 1 cm) on tall fescue to small lesions (about 1.5 mm) on bentgrass and bermudagrass. Turfgrass species on which leaf lesions have been observed include bentgrasses, bluegrasses, perennial ryegrass, tall fescue, bermudagrass, St. Augustinegrass, and zoysiagrass.

Disease Cycle. *Rhizoctonia* fungi survive from year to year, principally in the form of hard, often rounded, dark brown to black, resting bodies (bulbils) that measure about $\frac{1}{16}$ in. in diameter (Figure 5.55). The bulbils, which are seldom seen by turfgrass managers, occur largely in the thatch, diseased grass tissues, and the top $\frac{1}{2}$ in. of soil associated with organic debris. Bulbils, like sclerotia, are extremely resistant to heat, cold, drought, and fungicides. Each bulbil may germinate, cause infection up to 30 times or more, and survive in soil for a number of years. These fungi also survive as hyphae in grass plants and debris. Species of *Rhizoctonia* also grow saprophytically in soil and may invade roots, causing a dark decay.

During moist periods when the soil-thatch temperature is above 47 to 60°F, the bulbils may germinate by sending out hyphae radially through the upper soil and thatch. The result is a roughly circular spot of diseased grass. The hyphae penetrate and infect the grass plants through leaf pores (stomates), directly through leaf and stem tissue, or via mowing wounds. The lower leaves that touch the soil or turf mat are the first ones attacked. The fungus grows throughout the leaf tissues and grows up and over the grass leaves and sheaths. The spread from one grass blade to another occurs through droplets of dew or guttated water exuded at the leaf tips. Nutrients and organic compounds (primarily amino acids and sugars) in the guttated water stimulate rapid fungus growth.

As with bulbils, the mycelium within grass clippings or thatch may resume growth and initiate infections in a film of moisture, as long as the temperature is favorable. Infection and disease development are comparatively slow for *Rhizoctonia solani* at air temperatures below 70 to 75°F. (Brown patch is quite severe on bermudagrass and St. Augustinegrass in the southeast during the spring or fall, especially at temperatures of 60 to 75°F.) However, when the temperature is 80 to 85°F or somewhat above on most grasses and the air is moisture saturated, the fungus grows rapidly. Infection requires the foliage to be wet for more than 12 hours. Large areas of turf can become completely blighted. The pathogenic activity of *R. solani* ceases when the air temperature reaches about 90°F. Temperatures from about 85 to 100°F (optimum about 90°F) are ideal for growth of *R. zeae* and *R. oryzae*. The optimal temperatures for infection and disease development vary, however, for the different strains or races of these species.

Although brown patch may occur at low humidity levels, warm to hot rainy weather and a saturated atmosphere greatly speed disease development.

The severity of the disease is greatest in lush, succulent turf that has been highly fertilized with nitrogen and watered especially at night. Turfgrasses are more susceptible when grown at a moderate to high fertility level than at a low level of nitrogen fertilization. Resistance increases when the levels of phosphorus, and especially potassium, are increased.

Four conditions are necessary for brown patch to develop: the presence of the fungus in an actively growing state; a dense and well-watered stand of grass; prolonged periods of dew or the presence of a film of moisture on the foliage for 12 hours or longer; and a temperature of 70 to 95 °F for at least several hours.

If any of these conditions is lacking, the attack of brown patch will not be severe.

Yellow patch and winter brown patch. Yellow patch or Rhizoctonia yellow patch, formerly called cool-weather brown patch and winter brown patch, is caused by *Rhizoctonia cerealis* (sexual state or telomorph *Ceratobasidium* sp.). Like *R. solani,* it is a common soilborne fungus that can infect all northern turfgrass species. Yellow patch occurs mostly common in Kentucky bluegrass or perennial ryegrass sod that is 2 or more years old with a thatch layer over 1 in. thick. The fungus also attacks annual bluegrass, creeping bentgrass, tall fescue, bermudagrass, zoysiagrass, and probably other turfgrasses. Disease attacks occur in early spring, winter, or autumn during very moist weather when temperatures are cool (below 50 °F). The patches may be scattered and distinct or where numerous the patches may coalesce to involve large turfgrass areas.

Winter brown patch (Figure 5.58) often occurs on bentgrass golf greens from autumn through spring when temperatures are well above freezing. Attacks are usually superficial in that the grass crowns and roots are not usually killed.

Symptoms. Yellow patch and winter brown patch are commonly seen as light green to yellow green, yellow, tan, straw, or bronze-colored rings and crescent-shaped

Figure 5.58 Winter brown patch on a creeping bentgrass golf green. (Courtesy D. H. Scott.)

Key to Infectious Turfgrass Diseases

Figure 5.59 Yellow patch (*Rhizoctonia cerealis*) infecting a Kentucky bluegrass lawn. (Courtesy R. E. Partyka.)

patches, ranging from a few inches to about 3 ft in diameter, often with green grass in the center of the circles (Figure 5.59). Smaller yellow patches usually result from infections that occur under cold, wet conditions. The patches often have a distinctly sunken appearance due to rapid decomposition of the thatch. The leaves of infected grass plants, near the margins of diseased patches, frequently have a characteristic reddish or reddish-purple appearance (*Color plate 53*) which begins at the leaf tip. The symptoms of yellow patch and winter brown patch appear in cool to cold weather (optimum about 40 to 60°F) in the spring, autumn, and winter, and may resemble the "frogeyes" of summer patch and necrotic ring spot (pages 303 to 305). Attacks of summer patch and necrotic ring spot, however, occur in hot weather. Turf affected by yellow patch and winter brown patch often take several months to recover.

Disease Cycle. Relatively little is known about yellow patch. The *R. cerealis* fungus survives from year to year, much as does *Rhizoctonia solani* and other species of *Rhizoctonia,* primarily in the form of minute, dark brown to black bulbils or as mycelium in the thatch, diseased grass tissues, and soil near the surface.

Control. Brown patch, and to a lesser degree yellow patch and winter brown patch, can usually be controlled by following the cultural practices outlined on pages 212 to 214. If yellow patch is serious, applications of nitrogen fertilizer should be reduced in the spring and/or fall or try a slow-release form of nitrogen fertilizer. Avoid fall nitrogen applications on St. Augustinegrass and centipedegrass to reduce the risk of winter outbreaks of brown patch.

No species of turfgrasses are known to be highly resistant to brown patch or yellow patch. Perennial ryegrass cultivars reported to have some tolerance to *Rhizoctonia solani* include All-Star, Barry, Belle, Birdie, Birdie II, Blazer, Citation, Citation II, Derby,

Diplomat, Fiesta, Gator, Manhattan II, Omega, Omega II, Palmer, Pennant, Pennfine, Prelude, Premier, Regal, Repell, Tara, and Yorktown II. Susceptible perennial ryegrasses include Eton, Game, Linn, Manhattan, NK-100 and -200, Paramount, and Yorktown. Tall fescue cultivars that are more tolerant to brown patch include Apache, Arid, Chesapeake, Finelawn I, Galway, Houndog, Jaguar, Johnstone, Olympic, Pacer, and Tempo. Very susceptible tall fescues include Adventure, Barcel, Brookston, Chemfine, Festorina, 5GL, Maverick, NK–81425, Rebel, and Trident. Scaldis is a moderately resistant hard fescue. In a greenhouse study, the most resistant Kentucky bluegrass cultivars to yellow patch included Adelphi and Cheri. Very susceptible cultivars in the same study included A-34 (Bensun), Baron, Fylking, Merion, Parade, Shasta, and Touchdown.

When cultural practices do not check the development of brown patch, a preventive fungicide spray program (Table 5.4) may be needed. This is especially true for bentgrass cut at golf-green height and where a history of disease exists. The first fungicide application should be made when the temperature at night is expected to remain at 65°F or above, the daytime temperature will be 80°F or above, and the air is near the saturation point for 12 hours or longer. Repeat applications are needed at 5- to 14-day intervals during hot, humid weather. When the turf receives over 1.5 in. of water in a week as rain or irrigation, the interval between applications should be shortened to 5 days. Where feasible, the fungicide should be applied in the late afternoon or early evening when the temperature is 80°F or lower.

For the most effective control of brown patch, spray 1000 sq ft uniformly with 5 to 10 gal of fungicide suspension in water. Use the lower fungicide rates listed on the container labels in a routine *preventive* program; higher rates for a *curative* program after disease is evident. It is strongly suggested that a systemic fungicide (e.g., Tersan 1991, Fungo, or Cleary's 3336) be alternated or combined with one of the other chemicals listed in Table 5.4 to avoid future fungicide resistance problems. The use of any one of these products at the recommended rate per 1000 sq ft usually gives effective control for at least 2 weeks.

Alternate or combine any brown patch fungicide with a fungicide to control Pythium blight (page 265; Table 5.4) where it is a problem. Read and follow label directions.

Fungicide use and restrictions are subject to change without notice. When mixing or applying any fungicide, carefully read and follow all the manufacturer's directions and precautions.

Fungicide applications have *not* been completely successful in controlling yellow patch in the field. Based on field trials, two or more sprays of Bayleton, Daconil 2787, and Chipco 26019 gave good control. Applications need to be applied *before* symptoms appear. The most promising materials (Vorlan and Banner), based on a greenhouse study, were applied at a very early stage of infection.

Rhynchosporium Leaf Blotch

Rhynchosporium leaf blotch or scald, caused by the fungi *Rhynchosporium orthosporum* and *R. secalis,* occurs infrequently in prolonged, cool (39 to 71°F), damp weather on fescues, ryegrasses, bentgrasses, and bluegrasses. The same fungi attack a wide range of grass and cereal hosts. Perennial ryegrass is the most susceptible cultivated turfgrass, especially when it is cut infrequently.

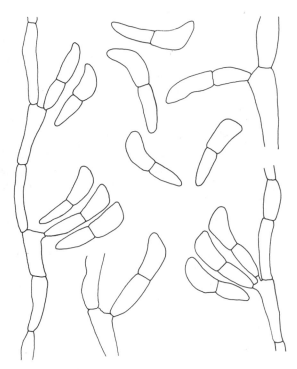

Figure 5.60 *Rhynchosporium secalis* one of two species causing Rhynchosporium leaf blotch or scald.

Symptoms. Distinctly defined, oval to irregular blotches, 2 to 3×10 to 20 mm, form on the leaves in early spring and late autumn. The blotches are grayish green to brown or are gray with a prominent dark brown margin. The lesions may enlarge and merge to blight large areas of a leaf. Diseased leaves often collapse and die back from the tip, becoming light gray to brown.

Disease Cycle. The *Rhynchosporium* fungi overseason as dormant mycelium in living or dead leaves and other grass debris. Large numbers of spores called conidia (Figure 5.60), produced in cool, wet weather in early spring and autumn, are splashed, blown, or carried to healthy leaves (on turfgrass equipment and shoes) where infection occurs. The cycle is repeated as long as the weather remains damp and cool.

Control. No special measures are usually needed to keep Rhynchosporium leaf blotch in check. Follow the suggested cultural control practices outlined on pages 212 to 214. Fungicides applied to control "Helminthosporium" diseases (Table 5.4) should provide adequate control if needed.

Rusts

Practially all commonly grown turfgrasses, including bluegrasses, fescues, ryegrasses, bermudagrass, zoysiagrasses, St. Augustinegrass, wheatgrasses, carpetgrass, turf timothy, weeping alkaligrass, kikuyugrass, bahiagrass, and buffalograss, are attacked by one or more rust fungi in the genera *Puccinia, Uromyces,* and *Physopella* (Table 5.3). Bentgrasses are usually not affected. Rust fungi are obligate parasites and infect only living grass plants. Two or more rusts may attack the same grass plant at the same time. Grass plants are most easily infected under stressful growing conditions.

TABLE 5.3 RUST FUNGI THAT INFECT CULTIVATED TURFGRASSES IN NORTH AMERICA

Rust fungus	Turfgrasses infected
Puccinia	
brachypodii var. *arrhenatheri*	Bluegrasses, fescues, wheatgrasses
brachypodii var. *poae-nemoralis*	Bentgrasses, bluegrasses, fescues, perennial ryegrass, turf timothy
chaetochloae	Bahiagrass, saltwater couch (*Paspalum*)
cockerelliana	Fescues
coronata var. *coronata*	Bahiagrass, bentgrasses, bluegrasses, fescues, perennial ryegrass, turf timothy, weeping alkaligrass (*Puccinellia*), wheatgrasses
coronata var. *himalensis*	Kentucky bluegrass
crandallii	Bluegrasses, fescues
cynodontis	Bermudagrasses
dolosa	Bahiagrass, saltwater couch (*Paspalum*)
graminis subsp. *graminicola*	Bentgrasses, bluegrasses, perennial ryegrass, turf timothy, wheatgrasses
graminis subsp. *graminis*	Bermudagrasses, wheatgrasses
hordei	Perennial ryegrass
kansensis	Buffalograss (*Buchloë dactyloides*)
levis	Bahiagrass, saltwater couch (*Paspalum*)
levis var. *panici-sanguinalis*	Bahiagrass, saltwater couch
montanensis	Wheatgrasses
pattersoniana	Wheatgrasses
poarum	Bentgrasses, bluegrasses, fescues, turf timothy (*Phleum nodosum*)
pygmaea	Bentgrasses
recondita	Bentgrasses, bluegrasses, fescues, perennial ryegrass, wheatgrasses
sessilis	Fescues
stenotaphri	St. Augustinegrass
striiformis	Bluegrasses, fescues, perennial ryegrass, turf timothy, weeping alkaligrass (*Puccinellia*), wheatgrasses
substriata var. *substriata*	Bahiagrass, saltwater couch (*Paspalum*)
zoysiae	Manilagrass (*Zoysia matrella*)
Physopella	
compressa	Bahiagrass, saltwater couch, tropical carpetgrass (*Axonopus compressus*)
Uromyces	
dactylidis var. *dactylidis*	Fescues
dactylidis var. *poae*	Bentgrasses, bluegrasses, weeping alkaligrass (*Puccinellia*)
fragilipes	Bentgrasses
setariae-italicae	St. Augustinegrass, kikuyugrass

Source: Adapted from Cummins (1971) and Smiley (1983). For illustrations of the urediospores and teliospores of these rust fungi, see Figures 5.63 and 5.64.

Rusts are most severe when water, fertility, and soil compaction are less than adequate for good growth. Most rust problems occur on Kentucky bluegrass, perennial ryegrass, tall fescue, and zoysiagrass. These diseases occur throughout the United States wherever susceptible grasses are grown.

Key to Infectious Turfgrass Diseases

Most rusts do not usually become a growth-limiting problem except during extended, warm to hot, humid, but droughty periods when grass grows slowly or not at all , and nights are cool with heavy dews. Some cultivars of Kentucky bluegrass (such as Birka, Delft, Eclipse, Lovegreen, Merion, Mystic, Prato, Touchdown, and Windsor), several of the newer perennial ryegrasses (Derby, Manhattan, Pennfine, and Regal), certain zoysiagrasses, Pennlawn spreading fescue, and Sunturf bermudagrass are particularly susceptible.

A continuous, heavy, rust infection causes many grass blades to turn yellow to brown, wither, and die. Such turf may be thinned and weakened and also be more susceptible to winterkill, drought, weed invasion, and other diseases.

Symptoms. During early infection, a close examination of the grass blades and leaf sheaths will show small light yellow flecks. These soon enlarge. In several days, the leaf epidermis ruptures and tears away to expose the round, oval, or elongated powdery, spore-filled pustules. These pustules may be reddish to chestnut brown, brownish yellow, bright orange, or lemon yellow (Figures 5.61 and 5.62). The powdery material rubs off easily on hands, shoes, clothing, and animals. Where severe, rust-affected leaves or even entire plants may turn yellow (orange on zoysiagrasses), wither, and die. Heavily rust-infected turf soon takes on a reddish-brown to a yellowish or orange appearance, depending on the rust involved. Affected turf becomes weakened, thin, and unsightly.

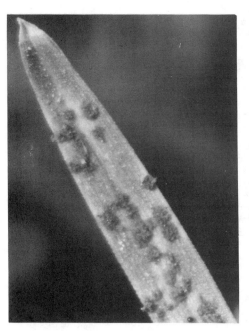

Figure 5.61 (left) Stem rust (*Puccinia graminis* subsp. *graminicola*) infecting a leaf blade of Merion bluegrass. (Courtesy O. M. Scott & Sons.)

Figure 5.62 (above) Leaf rust infecting three tall fescue leaves. (Courtesy L. T. Lucas.)

Severe rust development for most rust fungi is favored by 4 to 8 hours of low light intensity, temperatures of 70 to 75 °F, high humidity, heavy dews or light rains, followed by 8 to 16 hours of high light intensity, temperatures of 80 to 95 °F, and slow drying of leaf surfaces. Stripe rust (*Color plate 54*) is active during cool moist weather in early spring and fall. Along the Pacific coast it is active during the winter months.

Disease Cycle. The cycle of development for these rust fungi is very complex because of the many species involved (about 30 in the United States; see Table 5.3 and Figures 5.63 and 5.64) and the numerous alternate hosts, which are mostly woody shrubs and herbaceous ornamentals.

The powdery material that rubs off is composed of tremendous numbers of microscopic spores (urediospores, uredospores, or urediniospores), the reproductive structures of the rust fungi. A single pustule may contain 50,000 or more spores, each capable of producing a new pustule. These spores are readily transported by air currents, water, shoes, turf equipment, and infected sod, plugs, or sprigs. Some spores land on susceptible leaf tissue, where, in the presence of moisture, they infect by developing germ tubes that penetrate the leaves and sheaths through open stomates. A new generation of rust pustules and urediospores appear 7 to 15 days later, depending largely on the temperature. Urediospores constitute the repeating stage of the rust fungus. This cycle of spore production, release, penetration, and infection may be repeated a number of times during the summer and fall, or until environmental conditions become unfavorable for the growth and reproduction of the rust fungus.

In mild climates, the rust fungi overwinter as dormant mycelium and as urediospores in or on infected turfgrass foliage and equipment. When the temperature (usually between 60 and 90 °F) and moisture conditions are conducive to regrowth of the mycelium and germination of the urediospores, the leaves and leaf sheaths become infected and a new generation of uredial pustules and their urediospores are formed. These spores are readily transported over long distances by air currents, and those from southern regions of the United States may serve as sources of windblown inoculum for northern regions, where mycelium and urediospores cannot survive the winter.

Most rust fungi also produce another spore type, teliospores (Figures 5.63 and 5.64), when the leaves senesce or dry slowly. The brown to black telial stage, however, is minor on mowed turfgrasses growing under a good cultural management program. The teliospores, if produced, may serve as overwintering structures in the north, germinating in the spring to produce a third spore type, basidiospores. Basidiospores are transported by air currents to the leaves of nearby, alternate hosts (mostly woody shrubs and herbaceous ornamentals), where they may germinate and produce new infections that result in two more spore types, pycniospores, and later, the aeciospores. Cluster cups or aecia form on the alternate hosts and release aeciospores which are then capable of infecting grass plants giving rise to urediospores, thus completing the disease or life cycle. All spore types except the urediospores are rarely important in producing rust infections on turfgrasses.

Control. Grow locally adapted, rust-resistant grasses, blends, or mixtures. Check with your county cooperative extension office or your state extension turf specialist for suggested grass species and cultivars to grow. Kentucky bluegrass cultivars with moderate to good resistance to one or more rusts include A-20 and A-34 (Bensun), Adelphi, Admiral, America, Apart, Aquila, Argyle, Aspen, Banff, Bayside, Bonnieblue, Bono, Bristol,

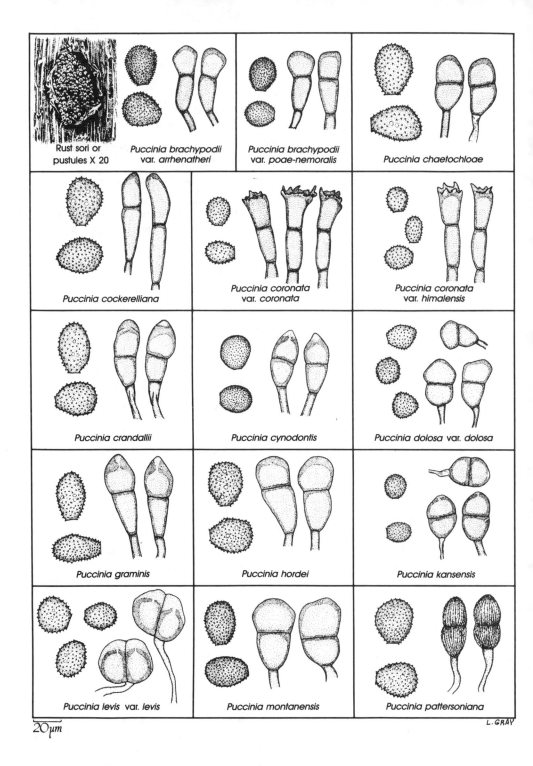

Figure 5.63 Fifteen species of *Puccinia* that cause rust diseases of turfgrasses; for each species the urediospores are on the left and the teliospores are on the right. [After Cummins (1971)].

Biology and Control of Diseases in Turfgrasses   Chap. 5

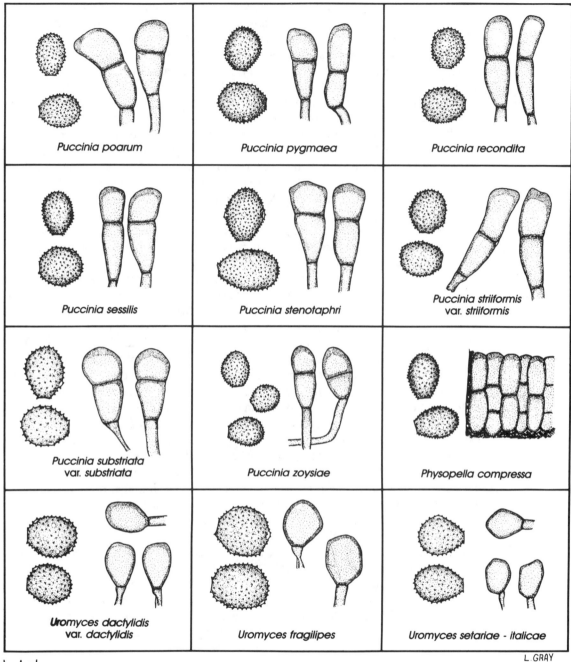

Puccinia poarum

Puccinia pygmaea

Puccinia recondita

Puccinia sessilis

Puccinia stenotaphri

Puccinia striiformis
var. striiformis

Puccinia substriata
var. substriata

Puccinia zoysiae

Physopella compressa

Uromyces dactylidis
var. dactylidis

Uromyces fragilipes

Uromyces setariae - italicae

L.GRAY

20 μm

Figure 5.64 Twelve species of rust fungi that cause rust diseases of turfgrasses; for each species the urediospores are on the left and the teliospores are on the right. [After Cummins (1971)].

Key to Infectious Turfgrass Diseases

Brunswick, Challenger, Charlotte, Classic, Columbia, Enmundi, Enoble, Escort, Fylking, Georgetown, Geronimo, Glade, Haga, Harmony, Holiday, Majestic, Merit, Midnight, Mona, Monopoly, Mosa, Nassau, Nugget, Parade, Park, Piedmont, Plush, Princeton 104, Ram I, Rugby, Shasta, Sodco, Sydsport, Trenton, Victa, Wabash, and Welcome. Resistant fine-leaved fescues include Ensylva, Flyer, and Shadow; Acclaim, All-Star, Birdie II, Blazer, CBS II, Cigil, Citation, Crown, Delray, Elka, Gator, Loretta, Manhattan II, Omega II, Ovation, Palmer, Pennant, Pippin, Prelude, Premier, Ranger, Repell, Tara, and Yorktown II perennial ryegrasses. Emerald and Meyer zoysiagrasses are very susceptible; Italian or annual ryegrass, bermudagrass, and tall fescue cultivars also differ in resistance. Common and hybrid bermudagrasses are tolerant or resistant while Sunturf is very susceptible. Tall fescue cultivars with improved crown rust resistance include Adventure, Apache, Falcon, Jaquar, Mustang, and Olympic. Resistance to rusts is limited by the presence of numerous physiological races of the rust fungi. A cultivar in one location may be resistant, whereas it appears susceptible in another turfgrass area.

Fertilize and irrigate to keep grass growing at a steady rate (about 1 in. a week for most turfgrasses) during summer or early fall drought periods. The growth of the grass blades pushes the rust-infected leaves outward, where they can be mowed off and removed. To increase vigor, maintain a proper balance of nitrogen, phosphorus, and potassium (N-P-K), according to local recommendations and a soil test report. These recommendations will vary with the grasses grown and their use. *Do not overfertilize,* especially with a readily available high-nitrogen source. Keep the phosphorus and potassium levels high.

During summer or early autumn droughts, water established turf thoroughly early in the day so that the grass can dry before night. Water infrequently and deeply, moistening the soil at each watering to a depth of 6 in. or more. Avoid frequent light sprinklings, especially in the late afternoon or evening. Free water on the leaf surface for several hours enhances the development of rusts and many other diseases.

Follow other cultural practices outlined on pages 212 to 214. These cultural practices and those outlined above should provide for a steady, vigorous growth of grass during extended, warm to hot, dry periods when rust attacks are most severe.

If rusts are serious year after year, these practices may need to be supplemented by a preventative fungicide spray program (Table 5.4). The initial application should be made when rust is first evident on the grass blades. Repeat applications are needed at 7- to 14-day intervals as long as rust is prevalent. Sterol-inhibiting fungicides such as Bayleton will provide several weeks of protection with a single application. For best results, apply the fungicide soon after mowing and removal of the clippings. Good coverage of the leaf surface is necessary for control. The addition of about ½ teaspoonful of a wetting-sticking agent or surfactant, such as liquid household soap or detergent, to each gallon of spray mixture will help spread the spray droplets over the grass surface. For the most effective control of rusts, uniformly spray 1000 sq ft of turf with 1 to 3 gal of water.

When mixing or applying any fungicide, follow the manufacturer's directions and precautions carefully.

St. Augustinegrass Decline

St. Augustinegrass decline (SAD) is caused by several strains of the panicum mosaic virus with several "serological types." This disease is causing serious damage to St. Augustinegrass. SAD and a different strain of panicum mosaic virus affecting centipedegrass are the only

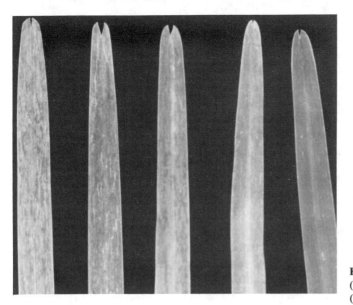

Figure 5.65 St. Augustinegrass decline (SAD); the right leaf is healthy. (Courtesy R. W. Toler.)

important viral diseases of cultivated turfgrasses. SAD is a potential threat wherever St. Augustinegrass is grown. Symptoms are more pronounced where the turf is under stress from lack of nitrogen, drought, nematode and insect injury, and shade. St. Augustinegrass and centipedegrass are the only turfgrasses presently known to be affected by the virus, which is spread through diseased sod or sprigs and from infected to healthy grass plants by contaminated mowers.

Symptoms. The first symptoms of SAD appear as pale green or yellowish spots, blotches, and a speckling or stippling in the leaves (Figure 5.65). The mottling gradually becomes more yellow as the spots and blotches merge, and by the second year infected turf has a uniform bright yellow appearance. Such turf lacks vigor and becomes thin as stolon growth is retarded. During the third year infected plants wither and die, producing irregular dead areas in the turf. Such areas are soon invaded by native grasses and broadleaf weeds. *Entire* turf areas may be killed by the end of the third year. Diseased St. Augustinegrass is much more susceptible to winterkill, drought, and pesticides.

SAD in its earlier stages may be confused with iron (page 39) or zinc deficiencies (page 34), mite-feeding damage (page 178), and downy mildew (page 232). Grass blades infected with St. Augustinegrass decline have a mosaic pattern with bright yellow stippling or streaking. Deficiency symptoms, on the other hand, appear as *continuous* yellow or pale stripes in the leaves parallel to the veins.

Control. Resprig or resod infected turf areas with a resistant or tolerant cultivar such as Floratam, Raleigh, or Seville. When establishing a new turf, purchase only disease-free sod that has been certified by the State Department of Agriculture. When SAD has been reported in your area, use your own mowing equipment.

Seed Decay, Damping-off, and Seedling Blights

Seeds of different turfgrasses require various periods of time to germinate. Cultivars of Kentucky bluegrass, bermudagrass, and buffalograss take 3 to 4 weeks to germinate, bentgrasses 1 to 2 weeks, fine-leaved fescues about a week, while seeds of perennial ryegrass germinate in just a few days. To ensure a good stand and seedling vigor, the properly prepared seedbed should be moist (not too wet or dry) during the entire germination period. Other requirements for the establishment of a healthy turf include adequate sunlight and oxygen. Optimum day-night temperatures for the germination of cool-season turfgrasses is 60 to 85 °F and 68 to 95 °F for warm-season species. As environmental factors (primarily moisture, light, oxygen, and temperature) become less favorable for seedling growth, the risk of seed decay, damping-off, and seedling blights increases.

This disease complex is most common when prolonged wet periods or overwatering follow seeding, where seeds were buried too deep or shallow, poor contact of seeds with soil due largely to a poorly prepared seedbed, and when seeding is done at other than suggested times (e.g., late summer or spring for most of the United States). Seed decay, damping-off, and seedling blights are caused primarily by numerous species of *Pythium, Rhizoctonia, Fusarium, Bipolaris, Drechslera, Exserohilum, Colletotrichum,* and *Microdochium* (Figures 5.2, 5.11, 5.29, 5.34, and 5.51).

Each of these fungal pathogens has its own requirements for optimal growth. For example, *Pythium ultimum, P. vanterpoolii, Fusarium nivale,* and *Rhizoctonia cerealis* grow best at a low temperature (50 to 72 °F), while other species of *Pythium (P. aphanidermatum* and *P. myriotylum), Rhozoctonia solani,* and *Bipolaris sorokiniana* are most pathogenic at a higher temperature (80 to 95 °F). Other seed and seedling blight fungi are capable of causing disease at low or high temperatures. The pathogenic capabilities of the various fungi mean that the prudent turfgrass manager plants at a time and under conditions where seed germination and seedling vigor will be strongly favored.

For problems with overseeding of warm-season turfs during the winter in the south, see under Pythium blight (page 265). Seeds sown into an existing turf face additional problems such as competition for light, water, space, and nutrients with larger, established plants; exposure to high levels of certain pathogens in the thatch; and toxins produced by the decomposition of organic matter in the thatch.

Symptoms.   Stands of newly seeded or overseeded turfgrass are thin, stunted, patchy, off-color, and slow to fill in when seed germination and seedling growth are slowed by environmental stresses (too cold, hot, dry, or wet) that favor the growth of pathogenic fungi. Seeds of all cultivated turfgrasses either decay in the soil or young seedlings become water-soaked at the soil line and below, turn yellow or bronzed to brown, wither, and die before *or* after emergence. Surviving plants are weakened and more susceptible to other diseases. Young seedlings often collapse and die (postemergence damping-off) from a decay at the ground line (Figure 5.66).

Disease Cycle.   Although most of the fungi that cause seed decay, damping-off, and seedling blights are common soil inhabitants and probably present in all unfumigated seedbeds, others are transported on or within seed. Infection occurs before emergence, especially when the seed lacks vigor and is slow to sprout due to unfavorable temperatures, an excess or lack of moisture, or other suboptimal conditions for seedling growth either above or below the soil surface.

Control.   Provide good surface and subsurface drainage and avoid compaction when establishing a new turf area. Fill in depressions where water may stand. Test the

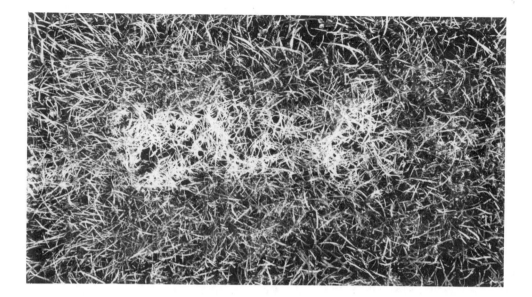

Figure 5.66 Close-up of seedling blight or postemergence damping-off of creeping bentgrass seedlings caused by *Rhizoctonia solani.*

soil reaction (pH) and follow the soil test report to obtain a pH between 6 and 7. Provide for good air movement over the turf.

Buy only top-quality, plump seed of locally adapted, disease-resistant grasses or combinations (blends and mixtures) of grasses. Except for southern grasses, which germinate best at slightly warmer temperatures, plant when the weather is cool (night–day temperatures of about 60 to 85 °F) and dry and therefore ideal for rapid seed germination and growth. The seedbed should be fertile and well prepared and the seed sown at the recommended rate and depth. Ensure that the soil–seed contact is good to speed germination. If you anticipate a problem, treat the seed with a seed-protectant fungicide (Table 5.4). Avoid overwatering, especially from seeding to seedling emergence or plant establishment.

Apply a suggested fungicide (Table 5.4) uniformly over the seedbed, using 5 to 10 gal of water to cover 1000 sq ft, immediately after seeding or at the *first* evidence of a patchy, uneven stand. Repeat the spray once or twice at 5- to 7-day intervals. Fungicide applications can be important in obtaining satisfactory stands of turfgrasses!

Mow the new turf area when the seedlings reach a height one-third greater than the anticipated cutting height. A light application of nitrogen fertilizer when grass seedlings reach 1½ to 2 in. tall will encourage vigorous growth. Apply approximately ½ lb of actual nitrogen per 1000 sq ft and water the fertilizer into the top 1 to 2 in. of soil.

Selenophoma Leaf Spot

Selenophoma leaf spot is caused by the fungi *Selenophoma donacis* and *S. everhartii* (*S. obtusa*). Other names for this minor disease include red eyespot, halo spot, and "frogeye." Susceptible cultivated turfgrasses include bentgrasses, fescues, bluegrasses, and weeping alkaligrass (*Puccinellia distans*).

Symptoms. Small (1 to 4 mm long), elliptical, brown to purple spots with a dark purplish margin form on the leaves and leaf sheaths during cool, wet weather in early spring and autumn. As the often numerous spots enlarge, the centers become bleached and dotted with minute, brown to black specks (pycnidia). When severe, individual leaves and affected turf have a purplish appearance.

Disease Cycle. The *Selenophoma* fungi overseason as pycnidia and mycelium in grass debris. During cool (60 to 70°F), damp weather large numbers of microscopic spores or conidia (Figure 5.14) are released from the pycnidia and are splashed or carried to healthy leaves on turfgrass equipment and shoes. The spores germinate in a film of water on the leaves. Infection results in the development of new leaf spots with pycnidia. The cycle may be repeated every week or two as long as the weather remains cool and moist, which promotes disease development.

Control. No special measures are usually needed to control Selenophoma leaf spot, due to its infrequent appearance in severe form. On cultivated turfgrasses the cultural and chemical control measures outlined for "Helminthosporium" diseases (page 248 and Table 5.4) should keep this disease in check.

Septoria Leaf Spot

Septoria leaf spot, sometimes called tip blight, is caused by about 15 species of the fungus *Septoria*. This is a minor disease that attacks many cultivated turfgrasses, including bentgrasses, bluegrasses, fescues, ryegrasses, redtop, bermudagrasses, and crested wheatgrass. Septoria leaf spot commonly occurs during cool, wet weather in the late winter or early spring and autumn. The disease is rare in warm to hot weather.

Symptoms. The overall appearance of a diseased turfgrass area often resembles damage from a dull mower (page 21). The grass leaves are often a pale yellow from the the tip downward. The spots, which may be scattered near the leaf tips, are gray to gray-green or brown before fading to a light straw color. On perennial ryegrass the spots are yellowish-green, later turning a chocolate-brown. All *Septoria* fungi produce dark brown to black, speck-sized, fruiting bodies (pycnidia) in the older lesions (Figure 5.67). They are easily seen with a magnifying lens and help to distinguish Septoria from dollar spot (page 228).

Disease Cycle. The *Septoria* fungi survive the winter and warm to hot dry weather as mycelium and pycnidia in grass debris. During cool rains, microscopic, needlelike spores formed within the pycnidia (Figure 5.14) are splashed and washed or carried on turfgrass equipment to healthy leaves. Here the spores germinate in a film of water and infection occurs, often in the freshly cut tips of the grass blades. The cycle can be repeated every week or two as long as the weather remains cool and moist (60 to 75°F).

Control. No special measures are usually needed to keep Septoria leaf spot in check. Where feasible, follow suggested cultural practices as outlined on pages 212 to 214. Fungicides Fungicides applied to control "Helminthosporium" diseases and dollar spot should provide adequate control (Table 5.4). Kentucky bluegrass cultivars differ in resistance.

Figure 5.67 (left) Septoria leaf spot (*S. macropoda*) lesions on Kentucky bluegrass leaves. Note the dark pycnidia embedded in the dead leaf tissue. (Courtesy R. W. Smiley.)

Figure 5.68 (above) Slime mold. Plasmodium of *Physarum cinereum* forming immature sporangia. (Courtesy Noel Jackson.)

Slime Molds

Slime molds (Figure 5.68) cause concern to many turfgrass managers when they occur suddenly in warm weather after heavy rains or watering. Numerous species may be involved, including the common *Physarum cinereum,* and occasionally *Mucilago spongiosa* and *Didymium crustaceum.* Other species of *Fuligo, Mucilago, Physarum,* and *Stemonitis* have also been reported on turfgrasses.

Slime molds are primitive organisms that lack cell walls and flow or move like amoebae over low-lying objects and vegetation, such as turfgrasses, strawberries, bedded flowers, ground covers, alfalfa and clovers, plantains, dandelions, mulches, bases of trees, and even sidewalks and driveways. These organisms are not parasitic on turf, but feed on decaying organic matter, fungi, and bacteria in the thatch layer and soil. Generally, slime molds cause little damage to living turfgrass, but may cause some yellowing by shading the affected leaves. Moist, warm weather and high soil moisture favor the fruiting of slime molds on turfgrasses.

Symptoms. The slimy amoebalike stage appears as watery white, gray, cream to light yellow, red, violet, blue, green, or greasy purple-brown masses in round to irregular-shaped patches from 1 in. to 2 ft in diameter. This stage is made up of a naked mass of protoplasm called a plasmodium, which simply "engulfs" its food. The plasmodium soon "heap ups" and the crusty (usually gray or yellow) fruiting bodies envelop individual grass blades with numerous small, purplish, blue gray, gray, black, dirty yellow, or white powdery structures called sporangia (Figure 5.68). Slime molds commonly reappear in the same areas each year.

Key to Infectious Turfgrass Diseases

Disease Cycle. Slime molds survive unfavorable conditions as microscopic spores in the soil and turfgrass thatch. The spores are spread about primarily by air currents, water, shoes, mowers, and other turf equipment. During or after warm, wet weather or deep watering from late spring to autumn, the spores absorb water, crack open, and a motile swarm spore emerges from each. The amoebalike swarm spores feed on fungi, bacteria, other microorganisms, and decaying organic matter in the soil and thatch while they undergo various changes and numerous fissions. Finally, they unite in pairs to form zygotes and become a shapeless, slimy plasmodium that increases in size. The plasmodium works its way to the soil surface and creeps over vegetation in round to irregular-shaped patches. Here the crustlike fruiting or reproductive stage is formed, which is the only stage that most of us ever see. The round, pinhead-sized fruiting structures (sporangia) are variously colored and range from white, gray to creamy white, purplish brown, bluish gray, tan to orange, brown, or black (Figure 5.68 and *Color plate 55*). They are filled with dark masses of powdery spores that are easily rubbed off the leaf or stem. Slime molds are nonparasitic and technically do not cause disease. They are much more unsightly than harmful and merely use grass leaves and stems as a means of support for their reproductive structures. However, slight damage may occur when leaves are smothered or shaded for several days to a week or longer. The weakened and somewhat yellow grass leaves are more susceptible to killing by secondary fungi and bacteria. An abundance of thatch favors slime molds by providing a ready source of organic matter plus high populations of microorganisms.

Control. No control measures are usually considered necessary. If the molds are abundant, break up the unsightly spore masses by vigorous raking, brushing, poling, or hosing down with a stream of water. Washing is suggested only after the onset of dry weather. Mowing the grass usually removes the spore masses. Spraying the turf with any suggested turf fungicide listed in Table 5.4 should also be beneficial in checking their growth but is usually not necessary.

Snow Molds

Snow molds are cold-tolerant fungi that grow at freezing or near freezing temperatures. Snow molds may damage turfgrasses from November or December to spring, especially in shaded or wet areas where the snow falls on unfrozen ground and is slow to melt. Roots, stems, and leaves may be rotted over a wide range of temperatures (about 25 to 60°F). Some snow molds may injure turf at snow melt or during cold, drizzly periods when snow is absent. When the grass surface dries out and the weather warms, snow mold fungi cease to attack; however, infection tends to reappear in the same areas year after year.

Snow molds are favored by excessive, early fall applications of nitrogenous fertilizers, excessive shade, a thick thatch, or mulches of straw, leaves, or other moisture-holding debris on the turf. Disease is most serious when air movement and soil drainage are poor and the grass stays wet for long periods or where the snow is deposited in drifts.

Most turfgrasses are susceptible to one or more snow mold fungi. They include Kentucky and annual bluegrasses, fescues, bentgrasses, ryegrasses, bermudagrass, and zoysiagrass. Bentgrasses are more often severely damaged than are coarser turfgrasses.

There are two principal snow molds over most of the northern half of the United States: pink snow mold or Fusarium patch (caused by the fungus *Fusarium nivale* or *Microdochium nivale;* sexual state *Calonectria graminicola* or *Monographella nivalis*), and gray or speckled snow mold, also known as Typhula blight (caused by several species of the fungus *Typhula*). The two types are found in the same geographical areas in the United States. Pink snow mold may be found farther south than gray snow mold and has been reported from Texas and southern California during cold and wet periods.

Gray snow mold or Typhula blight.   Gray or speckled snow mold is caused by the fungus *Typhula incarnata* and three varieties of *Typhula ishikariensis*: var. *canadensis,* var. *idahoensis,* and var. *ishikariensis.* A deep and prolonged snow cover on unfrozen soil, tall grass matted down, and unbalanced nitrogen fertilization produce favorable conditions for disease development. The fungus (or fungi) are less active while the turf and soil are frozen. In early spring, when the snow melts and the turf thaws, the fungus may again become active, and diseased patches may enlarge. As the weather warms and the turf dries, *Typhula* becomes dormant until middle to late autumn. The optimum temperature for infection is between 30 and 45 °F. All northern turfgrasses are susceptible, with bentgrasses and annual bluegrass being most susceptible. Kentucky bluegrass cultivars differ in resistance to the *Typhula* fungi. The fine-leaved fescues are commonly more resistant than are Kentucky bluegrasses and especially bentgrasses.

Symptoms.   After snow melt, gray snow mold appears as roughly circular, white to grayish-white areas with regular margins that coalesce to form areas up to 2 or 3 ft in diameter (Figure 5.69). The disease is active where the snow is melting. Several spots may merge, forming large, irregular, straw-colored dead areas. The wet grass may be matted together and covered at first with a fluffy, grayish-white mold (mycelium) that is speckled

Figure 5.69   Gray snow mold or Typhula blight at the edge of melting snow.

Figure 5.70 Gray snow mold. Close-up of the mycelium and sclerotia of *Typhula incarnata*. (Courtesy Noel Jackson.)

with numerous pale to dark brown sclerotia (Figure 5.70). The mold soon turns bluish gray to almost black. At other times a silvery membranous crust develops over the injured turf. When conditions favor disease development, large turf areas may be killed. More commonly, only the leaves are killed and new leaves form from the overwintered plant crowns.

Disease Cycle. After the period of active mycelial growth when the snow melts, the *Typhula* fungi produce small (0.2 to 5 mm), roundish or flattened, orange-yellow to tan or reddish, reddish-brown, chocolate-brown, or black survival structures called sclerotia. (The sclerotia of *T. ishikariensis* are tiny and black when mature.) The hard sclerotia are embedded in or attached to the leaves and crowns of diseased plants (Figure 5.70) and lie dormant during the following summer and early autumn. The sclerotia germinate in cold, wet weather or after autumn snow melt to produce delicate, pink to grayish-white, spore-bearing sporocarps up to 20 mm tall (Figure 5.71) or hyphae with clamp connections (Figure 5.2) that infect all tissues of the grass plant and start the disease cycle once again. The fungi spread by movement of sclerotia, or by windblown basidiospores produced by the clublike sporocarps, splashing or flowing water, turf equipment, and shoes. *Typhula* fungi that infect grasses are not seed-borne.

Cultivars of Kentucky bluegrass resistant to one or more *Typhula* fungi include Adorno, Bonnieblue, Galaxie, Monopoly, and Park. Very susceptible Kentucky bluegrasses include Fylking, Merion, Nugget, Prato, and South Dakota common. The red fescues are, in general, more resistant to gray snow mold than are Kentucky bluegrass and bentgrasses. Atlanta, Epsom, Ivalo, Magenta, and Weekend chewings fescues are resistant. Boreal and Reptans are highly resistant red fescues; Dawson is moderately resistant. Perennial ryegrasses that are resistant or moderately resistant include Delray, NK–200, and Pennfine.

Control. Follow the cultural controls outlined on pages 212 to 214. Follow a suggested fertilizer program for your area and the grass or grasses being grown. The risk of snow mold damage can be reduced by using balanced fertilization. Avoid straw mulches,

Figure 5.71 Gray snow mold. Close-up of sporocarps of *Typhula incarnata*. (Courtesy Noel Jackson.)

thatch accumulation, and fertilization with nitrogen within about 6 weeks of a killing frost or when the first heavy snow is expected. Slow-release forms of nitrogen fertilizer are recommended although soluble forms of nitrogen (such as ammonium sulfate) should work just as well in most situations. Turfgrasses should *not* go into the winter in a succulent condition. Use lime *only* when the need is indicated by a soil test; avoid excessive use of lime.

Prevent large snow drifts and excessive accumulation of snow on high-value turf areas by proper placement of snow fences, living evergreen windbreaks, and similar barriers.

Before the first heavy snow or cold, drizzly weather is forecast in autumn, apply *one* of the suggested turf fungicides (see Table 5.4) to areas with a history of snow mold infection. *Follow the manufacturer's directions and precautions carefully.* Reapply one or more times during late autumn, early winter, or midwinter as the snow melts.

Repair snow mold damage in spring by raking the matted grass and fertilizing. Reseed or resod as necessary. Fungicide sprays may be needed (see under Seed Decay, Damping-off, and Seedling Blights, page 287).

Pink snow mold or Fusarium patch.   Pink snow mold is caused by *Fusarium nivale* or *Microdochium nivale*. This disease is common and troublesome in western Washington and Oregon or other northern areas where prolonged periods of wet, cool weather occur from autumn to middle or late spring and early summer. Fusarium patch disease in these areas often occurs in the absence of snow and is favored by cool or cold wet weather when grass growth is retarded. Patches of the disease, which persist until a snow cover develops, may increase in size, especially if the snow falls on unfrozen ground. At snow melt, on exposure to light the fungus on diseased turf turns pink, hence the name "pink snow mold" (*Color plate 56*). Infection, spread, and disease development occur most rapidly when the turf moisture and air humidity are high and temperatures are 30 to 45 °F (maximum about 65 °F). Nearly all cool-season turfgrasses, bermudagrass, and zoysiagrass are susceptible. Fine-leaved fescues and tall fescue are usually not damaged as severely as annual bluegrass, bentgrasses, redtop, Kentucky bluegrass, and ryegrasses.

Symptoms. Fusarium patch disease first appears as round, water-soaked spots, 1 to 3 in. in diameter, that soon turn into yellow, orange-brown, or reddish-brown patches with sparse to abundant mold growth. Later, they may enlarge and become ringlike, light gray or light tan patches up to about 8 in. across with an orange-brown or brown border. The roughly circular patches, usually rounder and smaller than those of gray snow mold, are often pink after exposure to light. The spots may enlarge up to 8 or 12 in. across or merge to cover large areas.

Disease Cycle. The *Fusarium* or *Microdochium* fungus is inactive when the grass is dry and the weather is warm. It survives from one season to the next probably as dark aggregates of mycelium in infected grass plants or in dead grass debris and soil. There is also some evidence that the fungus is systemic within the grass plant. When temperature and moisture conditions are favorable, the fungus produces large numbers of crescent-shaped microscopic spores (macroconidia) in sticky masses (Figure 5.29). These spores are carried primarily by air currents, splashing or flowing water, turfgrass equipment, and shoes to grass leaves. Infection occurs through stomates. The fungus can exist and attack grasses in all soils from pH 5.5 to 7.5, but is favored by alkaline turf surfaces.

Control. Same as for gray snow mold (above). Follow a suggested fertilizer program for your area and the grasses grown. Use adequate amounts of a balanced fertilizer. In western Washington, excellent control of Fusarium patch has been obtained with a sulfur program similar to that outlined for take-all patch (page 306). Avoid sudden changes in surface pH, especially on *Poa annua* turf. Maintain high potassium and phosphorus soil test values and avoid overstimulation with any source of nitrogen. Somewhat resistant turfgrasses include Delray perennial ryegrass, Atlanta and Ruby chewings fescues, Dawson red fescue, and Emerald, Penncross, Penneagle, and Prominent creeping bentgrasses.

Fungicide treatments are required at 2- to 8-week intervals from late autumn, through the winter and into spring. See Table 5.4.

Coprinus or cottony snow mold [low-temperature basidiomycete (LTB) and sclerotial LTB (SLTB) snow molds]. Cottony or Coprinus snow mold, also known as winter crown rot, caused by the fungus *Coprinus psychromorbidus,* is most common in Canada and Alaska, where snow covers turfgrasses for prolonged periods from autumn well into spring. Two phases of the *Coprinus* fungus are known: nonsclerotial (LTB) and sclerotial (SLTB). The former is recognized only as a snow mold with a fine, sparse to

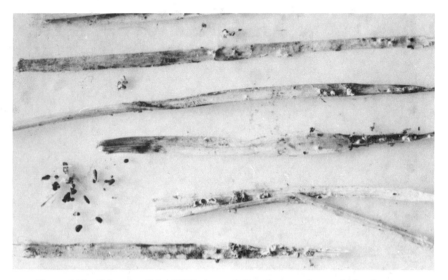

Figure 5.72 Sclerotia of the SLTB phase of *Coprinus psychromorbidus* the cottony snow mold fungus. (Courtesy J. D. Smith.)

abundant cottony white mycelium with clamp connections (Figure 5.2) at the septa (like *Typhula*). The individual patches often do *not* coalesce. The sclerotial strain produces a similar mycelium but with sclerotia that are white at first and then brownish-black, irregular-shaped, and up to 1 mm in diameter (Figure 5.72). Most common turfgrass species grown in Canada and Alaska, (e.g., creeping bentgrass, Kentucky bluegrass, red fescues and tall fescue) as well as forage grasses, wheat, rye, and alfalfa (winter crown rot), are susceptible to one or both phases of *Coprinus.*

Symptoms.   Round to irregular snow mold patches, 6 in. or more in diameter, are evident when the snow recedes. In the case of LTB the grass blades are covered with a white to gray, cottony or sparse mycelium (*Color plate 57*). In the SLTB, mycelial knots and later small, black, irregularly shaped sclerotia develop on the grass plants (Figure 5.72). Turfgrasses may be completely killed, particularly by the LTB phase, or recover very slowly. The SLTB phase is less pathogenic.

Disease Cycle.   The *Coprinus* fungus will grow at temperatures from a few degrees below to several degrees above freezing. Sclerotia in grass debris and soil may carry over the sclerotial (SLTB) phase of the pathogen until the following autumn or winter. The method of oversummering of the nonsclerotial or LTB phase is not known but is probably as dormant mycelium in infected plants. Small, white to grayish, mushroomlike structures of the causal fungus, *Coprinus psychromorbidus,* have been found in wet weather during late summer and early fall, but the function of the spores they produce in causing disease is unknown.

Control.   Follow the cultural controls outlined on pages 212 to 214 and for gray snow mold (above) and by applying a light coating of fine ashes or charcoal over the

Figure 5.73 Cottony snow mold, LTB phase, showing the differential effect on cultivars of Kentucky bluegrass. (Courtesy J. D. Smith.)

snow. Early snow melt should be encouraged on high-value turf areas, as for other snow molds, by spreading snow drifts, selective placing of snow fences or other barriers, and by snow removal with snow blowers.

Two or three applications of fungicides as for gray snow mold (Table 5.4) are needed during autumn and into early winter, with the last application being made just before the first permanent snow cover of winter. Resistant cultivars of Kentucky bluegrass (Dormie, Park) and red fescue (Arctared) have been identified (Figure 5.73).

Sclerotinia snow mold or snow scald. This snow mold disease, caused by the fungus *Myriosclerotinia* (*Sclerotinia*) *borealis,* affects turfgrasses (primarily Kentucky bluegrass, red fescue, and perennial ryegrass) in some parts of the northern continental United States, and is sometimes severe in areas of Canada and Alaska. The disease, also known as Sclerotinia patch, is favored by a damp autumn, and the early development of a permanent, deep, long-duration snow cover developing on unfrozen soil. However, the fungus is capable of causing damage at lower temperatures than other snow molds.

Symptoms. Patches of dead bleached grass about 6 or more inches across appear as the snow melts. The patches often coalesce to kill large irregular areas (Figure 5.74). Infected leaves are water-soaked at first and are covered with a sparse gray mycelium *without* clamp connections. Later, the leaves become bleached to almost white. Wrinkled,

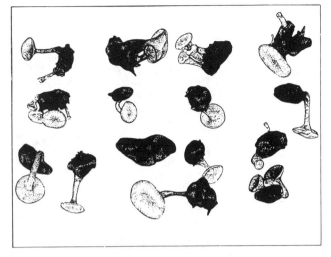

Figure 5.74 Snow scald or Sclerotinia snow mold. (Courtesy J. D. Smith.)

Figure 5.75 Apothecia on stalks from germinated sclerotia of the snow scald fungus, *Myriosclerotinia borealis*. The apothecia are rare in nature. (adapted from a photograph by J. D. Smith)

dull black sclerotia, which are round, oval, irregular, or almost flakelike, and 0.5 to 7 mm long, eventually form on the dead grass tissue near the soil line (Figure 5.75). Small, saucer-shaped spore-producing structures (apothecia) with short stalks are produced on the sclerotia in culture but are rarely observed in nature.

Disease Cycle.   The *Myriosclerotinia* fungus grows at temperatures between about 22 and 50°F. Sclerotia are the means by which the fungus oversummers.

Control.   Same as for Coprinus or cottony snow mold and gray snow mold (both above). Inorganic mercury fungicides (Calo-Clor and Calo-Gran) are usually ineffective in controlling the disease (Table 5.4).

Southern Blight

Southern blight, or Sclerotium blight, caused by the soilborne fungus *Athelia* (*Sclerotium*) *rolfsii*, attacks bentgrasses, bluegrasses, fescues, bermudagrass, and ryegrasses in the southern and western United States in warm, temperate regions during warm to hot weather (77 to 95°F). The fungus attacks the stems and roots of more than 500 plants, including field crops, fruits, ornamentals, vegetables, and weeds. The fungus also survives in soil as a saprophyte. The disease is most severe on heavily thatched turf that has previously been under drought stress. Dry conditions followed by a rainy or humid period enhances disease development.

Symptoms.   Yellow to white, thin, circular to crescent-shaped patches, up to about 12 in. across, appear in early summer. As the disease progresses, the patches increase in size. The grass at the border of the ring dies and turns reddish brown. The rings of

Key to Infectious Turfgrass Diseases   **299**

Figure 5.76 Southern blight in a bluegrass fairway. (Courtesy L. T. Lucas.)

dead grass grow outward up to 1 or 2 in. per day during hot, moist, overcast weather. Mature rings may be 3 to 6 ft or more in diameter (*Color plate 58* and Figure 5.76). Some patches have tufts of apparently healthy grass in the centers. An abundant, fluffy, white to grayish mycelium is usually evident in the thatch near the soil surface, growing on the dying grass at the edge of the patch. Clusters of small (1 to 3 mm in diameter), round, white, yellow, then tan to dark brown sclerotia form on the mycelium, dead grass, and the thatch in the ring. Sclerotia are formed in largest numbers when the soil is hot (86 °F), quite acid (pH 4), well aerated, and organic matter is abundant.

Disease Cycle. The numerous, small, round, dark brown sclerotia in the thatch and upper soil serve as overwintering structures. The sclerotia germinate in warm to hot (temperatures above 74 °F), moist weather. The hyphae (Figure 5.2) grow rapidly through the thatch or soil and into the grass leaves and stems. The foliage turns yellow and then reddish brown as it dies. Sclerotia formed on the dead grass and thatch may persist in the soil for several years. Cool temperatures and poorly aerated soils that are neutral to alkaline tend to restrict the growth of *Athelia* (*Sclerotium*) *rolfsii*. Aerifying and dethatching equipment spread the sclerotia.

Control. Follow cultural management practices (pages 212 to 214) to reduce thatch and drought stress. Aerify to avoid compaction where needed. Add lime, if needed, to raise the pH of the soil to 7.0 to 7.5. The fungicide Bayleton (Table 5.4) has given the best control of this disease.

Spermospora Blast

Spermospora blast, caused by four species of the fungus *Spermospora* (*S. ciliata, S. lolii, S. poagena,* and *S. subulata*), is known to infect bentgrasses, bluegrasses, fescues, ryegrasses, and turf timothy in cool temperate regions of the world. Like Selenophoma leaf spot (page 289), this minor disease is found primarily in early spring during cool, humid weather in coastal regions.

Symptoms. Round to elliptical (oval), straw, gray-brown, or reddish-brown spots with a brown border and surrounded by a yellowish halo appear on the leaves. The lesions often rapidly enlarge to involve much of the leaf blade, resulting in a dark brown or straw-colored "scald."

Disease Cycle. The *Spermospora* fungi probably overseason as dormant mycelium in the dark brown to black stromata at the surface of infected leaves or as long, tapering spores or conidia (Figure 5.77). During favorable conditions, conidia are produced which germinate in a film of water and penetrate the grass blades.

Control. Little is known about Spermospora blast, so no specific measures have been devised to control this disease. The cultural practices outlined on pages 212 to 214 should keep this minor disease in check.

Spring Dead Spot of Bermudagrass

Spring dead spot (SDS), caused by the fungi *Leptosphaeria korrae* and *L. narmari* is a widespread and serious disease of bermudagrass throughout its northern limit of adaptation, where winter temperatures are cold enough for the grass to go dormant. SDS occurs only in the "transition zone," where the average daily temperature during November is between 45°F and about 57°F. It is most common on compacted soils where the turf has been closely mowed, heavily fertilized during autumn and watered—often the best maintained. Golf fairways are usually the most severely infected. The disease can occur on greens

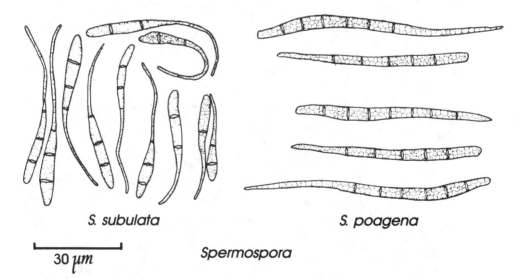

S. subulata   S. poagena

30 μm   *Spermospora*

Figure 5.77 Spores of two species of *Spermospora,* that cause Spermospora blast, as seen under a high-power microscope.

that have been overseeded, frosted, or covered with straw or plastic. Spring dead spot usually appears in turf 3 to 6 years or more old that has developed a thick thatch. The disease may be confused with snow molds (page 292), winter injury (page 44), or damage by insects (Chapter 4). SDS is usually more severe following very cold winters.

Symptoms. Roughly circular, bleached, dead spots appear with regrowth in the spring, varying in size from 2 in. to more than 3 ft in diameter (Figure 5.78). Sometimes the centers may survive after several years, resulting in "doughnuts." The sunken, circular, straw-colored spots usually remain dead for several months to a year or more, becoming invaded by weeds, such as crabgrass and annual bluegrass. The roots, crowns, and stolons of affected plants are brown to black and rotted. The spots often develop into rings and tend to reappear and enlarge in the same area for several years before disappearing.

Control. Remove excess thatch at least once a year during the summer when it accumulates to ½ in. or more. Use a "vertical mower," "power rake," or similar equipment. Dethatching machines may be rented at many large garden supply stores. Aerify to relieve compaction and promote deep root development.

Follow a suggested fertilizer program for bermudagrass in your area based on a soil test. Maintain *balanced* fertility and a soil reaction (pH) about 6.5. Avoid overfertilizing with nitrogen after late August, maintain high soil levels of potassium (K) and phosphorus (P).

The soil should be well drained. Good surface and subsurface drainage should be provided when establishing a new turf area. Low spots, where water may stand, should be filled in or drained.

Figure 5.78 Spring dead spot in a bermudagrass fairway. (Courtesy L. T. Lucas.)

U-3 bermudagrass, Tifton hybrids (e.g., Tifdwarf, Tiffine, Tifgreen, Tiflawn, Tifway), Sunturf, Texturf 1F, and other improved cultivars are usually more severely attacked than common bermudagrass and Midiron. Cultivars with a high level of winter hardiness are less affected by spring dead spot.

One or more fungicide sprays and drenches during the autumn (Table 5.4) are effective. Three or four monthly treatments may be needed, starting in October.

Summer Patch and Necrotic Ring Spot (Fusarium Blight)

Summer patch and necrotic ring spot are separate diseases that collectively were formerly called Fusarium blight. They are serious and widespread diseases of established Kentucky and annual bluegrass turfs that are managed intensively. These diseases are also difficult to control, primarily because we do not fully understand their biology and development. Summer patch, necrotic ring spot, and perhaps other components produce symptoms that are indistinguishable from each other.

The normally weakly pathogenic soilborne fungus *Phialophora graminicola* causes summer patch disease when hot (83 to 89 °F), sunny days follow warm to hot, very wet then dry periods. The soilborne fungus *Leptosphaeria korrae* causes necrotic ring spot and is favored by cool to mild temperatures and wet then dry conditions from spring to autumn. This disease is most severe in midsummer but may appear from spring to autumn and even during mild winters. *Phialophora* and *Leptosphaeria,* which are very closely related, also closely resemble the take-all fungus, *Gaeumannomyces graminis* var. *avenae* (page 306), in their dark brown mycelial growth ("runner hyphae") *over* the roots, crowns, and rhizomes of grass plants at the edges of the patches, and in their disease development. Also associated with these diseases are one or two presently unidentified primary pathogens as well as species of *Fusarium* (page 240), which are widely distributed but generally considered as secondary pathogens or saprophytes (see Figure 5.29). The *Fusarium* fungi may accelerate the expression of symptoms but are not essential to the final expression of disease. Many bacteria and such fungi as species of *Curvularia* (Figure 5.11), *Colletotrichum* (Figure 5.11), *Rhizoctonia* (Figure 5.2), *Alternaria, Stemphylium,* and yeasts, can also serve as secondary colonizers or saprophytes of the weakened grass plants, thereby substituting or coexisting with the *Fusarium* species.

Grasses susceptible to one or more parts of this disease complex include Kentucky and annual bluegrasses, several fescues (chewings, red, sheep, and tall), colonial and creeping bentgrasses, Italian and perennial ryegrasses, bermudagrass, zoysiagrass, centipedegrass, many other forage, wild, and weed grasses, and small grains.

Summer patch and necrotic ring spot can become severe when turfgrass, especially Kentucky bluegrass, is under stress and entering summer dormancy, although infection may have occurred several months earlier during cool weather. Prolonged periods of high humidity and warm to hot weather with temperature ranges of 75 °F to over 100 °F during the day and above about 70 °F during the night favor disease development. Moisture and heat stress, excessive watering, close mowing, a thick thatch with a soil reaction (pH) of above 7 or below 5, unbalanced applications of fertilizer (an excess of nitrogen and low levels of potassium and/or phosphorus), high populations of parasitic nematodes, such as the stunt nematode (*Tylenchorhynchus dubius,* page 259), compaction, applications of calcium arsenate herbicide, and other factors that predispose turf to stress condi-

Figure 5.79 Fusarium blight (summer patch and necrotic ring spot) in Kentucky bluegrass turf. (Courtesy R. E. Partyka.)

tions usually increase the severity to these diseases. The abiotic factors that most influence disease development appear to be related to the soil and thatch environments. In particular, the factors responsible for the rate of thatch decomposition, including good aeration under warm, moist conditions and an acidic or alkaline soil pH, are strongly implicated. These diseases of Kentucky bluegrass are generally not evident until the second or third years on newly laid sod and usually not for 4 years or more after seeding.

Symptoms.   Scattered light green patches, typically 2 to 6 in. in diameter, appear first. In warm to hot weather, they soon enlarge and rapidly fade to a dull reddish brown, then a light tan, and finally to a light straw color (Figure 5.79). The patches may become sunken elongated streaks, crescents, or roughly circular and 1 to 3 ft or more in diameter. The most characteristic symptom on Kentucky bluegrass in many areas of the United States is a roughly circular, doughnut-shaped area of dead or stunted grass up to 2 or 3 ft across, with tufts of apparently healthy grass in the center, giving a "frogeye" pattern (*Color plate 59*). Plants die as the basal stem, crown, root, and rhizome tissues are destroyed by a hard and tough, black, dark brown, or reddish-brown dry rot. Serious turf damage occurs when the blighted areas (necrotic ring spots) are numerous and overlap. The circular patches tend to increase in size for several years.

Frequently, more subtle symptoms develop. Irregular patches that resemble drought, sod webworm, or chinch bug injury contain living plants scattered among dead or weak plants. The turf in these areas is stunted and often a pale green to various shades of red, yellow or tan, eventually turns dull tan or brown, but does not usually develop distinct rings or patches. Such turf does not readily recover from mowing or adverse weather conditions.

When temperature and moisture are high, a white to pink mycelial growth and masses of *Fusarium* spores (Figure 5.29) can sometimes be found on the lower stem, crowns, and roots of diseased plants near the soil surface.

Disease Cycle.   The causal fungi are believed to have the same disease cycle as for the take-all patch fungus (page 306). The fungi radially grow outward at the rate of 2 to 4 in. per year for several years. Any one patch may "die out" or disappear after reaching a certain size.

Control.   Follow the suggested cultural control measures outlined on pages 212 to 214 to avoid as many environmental stresses as possible, promote root development, and keep the grass growing steadily. Heat stress can be reduced on hot and humid days by briefly sprinkling (syringing) the turf one or more times during midday, keeping the grass mowed to the recommended height, and removing no more than one-third of the leaf surface at one cutting. Grass height should be increased during the warmer months. Keep the soil and thatch pH between 6.5 and 7 by applying small amounts of lime or sulfur at frequent intervals based on a soil test. Avoid excessive applications. Maintain adequate moisture on south- and west-facing sunny slopes and other sites (such as near parking lots, driveways, and sidewalks) that dry faster and have higher thatch and soil temperatures than slopes facing east or north. Use soaker hoses on slopes where water tends to run off instead of slowly infiltrating the soil. Water in the morning so that the grass will dry before dusk. Restrict the use of herbicides.

Avoid pure stands of very susceptible cultivars of Kentucky bluegrass to summer patch and/or necrotic ring spot, such as Arboretum, Argyle, Delft, Delta, Enita, Entoper, Fylking, Galaxy, Garfield, Geronimo, Kenblue, Merion, Newport, Nugget, Park, Plush, Ram I, and South Dakota common or certified. Planting a blend of several Kentucky bluegrass cultivars that have good tolerance or resistance is recommended. Cultivars that have generally proven tolerant include A-20, Able 1, Adelphi, Admiral, America, Aquila, Banff, Baron, Bayside, Bristol, Brunswick, Burke, Campina, Challenger, Cheri, Classic, Columbia, Eclipse, Enmundi, Georgetown, Glade, Gnome, Haga, Majestic, Midnight, Monopoly, Mystic, Nassau, Parade, Piedmont, Princeton 104, Rugby, Shasta, Sydsport, Trenton, Victa, and Windsor. The blending of 15 to 20% seed (by weight) of a turf-type perennial ryegrass mix (e.g., All-Star, Birdie II, Blazer, Cigil, Citation II, Delray, Derby, Elka, Fiesta, Manhattan II, NK-200, Omega II, Palmer, Pennant, Pennfine, Prelude, Premier, Regal, Tara, and Yorktown II) with 80 to 85% seed of resistant Kentucky bluegrass cultivars will sharply reduce the incidence of summer patch and necrotic ring spot. Overseeding diseased turf with a blend of perennial ryegrasses, turf-type tall fescues, or resistant cultivars of Kentucky bluegrass also provides control. Cultivars of Kentucky bluegrass, perennial ryegrass, fine-leaved fescues, bentgrasses, and tall fescue differ in their resistance to *Phialophora graminicola* and *Leptosphaeria korrae*.

Where the cultural controls outlined above and on pages 212 to 214 are not feasible or do not adequately control this disease complex, a number of systemic fungicides are available (Table 5.4). The fungicides should be applied *before* disease symptoms become active again that season. Applications should start in mid to late spring when night temperatures first exceed 70°F and be repeated at intervals during the summer. Carefully follow the manufacturer's directions. Rubigan and Banner are the only fungicides that control both summer patch and necrotic ring spot (Table 5.4). Bayleton, another ergosterol-inhibiting fungicide, and Chipco 26019 are effective only against summer patch.

Key to Infectious Turfgrass Diseases

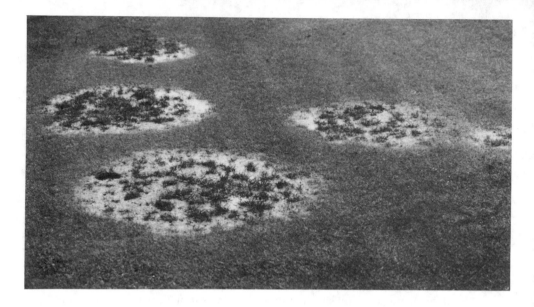

Figure 5.80 Take-all patch in a golf green. (Courtesy L. T. Jucas.)

Take-All Patch

Take-all patch, sometimes called Ophiobolus patch or Gaeumannomyces patch, is caused by the fungus *Gaeumannomyces graminis* var. *avenae*. The disease is largely restricted to cool, moist regions.

Bentgrasses are commonly and seriously attacked. Other cultivated turfgrasses that may become infected include Kentucky and annual bluegrasses, perennial and Italian ryegrasses, red fescues, tall fescue, and rough bluegrass.

The disease is most noticeable from spring to late summer on closely cut bentgrasses that have been excessively limed, improperly fertilized, and are overly wet. In the Pacific Northwest, take-all patch is most commonly associated with light sandy soils and on newly cleared land that was formerly in a Douglas fir/hemlock-type forest.

Symptoms. Take-all patch usually first appears in late spring as scattered, more or less circular, sunken, light yellow, reddish-brown, or bronzed patches of dead grass that continue to enlarge, turn a light brown color, and become dull gray in winter. Affected patches are 4 in. up to 2 to 3 ft or more across. Typically, the sunken centers are invaded by annual bluegrass, fescues, and other resistant grasses, or such broadleaf weeds as dandelions, clovers, and chickweeds, giving a "frogeye" or "doughnut" appearance (Figure 5.80). Around the margin of a patch, where the fungus is active, a bronzed to reddish-brown ring of infected grass plants have dark brown to blackened crowns, and dark, shallow, and rotted roots. Dead plants toward the center of the patch can easily be peeled off. Several patches may merge to kill fairly large, irregularly shaped areas that continue to enlarge up to 10 in. per year for several years. In mixed stands, bentgrasses become thinned and yellow-brown to brown and dominated by weeds and nonsusceptible grasses.

The base of shoots, crowns, stolons, rhizomes, and roots in affected areas become dark brown to black before dying; thus *Gaeumannomyces*-killed turf is very slow to recover. The results of disease may still be evident a year or more after an attack is first visible.

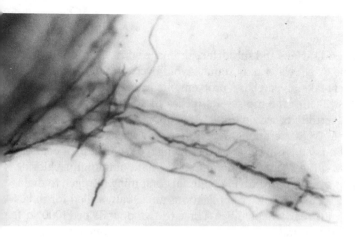

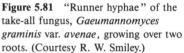

Figure 5.81 "Runner hyphae" of the take-all fungus, *Gaeumannomyces graminis* var. *avenae*, growing over two roots. (Courtesy R. W. Smiley.)

Disease Cycle. The causal fungus survives between seasons as mycelium in colonized but undecomposed grass debris in the thatch or soil and on perennial parts of living grass plants. Healthy crowns, stems, and underground parts of turfgrass plants are invaded by the characteristic dark brown to black mycelium in cool, moist weather. The fungus spreads from plant to plant by strands of dark brown mycelium (runner hyphae) growing *over* roots (Figure 5.81), crowns, rhizomes, or stolons and probably by infected plant debris adhering to mowers and other turf equipment. Associated with the mycelial mats, often embedded in leaf sheath tissue, are brown or black flask-shaped and beaked fruiting bodies (perithecia) that when mature contain large numbers of needlelike ascospores (Figure 5.82). Symptom-free but infected sod, sprigs, and plugs also serve to spread the disease.

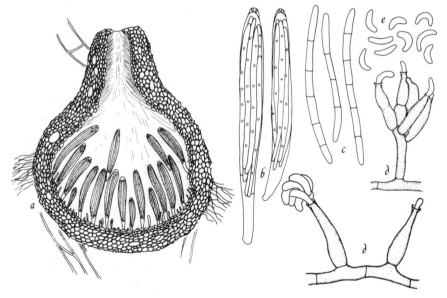

Figure 5.82 Take-all fungus *Gaeumannomyces* (*Ophiobolus*) *graminis*. a, Erumpent perithecium; b, two asci with eight ascospores each; c, three ascospores; d, asexual or *Phialophora* stage with conidiophores and conidia; e, nine conidia.

Control. Provide good surface and subsurface drainage when establishing a new turf area. Fill in depressions where water may stand. Avoid overwatering. Plant a mixture of grasses. In areas where take-all patch is a problem, incorporate 3 to 4 lb of *actual* elemental sulfur per 1000 sq ft into the top several inches of soil prior to planting.

Practice *balanced* soil fertility based on a soil test. Follow local recommendations for the grass or grasses grown. Avoid overliming! Apply lime *only* when absolutely needed on bentgrasses (pH below about 5.0), using a slowly dissolving type (100 mesh or coarser). For fertilizer, use ammonium sulfate, monoammonium phosphate, ammonium chloride, muriate of potash (KCL), or other sulfur-bearing material containing nitrogen to maintain the pH at 5.5 or slightly below. Fertilizer applications are usually called for in late March, mid-May, late June, and early September. Three to five pounds per 1000 sq ft of *actual* elemental sulfur (S) in several split applications is often recommended for each growing season where take-all patch is a serious problem. The disease can often not be stopped with one season of sulfur applications but must be continued for 2 or 3 years.

Take-all patch is often more severe where thatch has built up and the soil has been fumigated. This is probably due to the killing of organisms antagonistic or parasitic on the take-all fungus.

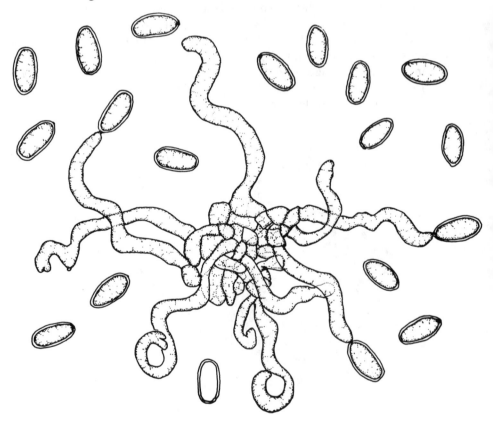

Figure 5.83 *Ovularia hordei,* one of the two fungi that cause tan leaf spot, as seen under a high-power microscope.

Single applications of Banner, Bayleton, and Rubigan in December have proven effective (Table 5.4).

Tan Leaf Spot

Tan leaf spot, caused by two species of the fungus *Ovularia* (*O. hordei* and *O. pusilla*), is known to infect bentgrasses, bluegrasses, fescues, ryegrasses, and wheatgrasses in cool, temperate climates. This is a widely distributed but very minor disease mostly of wild and forage grasses. Infections occur on the leaves, sheaths, and stems.

Symptoms. On fescues the spots are usually round to oval (but sometimes elongate) and tan to brown. On other grasses the spots are round to oval and ash white with reddish margins. The disease is commonly limited to scattered spots on the leaves.

Disease Cycle. The *Ovularia* fungi probably overseason as dormant mycelium in infected tissues and possibly as crystal white, egg-shaped spores or conidia (Figure 5.83). Little is known concerning the disease cycle, when infections occur, and how the fungus is disseminated.

Control. No specific measures have been devised to control tan leaf spot. The cultural practices outlined on pages 212 to 214 should keep tan leaf spot in check.

Tar Spot

Tar spot, also called black leaf spot, is caused by about 20 species of the fungus *Phyllachora*. Most turfgrass species (especially colonial bentgrass and tall fescue) are susceptible to this minor disease, which is most common in wet, shaded areas.

Symptoms. Small, round to oval or elongated, black spots (Figure 5.84) appear on the upper and/or lower leaf surface. Young lesions may be surrounded by a yellowish zone or halo. Heavily infected areas are a mottled yellow-green to bright yellow with black spots. As the leaves mature and age, the area around the black spots often remains green longer than the healthy tissue.

Disease Cycle. The *Phyllachora* fungi are believed to overseason as minute, black fruiting bodies (perithecia) under crusty, black, shieldlike coverings or spots on the leaves. Microscopic ascospores (Figure 5.84) formed in asci within the perithecia are released in the spring, germinate, and infect healthy leaves.

Control. No special measures have been suggested to control this very minor disease.

White Patch

White patches or rings, caused by one or more species of soilborne fungi (mainly *Trechispora* and *Melanotus*), may occur on any species of cultivated turfgrass mostly during cool, humid weather (see also Yellow Ring, page 312).

White patch, caused by *Melanotus phillipsi,* occurs primarily on tall fescue in the southeast in stands less than a year old. On the Atlantic coast from Maryland to Georgia,

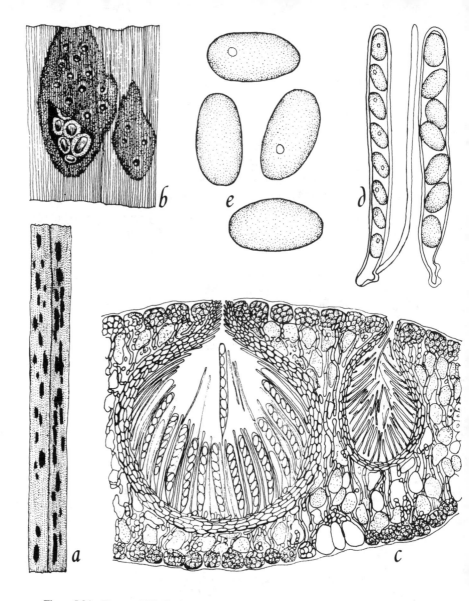

Figure 5.84 Tar spot (*(Phyllachora graminis)*). a, Typical leaf spots on a grass blade; b, close-up of two black "lesions" which are actually crusty, black shieldlike coverings (clypei) over the embedded perithecia; c, cross section of two perithecia within a leaf (one mature with asci and ascospores); d, two asci, each with ascospores; 3, ascospores. (b, as seen through a dissecting microscope; c–e, as seen through a high-power microscope.)

it is a problem on fine fescues and Kentucky bluegrass. This fungus is active during h humid weather when daytime air temperatures exceed 85°F, night temperatures do r fall below 70°F, and soil moisture is low.

Symptoms.   Superficial or distinctly off-white patches or rings, up to about 15 in diameter, appear mostly on bentgrasses and Kentucky bluegrass during cool, hun

Figure 5.85 White patch in a creeping bentgrass green. (Courtesy L. T. Lucas.)

weather or hot, humid weather, depending on the causal fungus (Figure 5.85). Individual patches often coalesce to involve large areas of turf. Distinguishing characteristics include small fruiting bodies ($\frac{1}{16}$ to $\frac{5}{16}$ in. in diameter) with gills on the leaf blades and a dense, white to pinkish mat of mycelium, 1 to 2½ in. across, at the margin of the ring. Sparse white mycelium is commonly observed within the ring. The aerial mycelium disappears when the weather warms in spring, but the creamy to mealy white mycelium can still be seen in the thatch during the summer months. Older leaves in the white patches may mat together, turn from tan to bleached white, and become closely pressed to the soil. Root growth is stunted. Grass in the centers of the rings may or may not appear healthy. When cooler weather returns the patches disappear.

Disease Cycle.   Several to many different fungi with clamp connections (Figure 5.2) in their hyphae cause white patch. Small, roundish mushrooms form in the dense white mycelium and bear spores (basidiospores) on the surfaces of their gills. The spores of *Trechispora* presumably germinate, and the hyphae grow out radially in the thatch during cool, wet weather to form a circular patch. Mycelial growth slows during warm, dry weather. *Melanotus,* unlike *Trechispora,* causes more severe damage in hot, humid weather, especially on sunny or droughty sites.

Control.   Remove thatch that is over ½ in. thick. See the cultural control suggestions outlined on pages 212 to 214. Fungicides effective against leaf smuts (page 249), Typhula blight (page 293), and Rhizoctonia diseases (page 273) should be of some help. See Table 5.4 on pages 323 to 327. Tall fescue cultivars differ in resistance.

Figure 5.86 White mycelium of *Trechispora alnicola* in thatch beneath the yellowed leaves in a yellow ring. (Courtesy H. T. Wilkinson.)

Yellow Ring

This disease of Kentucky bluegrass, caused by the soilborne fungus *Trechispora alnicola,* is evident from May into early autumn. It is most evident on heavily thatched (over ¾ in. thick) turf that has sufficient water and nutrients to remain green and lush during the entire growing season. The disease has been reported from a number of states in the midwest and northeast. Another species of *Trechispora* (*T. confinis*) is known to attack creeping bentgrass (*Agrostis palustris*).

Symptoms. Lemon to golden-yellow rings, 4 in. wide and up to 4½ ft in diameter, occur in otherwise healthy turf (*Color plate 60*). A dense, white mycelial growth is evident, up to an inch or more thick, in the thatch beneath the yellowed leaves (Figure 5.86). Diseased turf does not die. The rings enlarge from one year to the next.

Disease Cycle. *Trechispora alnicola* is largely a saprophyte that colonizes dead grass in the thatch and is therefore beneficial in breaking this debris down into elements available to the living grass. The fungus is believed to survive as dormant mycelium in plant debris and possibly in living plants and the soil. When favorable conditions of temperature, moisture, and nutrition return, the mycelium resumes growth and heavily colonizes the thatch, causing the leaves of living grass plants to turn yellow. The importance of spores produced by the fungus in possible spread and infection is unknown. The causal fungus appears to be disseminated in water and by equipment.

Control. Dethatch affected turf in early spring or fall when it accumulates to ½ in. Use a vertical mower, power rake, or similar dethatching equipment. Applications of PCNB or quintozene (sold as Terraclor, Turfcide, Lesco PCNB, Lawn Fungicide Spray, and Lawn Disease Preventer) have proven effective (see Table 5.5). Kentucky bluegrass cultivars differ in resistance.

Zoysia Patch

This newly recognized disease, whose cause is presently unknown, has been observed on sod farms and golf course fairways in the Mississippi Valley area of Missouri for more than 10 years. It has also been identified in Arkansas, Illinois, Indiana, Oklahoma, and Tennessee.

Figure 5.87 Zoysia patch. (Courtesy H. T. Wilkinson.)

Symptoms.   Roughly circular patches of dead grass, up to 18 ft or more in diameter, appear in the spring as the zoysiagrass begins to break dormancy (Figure 5.87). The patch often develops a red-yellow band up to 8 in. wide at the outer edge. The band disappears as temperatures rise above 75 to 80°F. The disease is again active in the fall as cooler temperatures start to slow down growth of the zoysiagrass. The patches grow out radially each season at the rate of up to 6 ft or more. Diseased patches, which persist for several years, can become irregular as individual patches merge, and may later be invaded by grassy and broadleaf weeds.

Disease Cycle.   Unknown. A temperature range of 60 to 70°F appears optimal for disease development.

Control.   Unknown.

TURFGRASS DISEASE CONTROL

Turfgrass disease control should begin with a rapid and accurate diagnosis of the problem. Diagnosis is based on knowledge of the turfgrass(es), its adaptation, growing requirements, and expected problems, such as insects (Chapter 4), diseases, and noninfectious disorders (Chapter 2). When other possible causes are eliminated, a disease problem should be considered.

Turfgrass diseases vary in severity from year to year and from one locality or region to another, depending on environmental conditions (principally moisture, temperature, humidity, and grass nutrition), the relative resistance or susceptibility of the turfgrass host, and the causal fungus or other pathogen. For disease to develop, all three factors must be present and in balance. For example, if the environment is favorable for a disease and the disease-producing fungus (bacterium or virus) is present but the host plant is highly resistant, little or no disease will develop. Similarly, if the causal agent is present and the host is susceptible but the environment is unfavorable, disease usually does not occur. A disease results from the right combination of a susceptible grass plant, a virulent pathogen, and an environment favorable for infection, growth, reproduction, and spread of the pathogen, plus the necessary time for the disease to develop.

We can put this relationship in the form of a simple equation:

$$\text{susceptible grass} \quad + \quad \text{disease-causing pathogen}$$
$$+ \qquad\qquad\qquad + \qquad\qquad = \text{disease}$$
$$\text{proper environment} + \text{spread of pathogen and time to develop}$$

If any one of the foregoing key ingredients is lacking, disease will not develop. Effective disease control measures are aimed at breaking this equation in one of three basic ways: (1) the susceptible turfgrass plant is made more resistant; (2) the air and soil environment is made less favorable for the causal pathogen and more favorable for growth of the grass plant; and (3) the pathogen is killed or prevented from reaching the plant, penetrating it, and producing disease. Integrated disease control involves the use of all of these management tools.

Three Basic Methods of Control

1. *The grass plant is made more resistant.* This is the ideal method of control. Grass breeders and other researchers are trying to develop more resistant grasses. Some progress has been made. We now have grass cultivars that are somewhat resistant to dollar spot, red thread, snow molds, one or more "Helminthosporium" diseases, one or more rusts, powdery mildew, summer patch and/or necrotic ring spot, gray leaf spot, St. Augustine-grass decline (SAD), spring dead spot of bermudagrass, and other diseases. This important control measure is still in its infancy. For some diseases, such as brown patch, Pythium blight, and rust diseases, where the causal fungi are composed of a large number of biotypes, strains, or races, the development of highly resistant or immune grass cultivars is many years in the future. Before such grasses can be developed and released, sources of resistance in wild or cultivated grasses must be found. Then comes the long, time-consuming process of breeding this resistance into otherwise desirable grasses. This resistance often "breaks down" in a few years as new races of the pathogen arise.

Grass cut at the proper height (1½ to 2½ in. for bluegrasses, ryegrasses, and fescues; 1 to ½ in. or less for bentgrasses, zoysiagrasses, and bermudagrass) usually has less disease than turf that is cut too short or is scalped. Without sufficient green leaf area to manufacture food to produce new leaves, roots, rhizomes, and stolons, the grass is definitely weakened or stressed. Grasses that are maintained as a mowed turf, such as in a lawn, athletic field, park, fairway, cemetery, or golf green are more subject to attack by disease-producing fungi and bacteria than they are in their natural environment. Exceptions are the rust diseases and pink patch, which are worse on unmowed grasses. Healthy, vigorously growing, adapted turfgrasses that are properly managed can best ward off disease attacks as well as insects, weeds, and other problems.

Another means of increasing tolerance to attack by pathogens is through properly balanced plant nutrition. Dollar spot, red thread and pink patch, pink snow mold or Fusarium patch, gray snow mold or Typhula blight, Pythium blight, powdery mildew, rusts, brown patch, summer patch and necrotic ring spot, anthracnose, take-all patch, spring dead spot, gray leaf spot, and "Helminthosporium" diseases are less serious when a moderate and uniform level of soil nutrients is maintained in the root zone. This may mean making fewer and lighter applications of fertilizer and keeping the three major nutrients—nitrogen (N), phosphorus (P), and potassium (K)—in balance. When N is high in relation to P and K, there may be disease trouble, especially in hot weather. A high level of potassium helps reduce injury from brown patch, dollar spot, Fusarium patch, gray snow mold, red thread and pink patch, take-all patch, Pythium blight, and "Helminthosporium"-caused diseases.

2. *The environment is made less favorable for the pathogen.* Fungi and bacteria that cause turf diseases thrive in the turf environment given an adequate supply of food, moisture, oxygen, and a favorable temperature. The basic concept in this method of control is to grow grass in an environment that will be unfavorable to the growth, multiplication, and spread of disease-producing organisms. This can be done by:

a. *Keeping the grass blades as dry as possible for as long as possible.* Fungi, with the exception of powdery mildew, require free moisture on the grass plant for 1½ to 12 hours or more to infect a plant. Poling, brushing, and hosing are means of removing dew and guttated water in which these organisms thrive.

Water established turf thoroughly during a drought. Moisten the soil to a depth of 6 in. or more with each irrigation. Water as infrequently as possible. Avoid daily light sprinklings, especially in the late afternoon or evening, that result in grass blades remaining wet overnight. Another way to speed drying of the grass is to increase light penetration and air movement by selectively pruning or removing dense trees, shrubs, or other barriers that border the turf area.

Poor surface and subsoil drainage lead to compaction and soil aeration problems. Roots suffocate from lack of oxygen. The indirect result, too frequently, is disease (e.g., Pythium blight, snow molds, Rhizoctonia diseases). Stagnant, humid air over a pocketed turf area causes disease problems because there is no wind to dry off the grass blades. If we could keep grass dry, we would have few foliar disease problems. Root rots that cause wilt of golf greens in July or August are commonly due to overwatering of the root zone. Keeping the soil near the saturation point prevents normal root growth and favors the growth of organisms that are common water molds (e.g., *Pythium*). Proper water management is the single biggest environmental factor in keeping disease in check on frequently watered and highly maintained turf areas.

b. *Eliminating the thatch or mat* in which disease organisms thrive. Removal of thatch removes the food supply for the fungi causing dollar spot, Pythium blight, brown patch, "Helminthosporium" diseases, fairy rings, red thread, pink patch, yellow ring, and white patch and forces them to compete unfavorably with the multitude of bacteria and fungi in the soil (4 to 8 billion organisms per pound of topsoil). Many of these soil-inhabiting organisms are antagonistic (suppressive) to or even parasitic on the disease-producing fungi that attack grass.

Periodic removal of thatch can greatly reduce the use of fungicides or other control measures. Remove thatch in early spring or in early autumn when it accumulates to ½ in. or more. You can buy or rent a "vertical mower," "power rake," or similar equipment at many large garden supply or equipment rental stores.

Although clippings contribute little to a buildup of thatch, their removal has helped in the control of several important diseases, including Pythium blight, rusts, leaf smuts, brown patch, dollar spot, summer patch or necrotic ring spot (Fusarium blight), various leaf spots, red thread, and "Helminthosporium" diseases. The removal of clippings from infected plants can also reduce the number of pathogens (such as rusts and leaf spots) and hasten recovery.

c. *Avoiding competition.* Keep large trees away from golf greens and tees or install root barriers.

d. *Not injuring the grass* by careless use of pesticides and fertilizers, using a mower that is dull or out of adjustment; compaction—walking or riding on turf that is soggy; removing more than one-third of the foliage at one mowing; and so on. Avoid dumping piles of mowed clippings on turf and remove tree leaves promptly. Remember that anything that weakens or stresses grass may lower its natural resistance, allowing a disease-producing fungus to "take over." Compacted turf areas should be aerified using a hand aerifier (hollow-tined fork) or power machine. This equipment can often be purchased or rented at large garden supply stores.

3. *The pathogen is killed or prevented from reaching the grass plant and producing disease.* This can be done by removing moisture from the grass blades, thus preventing a fungus from penetrating; using sand or other amendments to improve subsurface drainage and aeration; buying only top-quality seed, sod, sprigs, or plugs from a reputable dealer who has followed a sound disease management program; and by following suggested weed and insect control practices (see Chapters 3 and 4). The principal means of control here is chemical.

CHEMICAL CONTROL OF TURFGRASS DISEASES

The pesticides used to control diseases of turfgrasses include soil fumigants, nematicides, and fungicides.

Soil Fumigants

A soil fumigant (or biocide) can be applied to the turf area before planting to kill soilborne fungi, bacteria, nematodes, insects, and other soil fauna, and weed seeds at one time. Chemicals such as methyl bromide, chloropicrin, Vorlex, or Stauffer Vapam Soil Fumigant perform this function. The expense is fairly high, but more and more fumigation is being done before seeding or sodding golf and bowling greens, turfgrass nurseries, athletic fields, and even home lawns. Before application of a fumigant, the soil should be (1) at a moisture level for good seed germination (not too dry or wet); (2) thoroughly prepared as for a seedbed and free of large clods, roots, or other coarse organic debris; and (3) at a temperature of above 50°F, preferably 60 to 80°F. A gas-proof polyethylene cover is generally placed over the treated area for several days or longer to retain the toxic fumes of the fumigant. *Only experienced and licensed pesticide applicators are permitted to apply these toxic chemicals.* Because it takes 1 to 3 weeks or more for the fumes to dissipate in the soil, seeding, sodding, sprigging, or plugging must be delayed for 10 days to several weeks. (This is why fumigation is often done in early fall.)

Following fumigation, disease and nematode problems may become *more* severe because of the lack of competitive fungi, bacteria, nematodes, and other beneficial soil organisms in the treated area. Once a pathogen is introduced (blown, washed, tracked, or hauled) into a treated area, there is no "biological check and balance." As far as disease control is concerned, soil fumigation is most useful for controlling the fungi that cause brown patch, summer patch and necrotic ring spot, leaf smuts, gray snow mold, southern blight, Pythium blight, red thread, and dollar spot.

Nematicides

Nematode numbers in soil are greatly reduced before planting by application of a soil fumigant. A fumigant applied just to control nematodes is justified only where the turf has had a problem or history of high populations of plant-parasitic nematodes. When turfgrass is established, a liquid or granular contact nematicide (Table 5.4) properly applied uniformly to the turf will sharply reduce nematode numbers. Most nematicides will also control such insects as chinch bugs, cutworms, grubs, sod webworms, and other pests (Chapter 4). The nematicide-insecticide is drenched *immediately* into the thatch and soil using ½ to 1 in. of water (300 to 600 gal of water per 1000 sq ft of turf). Treatment is best done in the autumn or spring (or both, if nematodes are a serious problem) when the soil temperature is above 55 °F. (*Warning:* Do not apply nematicides at high temperatures (above 80 to 85 °F) due to the high potential for turf injury.) Core aerification of the turf before application improves the results. *This is not a treatment for newly established areas.* Since contact nematicides are highly toxic chemicals, it is important that all the manufacturer's directions and precautions be carefully followed. *These chemicals are for use only by certified and/or licensed pesticide applicators. Never apply a nematicide without first having a nematode analysis.*

Fungicides

Fungicides are formulated and sold to kill certain groups of fungi (true fungicides), or to inhibit the growth or reproduction of fungi (fungistats) for a period of days, weeks, or months.

The fungicides used to control diseases of turfgrasses are of two general types: protective-contact and systemic fungicides. *Protective-contact fungicides* are generally applied to the foliage to keep disease-causing fungal spores and mycelium from entering susceptible grass tissue. This type of fungicide prevents disease and usually cannot kill fungi after they have entered grass tissue. These fungicides must be applied fairly frequently to turf (usually at 5- to 14-day intervals) since mowing, rain, or irrigation remove much of the surface chemical barrier soon after application. Relatively high spray volumes (3 to 5 or 10 gal of water per 1000 sq ft of turf) are required to supply uniform and continous coverage of the foliage and thatch with the fungicide. Adding a spreader-sticker (or surfactant) to the spray mixture often facilitates better foliar coverage. Many available fungicides for turf use are of the protective-contact type; some also have limited systemic activity. These include cycloheximide (Acti-dione products), chlorothalonil (Daconil 2787, Thal-O-Nil), anilazine (Dyrene, Dymec, Lescorene, ProTurf Fungicide III), quintozene (PCNB, Terraclor,

Turfcide), cadmium compounds* (Cadminate, Caddy, Lebanon Fungicide Type C), zineb (Zineb), maneb (Dithane M-22), mancozeb (Fore, Formec 80, Lesco 4), captan (Captan 50, Orthocide), iprodione (Chipco 26019, ProTurf Fungicide VI), ethazole or etridiazole (Koban, Terrazole), mercury chlorides* (Calo-Clor, Calo-Gran), thiram (Thiramad, Spotrete, Lebanon Fungicide Type T), thiram plus a cadmium compound (Cad-Trete, Kromad, Cleary's Granular Turf Fungicide), phenylmercuric acetate (PMAS), and thiram plus PMA (ProTurf Broad Spectrum Fungicide).

Systemic fungicides are absorbed and translocated within the grass plant, destroying or suppressing established infections. The direction of movement within a grass plant depends on the type of systemic fungicide used. Most chemicals only move upward in the plant. Certain products control specific diseases for weeks or months. These fungicides are applied to the foliage or roots and are absorbed by the plant and distributed internally. For certain diseases, such as leaf smuts, summer patch, and necrotic ring spot, the fungicide needs to be drenched or watered in for best results, preferably following core cultivation. Examples of systemic fungicides include benomyl (Tersan 1991, Benomyl, Lebanon Fungicide Type B), thiophanate compounds (Fungo 50, Cleary's 3336, ProTurf Systemic Fungicide), propamocarb (Banol), triadimefon (Bayleton, ProTurf Fungicide 7), fenarimol (Rubigan), propiconazole (Banner), metalaxyl (Subdue, Apron), vinclozolin (Vorlan), thiophanate-ethyl plus thiram (Bromosan), and thiophanate-methyl + mancozeb (Duosan).

Both protective-contact and systemic fungicides are available as wettable powder (WP), flowable (F), and soluble (S) formulations for application as sprays or soil drenches. Some are also available in granular (G) formulations. Granular fungicides are mostly used on dormant grass to control snow molds and other cold-weather diseases or on closely cut golf and bowling greens. Granular products are *not* very efficient in covering the leaf surfaces of lawn-type turfs. Presumably, they act by suppressing fungus growth and spore production in the thatch, although several are systemic and taken up by the grass leaves and roots.

Most chemical control of turfgrass diseases is through the use of turf fungicides that are applied on a preventive schedule, *before* the disease strikes. *The manufacturer's directions on the container label should be carefully followed as regards rates to use, interval between applications, compatibility with other chemicals, grasses on which the fungicide is to be used, and safe use and handling.*

The method of application is also very important. If spraying, use about 5 gal of spray per 1000 sq ft to adequately wet the grass blades, thatch, and top ¼ in. or more of soil. Use 1 to 3 gal of spray against such diseases as powdery mildew, dollar spot, brown patch, red thread and pink patch, Septoria, Ascochyta and other leaf spots, and rusts. Other diseases, such as Pythium blight, "Helminthosporium" melting-out (crown, root, and rhizome rot), and snow molds, attack the crown and root area before growing on and over the grass surface. Here 3 to 5 gal per 1000 sq ft is usually adequate. For control of summer patch and necrotic ring spot (Fusarium blight) and leaf smuts, a soil drench using ½ to 1 in. of water (300 to 600 gal of water per 1000 sq ft) is needed to move the fungicide down into the root zone. This is best done by first spraying the turf with the recommended rate of fungicide, followed immediately by irrigation to deliver the desired amount of water.

*Cadmium compounds are not permitted to be used in certain states; and mercury chlorides can only be used on golf course greens, tees, and aprons.

Lawn-type grasses.   One or more broad-spectrum turf fungicides, such as Actidione Thiram or TGF, Daconil 2787, Dyrene, Chipco 26019, Duosan, and Kromad, may be used to maintain a lawn-type grass, such as a home or industrial lawn, municipal or state park, airport, athletic turf, school or church grounds, cemetery, sod farm, fairways and tees, highway shoulders, or median strip. All of these fungicides control *"Helminthosporium"-caused diseases* and *dollar spot* as well as other less important diseases (Table 5.4).

If *powdery mildew* is a problem in the shade, you may wish to add Cleary's 3336, Fungo 50, Tersan 1991 or Bayleton to the list above.

If *rusts* are serious in warm to hot weather, Fore, zineb, Duosan, Bayleton, Actidione Thiram or TGF, Dyrene, and Daconil provide good to excellent control.

Snow molds (primarily Fusarium patch or pink snow mold and Typhula blight or gray snow mold) damage turf in shady areas and where snow is slow to melt. Products that give control include Bayleton, Chipco 26019, Cad-Trete, Rubigan, or chloroneb (Teremec SP and Terraneb SP) *plus* PCNB or Terraclor. Duosan, Fungo 50, Tersan 1991, and Vorlan control Fusarium patch but not Typhula blight, while Daconil 2787 and Cadminate control Typhula blight but not Fusarium patch.

Summer patch and necrotic ring spot (formerly called Fusarium blight) are becoming more severe each year, especially in sunny, droughty areas where turf has a thick thatch. Banner and Rubigan applied as preventives give good to excellent control of both diseases where thatch has been removed, nitrogen is applied, and turf is thoroughly watered during dry periods. Bayleton and Chipco 26019 are other good preventive fungicides but one of these products should be combined with Tersan 1991, Fungo 50, or Cleary's 3336 to control both diseases (Table 5.4).

Seed decay (rot) and seedling blights are usually problems only with poorly germinating seed, or seed planted in an excessively wet seedbed, and/or at unseasonable temperatures. Treat seed with captan or thiram plus Koban or Apron before planting. Spray at early seedling emergence and repeat at 5- to 7-day intervals. Most turf fungicides (Table 5.4) do a good job of postemergence disease control, either alone or mixed with Koban, Terrazole, chloroneb, or Subdue.

Leaf smuts (largely stripe smut and flag smut) are of major concern in Kentucky bluegrass and creeping bentgrass turf areas over 2 or 3 years of age. The only materials to provide lasting (or eradicative) control are the fungicides Bayleton, Cleary's 3336, PCNB (Terraclor), Fungo 50, Rubigan, and Tersan 1991. These materials must be applied in late autumn, just before the grass goes into dormancy. These products need to be drenched into the soil (Table 5.4). Make two applications, 14 to 21 days apart. Carefully follow the label directions.

If you stock only one broad-spectrum turf fungicide, choose between Daconil 2787, Chipco 26019, Duosan, Vorlan, Dyrene, Kromad, and Acti-dione Thiram or TGF. When other disease problems are expected, supplement the broad-spectrum product with one or more disease-specific chemicals.

Bentgrasses.   If you are growing bentgrasses on golf greens, low-cut tees, fairways, or other areas, choose a broad-spectrum fungicide to control *"Helminthosporium" diseases, dollar spot,* and *brown patch* (e.g., Acti-dione Thiram or TGF, Daconil 2787, Dyrene, Chipco 26019, Duosan, Vorlan, or Kromad).

In hot, humid weather, when *Pythium* is active, Banol, Subdue, Koban, Terrazole, or chloroneb (Teremec SP and Terraneb SP) do an excellent job. In hot or very humid weather, Banol, Subdue, Koban, Terrazole, or chloroneb are often mixed with Daconil 2787, Dyrene, Fore, Tersan 1991, Chipco 26019, Duosan, Vorlan, Bayleton, Kromad, Cleary's 3336, or Fungo 50 to give a more broad-spectrum disease control.

Snow molds damage turf in shady areas, where snow is slow to melt and where no protective fungicide has been applied. Golf course superintendents who are certified can use Calo-Clor or Calo-Gran (both are restricted by the label) on golf course greens, tees, and aprons (Table 5.4). Otherwise, use one of the products mentioned for snow mold control under Lawn-Type Grasses.

Where *dollar spot* is a serious problem on creeping bentgrass, even where the turf has been adequately fertilized, the systemics (Tersan 1991, Bayleton, Banner, Vorlan, Cleary's 3336, Duosan, Fungo 50, Rubigan) and cadmium compounds (Cadminate, Caddy) provide the longest and best protection. Be alert, however, for evidence of resistant strains of the dollar spot fungus. Using a systemic fungicide in combination with Chipco 26019, Dyrene, Daconil, or Kromad and/or alternating fungicides that are chemically not related should solve the resistance problem. It is often suggested that Fore or zineb *not be added* in the same spray tank, since these products tend to stimulate dollar spot when used at normal rates (2 to 6 oz per 1000 sq ft), probably because they kill or suppress fungi that are antagonistic to the dollar spot fungi.

Leaf smuts are an uncommon problem. For control, see leaf smuts under Lawn-Type Grasses above.

Effective chemical control of turf diseases depends on a rapid and accurate diagnosis. Experienced golf course superintendents, sod growers, lawn care company personnel, and other turfgrass managers can usually recognize or predict the occurrence of common diseases and hence can promptly initiate proper chemical controls. Homeowners, however, are usually unable to diagnose turf diseases until substantial damage has occurred.

The use of fungicides is generally discouraged in most home lawn situations (unlike chemical control of weeds and insects) for several reasons: (1) proper diagnosis and selection of the right fungicide to apply is difficult, (2) it is usually too late for recovery after extensive damage has occurred, (3) homeowners often lack the proper application equipment or cannot purchase the suggested turfgrass fungicide(s) locally, (4) it is probably less expensive and more satisfactory in the long run to overseed or resod a diseased turf area with a mixture or blend of disease-resistant cultivars or species, and (5) lack of application experience and proper certification to handle pesticides.

Some negative effects of fungicides.* The indiscriminate use of fungicides or the employment of numerous preventative applications for many diseases, especially minor ones, should be discouraged. The reasons include: (1) Fungicides may reduce the populations of beneficial bacteria and fungi in the soil, which could lead to an excessive buildup of thatch. (2) Fungicides may upset the delicate balance among microorganisms in the soil and thatch that compete with and antagonize disease-causing fungi. This probably explains why certain diseases reoccur more commonly, rapidly, and cause more damage in turf previously treated with fungicides. (3) Continuous usage of a single

*Much of the material in this section has come from articles published by Peter H. Dernoeden.

fungicide or fungicides closely related chemically may lead to the development of fungal strains that are resistant to that particular fungicide or fungicides. (4) A fungicide may control one disease while encouraging the development of other diseases. (5) Phytotoxic or undesirable hormonal effects are possible. These effects include negative changes in shoot density, leaf growth, and root mass, changes in chlorophyll content, delay of senescence, and changes in the nonstructural carbohydrate content.

The repeated use of certain fungicides [e.g., Tersan 1991, Bromosan, Duosan, Fore, thiram (Thiramad and Spotrete), cadmium fungicides, and Chipco 26019] commonly leads to a buildup of thatch. Tersan 1991, Bromosan, Duosan, Fore, and thiram cause an accumulation of thatch by acidifying the soil, which inhibits decomposition of the thatch by beneficial microorganisms. Cadmium fungicides and Chipco 26019 enhance a buildup of thatch by directly inhibiting or killing the microorganisms that break down thatch into humus. Certain fungicides (Tersan 1991, Fore, Dyrene, and Daconil 2787) are toxic to earthworms, which mix soil with organic matter and also feed on the thatch.

The increasing resistance (more correctly called tolerance) of turfgrass pathogens to fungicides is of concern to turfgrass managers. Strains, races, or biotypes of the dollar spot, red thread, powdery mildew, summer patch and necrotic ring spot, Pythium blight, and pink snow mold organisms have become tolerant in recent years. For example, tolerant strains of the dollar spot fungi following repeated applications of cadmium fungicides, Tersan 1991, Fungo 50, Cleary's 3336, and Duosan is well documented. Scattered tolerance has also been reported to Dyrene and Chipco 26019. Tolerant strains of the fungi causing necrotic ring spot and powdery mildew are known to benzimidazole fungicides (Tersan 1991, Fungo 50, and Cleary's 3336). When a fungus becomes tolerant to benomyl (Tersan 1991) it is usually tolerant to the closely related thiophanate fungicides (Cleary's 3336 and Fungo 50). Tolerance to metalaxyl (Subdue) is known for strains of *Pythium aphanidermatum* causing Pythium blight. Strains of the pink snow mold fungus have been reported tolerant to Chipco 26019. The continued development of tolerant strains of turfgrass-infecting fungi is probably due to mutations and a selection process, whereby a small population of naturally occurring tolerant individuals eventually predominate in fungicide-treated turfgrass.

Fungicides applied to control one disease may encourage one or more other diseases to become troublesome. Examples include the use of Bayleton, Tersan 1991 and related fungicides, which enhance more severe attacks of "Helminthosporium"-caused diseases, Pythium blight, and white patch. Applications of Tersan 1991, Cleary's 3336, and Fungo 50 may make grass more susceptible to rust; Daconil 2787 may cause more severe injury to Kentucky bluegrass cultivars from summer patch and necrotic ring spot; applications of Chipco 26019 may increase yellow tuft; zineb, maneb, and mancozeb often stimulate attacks of dollar spot; benomyl and maneb have been reported to encourage red thread; and fungicides used to control snow molds have resulted in outbreaks of winter brown patch.

The buildup of a disease from continued use of a particular fungicide to control another problem has been attributed to an upset in the delicate balance between beneficial (antagonistic) and pathogenic microorganisms in the thatch–soil environment. Some researchers feel that continued use of certain fungicides may alter the physiology of a grass plant, making it more susceptible to a particular fungus or an environmental stress.

When used improperly, fungicides can also cause injury (phytotoxicity). Most reports of injury, generally not severe, have occurred when chemicals were applied during hot (above

85 to 90 °F) weather, especially to bentgrasses. Fungicides reported to cause yellowing or a tip dieback of bentgrass under high-temperature stress include Acti-dione products, PCNB (Terraclor and Acti-dione RZ), mercury products (Calo-Clor and PMAS), and Tersan 1991. Other fungicides (e.g., Banner, Rubigan, Bayleton, and PMAS) have given treated bentgrass a blue-green color when used repeatedly and at high rates. PCNB may cause Tufcote bermudagrass to turn purplish when applied in the autumn. Nematicides, such as Mocap, ProTurf Nematicide, Dasanit, and Nemacur, can seriously discolor or kill turfgrasses if not properly watered in immediately after application, especially in hot weather.

What does all this mean? Chemicals are an aid to disease control when the environment, coupled with stress conditions for the turf, "tip the balance" in favor of the pathogen. When fungicides or nematicides are applied strictly according to label directions on the turfgrasses specified, the chances of injury are remote. Most problems arise when repeated high rates are used in hot weather to grass that is already under stress. Tolerance to fungicides appears when the same fungicide, or one closely related to it chemically, is used repeatedly over one or more seasons on the same turf area. The answer to this problem is to combine two or three unrelated fungicides in the same spray tank to control the same disease or alternate among the fungicides listed to control a given disease (see Table 5.4).

Getting Ready to Spray*

Wettable powder products must be kept in suspension if they are to be applied accurately without equipment containing an agitator. The newer flowable and soluble products stay in suspension no matter what ground or air application equipment is used. Emulsifiable concentrate (EC) formulations and other water-soluble materials are easy to apply but may cause injury, especially in hot weather. Unlike insecticides, very few fungicides are formulated as emulsifiable concentrates. In general, wettable powders, flowables, and solubles should *not* be mixed with emulsifiable concentrates unless the product label states otherwise.

The time interval between spray applications will vary with the temperature, target disease(s), cultural management practices, grass cultivar and species, chemical used, and amount of rainfall or irrigation. The spray interval may be as short as 5 days in hot, wet weather or 2 weeks and longer if the weather is cool and dry. Some systemic fungicides give protection for 3 to 6 weeks, even when 4 to 6 in. of water has fallen as rain or has been applied by sprinkler. A protective-contact fungicide may last only a few days under similar conditions. The problem is complex and one that has to be "felt out," based on knowledge of the chemical and its past performance, the problem turf area involved, past fungicide and other records, and knowledge of the factors that cause a particular disease to flourish. It is only through adequate record keeping that you can hope to determine why a certain chemical failed or did a good job. Remember that even the best fungicide or fungicide mixture is only *one* tool in keeping turfgrass diseases in check. *All the fungicides in the world cannot compensate for or replace a poor turf management program.*

*For a complete discussion of pesticide application and equipment, read Chapter 6.

TABLE 5.4 CHEMICAL CONTROL OF TURFGRASS DISEASES

Disease (pathogen)[a]	Principal turfgrasses affected	Normal season and intervals of application[b] (remarks)	Fungicide[c]
"Helminthosporium" diseases			Materials listed below are somewhat to
Leaf spot, melting-out (*Drechslera poae*)	Kentucky bluegrass	March–June; September–November 7–21 days	very effective against *all* "Helmin-
Leaf spot, crown and root rot (*Bipolaris sorokiniana*)	All turfgrasses (except centipede, bahia, zoysia, and St. Augustine)	May–October 7–21 days	thosporium" diseases: Acti-dione RZ Acti-dione TGF
Zonate leaf spot or eyespot (*Drechslera gigantea*)	Bluegrasses, bermudagrass, bentgrasses	June–September 7–21 days	Acti-dione Thiram Bromosan Captan
Red leaf spot (*Drechslera erythrospila*)	Bentgrasses	April–September 7–21 days	Chipco 26019 Daconil 2787 Duosan
Net blotch, crown and root rot (*Drechslera dictyoides*)	Fescues, ryegrasses	March–July 7–21 days	Dyrene, Dymec Fore, Formec 80 Kromad PCNB, Terraclor 75
Brown blight (*Drechslera siccans*)	Ryegrasses	March–June 7–21 days	Thiram + PMAS Vorlan
Leaf blotch or blight, crown and root rot (*Bipolaris cynodontis, Exserohilum rostrata, Drechslera spicifer, D. triseptata, B. stenospila*)	Bermudagrass, St. Augustine, zoysia	March–June 7–21 days	
Leaf blight, crown rot (*Drechslera catenaria*)	Bentgrasses, redtop	March–June 7–21 days	
Summer patch (*Phialophora graminicola*) and necrotic ring spot (*Leptosphaeria korrae*) Fusarium leaf spot and crown rot (*Fusarium* species)	Bentgrasses, bermudagrass, bluegrasses, fine fescues, ryegrasses	April–September 14–21 days (Drench 300–600 gal per 1000 sq ft into the root zone. Water turf the day before.)	Banner, Rubigan, or Chipco 26019 *or* Bayleton[c] *plus* Cleary's 3336, Fungo 50, *or* Tersan 1991

TABLE 5.4 CHEMICAL CONTROL OF TURFGRASS DISEASES (Continued)

Disease (pathogen)[a]	Principal turfgrasses affected	Normal season and intervals of application[b] (remarks)	Fungicide[c]
Dollar spot *(Lanzia* and *Moellerodiscus* spp.; formerly called *Sclerotinia homoeocarpa)*	All turfgrasses	March–November 7–21 days (Resistance to cadmium compounds, benomyl, Dyrene, and other fungicides has been reported in some areas.)	Acti-dione TGF Acti-dione Thiram Acti-dione RZ Banner Bayleton Bromosan Cadmium compounds[d] Chipco 26019 Cleary's 3336 Daconil 2787
Red thread/ pink patch (Laetisaria fuciformis/ Limonomyces roseipellis)	Bentgrasses, bluegrasses, bermudagrass, fescues, ryegrasses	April–November 7–21 days	Duosan Dyrene, Dymec Fungo 50 Kromad PCNB, Terraclor 75 Rubigan Tersan 1991 Thiram, Spotrete Vorlan
Copper spot *(Gloeocercospora sorghi)*	Bentgrasses, redtop	April–November 7–21 days	
Rusts: leaf, crown, and stem *(Puccinia* and *Uromyces* spp. and *Physopella compressa)*	All turfgrasses (except bahia and centipede)	May–October 7–14 days (Follow fertility and irrigation practices to produce steady growth of grass— 1 in. per week— during summer or early fall droughts.)	Acti-dione RZ Acti-dione TGF Bayleton Daconil 2787 Duosan Dyrene Dymec Fore, Formec 80 Thiram, Spotrete Zineb
Brown patch *(Rhizoctonia solani* and possibly *R. zeae* and *R. oryzae)*	All turfgrasses	May–October 5–21 days	Acti-dione RZ Acti-dione Thiram Bromosan Chipco 26019 Cleary's 3336 Daconil 2787 Duosan Dyrene, Dymec Fore, Formec 80 Fungo 50 Kromad PCNB, Terraclor 75 Tersan 1991 Vorlan

TABLE 5.4 CHEMICAL CONTROL OF TURFGRASS DISEASES (Continued)

Disease (pathogen)[a]	Principal turfgrasses affected	Normal season and intervals of application[b] (remarks)	Fungicide[c]

Leaf smuts
Stripe smut (*Ustilago striiformis)* and Flag smut (*Urocystis agropyri)*
	Bentgrasses, bluegrasses, ryegrasses, redtop	Late fall or early spring (Drench 300–600 gal per 1000 sq ft into root zone immediately after application. Repeat 14 to 21 days later.)	Bayleton
			Cleary's 3336
			Fungo 50
			Rubigan *or*
			   Tersan 1991
			   plus PCNB,
			   Terraclor 75

Powdery mildew (*Erysiphe graminis)*	Bluegrasses, fescues, bermudagrass	March–November 7–21 days	Acti-dione TGF Acti-dione RZ Acti-dione Thiram Bayleton

Snow molds
Gray snow mold or Typhula blight (*Typhula* spp.) Pink snow mold or Fusarium patch *(Fusarium nivale* or *Microdochium nivale)* Snow scald (*Myriosclerotinia borealis)* Cottony snow mold (*Coprinus psychromorbidus)*
	All turfgrasses (except bahia, centipede, zoysia, and St. Augustine)	October–March (See label for intervals. Apply two or more of these products in combination to control snow-mold complexes.)	Bayleton[c]
			Calo-Clor,
			   Calo-Gran[e]
			Chipco 26019
			Daconil 2787
			Rubigan *or*
			   Teremec SP,
			   Terraneb SP
			   plus PCNB,
			   Terraclor 75

Pythium blight (Grease spot, spot blight, cottony blight) and root rot (usually *Pythium graminicola* and *P. aphanidermatum*)	All turfgrasses	March–December 5–21 days	Banol Chipco Aliette Koban Subdue Teremec SP, Terraneb SP Terrazole
Downy mildew, yellow tuft (*Sclerophthora macrospora*)	All turfgrasses	March–December 21 days	Subdue
Southern blight (*Sclerotium rolfsii*)	Bentgrasses, bermudagrass, bluegrasses, fescues, ryegrasses	May–July 60 days	Bayleton

TABLE 5.4 CHEMICAL CONTROL OF TURFGRASS DISEASES (Continued)

Disease (pathogen)[a]	Principal turfgrasses affected	Normal season and intervals of application[b] (remarks)	Fungicide[c]
Gray leaf spot (*Pyricularia grisea* and *P. oryzae*)	St. Augustinegrass, bermudagrass, centipedegrass, bahiagrass, ryegrasses	April–October 7–14 days	Acti-dione TGF Acti-dione Thiram Acti-dione RZ Daconil 2787 Dyrene, Dymec Fore, Formec 80 Kromad Thiram, Spotrete Zineb
Cercospora leaf spot (*Cercospora* spp.)	St. Augustinegrass	April–October 7–14 days	
Anthracnose (*Colletotrichum graminicola*)	All turfgrasses	May–October 7–21 days	Bayleton Daconil 2787 Duosan Fore Fungo 50 Rubigan Tersan 1991
Fairy rings (mostly caused by *Marasmius* spp., *Chlorophyllum (Lepiota)* spp., and *Agaricus (Psalliota) campestris* or *bisporus*)	All turfgrasses	(Soil temperature should be above 60°F for fumigation. Cover area with gas-proof plastic cover for several days.)	Methyl bromide, chloropicrin, Vapam, Vorlex, or formaldehyde fumigation *or* keep soil *wet* for several weeks
Spring dead spot (*Leptosphaeria korrae* and *L. narmari*)	Bermudagrass	October–December	Tersan 1991 Fungo 50 Rubigan
Seed rot, damping-off, seedling blights (many fungi, mostly species of *Pythium, Fusarium, Rhizoctonia, Bipolaris, Exserohilum, Drechslera,* and *Colletotrichum*)	All turfgrasses	Treat seed before planting. Spray just after seeding and twice more at 5- to 7-day intervals. (Apply fungicide in 5 to 10 gal of water per 1000 sq ft.)	Captan or thiram *plus* Koban or Apron Captan Chipco 26019 Daconil 2787 Dyrene, Dymec Kromad Thiram, Spotrete Zineb

TABLE 5.4 CHEMICAL CONTROL OF TURFGRASS DISEASES (Continued)

Disease (pathogen)[a]	Principal turfgrasses affected	Normal season and intervals of application[b] (remarks)	Fungicide[c]
Nematodes (many genera and species)	All turfgrasses	Fenamiphos (Nemacur), ethoprop (Mocap Nematicide-Insecticide, Proturf Nematicide-Insecticide), or fensulfothion (Dasanit): granules. Follow the manufacturer's directions carefully. Irrigate turf immediately (300 to 600 gal per 1000 sq ft) to ensure penetration of nematicide into soil and prevent toxic effects. Treat in spring or fall (or both, if nematodes are a serious problem) when soil temperature is above 55°F. Aerifying turf before application improves results. *Do not apply to newly seeded areas.* For use *only* by certified pesticide applicators.	
Algae, Green or black scum	All turfgrasses	Apply when first seen; reapply as needed.	Copper sulfate Daconil 2787 Fore, Formec 80 Sodium hypochlorite (0.01%)
Mosses	All turfgrasses	Apply when first seen; reapply as needed.	Ferrous ammonium sulfate; ferrous sulfate; ferric sulfate; ammonium sulfate

[a]Causal fungus or fungi given in parentheses.

[b]Calendar dates are approximate for the northern two-thirds of the United States. For the extreme south, start a month or more earlier and continue for a month or so later in the year. Follow local suggested spray schedules and dates.

[c]Denotes either the common (coined) name of that material, or representative trade names (see Table 5.5). Some fungicides listed may not be registered for a particular disease as listed or may be labeled for use only in selected states or on certain grasses. Mention of a trade name or proprietary product does not constitute warranty of the product by the authors or the publisher and does not imply approval of this material to the exclusion of comparable products that may be equally suitable. Except where indicated, all materials should be applied in 1 to 5 gal of water per 1000 sq ft. Use lower fungicide rates on container labels in *preventive* programs; higher rates for *curative* programs. Fungicide use and restrictions are subject to change without notice. Always read and follow the instructions and precautions on the current label. Check state extension recommendations each year. Bayleton controls summer patch but not necrotic ring spot and gives poor control of gray snow mold.

[d]Cadmium compounds cannot be used in certain states.

[e]Calo-Clor and Calo-Gran are cleared for use only on golf course greens, aprons, and tees by certified golf course superintendents.

TABLE 5.5 GUIDE TO FUNGICIDES CITED IN TABLE 5.4

Common or coined name	Trade names
Anilazine	Dyrene 50% WP, Dyrene 4, Dymec, Lescorene, ProTurf Fungicide III, Lofts Lawn Fungicide, Professional Lawn Disease Control
Benomyl	Lebanon Fungicide Type B, Tersan 1991, Benomyl, Ferti-lome Systemic Fungicide, Benomyl Turf Fungicide
Cadmium compounds	Caddy, Cadminate, Lebanon Fungicide Type C
Captan	Captan 50, Orthocide
Chloroneb	ProTurf Fungicide II, Teremec SP, Terraneb SP, Chloroneb
Chlorothalonil	Daconil 2787, Lebanon Fungicide Type D, ProTurf 101-V Broad Spectrum Fungicide, Green Gold Turf Fungicide, Ortho Lawn Disease Control, Lawn Fungicide 2787, Thal-O-Nil, Ferti-lome Broad Spectrum Liquid Fungicide, Fungi-Gard, The Andersons Daconil, Ornathol
Cycloheximide	Acti-dione TGF
Cycloheximide + PCNB	Acti-dione RZ
Cycloheximide + thiram	Acti-dione Thiram
Propiconazole	Banner
Ethazole or Etridiazole	Koban, Terrazole
Fenarimol	Rubigan
Fosetyl-Al	Chipco Aliette
Iprodione	Chipco 26019, ProTurf Fungicide VI
Mancozeb	Fore, Formec 80, Lesco 4
Maneb	Dithane M-22, Maneb Spray, Maneb Liquid Fungicide
Mercury chlorides	Calo-Clor, Calo-Gran
Metalaxyl	Subdue, Apron, ProTurf Pythium Control
PCNB or Quintozene	Lesco PCNB, Terraclor, Turfcide, Lawn Fungicide Spray, Lawn Disease Preventer
Phenylmercuric acetate	PMAS
Propamocarb	Banol
Thiophanate-ethyl	Cleary's 3336
Thiophanate-ethyl + thiram	Bromosan
Thiophanate-methyl	Fungo 50, ProTurf Systemic Fungicide
Thiophanate-methyl + iprodione	ProTurf Fluid Fungicide
Thiophanate-methyl + mancozeb	Duosan
Thiram	Lebanon Fungicide Type T, Lesco Thiram 75, Spotrete, Thiramad
Thiram + cadmium compound	Cad-Trete, Cleary's Granular Turf Fungicide, Lesco Snow Mold Turf Fungicide, Kromad, Lebanon Fungicide Type T
Thiram + PMA	ProTurf Broad Spectrum Fungicide
Triadimefon	Bayleton, ProTurf Fungicide 7
Vinclozolin	Vorlan
Zineb	Zineb, Zineb Spray, Zineb Garden Fungicide

SELECTED REFERENCES

BEARD, J. B. 1973. *Turfgrass: Science and Culture.* Englewood Cliffs, NJ: Prentice-Hall, Inc. 658 pp.

BEARD, J. B. 1979. *How to Have a Beautiful Lawn,* 2nd ed. College Station, TX: Beard Books. 113 pp.

BRUNNEAU, A. H., ed. 1985. *Turfgrass Pest Management. A Guide to Major Turfgrass Pests and Turfgrasses.* North Carolina State University Agricultural Extension Service Publication AG-348. 64 pp.

COUCH, H. B. 1973. *Diseases of Turfgrasses,* 2nd ed. Melbourne, FL: R. E. Krieger Publishing Co., Inc. 348 pp.

CUMMINS, G. B. 1971. *The Rust Fungi of Cereals, Grasses and Bamboos.* New York: Springer-Verlag New York, Inc. 570 pp.

FREEMAN, T. E. 1969. *Diseases of Southern Turfgrasses.* Florida Agricultural Experiment Station Technical Bulletin. 713A. 31 pp.

HANSON, A. A., and F. V. JUSKA, eds. 1969. *Turfgrass Science.* Agronomy Monograph 14. Madison, WI: American Society of Agronomy, Inc. 713 pp.

HOWARD, F. L., J. B. ROWELL, and H. L. KEIL. 1951. *Fungus Diseases of Turfgrasses.* Rhode Island Agricultural Experiment Station Bulletin 308. 56 pp.

LARSON, P. O., and B. G. JOYNER, eds. 1980. *Advances in Turfgrass Pathology.* New York: Harcourt Brace Jovanovich. 197 pp.

SHURTLEFF, M. C., and R. RANDELL. 1974. How to Control Lawn Diseases and Pests. Kansas City, MO: Intertec Publishing Corp., 97 pp.

SHURTLEFF, M. C., D. I. EDWARDS, J. W. COURTER, and R. RANDELL. 1983. *Soul Disinfestation—Methods and Materials.* University of Illinois Cooperative Extension Circular 1213. 36 pp.

SMILEY, R. W. 1983. *Compendium of Turfgrass Diseases.* St. Paul, MN: The American Phytopathological Society. 102 pp.

TURGEON, A. J. 1985. *Turfgrass Management,* 2nd ed. Englewood Cliffs, NJ: Prentice-Hall. 432 pp.

VARGAS, J. M., JR. 1981. *Management of Turfgrass Diseases.* Minneapolis, MN: Burgess Publishing Company. 204 pp.

WEIHING, J. L., M. C. SHURTLEFF, R. E. PARTYKA, J. M. VARGAS, JR., and J. E. WATKINS. 1978. *Lawn Diseases in the Midwest.* North Central Regional Extension Publication 12. 22 pp.

6

Application Equipment
and Calibration

INTRODUCTION

As mentioned in earlier chapters, successful control of turfgrass weeds, diseases, insects, and other animal pests is based on an *early and accurate diagnosis,* knowledge of the pest's life cycle, when and where the pest is most likely to attack, parts of the turfgrass plant involved, how the pest is disseminated, plus the cultural and chemical controls that have proven effective.

Pesticides should be applied *only* when the suggested management practices outlined earlier—proper planting, fertilization, watering, mowing, dethatching, and core aerification—are not providing the desired level of control. Turf protection chemicals are generally formulated as liquid concentrates—solutions (S), flowables (F), or emulsifiable concentrates (EC) –wettable powders (WP), and granules (G). Liquid concentrates and wettable powders are usually added to water and applied with a sprayer. Granular products are commonly applied with a drop (gravity) or rotary (centrifugal) fertilizer spreader.

The concentration of turf protection chemicals is usually expressed as a weight per unit volume or as a percent of the commercial product. Recommendations are usually given on a 1000-sq ft or acre basis. For example, a 50% wettable powder (50WP) contains 50% active ingredient (AI) and 50% inert material—emulsifying agent, carrier, diluent, and so on. If the manufacturer's recommended rate of application is 6 lb of

*Much of the material in this chapter has been adapted from Illinois Extension Circular 1192, *Equipment and Calibration: Low-Pressure Sprayers,* by L. E. Bode and B. J. Butler.

330

AI per acre, then 12 lb of the commercially formulated product (50 WP) is needed to treat an acre. This is roughly equivalent to ¼ lb (4 oz) per 1000 sq ft (1 acre = 43,560 sq ft).

Liquid formulations generally list the number of pounds of the active ingredient per gallon (lb AI/gal) on the container label. If the concentration is 4 lb/gal, then 2 pints (1 quart or 4 cups) is required per acre to supply 1 lb of active ingredient per acre.

Effective chemical control of any turfgrass pest involves using the *right* chemical at the *right* concentration at the *right* time and in the *right* way. Earlier chapters have provided detailed information concerning suggested chemicals for use against each turfgrass weed, insect, disease, or animal pest (Tables 3.3, 3.4, 4.1, and 5.4) plus information on the best timing of applications for optimum results. Additional precautions are given on page 350 and should be read before applying any turf protection chemical. The specific amount of material that should be applied to 1000 sq ft or an acre depends on the concentration of pesticide (the "active ingredient") in the preparation. For example, different manufacturers may sell the same insecticide in a half-dozen formulations where the percentage of AI may vary from 2 to 80%. All we can suggest is to read and follow the manufacturer's directions as printed on the container label.

WHAT APPLICATION EQUIPMENT SHOULD I HAVE?

At least three things should be considered when selecting equipment:

1. Consistent uniform distribution of chemicals is needed for efficient and maximum control.
2. The specific method of application is determined by the type of formulations you plan on using plus the size of the area or areas to be treated.
3. Your budget.

Liquid concentrates and wettable powders may be applied using a wide range of ground and air equipment satisfactory for spraying several thousand square feet once or twice a year to spraying of hundreds of acres every 7 to 10 days throughout the growing season. Before purchasing any piece of equipment, consider these points. Does it handle and operate efficiently on sloping or uneven ground? Is it simple to fill and clean? Is it big enough to do the job without frequent refilling? Does it have a mechanical or a hydraulic agitator? Is the manufacturer reliable? Are parts readily available? Is it well made with noncorroding parts? How long will it probably last if given proper cleaning and maintenance?

Many types and sizes of equipment, ranging from hose-end sprayers and small compressed-air sprayers to small or large power sprayers to helicopters, are used to apply pesticides to turf. Despite the many possible variations and combinations of equipment, however, most pesticides are applied to turf with manually operated sprayers, power-operated spray booms or spray guns, and granular applicators. Each sprayer or applicator has its distinct uses and features.

Figure 6.1 Hose-end sprayer of 20-gal capacity made of shatterproof polyethylene plastic.

HOSE-END SPRAYERS

A hose proportioner is attached to a garden hose and operated by water pressure (Figure 6.1). Concentrated pesticide added to a glass or polyethylene jar is metered out by suction. A jar of concentrate spray makes a specific number of gallons of dilute spray. Since accurate dosage control is difficult, the pesticide is often *not* applied at a uniform rate. Also, hose pressure may be insufficient to break up the spray into mist-size droplets that uniformly wet the grass blades and provide needed coverage. Adding a spreader-sticker (or surfactant) to the spray mix will help (see page 352). Wettable powder formulations do not work as well as solutions, flowables, and emulsifiable concentrates. Other disadvantages include dragging the hose wherever you go, being limited to the area you can reach with the hose, occasional drops in water pressure, and kneeling or stooping over to reach under shrubbery or flowers where insects and mites occur and disease-causing organisms infect. The outstanding advantages, of course, are convenience and simplicity of operation.

MANUAL SPRAYERS

Manual sprayers, such as compressed-air and knapsack sprayers for turf use, are designed for spot treatment and other areas unsuitable for power sprayers. They are relatively inexpensive, simple to operate, maneuverable, and easy to clean and store. Compressed-air or small, rechargeable cylinders of carbon dioxide are used in most manual sprayers to apply pressure to the supply tank and force the spray liquid through a nozzle.

Most manual sprayers have a number of accessories and special fittings available to meet practically every need. Spray tanks made of rust-free material (stainless steel, brass, copper, or fiberglass) will outlast the cheaper tinplate, aluminum, or galvanized steel models. Lightweight polyethylene plastic sprayers are also available.

Figure 6.2 A compressed-air sprayer is handy for spot spraying. (Courtesy H. D. Hudson Manufacturing Co.)

Figure 6.3 A knapsack sprayer is a convenient way to spray turf areas. (Courtesy Champion Sprayer Company.)

Compressed-Air Sprayers

Compressed-air sprayers (Figure 6.2) are popular, low-priced, easy to operate, and useful for a variety of jobs around the lawn, yard, and garden. Pressure for most sprayers is provided by a manually operated air pump that fits into the top of the tank and supplies compressed air to force the spray liquid out of the tank and through a hose. A valve at the end of the hose controls the flow of liquid. Agitation is provided by frequent shaking of the tank. Normal spraying pressure is between 30 and 60 pounds per square inch (psi) and is maintained by occasional pumping. The capacity of the tank ranges from 1 to 5 gal.

In some compressed-air sprayers, a precharged cylinder of air or carbon dioxide supplies the needed pressure. These units include a pressure-regulating valve to maintain uniform pressure. Some models are mounted on wheels for easy portability. Pesticides are applied through a spray gun or a short boom with several nozzles.

Knapsack Sprayers

Knapsack sprayers (Figure 6.3) that strap on the back are more expensive and heavier to carry, but do a faster and better job of applying a uniform spray. The hose and nozzle are similar to those used on compressed-air sprayers. Pressure is maintained by a piston or diaphragm pump that is either operated by easy hand pumping or by a small gasoline engine. An air chamber helps to "smooth out" pump pulsations. Tank capacity ranges from 2 to 6 gal, and pressures up to about 150 psi can be developed. Spray material in the tank is kept in suspension by a mechanical agitator or by bypassing part of the pumped solution back into the tank.

Figure 6.4 A small power sprayer equipped with a short spray boom. (Courtesy H. D. Hudson Manufacturing Co.)

Figure 6.5 Applying fungicide with a spray boom on a golf course. (Courtesy The Broyhill Co.)

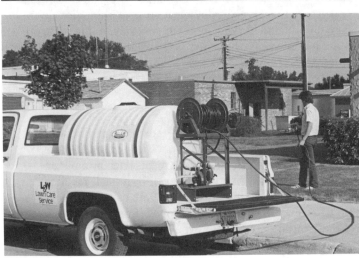

Figure 6.6 Typical spray truck and the equipment widely used by lawn care companies. (Courtesy The Broyhill Co.)

Calibration of Manual Sprayers

Because compressed-air and knapsack sprayers are generally used on small areas, the amount of spray volume should be determined on an area such as 1000 sq ft. Most of these sprayers do not have pressure gauges or pressure controls. The pressure in the tank drops as the material is sprayed. This pressure drop can be partially overcome by (1) filling the tank only two-thirds full with spray material so that considerable air space remains above the spray mix; and (2) repressurizing the tank at frequent intervals. If the sprayer has a pressure gauge, repressurize when the pressure drops approximately 10 psi from the initial reading. When spraying, either hold the nozzle steady at a constant height and walk back and forth, or swing the nozzle in a steady, sweeping, overlapping motion. Maintain a uniform walking speed during application.

Step 1. Measure and mark an area of 1000 sq ft (such as 20 ft × 50 ft). Practice spraying the area with water. For uniform application, always spray the area twice, each with one half the spray, with the second application at right angles to the first.

Step 2. Add a measured amount of water to the tank, spray the area in two directions, then measure the amount of water remaining in the tank. Obviously, the difference between the amount in the tank before and after spraying is the amount used.

You can also determine the time in seconds to spray this area in a normal manner. In this method catch the spray from the nozzle (or nozzles) used for the time period you have determined (see Table 6.1). You can calculate the rate per acre as follows: pints caught × 20 = gallons per acre.

TABLE 6.1 MANUAL-SPRAYER CALIBRATION

Pints of spray caught in 1 minute	Rate (gal/acre)
¼	5.0
⅜	7.4
½	10.0
⅝	12.5
¾	15.0
1	20.0
1¼	25.0
1½	30.0
1¾	35.0
2	40.0

POWER SPRAYERS

Several types of power sprayers (Figures 6.4, 6.5, and 6.6) are available that are capable of delivering 1 to 3 gal/min at pressures up to 150 to 300 psi. But you will not need anywhere near these pressures (at the nozzle) to spray turf, 30 to 90 psi is all that is normally required. Adjustable spray guns are commonly used with these units, but spray booms are also available.

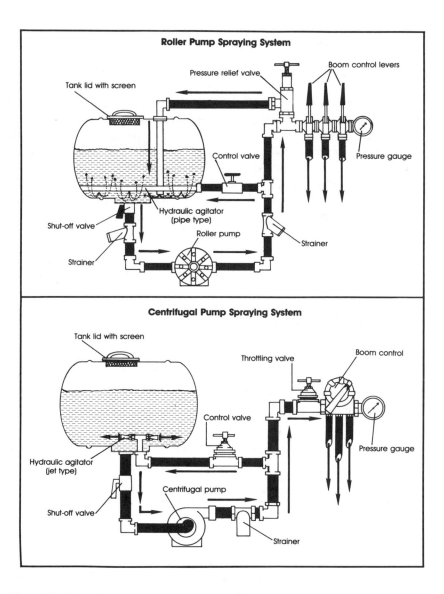

Figure 6.7 Two principal types of low-pressure spraying systems used to apply pesticides and fertilizers to turfgrasses.

Most sprayers for applying pesticides to turf areas use a power source (portable or self-propelled) to develop the pressure required to meter and distribute the spray liquid. Spray pressure ranges from nearly zero to 500 psi or more. Tractor-mounted, pull-type, and self-propelled sprayers are available in many models. Application rates can vary from 10 to 200 gal/acre.

All power sprayers used by turfgrass managers have several basic components: a pump, a tank, an agitation system, a flow-control assembly, and a distribution system

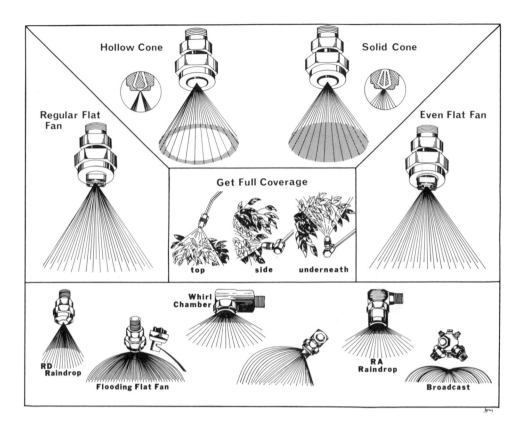

Figure 6.8 Various types of spray nozzles. The most widely used nozzles on turf are the regular flat-fan, flooding flat-fan, and hollow cone. The hollow-cone nozzle is preferred if you are also spraying flowers, shrubbery, and other vegetation.

(Figure 6.7). We suggest a large-wheeled, easily maneuverable model with extra chemical-resistant hose, and a spray boom or multinozzle, trigger-type spray gun.

Roller and centrifugal pumps are used in low-pressure sprayers for turf use. Sprayers with piston pumps can deliver pressures up to the 800 or 1000 psi needed to reach the tops of tall trees but greatly increase drift.

Nozzles

Regardless of the type of sprayer, the proper selection of nozzle type and size is important in applying pesticides to turf (Figure 6.8). The nozzle determines how much spray is applied to a particular area, the uniformity of the spray applied, the coverage obtained on the grass surface, and the amount of drift. You can minimize drift by selecting nozzles that give the largest drop size while still providing adequate coverage at the intended application rate and pressure. Although nozzles have been developed for almost every spray application, only a few types are commonly used for applying pesticides to turfgrasses.

Regular flat-fan nozzles are widely used for broadcast spraying of herbicides and for certain insecticides and fungicides when foliar penetration and complete coverage

Power Sprayers   **337**

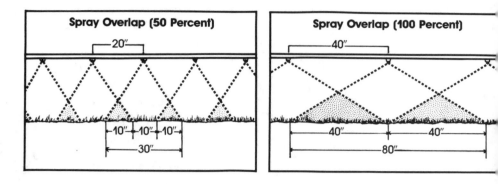

Figure 6.9 Two spray booms showing 50 and 100% overlap; flat-fan nozzles on the left boom and flooding-fan nozzles on the right boom.

are not required. These nozzles produce a tapered-edge, flat-fan spray pattern, and are available in several spray-fan angles (80° spray-angle tips are most commonly used). The nozzles are generally on 20-in. centers at a boom height of 10 to 23 in. (Figure 6.9). The boom heights for various spray angles are given in Table 6.2.

TABLE 6.2 SPRAY ANGLES AND BOOM HEIGHTS

Spray angle (deg)	Boom height, 20-in. spacing (in.)
65	21 to 23
73	20 to 22
80	17 to 19
110	10 to 12

When applying herbicides with flat-fan nozzles, keep the operating pressure between 15 and 30 psi. At these pressures, flat-fan nozzles produce medium-to-coarse droplets that are not as susceptible to drift as the finer droplets produced at pressures of 40 psi and above. Regular flat-fan nozzles are recommended for some foliar-applied pesticides at pressures from 40 to 60 psi. These pressures will generate fine droplets for maximum coverage on the grass surface.

Because the outer edges of the spray pattern have tapered or reduced volumes, it is necessary to overlap adjacent patterns along a boom to obtain uniform coverage. For maximum uniformity, this overlap should be about 40 to 50% of the nozzle spacing (Figure 6.9).

The LP or "low-pressure" flat-fan nozzle (Spraying Systems Co., North Avenue, Wheaton, IL 60188) develops a normal fan angle and distribution pattern at spray pressures from 10 to 25 psi. Operating at a lower pressure results in larger drops and less drift than the regular flat-fan nozzle designed to operate at pressures of 15 to 30 psi.

Flooding flat-fan nozzles produce a wide-angle, flat-fan pattern, and are used for applying herbicides and mixtures of herbicides and liquid fertilizers. The nozzle spacing for applying herbicides should be 60 in. or less. These nozzles are most effective in reducing drift when they are operated within a pressure range of 8 to 25 psi. Pressure changes affect the width of the spray pattern more with the flooding flat-fan nozzle than with the regular flat-fan nozzle. In addition, the distribution pattern is usually not as uniform as that of the regular flat-fan. The best distribution is achieved when the nozzle is mounted at a height and angle to obtain at least double coverage or 100% overlap (Figure 6.9).

Flooding flat-fan nozzles can be mounted so that they spray down, straight back, or at any angle in between. The position of the nozzles is not critical as long as double coverage is obtained. You can determine nozzle position by rotating the nozzle to the angle required to obtain double coverage at a convenient nozzle height.

Hollow-cone nozzles (disc and core type) are used primarily when foliar penetration is essential for effective insect and disease control and when drift is not a major concern. At pressures of 40 to 60 psi, hollow-cone nozzles produce small droplets that penetrate grass foliage and thatch and cover the leaves more effectively than does spray from other nozzles. If penetration is not required, a pressure of 30 to 40 psi is sufficient for most turfgrass areas. The most commonly used hollow-cone nozzle is the two-piece, disc-core, hollow-cone spray tip. The core gives the fluid a swirling motion before it is metered through the orifice disc, resulting in a circular, hollow-cone spray pattern.

Other types of nozzles, such as the solid cone, even flat-fan, whirl chamber, RA and RD raindrop, off-center flat-fan, and broadcast (boomless) nozzles (Figure 6.8) have little place in applying pesticides to turf.

Spray guns for spraying turf areas range from those that produce a low flow rate with a wide-cone spray pattern to those that produce a high flow rate with a straight-stream spray pattern. Spray guns are *not* usually recommended for spraying turf areas such as lawns or golf course greens. It is difficult to obtain uniform coverage of turf areas using a spray gun. If you cannot use a conventional sprayer with a boom, use a hand or walking boom with conventional nozzles (Figure 6.10). When the spray gun must be used, because of rough or irregularly shaped areas, be aware of the difficulty in obtaining uniform spray coverage over the area. Pressure gauges at the pump and on the spray gun are recommended to indicate line pressure loss and give some indication of output.

Figure 6.10 Spray-Hawk applying fungicide to a golf green. (Courtest Mallinckrodt, Inc.)

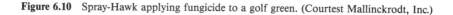

Power Sprayers

Nozzle-tip materials. Nozzle tips are available in hardened stainless steel, stainless steel, nylon, brass, ceramic or procelain, Kematal, and aluminum. Hardened stainless steel is the most wear-resistant material, but also the most expensive. Stainless steel tips have excellent wear resistance with either corrosive or abrasive materials. Nylon and other synthetic plastics are resistant to corrosion and abrasion, but may swell when exposed to some solvents. Brass tips are widely used, but they wear rapidly when used to apply abrasive materials, such as wettable powders, and are corroded by some liquid fertilizers. Nevertheless, brass tips are probably the most economical for limited use. Other types should be considered for more extensive use. Ceramic or porcelain nozzle tips are highly resistant to abrasion and corrosion. Kematal tips have excellent chemical and wear resistance to abrasive materials. Aluminum tips are subject to corrosion and have a short thread life.

Calibration of Power Sprayers

The performance of any pesticide depends on the proper application of the correct amount of chemical. Most performance complaints about turfgrass pesticides relate directly to errors in dosage or to improper application. The purpose of calibration is to ensure that your sprayer is applying the correct amount of material uniformly over a given area.

Three variables affect the amount of spray mixture applied per 1000 sq ft or per acre: (1) the nozzle flow rate; (2) the ground speed of the sprayer; and (3) the effective sprayed width per nozzle. To calibrate and operate your sprayer properly, you must know how each of these variables affects the sprayer output.

Nozzle flow rate. The flow rate through a nozzle varies with the size of the tip and the nozzle pressure. You can increase the flow rate by installing a nozzle tip with a larger orifice or by increasing the pressure. Nozzle flow rate varies in proportion to the square root of the pressure. *Doubling the pressure will NOT double the flow rate. To double the flow rate, you must increase the pressure four times.* For example, to double the flow rate of a nozzle from 0.28 gallon per minute (GPM) at 20 psi to 0.56 GPM, you must increase the pressure to 80 psi (4 × 20).

Pressure cannot be used to make major changes in the application rate, but it can correct minor changes due to nozzle wear. To obtain a uniform spray pattern and minimize drift, you must keep the operating pressure within the recommended range for each nozzle type. Remember: if you use check valves to prevent nozzle drip, the pressure at the nozzle is 5 to 7 psi lower than the boom pressure indicated on the pressure gauge.

Ground speed. The spray application rate varies *inversely* with the ground speed. *Doubling the ground speed of the sprayer reduces the application rate by one-half.* For example, a sprayer applying 20 GPA at 3 mph would apply 10 GPA if the speed were increased to 6 mph and the pressure remained constant.

Some power sprayers come equipped with control systems that maintain a constant spray application rate (GPA) over a range of ground speeds. The pressure is changed to vary the nozzle flow rate according to changes in the ground speed. These systems require calibration at a set ground speed. In the field, speed changes must be limited to those that maintain the nozzle pressure within its recommended range.

Sprayed width per nozzle.   The effective width sprayed per nozzle also affects the spray application rate. *Doubling the effective sprayed width per nozzle decreases the application rate by one-half.* For example, if you are applying 40 GPA with flat-fan nozzles on 20-in. spacings, and change to flooding nozzles with the same flow rate on 40-in. spacings, the application rate decreases from 40 GPA to 20 GPA.

The gallons of spray applied per acre can be determined by using the following equation:

$$GPA = \frac{GPM \times 5940}{mph \times W} \tag{1}$$

where   GPM = output per nozzle, gallons per minute
      mph = ground speed, miles per hour
         W = effective sprayed width per nozzle, inches
      5940 = a constant used to convert gallons per minute, miles per hour, and inches to gallons per acre

Selecting nozzle tips for boom sprayers.   The size of the nozzle tip depends on the application rate (GPA), ground speed (mph), and effective sprayed width (W) that you plan to use. An exact method for choosing the correct nozzle tip is to determine the gallons per minute (GPM) required for your conditions; then select nozzles that, when operated within the recommended pressure range, provide this flow rate. By following the five steps below, you can select the nozzles required for each application well ahead of the spraying season.

Step 1. Select the spray application rate in gallons per acre (GPA) that you want to use. Pesticide labels recommend ranges for various types of equipment. The spray application rate is the number of gallons of carrier (water, fertilizer, etc.) and pesticide that you want to apply per acre.

Step 2. Select or measure an appropriate ground speed in miles per hour (mph) according to existing field conditions. Do *not* rely on speedometers as an accurate measure of speed. Slippage and variation in tire sizes can result in speedometer errors of 30% or more. If you do not know the actual ground speed, you can easily measure it (see Measuring Ground Speed and Tractor Speed Conversions in Appendix B).

Step 3. Determine the effective sprayed width per nozzle (W) in inches. For broadcast spraying, W equals the nozzle spacing.

Step 4. Determine the flow rate required from each nozzle in gallons per minute (GPM) by using a nozzle catalog, tables, or the following equation:

$$GPM = \frac{GPA \times mph \times W}{5940} \tag{2}$$

where   GPM = gallons per minute of output required from each nozzle
      GPA = gallons per acre from step 1
      mph = miles per hour from step 2
        W = inches sprayed per nozzle from step 3
      5940 = a constant to convert gallons per minute, miles per hour, and inches to gallons per acre

Step 5. Select a nozzle that will give the flow rate determined in step 4 when the nozzle is operated within the recommended pressure range. You should obtain a catalog that lists available nozzle tips. These catalogs may be obtained free of charge from equipment dealers or nozzle manufacturers (e.g., Spraying Systems, Co., North Avenue, Wheaton, IL, 60188 or Delavan Corp., 811 4th Street, Des Moines, IA 50265). If you decide to use nozzles that you already have, return to step 2 and select a speed that allows you to operate within the recommended pressure range.

Example: You want to broadcast a herbicide at 25 GPA (step 1) at a speed of 5 mph (step 2), using regular flat-fan nozzles spaced 20 in. apart on the boom (step 3). What nozzle tip should you select? First, determine the required flow rate for each nozzle by using equation (2) in step 4:

$$\text{GPM} = \frac{\text{GPA} \times \text{mph} \times W}{5940} \quad \text{where} \quad \text{GPM} = \frac{25 \times 5 \times 20}{5940} = \frac{2500}{5940} = 0.42$$

The nozzle you select must have a flow rate of 0.42 GPM when operated within the recommended pressure range of 15 to 30 psi. Table 6.3 shows the GPM at various pressures for several Spraying Systems and Delavan nozzles. For example, the Spraying Systems 8006 and Delavan LF-6 nozzles have a rated output of 0.42 GPM at 20 psi (step 5). Either nozzle would be suitable for this application.

TABLE 6.3 REGULAR FLAT-FAN NOZZLES

Manufacturer		Liquid pressure (psi)	Capacity (GPM)
Delavan	Spraying Systems		
LF-1	8001	20	0.07
(100-mesh)	(100-mesh)	25	0.08
		30	0.09
		40	0.10
		50	0.11
LF-1.5	80015	20	0.11
(100-mesh)	(100-mesh)	25	0.12
		30	0.13
		40	0.15
		50	0.17
LF-2	8002	20	0.14
(50-mesh)	(50-mesh)	25	0.16
		30	0.17
		40	0.20
		50	0.23
LF-3	8003	20	0.21
(50-mesh)	(50-mesh)	25	0.24
		30	0.26
		40	0.30
		50	0.34
LF-4	8004	20	0.28
(50-mesh)	(50-mesh)	25	0.32
		30	0.35
		40	0.40
		50	0.45

TABLE 6.3 REGULAR FLAT-FAN NOZZLES (continued)

Manufacturer		Liquid pressure (psi)	Capacity (GPM)
Delavan	Spraying Systems		
LF-5	8005	20	0.35
(50-mesh)	(50-mesh)	25	0.40
		30	0.43
		40	0.50
		50	0.56
LF-6	8006	20	0.42
(50-mesh)	(50-mesh)	25	0.47
		30	0.52
		40	0.60
		50	0.67
LF-8	8008	20	0.57
(50-mesh)	(50-mesh)	25	0.63
		30	0.69
		40	0.80
		50	0.89
LF-10	8010	20	0.71
(No strainer)	(No strainer)	25	0.79
		30	0.87
		40	1.00
		50	1.12
LF-15	8015	20	1.06
(No strainer)	(No strainer)	25	1.19
		30	1.30
		40	1.50
		50	1.68

Selecting nozzle tips for hand-held spray booms. The size of the nozzle tip will depend on the application rate (gallons per 1000 sq ft), walking speed (minutes per 1000 sq ft), and effective spray width (the number of feet between the nozzles multiplied by the number of nozzles).

Choose the correct nozzle tip by determining the gallons per minute required for your conditions; then select nozzles from a nozzle manufacturer's catalog that, when operated within the recommended pressure range, provide this flow rate. By following the steps below, you can select the nozzles required for each application well ahead of the spraying season.

Step 1. Determine the application rate in gallons per 1000 sq ft. Pesticide labels indicate recommended ranges for various types of equipment and pests. The spray application rate may be given in gallons of carrier (water, fertilizer, etc.) and pesticide applied per acre rather than in gallons per 1000 sq ft. Gallons per acre (GPA) can be converted to gallons per 1000 sq ft by using the following equation:

$$\text{Gallons per 1000 sq ft} = \frac{\text{GPA} \times 1000}{43{,}560} \tag{3}$$

where $43{,}560$ = number of square feet per acre

Example: A rate of 50 GPA is recommended on the herbicide label. What is the application rate in gallons per 1000 sq ft?

$$\text{Gallons per 1000 sq ft} = \frac{50 \times 1000}{43,560} = \frac{50,000}{43,560} = 1.15$$

Step 2. Determine the effective swath width in feet. For hand-held booms, the swath width is the distance between the nozzles multiplied by the number of nozzles on the spray boom.

Example: Your walking boom has three nozzles spaced 20 in. apart (20 in. equals 1.67 ft). The effective swath width is

$$\text{Swath width} = 3 \text{ nozzles} \times 1.67 \text{ ft} = 5 \text{ ft}$$

Step 3. Measure the time in minutes required to spray 1000 sq ft. The time can easily be measured by using your swath width from step 2 and laying out a course measuring 1000 sq ft. To lay out a single-pass course that contains 1000 sq ft, use the following equation:

$$\text{Distance of course} = \frac{1000 \text{ sq ft}}{\text{swath width (ft)}} \tag{4}$$

Example: Your boom has an effective swath width of 5 ft. What length course is required for a 1000-sq ft, single-pass course?

$$\text{Distance of course} = \frac{1000}{5} = 200 \text{ ft}$$

Mark off a 200-ft course and time your walking speed, walking steadily along this in both directions; then calculate your average time. For example, if one timing took 44 seconds, and a second took 46 seconds, the average time would be 45 seconds. To convert seconds to minutes, divide the average time by 60 seconds per minute. In this example, the time to spray a 200-ft course with your three-nozzle boom equals

$$\frac{45 \text{ seconds}}{60 \text{ seconds per minute}} = 0.75 \text{ minute}$$

Step 4. Use the following equation to determine the flow rate required from each nozzle in gallons per minute (GPM):

$$\text{GPM} = \frac{\text{gallons per 1000 sq ft}}{\text{minutes per 1000 sq ft}} \tag{5}$$

Example: If the application rate is 1.15 gal per 1000 sq ft (step 1) and the time required to spray 1000 sq ft is 0.75 minute (step 3), what is the required nozzle flow rate from the boom using equation (5)?

$$\text{GPM} = \frac{1.15}{0.75} = 1.5$$

Since there are three nozzles per boom, the required flow rate from the boom (1.5) would be divided by 3: 1.5 ÷ 3 = 0.5. The required flow rate per nozzle would be 0.5 gal (or 2 quarts) per minute.

Step 5. Select a nozzle that will provide the flow rate determined in step 4 when the nozzle is operated within the recommended pressure range.

Example: Which regular flat-fan nozzle would you select for your three-nozzle boom? The nozzle you select must have a flow rate of 0.5 GPM when operated within the recommended pressure range of 15 to 30 psi. Table 6.3 shows gallon-per-minute rates at various pressures for several Spraying Systems and Delavan nozzles. For example, the Spraying Systems 8006 and Delavan LF-6 nozzles have a rated output of 0.52 GPM at 30 psi. Either of these nozzles would be suitable for your boom.

Precalibration checking.   After making sure that your sprayer is clean, install the selected nozzle tips, partially fill the tank with clean water, and operate the sprayer at a pressure within the recommended range. Place a quart jar or other suitable container under each nozzle. Check to see whether all the jars fill in about the same time. Replace any nozzle with an output 5% more or less than the average of all the nozzles, an obviously different fan angle, or a nonuniform appearance in spray pattern.

To obtain uniform coverage, you must consider the spray angle, spacing, and height of the nozzle(s). The height must be readjusted for uniform coverage with various spray angles on the same boom for broadcast spraying. Do *not* use nozzles with different spray angles on the same boom.

Worn or partially plugged nozzles and misalignment of nozzle tips will produce nonuniform patterns. Skips and uneven coverage also result if one end of the boom is allowed to raise or droop. A practical method for determining the exact nozzle height that will produce the most uniform coverage is to spray a warm surface (such as a driveway or road) and observe the drying rate. Lower or raise the height to eliminate excess streaking.

Calibrating your sprayer.   After selecting and installing the proper nozzle tips (steps 1 to 5 above) you are ready to complete the calibration of your sprayer (steps 6 to 10 below). Check the calibration every few days during the season or when changing the pesticides being applied. New nozzles do *not* lessen the need to calibrate because nozzles "wear in" and their flow rate increases most rapidly during the first few hours of use. Once you learn the following calibration method, you can check application rates quickly and easily.

Step 6. Determine the required flow rate for each nozzle in ounces per minute (OPM). To convert the GPM (step 4) to OPM, use the following equation:

$$\text{OPM} = \text{GPM} \times 128 \qquad 128 = \text{number of ounces in 1 gal} \qquad (6)$$

Example: If the required nozzle flow rate = 0.56 GPM, what is the required OPM?

$$\text{OPM} = 0.56 \times 128 = 71.7$$

Step 7. Collect the output from one of the nozzles in a container marked in ounces. Adjust the pressure until the amount you collect is within plus or minus 5% of the desired number of ounces per minute (OPM) you determined in step 6. If it is impossible to obtain the desired output within the recommended range of operating pressures, select larger or smaller nozzle tips, and recalibrate. It is important that spray nozzles be operated within the recommended pressure range. (The range of operating pressures is for pressure at the nozzle tip. Losses within hoses or booms, nozzle check valves, and so on, may cause the pressure gauge to read much higher.)

Step 8. Determine the amount of pesticide needed for each tankful or for the acreage to be sprayed (see Mixing Pesticides, pages 347 to 352). Add the pesticide to a tank partially filled with a carrier (water, fertilizer, etc.); then add more carrier to the desired level with continuous agitation.

Step 9. Operate the sprayer in the field at the measured ground speed and pressure you determined in step 7. You will be spraying at the application rate selected in step 1. After spraying an area of known size, check the liquid level in the tank to verify that the application rate is correct.

Step 10. Check the nozzle flow rate frequently. Adjust the pressure to compensate for small changes in nozzle output resulting from nozzle wear or variations in other spraying components. Replace the nozzle tips and recalibrate when the output has changed 10% or more from that of a new nozzle, or when the pattern becomes uneven.

Determining the spray rate with installed nozzle tips.   You may already have nozzle tips in your boom, and you want to know the spray rate (GPA) when operating at a particular nozzle pressure and speed.

Add water to the spray tank and make a precalibration check to see that all spray components are working properly. Remember that the type, size, and fan angle of all nozzle tips must be the same, and the flow rate from each nozzle must be within 5% of the average flow rate from the other nozzles.

Step 1. Operate the sprayer at the desired operating pressure. Use a container marked in ounces to collect the output from a nozzle for a measured length of time (such as 1 minute). Check the other nozzles to determine the average number of ounces per minute of output from each nozzle.

Step 2. Convert ounces per minute (OPM) of flow to gallons per minute (GPM) by dividing the OPM by 128 (the number of ounces in 1 gal).

Step 3. Determine the spraying speed. For mounted boom sprayers, the speed in mph can easily be measured (see Measuring Ground Speed in Appendix B, page 389). For hand-operated booms, lay out 1000 sq ft and record the time required to cover the area uniformly.

Step 4. Determine the sprayed width per nozzle (W) in inches. For broadcast spraying, W equals the nozzle spacing.

Step 5. For mounted boom sprayers, use equation (1) (page 341) to calculate the sprayer application rate in gallons per acre (GPA):

$$GPA = \frac{GPM \times 5940}{mph \times W}$$

Example: If the measured nozzle output is 54 ounces per minute (OPM), the measured ground speed is 6 mph, and the nozzle spacing (*W*) is 20 in., what is the sprayer application rate?

First, convert OPM to GPM (step 2) by dividing the OPM by 128 (the number of ounces in 1 gal):

$$GPM = \frac{54}{128} = 0.42$$

Using equation (1) (page 341), calculate the application rate in GPA as follows:

$$GPA = \frac{0.42 \times 5940}{6 \times 20} = 20.8$$

For hand-operated walking booms, use the following equation to calculate the application rate:

$$Gallons\ per\ 1000\ sq\ ft = GPM \times minutes\ per\ 1000\ sq\ ft \qquad (7)$$

Example: The measured nozzle output is 0.61 GPM and 2 minutes is required to spray 1000 sq ft. The application rate equals 1.2 gal per 1000 sq ft (0.61 × 2).

The application rate (step 5) can be adjusted by changing the ground speed or nozzle pressure and recalibrating. Changes in nozzle pressure should be used *only* to make small changes in output, and these changes must be within the recommended pressure range.

A final caution: You should check your use patterns frequently. If you know the size of your turf areas (see page 393) and how much spray should be applied, does this match your uses?

For information on Sprayer Calibration by the Quart Jar Method and an Operating Chart for Tractor Boom Sprayers, see Appendix B, page 388.

Mixing Pesticides

To determine the amount of pesticide to add to the spray tank, you need to know the recommended rate of pesticide, the capacity of the spray tank, and the calibrated output of the sprayer.

The recommended application rate of the pesticide is given on the container label. The rate is usually indicated as pounds per acre or ounces per 1000 sq ft for wettable powders, and as pints, quarts, or gallons per acre for liquids. Sometimes the recommendation is given as pounds of active ingredient (lb AI) per acre rather than the amount of total product per acre. The active ingredient must be converted to actual product.

Dry formulations

Example 1

A carbaryl recommendation calls for 2 lb AI per acre. You have Sevin (80% wettable powder). Your sprayer has a 200-gal tank and is calibrated to apply 20 GPA. How much Sevin should you add to the spray tank?

Step 1. Determine the number of acres that you can spray with each tankful. Your sprayer has a 200-gal tank and is calibrated to apply 20 GPA.

$$\frac{\text{tank capacity (gallons per tank)}}{\text{spray rate (gallons per acre)}} = \frac{200}{20} \tag{8}$$
$$= 10 \text{ acres sprayed per tankful}$$

Step 2. Determine the pounds of pesticide product needed per acre. Because not all the Sevin in the bag is an active ingredient, you will have to add more than 2 lb of the product to each "acre's worth" of water in your tank. The calculation is simple: Divide the percentage of active ingredient (80) into the total (100):

$$2 \text{ lb AI per acre} \times \frac{100\%}{80\%} = 2 \times 1.25 = 2.5 \text{ lb of product per acre}$$

Step 3. Determine the amount of pesticide to add to each tankful. With each tankful, you will cover 10 acres (step 1), and you want 2.5 lb of product per acre (step 2). Add 25 lb (10 acres × 2.5 lb per acre = 25 lb) of Sevin to each tankful.

Example 2

The recommendation for the insecticide diazinon is 4 lb/acre. Your 5-gal compressed-air sprayer applies 1.25 gal per 1000 sq ft. How many ounces should you add to the spray tank?

Step 1. Convert the recommended rate to ounces per 1000 sq ft by the following formula:

$$\text{Ounces per 1000 sq ft} = \frac{\text{recommended amount of product} \times 1000 \text{ sq ft}}{2722} \tag{9}$$

where 2722 is a constant derived from 43,560 sq ft per acre divided by 16 oz per pound or per pint.

$$\text{Ounces per 1000 sq ft} = \frac{4 \times 1000}{2722} = \frac{4000}{2722} = 1.5$$

Step 2. After converting the recommended rate to ounces per 1000 sq ft, you can find the amount of pesticide you should add to each tankful by the following formula:

$$\text{Ounces per tankful} = \frac{\text{tank size in gallons} \times \text{ounces per 1000 sq ft}}{\text{application rate in gallons per 1000 sq ft}} \tag{10}$$

$$= \frac{5 \times 1.5}{1.25} = 6$$

Liquid formulations

Example 1

A trichlorfon recommendation is 1 lb AI per acre. You have purchased Dylox 4E (4-lb/gal formulation). Your sprayer has a 150-gal tank and is calibrated at 15 gallons per acre. How much Dylox should you add to the spray tank?

Step 1. Determine the number of acres that you spray with each tankful by equation (8):

$$\text{Acres sprayed with each tankful} = \frac{150}{15} = 10$$

Step 2. Determine the amount of product needed per acre by dividing the recommended active ingredient per acre by the concentration of the formulation.

$$\frac{1 \text{ lb AI per acre}}{4 \text{ lb AI per gallon}} = \frac{1}{4} \text{ GPA}$$

One-fourth gallon (1 quart) of product is needed for each "acre's worth" of water in the tank to apply 1 lb AI per acre.

Step 3. Determine the amount of pesticide to add to each tankful. With each tankful, you will cover 10 acres (step 1), and you need 1 quart of product per acre (step 2). Add 10 quarts (10 acres × 1 quart per acre) of trichlorfon to each tankful.

Example 2

The insecticide malathion recommendation calls for 1 gal of product per acre. You have a 4-gal knapsack sprayer calibrated to apply ½ gal per 1000 sq ft. How many ounces should you add to the spray tank?

Step 1. Convert the recommended rate to pints per acre (8 pints = 1 gallon):

$$\text{Pints per acre} = \text{gallons per acre} \times 8 = 1 \times 8 = 8$$

Step 2. Convert the required pints per acre to ounces per 1000 sq ft by using equation (9):

$$\text{Ounces per 1000 sq ft} = \frac{8 \times 1000}{2722} = 2.9$$

Step 3. Determine the amount of pesticide to add to each tankful by using equation (10):

$$\text{Ounces per tankful} = \frac{4 \times 2.9}{0.5} = 23.2$$

Problems of Mixing Pesticides

Combining chemicals to do several jobs with a single spray saves time and labor. In light of the many thousands of pesticides, soluble fertilizers, growth regulators, sticking-wetting agents (see Surfactants, page 352), and other chemicals that can be sprayed on turf, it is surprising that plant injury (or phytotoxicity) does not occur more often. There are over 60,000 proprietary pesticides formulated in various ways from some 1200 basic active ingredients. The end products are used as bactericides, fungicides, herbicides, insecticides, miticides, nematicides, and so on. Sometimes, sludges will form in the tank, spray nozzles will plug up, and turf will be damaged as a result of the indiscriminate mixing of two or more of these pesticides. An understanding of pesticide compatibilities is essential to avoid these problems.

Compatibility. When pesticides are used in combination or as components of a mixture, they will be either compatible or incompatible.

Compatible refers to the reaction when two or more chemicals are mixed together without impairing their toxicity to pests, causing undesirable physical properties, or making the combination more toxic to plants than the individual chemicals when used alone.

Incompatible refers to the reaction of pesticides that cannot be mixed safely without impairing the effectiveness of one or more of the chemicals, developing undesirable physical properties, or causing plant injury.

There are two basic types of incompatibility: chemical and physical. It is possible to get one or both from the same mix. *Chemical incompatibility* involves the breakdown and loss of effectiveness of one or more products in the spray tank and possible formation of one or more new chemicals that are insoluble or phytotoxic. *Physical incompatibility* involves an unstable mixture that settles out, flocculates, foams excessively, or disperses poorly and reduces efficiency and causes the clogging of sprayer nozzles and screens. This type of incompatibility may result from the use of hard water.

General rules and principles

1. Follow all label instructions and precautions regarding dosage, method of application (gallons of water to apply to 1000 sq ft or per acre), and all incompatibilities. Practically all pesticide companies and experienced specialists recommend that chemicals should be applied *separately* and for a specific purpose, if there is any doubt.

2. If chemicals can be mixed, pour each separately into the spray tank with agitation (shaking). This frequently prevents settling out and nozzle plugging. A common practice is to make up a thin, uniform "batter" or slurry of the spray powder, diluting it with water. Some specialists suggest straining the spray solution through fine cheesecloth while it is being added to the tank.

3. Never tank-mix emulsifiable insecticide concentrates.

4. Mix only one soluble chemical (such as an emulsifiable concentrate, soluble, or soluble powder formulation) with any number of insolubles (such as wettable powders and flowable formulations).

5. Soluble fertilizers and trace elements can usually be added individually or mixed provided that the amount will not exceed 1 oz of solid material per gallon of tank spray mix.

6. Apply spray solutions as soon after mixing as possible. The longer a spray combination remains in the tank, the greater the number of problems that can arise. The iprodione (Chipco 26019) label, for example, specifically warns against premixing 12 hours or more before use due to possible fungicide breakdown.

7. To determine the physical compatibility of a tank mix, you should check it yourself. Two steps are important: (1) Place a mixture of the precise dosage of pesticide plus the proper volume of water in a quart glass jar, shake it briskly for 30 seconds, and then let it stand for 30 minutes. If the chemical mixture separates or settles out, it is unwise

to use the mixture. Regardless of the results in step 1, step 2 should be carried out if the material is at all sprayable.

In step 2 the mixture is applied to a turf area, preferably during adverse conditions such as heat (above 85 to 90 °F) and moisture stress and overlapped to determine phytotoxicity. A minimum of 48 hours should elapse before you can properly evaluate whether or not injury has occurred.

8. If you are determined to apply a mixture of different pesticides, we suggest this order of adding them to the spray tank: wettable powders first, flowables second, solubles third, powders fourth, surfactants fifth, and emulsifiable concentrates last. Always remember that pesticides should be placed in a spray tank that has been filled with *clean* water and with the agitator running.

9. Use caution when mixing wettable powders with emulsifiable formulations or a soluble fertilizer. Wettable powders and emulsions both suspend in water. Depending on the concentration and water used, such mixtures may cause a breakdown of the emulsion, the formation of sludges, flocculation, and reduced efficiency. In most cases the active ingredients are *not* at fault; the emulsifiers, solvents, fillers, and surfactants are responsible. Sometimes, the products of a single company will be compatible but the same materials from two different companies will not be. Yet many (or most) such formulations are compatible.

Plant damage is most common and severe at high temperatures or under slow-drying conditions. Soluble fertilizers or nutrient mixes, such as zinc or iron sulfate and chelated compounds, added to a pesticide mix can destroy the emulsification or suspension of other chemicals. However, urea is compatible with most pesticides.

10. Do not mix strongly alkaline and acid materials together! Strongly acid or alkaline materials (sulfur, lime, calcium arsenate, zinc sulfate and lime, ferrous sulfate, and ammonium sulfate) commonly cause acute compatibility problems. For example, no fungicide containing Acti-dione should ever be mixed with alkaline materials such as lime.

11. The pH and chemical composition of the water may be important. City water that has been softened may be strongly alkaline (pH 8 to 9+). Hard water from deep wells may cause pesticides to precipitate. Water pumped from a stream may contain chemical wastes. These factors can have a great influence on how pesticides perform individually and in mixes.

12. Do not experiment with new combinations. If you must try out a new mix, apply it on a small area first. Whenever possible, spray an out-of-the-way area with each product alone alongside a turf area sprayed with the test mixture. Apply these sprays several times at various strengths and different air temperatures. Check to see if the mix performs as well as when the materials are applied separately. Write your findings in a record book—do not trust your memory. Remember, no chemical company can possibly test all its products and those of its competitors in all possible combinations. The product bought today may have different "fillers," emulsifiers, solvents, or surfactants than the same product bought a year or two ago.

13. As a general rule, insoluble and wettable powder fungicides do not produce chemical injury when used as recommended. Many soluble fungicides can be phytotoxic, should be applied within their safety ranges, and should not be combined with other chemicals unless the package label states otherwise.

14. Turfgrass in a low state of vigor is more easily injured than vigorously growing grass by chemicals and mixes. Plants may be predisposed to damage by winter or herbicide injury, drought, waterlogging of the soil, poor soil, disease or insect damage, or an imbalance of nitrogen, potassium, phosphorus, or other elements.

15. Do not mix a foliar fungicide or insecticide with fertilizers or other chemicals that require watering in. Incorrect placement of pesticides sometimes explains poor disease or insect control. For example, a combination of a Dyrene spray to control leaf spot and an Oftanol drench to control grubs applied at the same time to turf.

16. Use caution when mixing chemicals that may be toxic by themselves with other materials. Such combinations commonly injure sensitive grasses at considerably lower concentrations than individual products in the mix.

17. Plant injury can sometimes be avoided by spraying when temperatures are between 40°F and 90°F. Emulsifiable materials are more likely to cause injury than wettable powders.

18. Buy pesticides only in amounts you expect to consume in the current year. Different pesticides, especially in combination, vary greatly in their shelf life, particularly once the container has been opened. The same basic chemical, manufactured by different companies, may vary in stability because of differences in formulation. Storage temperature and humidity can also have important effects. Many fungicides and insecticides last indefinitely if kept dry with the container sealed.

19. Store chemicals only in their original, tightly closed containers so that contamination cannot occur. Clean up sprayers, hose lines, nozzles, and mixing containers thoroughly after each use. Numerous cases of plant injury can be traced back to the contamination of equipment with potent weedkillers or to carelessness.

20. Be sure of the identity of the material. It may seem incredible, but whole towns have actually been "fogged" with 2,4-D (instead of with an insecticide) for mosquito control. Liability damages amounting to hundreds of thousands of dollars could have been avoided by simply reading the label—if the old container still had one.

Commercial products that contain a mixture of ingredients are the result of many years of testing under a wide variety of environmental conditions. Many such mixes (tested by company representatives, the USDA, state experiment stations, consultants, and extension service specialists) are never sold, because of reduced efficiency, short shelf life, or other problems. Yet many "practical" people, with limited time and facilities, think they can come up with an even better mix. The odds are not good.

Surfactants

When added to a pesticide, a surfactant reduces the surface tension between two unlike materials, such as a spray film and a solid surface. For example, by adding a surface-active agent to a tank mix, oil and water will mix and can be sprayed on plant surfaces.

With increasing emphasis on safe application of pesticides, such factors as particle size, spray pattern, and pesticide drift have focused more attention on surfactants to give ideal coverage for specific pesticides and plants. There are numerous terms that designate the surface-active components of a pesticide; these are often closely related and commonly perform two or more of the same functions.

Surfactants include: activators, deflocculators, dispersants, compatibility agents, detergents, emulsifiers, foam and drift suppressants, and spreading, sticking, and wetting agents. These materials are added to a spray mix to help keep the pesticide in suspension; improve cohesiveness and dispersion of the spray; and increase the wetting (or coverage) of the foliage and thatch.

Whether a spray rolls off or sticks to a plant surface depends on the physical and chemical properties of the spray mixture and the physical properties of the surface itself. If the surface tension of the mixture is high or if the plant surface is waxy, the spray droplets will roll off.

Spreader or film extender (spreader-activator): a substance that when added to a pesticide mix increases the area that a given volume of spray will cover and improves the contact between the pesticide and the plant surface. A spreading agent builds spray deposits and improves weathering ability. Most wettable powder fungicides and insecticides benefit from the addition of a spreader.

Sticker or adhesive: a material that when added to a spray mix improves the adherence (tenacity) to a plant surface rather than increasing the initial deposit. Commercial sticking agents are oily in consistency and increase the amount of suspended solids retained on plant surfaces by coating the particles in a resin or varnish-like film. (Most fungicides and insecticides already contain an adequate amount of sticker in the formulation.) Stickers may be measured in terms of resistance to wind and water, length of adherence, and mechanical or chemical action.

Spreader-sticker: an agent that combines the functions of both spreader and sticker.

Wetting agent: a material that when added to a pesticide lowers the interfacial tension between liquid and a solid; in this case, a plant surface. The effectiveness is measured by the increase in spread of a liquid over a solid surface and the ability of the spray film to make complete contact with it. When a wetting agent reduces surface tension, spreading naturally occurs.

All commercial spreading, sticking, and wetting agents should be mixed strictly according to label direction. Adding more surfactant than recommended may cause excessive runoff, resulting in a poor spray deposit and reduced pest control. In general, if the spray mix contains one or more pesticides produced or formulated by the same company, use a surfactant sold or recommended by that company.

When selecting a product to add to a spray mix, consider such factors as the homogeneity of the surfactant concentrate or powder, its stability in storage, ease of mixing in water, effect of water hardness on the emulsion stability or dispersion, and the added cost.

In a study of 70 surfactants, 80% actually *reduced* the weedkiller's effectiveness, 10% had no effect at all, and only 10% increased the herbicide's efficiency. Many turfgrass specialists do *not* favor adding a surfactant to the spray mix unless it is specifically needed.

Surfactants are sold separately from pesticides and are not subject to EPA registration. The lack of authority to regulate performance standards has resulted in some misleading product claims and misunderstandings.

An example of this involves the application of a surfactant as a wetting agent, spreading the herbicide over the entire surface of a weed, a desirable characteristic when a contact herbicide is being applied with water in a low gallonage rate. Without a wetting agent, the spray droplets will concentrate on small sections of the leaf surface, resulting in local tissue burning without killing the weed.

But when a *high* gallonage rate of the herbicide and water mixture is being applied, a wetting agent used by itself can cause up to two-thirds of the spray to run off the plant. Under these circumstances a specially compounded product is required that also contains a sticking agent to aid spray retention.

The foaming characteristics of a surfactant are important to its performance. When you reduce surface tension with a surfactant, you get foaming. When surface tension is too low the spray tank fills up with foam, you get poor distribution of the pesticide(s), and you are left with a mess on your hands.

A few examples of surfactants that act as spreading, sticking, and/or wetting agents include Activate 3, Adsee, Ag-Chem Activator, AIM Spreader Activator, Bio-Film, Chevron Spray Sticker, Citowett Plus, Exhalt 800, Igepal surfactants, Multi-Film L and X-77, Nu-Film-P and -17, Pinolene, Plyac Non-Ionic Spreader-Sticker, Triton B-1956, and X-77 Spreader.

Choosing a surfactant is not simply a matter of finding something that works with one pesticide and using it with all your pesticides. Unless you have evaluated a spreader-sticker, you have no way of knowing how it might affect the performance of a product or spray mixture. Although choosing an effective surfactant to accompany a specific pesticide is no simple task, the container label should state whether a surfactant is needed and the brand or brands that should be used. Practically all turf protection chemicals have one or more of these materials already in the spray mix. The Daconil label specifically warns against the use of any surfactant with the fungicide.

Sprayer Maintenance and Cleaning

A sprayer is a long-term investment and should provide many years of satisfactory service—if. Carefully follow *all* the manufacturer's instructions, as printed in the sprayer service and maintenance manual, as regards operation, maintenance, and lubrication. The spray tank should be kept *clean*—free of rust, scale, dirt and sand, grass clippings, and other trash. Nothing wears out nozzle tips or a pump faster than sand particles and rust. Do not make the mistake of laying sprayer parts where they can pick up sand or dirt particles and grass clippings.

Have you had problems with spray nozzles clogging? Everyone has. Liquid concentrates, solubles, and flowables should present no problems. Clogging of wettable powders can often be prevented by making up a spray mix into a thin, smooth batter of water and spray powder before pouring into the spray tank through a fine screen or cheesecloth.

Check and clean the strainers after use each day. Partially plugged strainers create a pressure drop and reduce the nozzle flow rate. Most power sprayers contain strainers: (1) on the suction hose to protect the pump, (2) in the line between the pump and the boom, and (3) in the nozzle (Figure 6.7).

All types of sprayers should be thoroughly rinsed after *each* use. Give the tank a general flushing then add clean water (warm, if possible) containing a teaspoonful of liquid detergent, household ammonia, trisodium phosphate (TSP), or washing soda per gallon (1 quart of ammonia or TSP to 25 gal). Seal the sprayer and circulate the solution through the system for a few minutes, letting a small amount go through the nozzle(s). The remainder of the solution should stand in the sprayer for at least 6 hours before pumping it through the nozzles.

Shake manual sprayers well before pumping a little pressure and flushing the discharge line with the nozzle cap off. Drain, pump some clean water through the system, and hang upside down. Lock the spray-control valve open for drainage. Where possible, take the pump out and hang separately.

For power sprayers, pump soapy water through the discharge system, followed by one or more rinses of clean water. Periodically, remove the nozzles and strainers and wash with kerosene followed by hot, soapy water. Store dry and where the tank and discharge system will drain properly.

Before starting a new power sprayer, check all lubrication points. Flush out the system thoroughly before starting the pump to remove metal chips and dirt accumulated during the manufacturing process. Then add water to the tank and operate at slow speed while checking the delivery system, control valves, pressure regulator, and other parts.

Occasionally during the season, and definitely before winter storage, clean hand-operated and power sprayers more thoroughly. Clean, flush, and drain as outlined, then disconnect the hose(s) and soak nozzles, strainers, and screens with kerosene. Scrub these with an old toothbrush or fine bristle brush (*not* with anything metal) before rinsing with hot, soapy water. Replace nozzle discs with enlarged holes and other worn parts. Rinse hoses clean.

Before winter storage. *Manual sprayers* should be taken apart and the pump cleaned, where possible. Add a few drops of light oil in the top of the pump cylinder to keep the plunger cup pliable and lubricate the cylinder. For winter storage, leave partially unassembled. Lightly oil all metal parts and wrap in newspaper. When reassembling the sprayer, pump clean water through the open nozzle head to flush out the discharge line. Finally, pump to nearly full pressure and check hose and gaskets for leaks; maybe the shutoff valve needs a drop of oil. If the pump fails to develop full pressure, remove the plunger from the cylinder and replace the cup so that it seals tightly. It may need more lubrication or replacement.

Power sprayers should be thoroughly drained, flushed, and cleaned as outlined by the manufacturer. Pour a pint to 5 gal of lightweight engine oil or radiator rust inhibitor (depending on its size) into the tank, fill with water, and pump for a minute or two. This provides a protective coating to the inside of the tank, pump, valves, and circulating system. Finally, drain and dry the sprayer completely and store where clean and dry. To prevent corrosion, remove the nozzle tips and strainers, dry them, and store in a can of diesel fuel or kerosene. The hose(s) should be stored unkinked inside in the dark and free from freezing. When reassembling in the spring, check the hose carefully for deep cuts and cracks. Are the hose clamps tight and gaskets still pliable?

Corrosive fertilizers should not be used in certain sprayers. For example, liquid fertilizers are corrosive to copper, galvanized surfaces, brass, bronze, and steel. An ordinary sprayer can be ruined by using a liquid fertilizer just once. If you apply liquid fertilizers, use a sprayer made completely of stainless steel or aluminum. Aluminum is satisfactory for some nitrogen fertilizers but not for mixed fertilizers.

Figure 6.11 A drop-type (gravity) spreader is convenient for applying fertilizers and pesticides. (Courtesy O. M. Scott & Sons.)

Figure 6.12 Popular rotary (centrifugal) spreader. (Courtesy O. M. Scott & Sons.)

GRANULAR APPLICATORS

More and more pesticides are becoming available in granular form for turf use (Figures 6.11 and 6.12). Some come premixed with fertilizers or as mixtures to control a variety of pests. This is a fast, simple, and convenient way to apply chemicals to kill weeds, many soil insects, and nematodes. Granules, however, are *not* generally satisfactory for controlling disease-causing fungi that invade through the leaf blades unless you use a systemic fungicide. Here you need the uniform coverage obtainable with a fine spray. Proper selection, care, calibration, and use of granular applicators can minimize costs and maximize the results obtained.

Drop (gravity) and *rotary (centrifugal) spreaders* are available for applying granules to turf. Drop spreaders are usually more precise and deliver a more uniform pattern than rotary spreaders. Because the granules drop straight down, there is also less drift. Some drop spreaders will not handle larger granules, however, and ground clearance in high-cut wet turf can be a problem. Because the edges of a drop-spreader pattern are sharp, any steering error will cause missed or doubled strips. Drop spreaders also usually require more effort to push than rotary spreaders.

Operating Procedures

First, read the operator's manual and follow the instructions carefully. Second, read the product label, and select the appropriate rate and pattern settings for specific conditions. Third, operate the spreader the long way of the turf area, but first apply header strips across each end or around an irregular area (Figure 6.13).

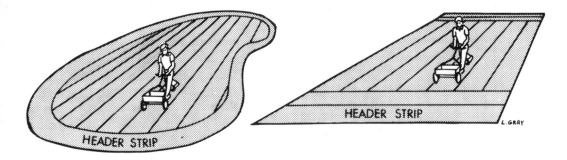

Figure 6.13 Header strips help to obtain uniform coverage with a drop-type spreader.

Header strips provide an area in which to turn around and realign the spreader. Always move the spreader at normal operating speed on the header strips, and then activate the spreader as it enters the untreated turf area. When you reach the other end, the spreader should be shut off while moving, and then stopped and turned in the header strip. A spreader should *never* be open while stopped. In addition, the end turns should not be made with the spreader open because the pattern will be very irregular while the spreader is turning.

Occasionally, it may be impossible to obtain an acceptable pattern with a rotary spreader, and streaking of the turf may result. A common solution to this problem is to reduce the setting by one-half and go over the area twice at right angles. However, it is better to reduce the setting and swath width by one-half and go back and forth in parallel swaths.

Do not operate your spreader backwards. When pulled backwards, most rotary spreaders deliver an unacceptable pattern and drop spreaders will not maintain a constant application rate.

Finally, set and fill the spreader on a paved surface rather than on turf. If a spill occurs, a driveway is much easier to sweep clean than turf. Some rotary spreaders are provided with a means of shutting off one side of the pattern. This feature is desirable when edging a driveway, sidewalk, or other nonturf area.

Uniform Application

There are two important aspects to precise application of granular products. The first is the application rate (the amount of product applied in pounds per 1000 sq ft). Every product, whether a fertilizer or pesticide, is designed and recommended for application at a specific rate. Overapplication is costly, increases the risk of grass injury, and may be illegal if label recommendations are exceeded. Underapplication may mean poor pest control.

The flow rate from granular applicators will not change in the same proportion as changes in speed. For example, doubling the speed will *not* double the flow rate. A constant ground speed is necessary to maintain a uniform application rate.

Even distribution of the product is as important as the application rate. For example, the pesticide label may indicate an application rate of 4 lb per 1000 sq ft, and the spreader may apply that amount; however, the pesticide may not be applied uniformly over the 1000 sq ft. It is very important to obtain uniform distribution of granules on turf since even small differences in the application rate can result in obvious streaks or lack of control.

Granular Applicators

The pattern applied by a rotary spreader depends upon impeller characteristics (height, angle, speed, shape, and roughness), ground speed, the drop point of the product on the impeller, the physical properties of the product, and environmental conditions (temperature, humidity, wind, etc.). Methods for adjusting the pattern include blocking off part of the metering port or ports on some units and moving the metering point or impeller on other units. If pattern skewing cannot be corrected by following the manufacturer's recommendations, try varying the speed or tilting the impeller. When a product is so heavy or light that skewing cannot be eliminated, it may be necessary to use a wider swath width on one side than on the other.

Calibration of Granular Applicators

Most suppliers recommend spreader settings and swath widths for their products and several products of their principal competitors, but these are only initial guides for calibration runs prior to actual use. Every spreader should be calibrated for proper delivery rate with a particular product and operator because of variability in the product, the operator's walking speed, and environmental conditions. Calibration should be checked and corrected according to the manufacturer's directions at least once a week; more often if the spreader has received mechanical damage.

An easy method for checking the delivery rate of a spreader is to apply (spread) a weighed amount of product on a measured area (at least 1000 sq ft for a drop spreader and 5000 sq ft for a rotary spreader), and then weigh the product remaining in the spreader to determine the actual rate delivered.

To avoid contamination of the turf area during initial calibration, hang a catch pan or bag under the spreader and push the spreader a measured distance at the proper speed. Hang the catch container so there is no interference with the shutoff bar or rate-control linkage.

Check both the distribution pattern and the flow rate of a rotary spreader. The product manufacturer may recommend a particular swath width, but verify this width before treating a large turf area. Check the pattern by laying out a row of shallow pans at right angles to the direction of travel. For commercial, push-type, rotary spreaders, the pans should be 1 to 2 in. high, with an area of about 1 sq ft, and be spaced on 1-ft centers. The row of pans should cover 1½ to 2 times the anticipated effective swath width. Add granules to the spreader, set it at the recommended setting for rate and pattern, and make three passes in the same direction over the pans. The material caught in the individual pans can then be weighed and a distribution pattern plotted.

For a Conversion Table for Granular Rates, see Appendix B, page 381.

Maintenance and Care of Spreaders

A spreader should provide many years of satisfactory service if the following maintenance techniques are practiced: (1) Carefully follow *all* the manufacturer's instructions, as printed in the service manual, that came with the spreader, as regards operation, maintenance, and lubrication; (2) the spreader should be empty after each usage; (3) rinse the outside and especially the inside of the hopper with a stream of water to remove any pesticide or fertilizer clinging to the surface of the spreader; (4) allow the spreader to dry thoroughly;

(5) oil the bottom hopper surface of drop spreaders, plus the spring and rod inside the control housing, axle bearing, and other lubrication points; (6) store the spreader *wide open*; and (7) check the calibration periodically as outlined above.

SAFETY PRECAUTIONS

There are other safety hints concerning the use of pesticides that are not mentioned above or in earlier chapters:

1. Reread the instructions, precautions, and warnings on the container label before opening. Use the product strictly according to package directions, on the *grasses* specified, in the *amounts* specified, at the *times* specified, and *only* when needed. Keep the container tightly closed except when preparing the mix.

2. Store all chemicals in their original containers—with a label securely attached—in a dry, locked, orderly-kept, and well-ventilated cabinet or building, outside the home. Place warning signs to indicate that pesticides are stored there. Never leave pesticides open to children, irresponsible or unauthorized adults, or pets. Do not store them near human food, animal feed, fertilizers, or other commonly used chemicals such as fuels, lubricants, and motor oil. A few minutes spent studying the directions and precautions on a product label will prevent misuse and needless accidents.

3. Do not breathe mists, vapors, or dusts of pesticides when mixing, handling, or applying. Do not allow smoking, eating, or drinking in or near pesticide handling, mixing, or storage areas. Mix and prepare pesticides in the open or in a well-ventilated place. Avoid spilling on the skin, shoes or clothing. Immediately flush with warm soapy water any part of the skin contacted. Promptly remove all contaminated clothing and launder before wearing. Bathe promptly after spraying.

4. When applying turf protection chemicals, wear full protective clothing where called for. For a minimum, wear unlined rubber gloves, keep sleeves and trouser legs rolled down, collar buttoned, and wear a washable cap.

5. Wash hands and face thoroughly before eating, drinking, or smoking.

6. Cover birdbaths, pet dishes, and fish pools before applying any pesticide to turf. Avoid drift to fish ponds, streams, or other water supplies. Keep all chemicals away from herbs, fruits, and vegetables if these plants are not specifically mentioned on the label.

7. Do not mix emulsifiable concentrates (EC) with wettable powder (WP) formulations unless the label states otherwise. Before mixing any two or more chemicals together, check the label for instructions.

8. Do not apply any spray when the temperature is above 85 to 90°F or below 40°F, or injury to turf may result.

9. What to do with leftover spray? First, check the label for instructions. It may be possible to pour leftover spray into a gravel drive or hole in waste soil; or

dilute and spray on another area. Use extra spray on a labeled crop if possible. Never leave puddles on a hard surface that could attract pets or birds.

10. Promptly destroy empty or old pesticide containers so that they are not a hazard to people or pets. Wash out glass and metal containers before putting in the trash can.

11. Do not contaminate a sprayer used to apply insecticides and fungicides with herbicides, especially those used for broadleaf weed control, such as 2,4-D, mecoprop, and dicamba.

12. Keep the sprayer or granular applicator in good repair by following a regular maintenance program (pages 354 to 359).

7

Integrated Pest Management

INTRODUCTION

Integrated pest management (IPM) is both a concept and a philosophy. It is a broad, multidisciplinary, systematic approach to controlling all pests. All types of control methods (biological, cultural, regulatory, physical, and chemical) are utilized. Use of IPM strategies should result in effective and economical suppression of pests with a minimum effect on nontarget organisms and the environment. IPM is based on understanding the biology and ecology of the turfgrass plant or community to be protected and the pests to be controlled.

IPM might be defined as the optimization of pest control in an economically and ecologically sound manner through the use of multiple tactics compatible in keeping pest damage below the economic injury level while minimizing hazards to human beings, domestic and wild animals, plants, and the environment. (The economic injury level is the lowest population density of pests that will cause economic damage.) Others might define IPM as an organized and comprehensive approach to the management of key pests in an ecologically sound crop production system. Integrated management of turfgrass pests is much more than chemical pest management, although this is an important part. We should not depend on a single method or tactic to control any pest.

The amount of pest damage that can be tolerated—the economic injury level—depends on the cost of maintenance which, in turn, depends on the value of the turf. Obviously, a highway right-of-way is not as expensive to maintain or as valuable as a golf green, fairway, or home lawn.

There are two other concepts that are widely used in IPM. These are the economic threshold and damage threshold levels. The economic threshold level is a fundamental concept of IPM. It is the point at which the density of the pest infestation in the turf requires a control measure (usually chemical) to prevent economic loss. The damage threshold level is the lowest pest population density at which damage occurs. Both concepts are important when planning pest management at low, medium, and high levels of maintenance. At present, economic threshold levels have not been accurately determined for most turfgrass pests.

As far as turfgrass managers are concerned, IPM is based on six basic principles:

1. *Identify the pests* (including all insects and other animal pests, weeds, fungi, nematodes, bacteria, and viruses) to be managed in the turfgrass ecosystem. What are the key pests, potential pests, and those that may migrate in or be introduced with seed, sod, sprigs, plugs, or soil?

After successfully identifying all pests to be managed in the turfgrass ecosystem, an assessment of the potential damage from these pests must be made. With this knowledge the pests can then be ranked according to their potential importance and grouped into those that can potentially cause severe or irreversible damage, those that cause occasional minor damage or injury, and a third group of pests that cause little or no damage to the turf.

2. *Define the turfgrass management unit*—the agroecosystem. For some pests it may be a single unit of turfgrass (an athletic field, park, lawn, or golf course fairway or green). A whole subcontinent may be involved in the case of greenbugs or certain rusts that can blow hundreds of miles through the air within a relatively few hours. The size of the management unit depends on the mobility of the pest and its dispersal potential.

3. *Develop reliable monitoring techniques;* a critical component of any IPM program. Do we know how to accurately assess the turfgrass pest populations present, and measure the loss caused by each? The IPM system depends heavily on monitoring or scouting turfgrass areas on a regular basis for insects, weeds, and diseases. This information, in conjunction with data on related matters such as recent weather conditions, past cultural practices, the grass or grasses being grown, and desired turf quality enables the turfgrass manager to select the best strategies for reducing pest damage effectively and as economically as possible.

4. *Establish economic thresholds.* These thresholds will vary with the level of maintenance (low, medium, or high), the turfgrass(es) grown, and the pests that need to be controlled. Much more research needs to be done in determining the economic threshold levels for turfgrass pests. Other factors to consider are budget restrictions, availability of water, fertilizer, pesticides, dethatching and coring equipment, and so on.

5. *Evolve descriptive and predictive models* of what pests are most likely to occur, when they would be expected to appear, and the amount of damage that may take place. We need to identify and fill the knowledge gaps in the life cycles of many different turfgrass pests. We need to know more about the biology, ecology, and epidemiology of these pests.

6. *Develop an effective and economical pest management strategy.* This should involve the coordinated use of multiple tactics or control strategies into an integrated system. A pest management strategy should be developed for each uniform management area. Although these areas generally include the boundaries of a given turf area, they sometimes can be in smaller units. A good example might be the landing area in a golf course fairway, which would vary from the usual fairway management program to

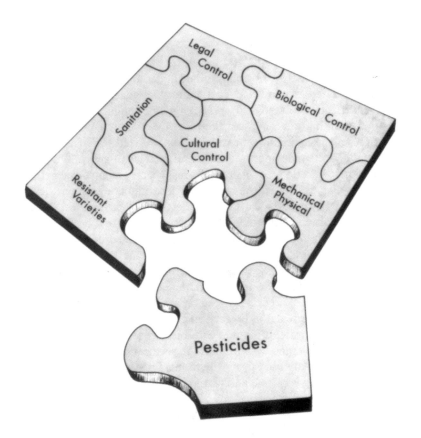

Figure 7.1 Integrated pest management (IPM) puzzle.

anticipate a higher degree of use. The same might be true for a general park area where concentrated traffic is anticipated. It is important that the strategy covers a very uniform management area to minimize variation in response to the program.

As shown in Figure 7.1, there are a number of pieces to the IPM puzzle. These pieces are interlocked and must be fitted together in a certain way. This integration of techniques must be compatible with sound turf management practices (see Chapters 2 to 5). We should also consider the costs of control measures over a period of years. We must remember that pest control is but *one* cost in producing a vigorous and aesthetically pleasing turf. Which pest management tactics or control measures are the most cost-effective over 5, 20, or more years? The management strategies selected must be economical and practical based on the labor, equipment, and money available. When should these measures be applied? Is protective action always the best? These are tough questions that every turfgrass manager must answer sooner or later.

MANAGEMENT TACTICS

The tactics used to manage turfgrass pests encompass legal or regulatory, genetic, cultural, biological, physical or mechanical, and chemical areas.

Legal

Regulatory measures are normally aimed at excluding turfgrass pests from an area, state, or country. These may involve federal and state quarantines or embargoes; seed inspections; certification of seed, sod, sprigs, or plugs; regulations regarding the quality of seed or other planting material; and the planting of certain very susceptible species.

Of all the regulatory measures available, seed certification is probably the most active and covers the widest range of use. Seed certification is a program covering seed production fields and seed lots, which are inspected to ensure genetic purity of seed. Different state agencies have the responsibility for conducting the certification program, which is coordinated by the Association of Official Seed Certification Agencies (AOSCA). The certification process generally involves controlled growth of regulated seed stock in a given field, with buffer strips of similar seed stock adjacent to the field to be harvested to ensure the direct pollination of seed within the field.

There are four classes of seed meeting or exceeding the standards established by AOSCA: breeder, foundation, registered, and certified seed. *Breeder seed* is the original source of all classes of certified seed. It is maintained by sponsoring plant breeders or institutions and provides a direct source of seed for foundation materials. *Foundation seed* is produced in fields planted with breeder seed, and is tagged with white certification tags. Fields planted with foundation seed can be harvested and tagged as *registered seed*. These fields are use ! primarily to increase the supply of a particular cultivar. The registered seed tag is purple and is the source for planting certified seed. *Certified seed* is the seed available to the consumer. It is produced in fields planted with either registered or foundation seed. Bags of certified seed carry a blue certification tag. It is important to note that the certification program does *not* guarantee that the seed is of the highest quality as to germination, purity, or freedom from disease or pathogens. However, it does ensure that the cultivars listed on the label are true to type.

Genetic

Genetic control tactics have been widely used for generations. They involve (1) the selection, identification, and planting of adapted turfgrass species and cultivars with naturally occurring resistance to insects or other animal pests and/or diseases; or (2) the introduction of specific genes for resistance into an otherwise desirable turfgrass species or cultivar. The development of multiple disease-resistant cultivars of turfgrasses has been an important step in reducing losses from major diseases. These concepts have been demonstrated in thousands of species/cultivar evaluation studies in the United States, Canada, Europe, and elsewhere (Figure 5.73).

Besides genetic selection and breeding for resistance, the identification and use of highly vigorous and competitive turfgrass species, mixes, and blends can offer successful competition with weed species leading to the elimination of those weeds.

In many variety trials a fast-germinating turfgrass species, such as perennial ryegrass, has provided superior seedling weed control when compared to slower-germinating species, such as Kentucky bluegrass. A turfgrass species seeded at its optimum rate will also have significantly fewer weed problems during its establishment stage than the same turfgrass seeded at a suboptimum rate.

Cultural

Cultural management tactics are the oldest and most widely used procedures to keep down pest losses. They include sanitation (the removal of dead or living material harboring a pest, thereby disrupting the life cycle of the pest), plus proper planting, watering, fertilizing, mowing, and cultivation practices that stimulate the vigorous growth of turfgrasses to better resist pests (see Chapter 2). The essence of cultural controls is to adjust turf maintenance procedures to the current growth rate of the turf. This growth rate will fluctuate during the growing season, creating different levels of demand which must be met to minimize stress on the turf. The time of planting is also important in cultural control. Poor or incorrect maintenance results in a weakened turf that lacks density and vigor thereby encouraging pest activity and weed invasion.

Water is the single most important factor governing the incidence and severity of a disease attack because a film of moisture on the susceptible plant surface is needed before spore germination, infection, and disease development can occur. The severity of disease can be considerably reduced with proper irrigation (e.g., watering early in the morning, *not* during the late afternoon and evening). Any practice that shortens the time period that the grass is wet will restrict the spread and growth of practically all turfgrass pathogens.

An excess of water may increase the succulence of turfgrass plants, stress them by preventing oxygen uptake by their roots, and thus increase the plant's susceptibility to disease. Good examples of diseases aided by irrigation practices include Pythium blight and yellow tuft or downy mildew. The fungi causing these diseases release zoospores that swim through films of water to infect new plants. Water flowing over a grass surface rapidly transports zoospores and other fungus spores over wide areas, where they can infect more turfgrass plants.

Turf that is healthy requires enough water to meet its evapotranspiration and growth requirement needs. Too much or too little water, and too frequent or too infrequent irrigations, provide the conditions that favor growth and development of unwanted weed species. Poor irrigation practices can decrease turfgrass roots, grass vigor, and density, which leads to weed seed germination, growth, and survival of the adapted species. Weed colonization follows, which leads to the need for herbicides and renovation or reestablishment.

Excessive thatch and compaction must be controlled to maintain a weed-free turf. Soil that is compacted and turf that is heavily thatched restrict the entry of water, air, and nutrients into the soil, thereby reducing root growth and eventually, the vigor of turfgrasses. The presence of knotweed, a summer annual, is a good indicator of compaction due to its tolerance and competitive advantage in compacted soils. Turf with a thick thatch commonly has high populations of shallow-rooted weeds, such as crabgrass, goosegrass, and annual bluegrass, that prefer high-moisture sites. The correct timing and frequency of core aerification and thatch removal (vertical mowing) is a relatively easy means to maintain a healthy stand of grass.

Core aerification helps to reverse the effects of compaction by allowing a better exchange of oxygen by the roots and better water penetration. Aerification also increases a turfgrass plant's resistance to disease and insect attack by enabling it to maintain more vigorous growth through an increased root system.

Thatch is an excellent food base for numerous turfgrass-infecting fungi. Thatch removal reduces the food base of weakly pathogenic organisms, thereby lessening the opportunity for fungi to produce disease. An accumulation of thatch can also lead to an increase in insect damage. Thatch provides a haven for insects to hide and for their populations to increase. Insecticide and fungicide activity is also inhibited because the chemicals become bound to the organic matter in the thatch. A buildup of thatch results in poor penetration of water and air, thus weakening the grass and making it more susceptible to insect damage. Many severe insect problems are associated with a thick thatch (Chapter 4).

Mowing affects turfgrass plants by providing wounds through which pathogens (such as those causing bacterial wilt, Rhizoctonia diseases, dollar spot, red thread, and Septoria leaf spot) may infect a plant. Close mowing removes much of the photosynthetic area, thereby decreasing the stress resistance of the grass plant and its ability to recover from all types of pest damage. Why? After severe clipping the grass plant's regenerative processes are mobilized into repairing the damage. With the need for additional resources for pest resistance, the plant definitely goes under stress.

Mowing turf at or near its optimal height for a particular use causes less depletion of food reserves, thereby allowing the plants to remain more resistant to pest attack. Mowing at the optimal height also shades out the seedlings of many weed species. Long-term close mowing results in shallow and reduced root systems, and an invasion of such weeds as annual bluegrass, oxalis, and spotted spurge.

The effects of fertilization on the development of turfgrass diseases varies. Many diseases become more damaging when grass is grown under higher or lower than normal levels of nitrogen (page 213). Brown patch and Pythium blight are examples of diseases which are more severe where nitrogen levels are excessive while the levels of phosphorus and potassium are normal. Dollar spot, pink patch, and red thread, however, are more severe where the turf is deficient in nitrogen. With a knowledge of what diseases are most likely to occur in a given turf, under what environmental conditions these diseases occur (Chapter 5), and their response to different fertilizer levels, the turfgrass manager can thus adjust the fertilizer program to minimize the effects of disease.

Fertilization practices also greatly affect the invasion of weeds into turf. The area covered by many broadleaf weeds often decreases as the annual amount of nitrogen increases. A fertilization program that results in a nutrient imbalance (i.e., a low level of phosphorus, potassium, or other essential element) may also hasten weed invasion. An excellent example is the rapid development or increase in annual bluegrass populations in areas that receive a high level of phosphorus fertilization. This is most evident in closely cut turfs. Unfortunately, weeds are better able to compete in poorly fertilized turf than in turf that is well fertilized due to the greater density, vigor, and competitiveness of properly fertilized turf.

The importance of sound fertilization, watering, and cultivation programs cannot be overemphasized. Healthy, vigorous turf can often outgrow the effects of insect or weed infestations and disease attacks, while poor conditions result in more severe damage and a slower recovery. Healthy turf therefore usually requires fewer treatments of pesticides to control insects, diseases, and weeds. It also follows that turf under water, heat, compaction, thatch, fertilization, or other stresses stands a greater chance of being damaged by chemicals applied for pest control.

Biological

Biological control can be defined as the regulation or control of pest populations by their natural enemies (antagonists, parasites, and predators). The only successful biological control program for turfgrass insects at present is the use of the spore-forming bacterium (*Bacillus popilliae*), or milky disease, in the control of Japanese beetle grubs. The Japanese beetle is apparently the main host of this bacterium, although the larvae of other scarabacid insects are known to be susceptible. The bacterium is widely sold and applied as a dust which contains countless numbers of its spores. It takes several years for the milky disease to appreciably reduce beetle-grub populations. Although there are naturally occurring parasites and predators of turfgrass insects and mites, their success in reducing damaging pest populations has not been proven. For predators and parasites to be effective, pest insects must be present in the turf at high enough population levels to sustain populations of parasites and predators. The only problem is that biological control measures take a long time and turfgrass managers must be willing to accept a certain level of damage to the turf.

An insect called the big-eyed bug is often found in turfgrass with infestations of chinch bugs. This predator insect attacks chinch bug eggs and nymphs and reduces their populations. Big-eyed bugs and chinch bugs are similar in appearance except for the pair of oversized eyes on the adult big-eyed bug.

Lady beetle and syrphid fly larvae commonly attack populations of greenbug in a lawn. The number of greenbug aphids builds up rapidly and rust-colored damaged areas appear. The predator lady beetles and syrphid flies appear and reduce the numbers of greenbugs.

Other predator insects include the adults and larvae of ground beetles, which attack a number of soil insects. Noninsect predators include birds that feed on leaf-feeding caterpillars such as cutworms and sod webworms.

Insect control by disease-causing organisms other than *Bacillus popilliae* include species of *Beauvaria*. This fungus produces a disease that is quite effective in regulating chinch bug populations. Another species of *Beauvaria* attacks billbugs. Species of *Beauvaria* have been also tested as applied controls for sod webworms.

An endophytic fungus (*Acremonium*) found in fescues and perennial ryegrass has provided resistance of these grasses to sod webworms and billbugs. The endophytic fungus grows systemically from the seed throughout the growing plant. Seeds can be examined in a laboratory to determine the presence or absence of the endophyte. Future plans call for seed tags to be marked as to the percentage of the seeds within the sack that contain the endophytic fungus. Future research may show control of other pests by *Acremonium* or other endophytes.

Although the biological balance of fungi, bacteria, nematodes, and other microorganisms in the turf thatch–soil environment undoubtedly plays a major role in the development of disease, there are no outstanding examples of biological control of turfgrass diseases using organisms antagonistic or parasitic to disease-causing fungi. Biological control of nematodes, dollar spot, and possibly other diseases is enhanced by using an activated sewage sludge fertilizer. Current research in this area, however, may result in the future marketing of biological disease-control agents.

Biological control of weeds using allelopathic plants (plants that are naturally toxic to other species) in turf establishment and maintenance is in its infancy but offers promise for the future.

Physical or Mechanical

Management tactics that use physical means of control include traps for insects, moles, or other vertebrate pests. Various noise devices that discourage injurious birds might have a place in seed-producing fields and other turfgrass areas. Providing good surface and subsurface water drainage is another valuable physical control tactic, as is having sharp mowers, to reduce excessive wounding of the leaf tips.

Chemical

The use of pesticides has been discussed in Chapters 3 to 6, and involves the use of chemicals applied as sprays, drenches, granules, seed treatments, and the preplant use of soil fumigants. The selective use of herbicides, insecticides, fungicides, and nematicides must remain the first line of defense against most turfgrass pests in medium- and especially high-maintenance turfs.

Although sound turfgrass management practices (Chapter 2) can significantly reduce weed, insect, and disease activity, it does not eliminate the necessity of using pesticides when serious problems develop. In practice, sound management procedures reduce the number of pesticide applications needed to control pest outbreaks when they do occur. When, by pest monitoring, you determine that a pest has equaled or exceeded the economic threshold, thereby requiring pesticide applications, the proper timing of these applications is crucial. With proper timing, additional applications will not be necessary, resulting in a reduction in total pesticide use.

Ideally, when a disease appears, the identity of the pathogen is determined, cultural practices are investigated to determine if they are creating or intensifying the problem, and the history of the turf is reviewed to determine if it has occurred in the past. This is where the keeping of a "turfgrass diary" comes in handy.

Once it is determined that cultural management practices—watering, fertilizing, mowing, dethatching, core aerification, and the pruning or removal of dense trees and shrubs bordering the turf area—cannot be modified to help suppress a disease outbreak, the use of fungicides becomes necessary. The fungicide selected should be specific for the fungus involved (Table 5.4) and be applied strictly according to label instructions. Fungicides should be regarded as only one component of an integrated pest management program.

For weed control, specific herbicides are registered for most turfgrass weeds (Tables 3.3 and 3.4) and can be used on the common turfgrass species without injury. Of course, the weeds must be correctly identified as well as the desirable turfgrass species. The most effective herbicide for a specific weed problem should be applied according to label instructions when maximum control can be obtained. The cause(s) of the weed problem should be determined, and cultural practices should be modified to minimize the reinvasion of the weed (see Chapter 3).

To avoid turfgrass damage from weeds, insects, and diseases, regular inspections are necessary. For diseases such as Pythium blight, daily examinations of golf course greens are necessary in hot wet weather. Insects may cause the turfgrass to die back, be stunted, or develop growth distortions. The leaves may be bleached or turn yellow or brown. If such symptoms are observed, immediate action should be taken in medium- and high-maintenance turf. Insect populations can increase rapidly under the right conditions (Chapter 4). Some insects, such as cutworms, feed only at night. Unless a special effort is made to look for them during darkness, they may go undetected for some time.

Leafhoppers, scale insects, greenbugs, sod webworm larvae, and spider mites can be detected by carefully examining the leaves, stems, and crowns of grasses. Chinch bugs are found by carefully examining the crowns and thatch. An easy method to detect many insect pests in turf is called the "pyrethrum test." One tablespoon of a garden insecticide containing 1 to 2% pyrethrins is added to a gallon of water. One square yard of turf, including both damaged and "healthy" grass, is marked off. The gallon of pyrethrum mix is then applied with a sprinkling can as uniformly as possible over the marked area. Since pyrethrum is very irritating to most insects, this treatment will quickly bring cutworms, sod webworms, lucerne moths, skipper larvae, and other insects to the grass surface, where they can be seen and counted (if needed). Several areas within the turf should be checked to get an indication of the extent of the infestation. If pyrethrum is unavailable, you can get similar results by flooding the suspected turf area with water for 5 to 10 minutes.

White grubs and billbug larvae will not surface using the pyrethrum test or flooding. If grubs are present, they can be found by carefully digging around the roots of grass during the warm spring and fall months (Figures 4.4 to 4.7). If the white grub or billbug infestation is heavy, the grass roots will be eaten away, allowing you to roll the grass back like a carpet.

When a pest problem appears, consider several factors before applying any chemical. Accurate identification of the disease, insect or weed in the turf is important; many of the insects are not pests. Of the insects that are pests, knowledge of their behavior and biology is critical in determining what chemical(s) should be applied for their control. Different turfgrass pests require different chemical treatments and management methods to be effective (Tables 3.3, 3.4, 4.1 and 5.4).

Such factors as temperature, humidity, soil moisture, soil type, and location all influence the outbreaks of disease and buildup of insect populations. Some insect pests thrive in a warm, dry environment; others prefer a moist one. Some insect pests of turf are influenced by cycles of drought. For example, the frit fly is more prevalent during droughts. Certain turf areas may be more susceptible to insect pest populations than others due to the grass(es) being grown, management practices, exposure to sun, slope, and soil types. All of these factors should be considered when checking for the presence of insect pests and whether a chemical control is warranted. Remember that insect pests are commonly found first in isolated spots, most commonly at the edge of a turf. It would be unusual to find insects uniformly distributed throughout a turf area.

Turfgrass should be well watered before applying an insecticide to control pests that feed on the leaves, stems, and crowns. Apply the insecticide as soon as the turf has dried. Withhold further watering until it is necessary to water the grass to prevent wilting. This procedure allows the insecticide to remain on the turfgrass as long as possible, thereby getting maximum effectiveness from the treatment.

Sprays are the preferred application method to control turfgrass weeds, insect pests, and diseases. Granular formulations of many pesticides are available to control annual weeds, white grubs, sod webworms, chinch bugs, cutworms, billbugs, skipper larvae, slugs and snails, snow molds, leaf smuts, and other diseases.

When areas are to be treated for pests and disease-causing fungi that "operate" below ground, such as white grubs, billbug larvae, leaf smuts, summer patch and necrotic ring spot (Fusarium blight), the pesticide should be uniformly applied to the turfgrass surface and the area then heavily irrigated (using 1 in. of water or about 600 gal per 1000 sq ft) to move the chemical down into the top several inches of soil.

No turfgrass planting is infected with every disease, weed, or insect pest to which it is susceptible. Commonly, a history of pest infestation develops in a given turf area where a single pest or a few pests occur year after year. Thorough knowledge of what weeds, insects, and diseases occur in that turfgrass area and the time of year that the pests normally appear can contribute greatly to their control. Some states, as well as pesticide companies, have developed "insect and disease calendar guides" that are useful aids in turfgrass insect and disease control. They provide a turfgrass manager with a ready reference as to when to monitor for turfgrass pests and when chemical treatments are most desirable. Highly sophisticated IPM programs that involve plant growth modeling and the integration of all weed, insect pest, and disease control tactics into a cohesive system have not been developed for turfgrass managers, although several computer programs are being developed, for various states. Many factors of this multidisciplinary pest control approach, however, are well understood and can lead to setting priorities for management practices based on the level of maintenance desired.

Selecting the best adapted turfgrass species and cultivars based on the climatic zones (Figure 2.1) and the on-site use is very important. Other major considerations might include providing for a means of irrigation, an adequate soil-fertility level, and the proper soil reaction (pH). The ideal time to plan for the solution of future weed, insect, disease, and nematode problems is before the turf is planted.

The next critical stage in a pest management system is proper planting and seedling establishment. The planting of vigorous seed, sod, sprigs, or plugs free of weeds, insects, and diseases (certified and/or inspected, if possible), planted correctly to produce a uniform dense turf, is basic to proper establishment regardless of the level of maintenance.

Following planting and establishment, one of the most important and effective IPM practices is frequent observations of the turf to monitor or scout rigorously for weed, insect pest, and disease problems. Close observations, assessment of pest and environmental problems, and detailed record keeping will help ensure that proper pest control action is taken at the most opportune time. Scouting combined with information written in a "turfgrass pest diary" can lead to adjusting or changing one or more management practices that will alleviate or moderate most pest problems.

If pesticides must be applied, and they are necessary in many situations, choose the most effective and least toxic chemical to nontarget plant and animal species, and the least persistent in the environment.

WEED MANAGEMENT FOR DIFFERENT LEVELS OF TURFGRASS MANAGEMENT

A turfgrass manager should first determine the level of maintenance necessary to achieve the desired turf quality and utility (see Chapter 2). The appropriate low, medium, or high maintenance level can then be chosen to achieve that goal. Although only three maintenance levels may be too narrow in scope, most levels of maintenance can be adjusted to fit within one of these broad classifications. Although total weed eradication is generally not possible, higher-maintenance turfs require minimal weed populations. Similarly, low-maintenance turf will tolerate greater populations of weeds. In fact, for the most minimally maintained turfs, some weed growth is necessary to maintain a continuous living cover of reasonable density.

The initial maintenance plan or calendar should be developed solely with turfgrass requirements in mind (see Table 2.11, page 37). This maintenance schedule is rarely sufficient and must be modified to accommodate weed populations that develop on the site. An example might be in areas of poor drainage. Where soil moisture levels are at field capacity or slightly less for extended periods of time, populations of crabgrass, goosegrass, *Poa annua,* or other weeds with high moisture requirements will develop. Here, less irrigation will be necessary to hold weed populations in check.

In acidic or low pH soils, weed populations such as red sorrel will predominate. Therefore, pH amendments will be required for optimal control. Just as soil compaction can have a direct effect on turf density, the same effect influences weed populations. Many turfgrass weeds can tolerate compacted soil conditions better than do turfgrass(es). To benefit the turf and minimize weed development, some alleviation from soil compaction is necesasry, usually through core aerification (Chapter 2).

Successful preemergent weed control is dependent on a continuous chemical barrier in the upper soil surface to intercept developing weed seedlings. Core aerification disrupts this barrier allowing the emergence of weed seedlings. Therefore, preemergent herbicide applications should be delayed until after core aerification.

The cycle of applying cultural controls to benefit turf development and minimize weed encroachment should be followed by effective physical or chemical weed management procedures. The cycle is repeated with additional necessary cultural practices followed by direct weed control measures. Close evaluation of turfgrass growth performance and weed populations after each step is crucial in determining necessary future operations. Again, it is necessary to keep this information in a turfgrass-pest diary to follow changes in turfgrass performance as affected by weed populations. Corrective measures can then be taken to reduce weed populations. Integrated weed control is therefore a reactive procedure where the turf manager formulates new strategies based on an evaluation of previous efforts.

INSECT PEST MANAGEMENT FOR THREE LEVELS OF TURFGRASS MAINTENANCE

Low Maintenance

Turfgrass insect pests favor high-maintenance turf for their host rather than poor-quality turf. The leaf feeders, including sod webworms, cutworms, armyworms, and other chewing insects, prefer to feed in areas of high fertility and irrigation than on low-maintenance turf such as airports, highway rights-of-way, industrial grounds, land reclamation or waste sites, and waterway banks.

Insect control in low-maintenance areas consists of applying an insecticide to an outbreak situation. For example, a population of a general feeder, such as grasshoppers or crickets, builds up in large numbers in an industrial site; or leafhoppers attracted to lights are found in large numbers along a highway median. These turf areas could be treated if the insect population is causing severe damage or is a nuisance to people using the area.

Only in unusual situations would areas of low maintenance need to be treated to control insects. Table 4.1 gives control suggestions.

Medium Maintenance

Home and industrial lawns, athletic fields, parks, cemeteries, and golf course roughs are often infested with insect pests. The numbers of these pests fluctuate yearly with visible damage appearing in periods of moisture stress. White grubs, billbugs, chinch bugs, webworms, and greenbugs are often found in these medium-maintenance areas, and their damage appears in mid to late summer. In most instances, treatment is applied when severe or not so severe damage is evident. Treatments, however, should be made when damage *first* appears. The application of an effective insecticide, combined with additional fertility and supplemental irrigation, will usually solve most insect pest problems in medium-maintenance turfs. Where a history of repeated annual damage from a pest insect, such as Japanese beetles or bluegrass billbugs occurs, treatments may need to be made to prevent economic populations and provide season-long control. Table 4.1 lists the effective insecticides for specific insect pests.

High Maintenance

High-quality, vigorous turfgrass that is well fertilized and irrigated with frequent mowings are inviting to certain insect pests. For example, black cutworms spend repeated generations in high-quality golf greens and tees, black turfgrass ataenius grubs can appear in high numbers in fairways, and various species of white grubs may infest fairways and other fine-turf areas.

Managers of high-quality turfs soon learn which insect pests frequent these areas. He or she also learns when damage, if any, is most likely to appear. There are many turf areas that receive an insecticide treatment at regular intervals throughout the growing season. It is very important to identify the pest insect that appears regularly in the area, note symptoms of its early damage and its potential for serious damage, and the life cycle of the insect. The most vulnerable stage of the insect must also be understood. For example, black turfgrass ataenius grubs hatch from eggs laid on the golf course fairway by adult beetles which migrated into the area in the spring. Grubs, if a problem, will appear in early summer, and fewer than 30 to 40 grubs per square foot will usually not exhibit damage in well-managed turf.

Insecticides for both prevention of insect pests as well as treatment of a damaging population on high-maintenance turf are given in Table 4.1.

Low Maintenance

Disease control is achieved most economically in low-maintenance turfs (Chapter 2) by planting mixtures or blends of locally adapted, disease-resistant grasses (see in Chapter 5). In certain situations light applications of fertilizer, mowing as high as practical, and supplemental irrigation might be feasible. Diseases are rarely unsightly enough in low-maintenance turfs to warrant other cultural or chemical measures. Chapter 5 discusses desirable cultural management practices (pages 212 to 214) to minimize disease attacks, and chemical control suggestions are given at the end of Chapter 5.

Medium Maintenance

Disease control in lawns, parks, cemeteries, athletic fields, and golf course roughs should start with providing good surface and subsurface drainage plus a well prepared and fertile seedbed. Seed, sod, sprigs or plugs should be of locally adapted, disease-resistant grasses (see in Chapter 5) and be of top quality. Other cultural controls would include late spring and early fall applications of slow-release fertilizers, mowing at the suggested height and frequency (Chapter 2), watering deeply during droughts but only to prevent permanent injury. Dethatching and core aerification may be warranted when the thatch is over ½ in. thick and compaction is a problem. Light penetration and air movement across the turf may be increased by selectively pruning or removing dense trees, shrubs, or other barriers bordering the turf area(s). More light and air means that the grass will dry more quickly and disease attacks should not be as severe. Fungicides may be called for on a preventive basis (Table 5.4). Their use is discussed on pages 317 to 322.

High Maintenance

Golf and bowling greens, tees, fairways, and high-quality athletic fields require the full spectrum of cultural and chemical disease control practices outlined for medium maintenance turf plus the others listed in Table 5.1. Proper and timely planting, fertilization, mowing, watering, dethatching, and core aerification practices are needed to maintain turf vigor, density, and uniformity. With high maintenance will come increased disease pressure. The full spectrum of cultural controls outlined in Chapters 2 and 5 and chemical controls (pages 316 to 322 and Table 5.4) will be needed to keep damaging diseases in check. These cultural, chemical, and other management practices need to be integrated with practices to keep down damaging populations of weeds, insects, and other animal pests.

Appendix A:
Measurements and Conversions

WEIGHTS

1 gram (g) = 1000 milligrams = 0.035274 oz avoirdupois = 0.0022046 pound = 0.001 kilogram

1 ounce avoirdupois (oz av) = 0.911458 troy oz = 28.349527 grams = 0.0625 pound

1 ounce (troy) = 1.097 oz av = 31.10348 grams

1 kilogram (kg) = 1000 grams = 35.273957 oz av = 2.20462 pounds (av)

1 pound avoirdupois (lb av) = 16 oz av = 14.5833 troy oz = 453.5924 grams = 0.4535924 kilogram

1 ton (short, U.S.) = 2000 pounds (av) = 2430.56 troy pounds = 0.892857 long ton = 0.907185 metric ton = 907.18486 kilograms = 32,000 oz

1 ton (long, U.S.) = 2240 pounds = 2722.22 troy pounds = 1.120 short tons = 1.016 metric tons = 1016.04 kilograms

1 ton (metric) = 2204.6 pounds = 1.1023 short tons = 0.984 long ton = 1000 kilograms

SQUARE (OR SURFACE) MEASURES

1 square millimeter (sq mm) = 0.01 sq centimeter = 0.000001 sq meter = 0.00155 sq in.

1 square centimeter (sq cm) = 100 sq millimeters = 0.155 sq inch = 0.001076 sq foot

1 square inch (sq in.) = 6.451626 sq centimeters = 0.0069444 sq ft

1 square foot (sq ft) = 144 sq inches = 0.111111 sq yard = 0.0929 sq meter = 0.003673 sq rod

1 square yard (sq yd) = 9 sq ft = 1296 sq inches = 0.83613 sq meter = 0.03306 sq rod

1 square meter (sq m) = 10.76387 sq ft = 1550 sq inches = 1.195985 sq yards = 0.039537 sq rod = 1 million sq millimeters = 10,000 sq centimeters

1 square rod (sq rod) = 30.25 sq yards = 25.29295 sq meters = 272.25 sq feet = 0.00625 sq acre = 0.0025293 hectare

1 acre = 43,560 sq feet = 4840 sq yards = 160 sq rods = 4046.873 sq meters = 0.404687 hectare = 0.0015625 sq mile = strip 8 ft wide and 1 mile long (approximate)

1 hectare = 2.471 acres = 395.367 sq rods = 10,000 sq meters = 0.01 sq kilometer = 0.0039 sq mile

1 square kilometer = 0.3861 sq mile = 247.1 acres = 100 hectares = 1 million sq meters

1 square mile = 640 acres = 1 section = 258.9998 hectares = 102,400 sq rods = 3,097,600 sq yards = 2.589998 sq kilometers

CUBIC MEASURES

1 cubic centimeter (cc) = 0.06102 cu inch = 1000 cu milliliters = 0.000001 cu meter

1 cubic inch (cu in.) = 16.38716 cubic centimeters = 0.0005787 cu foot = 0.004329 gallon (U.S.)

1 cubic foot (cu ft) = 0.80356 bushel = 1728 cu inches = 0.037037 cu yard = 0.028317 cu meter = 7.4805 U.S. gallons = 6.229 British or Imperial gallons = 28.317 liters = 29.922 quarts (liquid) = 25.714 quarts (dry)

1 cubic foot of water = 62.43 pounds (1 pound of water = 27.68 cu inches = 0.1198 U.S. gallon = 0.01602 cu foot)

1 cubic foot (cu ft) of *dry* soil (approximate) = sandy (90 lb), loamy (80 lb), clayey (75 lb)

1 bushel (bu) *dry* soil (approximate) = sandy (112 lb), loamy (100 lb), clayey (94 lb)

1 cubic yard (cu yd) = 27 cu ft = 46,656 cu inches = 764.559 liters = 292 U.S. gallons = 168.176 British gallons = 1616 pints (liquid) = 807.9 quarts (liquid) = 21.694 bushels = 0.764559 cubic meter

1 cubic meter (cu m) = 1.30794 cu yard = 35.3144 cu feet = 28.3776 bushels = 264.173 gallons = 1056.7 quarts (liquid) = 2113.4 pints (liquid) = 61,023 cu inches

VOLUMES

Dry

1 quart (U.S.)* = 67.2 cu inches = 2 pints = 1.1012 liters = 0.125 peck = 0.03125 bushel = 0.038889 cu foot = 67.2 cu inches

1 peck (U.S.) = 0.25 bushel = 2 gallons = 8 quarts = 16 pints = 32 cups = 8.80958 liters = 537.605 cu inches

1 bushel (U.S.) = 4 pecks = 32 quarts = 64 pints = 128 cups = 1.2445 cu feet = 35.2383 liters = 0.304785 barrel = approximately ½₀ cubic yard

Liquid

1 milliliter (ml) = 1 cubic centimeter (approximate) = 0.001 liter = 0.061 cu inch = 0.03815 fluid ounce

*1 pint or quart dry measure is about 16% larger than 1 pint or quart liquid measure.

1 teaspoonful (tsp) = 5 milliliters = 0.17 fluid ounce

1 tablespoonful (Tbsp) = 3 teaspoons = 14.8 milliliters or cubic centimeters = ½ fluid ounce = 0.902 cu inch = 0.063 cup

1 fluid ounce (fl oz, U.S.) = 2 tablespoons = 0.125 cup = 0.0625 pint = 0.03125 quart = 0.00781 gallon = 29.573 millimeters = 1.80469 cu inches = 0.029573 liter

1 cup = 16 tablespoons = 8 fluid ounces = 0.5 pint = 236.6 cubic centimeters or milliliters

1 pint (U.S.)* = 16 fluid ounces = 32 tablespoons = 2 cups = 0.125 gallon = 473.167 milliliters = 1.04 pounds of water = 28.875 cu inches = 0.473167 liter = 0.01671 cu foot

1 liter = 2.1134 pints = 1.0567 liquid quarts (U.S.) = 0.9081 dry quart (U.S.) = 0.264178 gallon (U.S.) = 1000 milliliters or cubic centimeters = 33.8147 fluid ounces = 61.025 cu inches = 0.0353 cu foot = 0.028378 bushel

1 quart (U.S.)* = 2 pints = 4 cups = 32 fluid ounces = 57.749 cu inches = 64 table-spoons = 0.25 gallon = 0.946333 liter = 0.3342 cu foot

1 gallon (U.S.) = 4 quarts = 8 pints = 16 cups = 128 fluid ounces = 0.1337 cu foot = 0.83268 British or Imperial gallon = 3785.4 milliliters or cubic centimeters = 231 cu inches = 8.337 pounds water = 3.782 kilograms

1 barrel (U.S.) = 31.5 gallons = 7056 cu inches = 0.11924 cu meter

LINEAR (OR DISTANCE) MEASURES

1 millimeter (mm) = 0.1 centimeter = 0.01 decimeter = 0.001 meter = 1000 microns = 0.03937 inch (about ⅟₂₅ inch).

1 centimeter (cm) = 10 millimeters = 0.01 meter = 0.3937 inch = 0.03281 foot = 0.010936 yard (U.S.)

1 inch (in.) = 25.4 millimeters = 2.54 centimeters = 0.0254 meter = 0.083333 foot = 0.027778 yard = 0.00505 rod

1 foot (ft) = 12 inches = 0.333 yard = 30.48 centimeters = 0.3048 meter

1 yard (yd) = 36 inches = 3 feet = 0.181818 rod = 0.9144 meter

1 meter (m) = 100 centimeters = 39.37 inches = 3.2808 feet = 1.09361 yards = 0.1988 rod = 0.001 kilometer

1 rod = 5.5 yards = 16.5 feet = 198 inches = 5.02921 meters = 0.003125 mile

1 kilometer (km) = 1000 meters = 3280.8 feet = 1093.6 yards = 0.62137 statute mile = 0.53961 nautical mile

1 mile (statute) = 5280 feet = 1760 yards = 1609.35 meters = 320 rods = 0.86836 nautical mile

DILUTIONS

1 part per million (ppm) = 1 milligram per liter or kilogram = 0.0001% = 0.013 ounce by weight in 100 gallons = 0.379 gram in 100 gallons = 1 inch in nearly 16 miles = 2 crystals of sugar in a pound = 1 ounce of salt in 62,500 pounds of sugar = 1 minute of time in about 2 years = a 1-gram needle in a 1-ton haystack = 1 ounce of sand

*1 pint or quart dry measure is about 16% larger than 1 pint or quart liquid measure.

in 34¼ tons of cement = 1 ounce of dye in 7530 gallons of water = 1 pound in 500 tons = 1 penny of $10,000
1 part per billion (ppb) = 1 inch in nearly 16,000 miles = 1 drop in 20,000 gallons = 1 ounce in 753 million gallons = 2 crystals of sugar in 1000 pounds
1 percent (%) = 10,000 parts per million = 10 grams per liter = 1.28 ounces by weight per gallon = 8.336 pounds per 100 gallons

MISCELLANEOUS WEIGHTS AND MEASURES

1 micron = 0.00039 inch
1 acre inch of water = 27,154 gallons = 624.23 gallons per 1000 sq feet
1 pound per cubic foot = 0.26 gram per cubic inch
1 gram per cubic inch = 3.78 pounds per cubic foot

WEIGHTS PER UNIT AREA

1 ounce per square foot = 2722.5 pounds per acre
1 ounce per square yard = 302.5 pounds per acre
1 ounce per 100 square feet = 27.2 pounds per acre
1 ounce per 1000 square feet = 2.72 pounds per acre
1 pound per 100 square feet = 435.6 pounds per acre
1 pound per 1000 square feet = 43.56 pounds per acre
1 pound per acre = 1 ounce per 2733 square feet (0.37 oz/1000 sq ft) = 0.0104 g per sq ft = 1.12 kilograms per hectare
100 pounds per acre = 2.5 pounds per 1000 square feet ≡ 1.04 g per sq ft
5 gallons per acre = 1 pint per 1000 square feet = 0.43 ml per square foot
100 gallons per acre = 2.5 gallons per 1000 square feet = 1 quart per 100 square feet = 935 liters per hectare
1 quart per 100 gallons (approximate) = 10 ml per gallon
1 pound per gallon = 120 grams per liter
1 kilogram per 100 square meters = 2.05 pounds per 1000 square feet = 1 kilogram per hectare = 89 pounds per acre
1 kilogram per hectare = 0.0205 pound per 1000 square feet = 0.1 kilogram per 100 square meters = 0.89 pound per acre

CONVERTING TEMPERATURE FROM FAHRENHEIT TO CELSIUS (CENTIGRADE), AND VICE VERSA

To convert from *Fahrenheit* to *Celsius:* Subtract 32 from the Fahrenheit reading, multiply by 5, and divide the product by 9. *Example:* 131°F − 32 = 99 × 5 = 495; 495 ÷ 9 = 55°C.

To convert from *Celsius* to *Fahrenheit:* Multiply the Celsius reading by 9, divide the product by 5, and add 32. *Example:* 25°C × 9 = 225 ÷ 5 = 45; 45 + 32 = 77°F.

EQUIVALENT VOLUMES (LIQUID) FOR COMMON MEASURES

Measuring Unit Used	Number of Units to Fill Measure in the First Column					
	tsp	Tbsp	cup	pint	cc	liter
1 teaspoonful	1.00	0.33	0.021	0.010	4.9	0.0049
1 tablespoonful	3.00	1.00	0.663	0.031	14.8	0.0148
1 fluid ounce	6.00	2.00	0.125	0.062	29.6	0.0296
1 cup	48.00	16.00	1.000	0.500	236.6	0.2366
1 pint	96.00	32.00	2.000	1.000	473.2	0.4732
1 quart	192.00	64.00	4.000	2.000	946.3	0.9463
1 gallon	768.00	256.00	16.000	8.000	3,785.3	3.7853
1 liter	202.88	67.63	4.328	2.164	1,000.0	1.0000
1 milliliter (cc)	0.20	0.068	0.0042	0.0021	1.0	0.0010

METRIC–ENGLISH CONVERSION FACTORS

To Change:	To:	Multiply by:
Inches	Centimeters	2.54
Centimeters	Inches	0.3937
Feet	Meters	0.3048
Meters	Inches	39.37
Square inches	Square centimeters	6.452
Square centimeters	Square inches	0.155
Square yards	Square meters	0.836
Square meters	Square yards	1.196
Cubic yards	Cubic meters	0.765
Cubic meters	Cubic yards	1.308
Cubic inches	Cubic centimeters	16.387
Cubic centimeters	Cubic inches	0.061
Cubic centimeters	Fluid ounces	0.034
Fluid ounces	Cubic centimeters	29.57
Quarts	Liters	0.946
Liters	Quarts	1.057
Grams	Ounces (avoirdupois)	0.0352
Ounces (avoirdupois)	Grams	28.349
Pounds (avoirdupois)	Kilograms	0.454
Kilograms	Pounds (avoirdupois)	2.2046
Pounds (apothecary)	Kilograms	0.373
Kilograms	Pounds (apothecary)	2.205
Ounces (apothecary)	Grams	31.103
Grams (sq ft)	Pounds (acre)	96

Appendix B:
Calculating Application Rates

CONVERSION TABLE FOR USE OF MATERIALS ON SMALL AREAS

Rate per Acre	Rate per 1000 Square Feet	Rate per 100 Square Feet
Liquid Materials[a]		
1 pt	¾ Tbsp	¼ tsp
1 qt	1½ Tbsp	½ tsp
1 gal	6 Tbsp	2 tsp
25 gal	4½ pt	1 cup
50 gal	4½ qt	1 pt
75 gal	6½ qt	1½ pt
100 gal	9 qt	1 qt
Dry Materials[b]		
1 lb	2½ tsp	¼ tsp
3 lb	2¼ Tbsp	¾ tsp
4 lb	3 Tbsp	1 tsp
5 lb	4 Tbsp	1¼ tsp
6 lb	4½ Tbsp	1½ tsp
8 lb	⅔ cup	1¾ tsp
10 lb	½ cup	2 tsp
100 lb	2¼ lb	¼ lb

[a]1 pt/100 gal = 1 fl oz/6¼ gal = ½ fl oz/3 gal = 1 tsp/gal.
  1 qt/100 gal = 10 tsp/5 gal = 2 Tbsp/3 gal = 2 tsp/gal.
  1 gal/100 gal = ¾ cup and 4 tsp/5 gal = ½ cup/3 gal = 8 tsp/gal.
[b]1 lb/100 gal = 1 oz/6¼ gal = ½ oz/3 gal = 4.5 g/gal.

HOW TO CALCULATE NOZZLE FLOW RATES

Gallons per minute	Seconds for 1 Pint	Gallons per Minute	Seconds for 1 Quart
0.05	150	0.175	86
0.06	125	0.20	75
0.07	107	0.225	67
0.08	94	0.25	60
0.09	84	0.30	50
0.10	75	0.325	46
0.11	68	0.35	43
0.12	62	0.40	38
0.13	58	0.425	35
0.14	53	0.45	33
0.15	50	0.50	30

CONVERSION TABLE FOR GRANULAR RATES

If Percent of Active Ingredients in Granules is:	And Recommended Rate of Active Ingredients is:	Then Apply This Amount of Granules:
5	½ lb/acre	10 lb/acre
	1 lb/acre	20 lb/acre
	1½ lb/acre	30 lb/acre
	2 lb/acre	40 lb/acre
	3 lb/acre	60 lb/acre
	4 lb/acre	80 lb/acre
10	½ lb/acre	5 lb/acre
	1 lb/acre	10 lb/acre
	1½ lb/acre	15 lb/acre
	2 lb/acre	20 lb/acre
	3 lb/acre	30 lb/acre
	4 lb/acre	40 lb/acre
20	½ lb/acre	2½ lb/acre
	1 lb/acre	5 lb/acre
	1½ lb/acre	7½ lb/acre
	2 lb/acre	10 lb/acre
	3 lb/acre	15 lb/acre
	4 lb/acre	20 lb/acre
25	½ lb/acre	2 lb/acre
	1 lb/acre	4 lb/acre
	1½ lb/acre	6 lb/acre
	2 lb/acre	8 lb/acre
	3 lb/acre	12 lb/acre
	4 lb/acre	16 lb/acre

QUANTITIES OF MATERIAL GIVING THE SAME CONCENTRATION IN VARIOUS QUANTITIES OF WATER

Water	Spray Material									
	Powder					Liquid				
100 gal	1 lb	2 lb	3 lb	4 lb	5 lb	½ pt	1 pt	1 qt	2 qt	1 gal
50 gal	½ lb	1 lb	1½ lb	2 lb	2½ lb	¼ pt	½ pt	1 pt	1 qt	2 qt
25 gal	4 oz	8 oz	12 oz	1 lb	1¼ lb	2 fl oz	4 fl oz	8 fl oz	1 pt	1 qt
12½ gal	2 oz	4 oz	6 oz	8 oz	10 oz	1 fl oz	2 fl oz	4 fl oz	8 fl oz	1 pt
6¼ gal	1 oz	2 oz	3 oz	4 oz	5 oz	½ fl oz	1 fl oz	2 fl oz	4 fl oz	8 fl oz
3⅛ gal	½ oz	1 oz	1½ oz	2 oz	2½ oz	¼ fl oz	½ fl oz	1 fl oz	2 fl oz	4 fl oz
1 gal	4.5 g	9.1 g	13.6 g	18.1 g	22.7 g	2.4 ml	4.7 ml	9.5 ml	18.9 ml	37.9 ml
1 qt	1.1 g	2.3 g	3.4 g	4.5 g	5.7 g	0.59 ml	1.18 ml	2.36 ml	4.73 ml	9.46 ml
1 liter	1.2 g	2.4 g	3.6 g	4.8 g	6.0 g	0.62 ml	1.25 ml	2.50 ml	5.00 ml	10.0 ml

AMOUNT (VOLUME) OF LIQUIDS REQUIRED TO PREPARE DIFFERENT AMOUNTS OF SPRAY MIXTURES AT DIFFERENT DILUTIONS

Dilution of Spray Required	Recommended Dosage of Chemical in 100 Gallons of Water			Amount of Material Required to Prepare Spray for:					
				20 gal		5 gal		1 gal	
	Cups	Pints	Quarts	Pints	cc	cc	tsp	cc	tsp
1:3200	0.5	0.25	0.12	0.050	23.7	5.9	1.2	1.18	0.2
1:1600	1.0	0.50	0.25	0.100	47.7	11.8	2.4	2.37	0.5
1:800	2.0	1.00	0.50	0.200	94.6	23.7	4.8	4.73	1.0
1:400	4.0	2.00	1.00	0.400	189.3	47.3	9.6	9.46	1.9
1:200	8.0	4.00	2.00	0.800	378.6	94.6	19.2	18.93	3.8
1:100	16.0	8.00	4.00	1.600	757.1	189.3	38.3	37.86	7.7
1:50	32.0	16.00	8.00	3.200	1514.2	378.6	76.6	75.71	15.3
1:25	64.0	32.00	16.00	6.400	3028.5	757.1	153.2	151.42	30.6
1:10	160.0	80.00	40.00	16.000	7571.0	1893.0	383.0	378.60	76.5

EQUIVALENT AMOUNTS OF POWDERS FOR VARIOUS QUANTITIES OF WATER

Recommended Dose per 100 Gallons		Amount of Material Required to Prepare Spray for:												
		50 gal		20 gal		10 gal		5 gal		1 gal	
lb	oz	g	oz	g	oz	g	oz	g	oz	g	oz	g
0.25	4	113	2	56	0.8	23	0.4	11	0.20	6	0.04	1
0.50	8	227	4	113	1.6	45	0.8	23	0.40	11	0.08	2
1.00	16	454	8	227	3.2	91	1.6	45	0.80	23	0.16	5
1.50	24	681	12	340	4.8	136	2.4	68	1.20	34	0.24	7
2.00	32	908	16	454	6.4	182	3.2	91	1.60	45	0.32	9
3.00	48	1362	24	681	9.6	272	4.8	136	2.40	68	0.48	14
4.00	64	1816	32	908	12.8	363	6.4	182	3.20	91	0.64	18
5.00	80	2270	40	1135	16.0	454	8.0	227	4.00	113	0.80	23

AMOUNT (GRAMS) OF CHEMICAL REQUIRED TO PREPARE DIFFERENT AMOUNTS OF SPRAY MIXTURE

Recommended Dose per 100 Gallons		Grams of Material to Prepare:[a]				
Ounces	Pounds	100 gal	50 gal	20 gal	5 gal	1 gal
2.0	0.12	56.7	28.3	11.3	2.8	0.6
4.0	0.25	113.4	56.7	22.7	5.7	1.1
8.0	0.50	226.8	113.4	45.4	11.3	2.3
12.0	0.75	340.2	170.1	68.0	17.0	3.4
16.0	1.00	453.6	226.8	90.7	22.7	4.5
20.0	1.25	566.9	283.5	113.4	28.4	5.7
24.0	1.50	680.3	340.1	136.1	34.0	6.8
28.0	1.75	793.7	396.8	158.7	39.7	7.9
32.0	2.00	907.1	453.6	181.4	43.4	9.1
40.0	2.50	1133.8	566.9	226.8	56.7	11.3
48.0	3.00	1360.6	680.3	272.2	68.0	13.6
64.0	4.00	1814.1	907.1	362.8	90.7	18.1
80.0	5.00	2267.7	1133.8	453.6	113.4	22.7
96.0	6.00	2721.2	1360.6	544.2	136.1	27.2
112.0	7.00	3174.7	1587.4	634.9	158.7	31.7
128.0	8.00	3628.3	1814.1	725.7	181.4	36.3
144.0	9.00	4081.8	2040.9	816.4	204.1	40.8
160.0	10.00	4535.3	2267.7	907.1	226.8	45.4

[a]To convert to ounces or pounds, divide by 28.35 or 453.59, respectively.

**QUANTITY OF PESTICIDE FORMULATION TO USE PER ACRE
TO GIVE DESIRED DOSAGE OF ACTUAL CHEMICAL PER ACRE**

Formulation of Pesticide[a]	Pounds per Acre of Pesticide Needed							
	⅛	¼	½	¾	1	2	3	4
10–12% E.C. containing 1 lb chem. per gal	16.00 oz	2.00 pt	2.00 qt	3.00 qt	1.00 gal	2.00 gal	3.00 gal	4.00 gal
15–20% E.C. containing 1.5 lb chem. per gal	11.00 oz	1.33 pt	1.33 qt	2.00 qt	5.33 pt	5.33 qt	2.00 gal	2.76 gal
25% E.C. containing 2 lb chem. per gal	8.00 oz	1.00 pt	1.00 qt	3.00 pt	2.00 qt	1.00 gal	1.50 gal	2.00 gal
40–50% E.C. containing 4 lb chem. per gal	4.00 oz	8.00 oz	1.00 pt	1.50 pt	1.00 qt	2.00 qt	3.00 qt	1.00 gal
60–65% E.C. containing 6 lb chem. per gal	3.00 oz	6.00 oz	10.00 oz	1.00 pt	1.33 pt	1.33 qt	2.00 qt	2.67 qt
70–75% E.C. containing 8 lb chem. per gal	2.00 oz	4.00 oz	8.00 oz	0.75 pt	1.00 pt	1.00 qt	3.00 pt	2.00 qt
15% Wettable powder	13.00 oz	1.67 lb	3.33 lb	5.00 lb	6.50 lb	13.00 lb	20.00 lb	26.50 lb
25% Wettable powder	8.00 oz	1.00 lb	2.00 lb	3.00 lb	4.00 lb	8.00 lb	12.00 lb	16.00 lb
40% Wettable powder	5.00 oz	10.00 oz	1.25 lb	1.75 lb	2.50 lb	5.00 lb	7.50 lb	10.00 lb
50% Wettable powder	4.00 oz	8.00 oz	1.00 lb	1.50 lb	2.00 lb	4.00 lb	6.00 lb	8.00 lb
65% Wettable powder	3.00 oz	6.00 oz	12.00 oz	1.12 lb	1.50 lb	3.00 lb	4.50 lb	6.00 lb
75% Wettable powder	2.67 oz	5.33 oz	11.00 oz	1.00 lb	1.33 lb	2.67 lb	4.00 lb	5.33 lb
80% Wettable powder	2.50 oz	5.00 oz	10.00 oz	14.00 oz	1.25 lb	2.50 lb	3.75 lb	5.00 lb
1% Dust	12.50 lb	25.00 lb	50.00 lb	75.00 lb	100.00 lb	200.00 lb	300.00 lb	400.00 lb
5% Dust	2.50 lb	5.00 lb	10.00 lb	15.00 lb	20.00 lb	40.00 lb	60.00 lb	80.00 lb
10% Dust	1.25 lb	2.50 lb	5.00 lb	7.50 lb	10.00 lb	20.00 lb	30.00 lb	40.00 lb

[a]E.C., Emulsion or liquid concentrate.

DILUTION TABLE FOR CHEMICAL RECOMMENDATIONS GIVEN IN POUNDS PER 100 GALLONS

Amount of Active Chemical Recommended per Acre

⅛ lb	¼ lb	½ lb	¾ lb	1 lb	1½ lb	2 lb	2½ lb	3 lb	5 lb
Amount of Formulation Needed to Obtain the Above Amounts of Active Chemical									
10–12% Emulsion Concentrate (contains 1 lb chemical per gal)									
½ qt	1 qt	2 qt	3 qt	1 gal	1½ gal	2 gal	2½ gal	3 gal	5 gal
15–20% Emulsion Concentrate (contains 1¼ lb chemical per gal)									
⅓ qt	⅔ qt	1⅓ qt	2 qt	2⅔ qt	1 gal	1⅓ gal	1⅔ gal	2 gal	3⅗ gal
25% Emulsion Concentrate (contains 2 lb chemical per gal)									
½ pt	1 pt	1 qt	3 pt	2 qt	3 qt	1 gal	5 qt	1½ gal	2½ gal
40–50% Emulsion Concentrate (contains 4 lb chemical per gal)									
¼ pt	½ pt	1 pt	1½ pt	1 qt	3 pt	2 qt	5 pt	3 qt	5 qt
60–75% Emulsion Concentrate (contains 6 lb chemical per gal)									
⅙ pt	⅓ pt	⅔ pt	1 pt	1⅓ pt	1 qt	2⅔ pt	3⅓ pt	2 qt	3⅓ qt
70–75% Emulsion Concentrate (contains 8 lb chemical per gal)									
⅛ pt	¼ pt	½ pt	¾ pt	1 pt	1½ pt	1 qt	2½ pt	3 pt	2½ qt
15% Wettable Powder									
¾ lb	1½ lb	3⅓ lb	5 lb	6⅔ lb	10 lb	13½ lb	16⅔ lb	20 lb	33⅓ lb
25% Wettable Powder									
½ lb	1 lb	2 lb	3 lb	4 lb	6 lb	8 lb	10 lb	12 lb	20 lb
40% Wettable Powder									
5 oz	10 oz	1¼ lb	1⅞ lb	2½ lb	3¼ lb	5 lb	6¼ lb	7½ lb	12½ lb
50% Wettable Powder									
¼ lb	½ lb	1 lb	1½ lb	2 lb	3 lb	4 lb	5 lb	6 lb	10 lb
75% Wettable Powder									
⅙ lb	⅓ lb	⅔ lb	1 lb	1⅓ lb	2 lb	2⅔ lb	3⅓ lb	4 lb	6⅔ lb
80% Wettable Powder									
2½ oz	5 oz	⅝ lb	15⁄16 lb	1¼ lb	1⅞ lb	2½ lb	3⅛ lb	3¾ lb	6¼ lb

DILUTION TABLE

Concentration of formulation	Recommended Pesticide Active Ingredient (AI) per Acre or 100 Gallons of Water:				
	¼ lb	½ lb	1 lb	2 lb	3 lb
Amount of Liquid Pesticide Product Required to Obtain Recommended Rate					
1 lb/gal	1 qt	2 qt	1 gal	2 gal	3 gal
1½ lb/gal	1⅓ pt	1⅓ qt or 2⅔ pt	5⅓ pt	5⅓ qt	2 gal
2 lb/gal	1 pt	1 qt	2 qt	1 gal	6 qt
4 lb/gal	8 oz	1 pt	1 qt	2 qt	3 qt
6 lb/gal	6 oz	10 oz	1⅓ pt	1⅓ qt	2 qt
8 lb/gal	4 oz	8 oz	1 pt	1 qt	3 pt
Amount of Dry Pesticide Product Required to Obtain Recommended Rate					
15%	1⅔ lb	3⅓ lb	6½ lb	13 lb	20 lb
25%	1 lb	2 lb	4 lb	8 lb	12 lb
40%	10 oz	1¼ lb	2½ lb	5 lb	7½ lb
50%	8 oz	1 lb	2 lb	4 lb	6 lb
65%	6 oz	12 oz	1½ lb	3 lb	4½ lb
75%	5⅓ oz	11 oz	1⅓ lb	2⅔ lb	4 lb
80%	5 oz	10 oz	1¼ lb	2½ lb	3¾ lb

DILUTIONS OF ACTIVE INGREDIENTS, PERCENTAGE SOLUTION, PARTS PER MILLION, AND GRAMS PER LITER

Percent	Dilution or Rate	Parts per Million (ppm)	Grams per Liter
10.0	1.10	100,000	100.00
1.0	1:100	10,000	10.0
0.2	1:500	2,000	2.0
0.1	1:1,000	1,000	1.0
0.05	1:2,000	500	0.5
0.03	1:3,000	300	0.3
0.02	1:5,000	200	0.2
0.01	1:10,000	100	0.1
0.005	1:20,000	50	0.05
0.001	1:100,000	10	0.01
0.0001	1:1,000,000	1	0.001

SPRAY CALIBRATION BY THE QUART JAR METHOD

Nozzle Spacing (in.)	Distance in Feet Required to Catch One Quart per Nozzle at Various Rates of Application[a]							
	5 gal/ acre	7½ gal/ acre	10 gal/ acre	12½ gal/ acre	15 gal/ acre	20 gal/ acre	25 gal/ acre	35 gal/ acre
6	4356	2904	2178	1742	1452	1089	871	623
8	3265	2180	1633	1305	1089	816	652	466
10	2610	1744	1305	1045	871	652	522	373
12	2178	1452	1089	871	726	544	435	311
14	1868	1245	934	747	624	466	374	267
16	1633	1089	816	652	544	407	326	233
18[b]	1452	968	726	580	484	363[b]	290	207
20	1306	871	653	522	435	327	261	187
21	1245	830	622	498	415	311	249	178
22	1188	792	594	475	396	297	238	170
24	1089	726	545	436	363	272	218	156
30	871	581	436	348	290	218	174	124
36	726	484	363	290	242	182	145	104
42	622	415	311	249	207	156	124	89
48	545	363	272	218	182	136	109	78

[a]*Caution:* Check output of *all* nozzles, and select an *average* nozzle to calibrate by.

[b]Example: Using a boom sprayer with nozzles spaced 18 in. apart on the boom, if a quart of spray material or water is collected from one nozzle while the sprayer is traveling a distance of 363 ft, the rate of application is 20 gal per acre. The *speed* is accounted for in the distance.

OPERATING CHART FOR TRACTOR BOOM SPRAYERS

TeeJet Tip No.	Pressure (lb)	Gallons per acre at:[a]				
		2 mph	3 mph	4 mph	5 mph	7½ mph
¼ T 80015 or	20	15.7	10.5	7.8	6.3	4.3
¼ TT 80015	25	17.5	11.7	8.8	7.1	4.7
100-mesh screen	30	19.2	12.9	9.7	7.7	5.2
	40	22.0	14.9	11.1	8.9	6.0
	50	25.0	16.7	12.4	10.0	6.7
	60	27.0	18.2	13.6	10.9	7.4
¼ T 8002 or	20	21.0	14.0	10.5	8.4	5.6
¼ TT 8002	25	23.0	15.7	11.8	9.4	6.3
50-mesh screen	30	26.0	17.2	12.9	10.3	6.9
	40	30.0	19.8	14.8	11.8	7.9
	50	33.0	22.0	16.5	13.2	8.8
	60	36.0	24.0	18.1	14.4	9.7
½ T 8003 or	20	32.0	21.0	15.7	12.6	8.4
¼ TT 8003	25	35.0	23.4	17.6	14.1	9.4
50-mesh screen	30	38.0	25.8	19.3	15.4	10.3
	40	45.0	29.6	22.2	17.8	11.8
	50	50.0	33.0	25.0	20.0	13.2
	60	55.0	36.0	27.0	22.0	14.4

[a]Mph, miles per hour.

To measure ground speed, stake out a known distance in the area to be sprayed or in an area with similar surface conditions. Suggested distances are 100 ft for speeds up to 5 mph, 200 ft for speeds from 5 to 10 mph, and at least 300 ft for speeds above 10 mph. At the engine throttle setting and gear that you plan to use during spraying with a loaded sprayer, determine the travel time between the measured stakes in each direction. Average these speeds and use the following equation or the table on this page to determine ground speed.

$$\text{speed (mph)} = \frac{\text{distance (feet)} \times 60}{\text{time (seconds)} \times 88} \qquad (1 \text{ mph} = 88 \text{ feet in } 60 \text{ seconds})$$

Example:

You measure a 200-ft course and discover that 22 seconds are required for the first pass and 24 seconds for the return pass.

$$\text{average time} = \frac{22 + 24}{2} = 23 \text{ seconds}$$

$$\text{mph} = \frac{200 \times 60}{23 \times 88} = \frac{12,000}{2024} = 5.9$$

Once you have decided on a particular speed, record the throttle setting and drive gear used.

MEASURING GROUND SPEED

Ground Speed (mph)	Time (sec) to Travel a Distance of (ft):		
	100	200	300
3	23	45	68
4	17	34	51
5	14	27	41
6	—	23	34
7	—	19	29
8	—	17	26
9	—	15	23
10	—	14	20
12	—	—	17
15	—	—	14
20	—	—	10

TRACTOR SPEED CONVERSIONS

Miles per Hour	Feet per Minute	Time Required in Seconds to Travel:		
		100 ft	200 ft	300 ft
1[a]	88[a]	68.0	137	205
1.5	132	45.0	91	136
2	176	34.0	68	102
2.5	220	27.0	54	81
3	264	23.0	46	68
3.5	308	20.0	40	60
4	352	17.0	34	51
4.5	396	15.0	30	45
5	440	13.6	27	41
6	528	11.3	23	34
7	618	9.7	20	29
8	704	8.5	17	26

[a]1 mph = 88 feet per minute or 1.467 feet per second (88 feet = $\frac{1}{60}$ of a mile).

HOW TO FIGURE TRACTOR SPEED AND SPRAY RATES

$$\text{tractor speed (mph)} = \frac{\text{gallons/minute} \times 495}{\text{gallons/acre} \times \text{width of spray}}$$

$$\text{gallons per acre} = \frac{\text{gallons/minute} \times 495}{\text{mph} \times \text{width of spray}}$$

$$\text{tractor speed (mph)} = \frac{0.682 \times \text{distance}}{\text{seconds}}$$

$$\text{gallons/minute} = \frac{\text{gallons/acre} \times \text{mph} \times \text{nozzle spacing (in.)}}{5940}$$

CALIBRATING A MANUAL SPRAYER

1. Mark out a square rod (16½ ft × 16½ ft) or an equivalent area with other dimensions.
2. Determine the time in seconds to spray this area in a normal manner.
3. Catch the spray from the nozzle (or nozzles) used for the time period determined in step 2.
4. Calculate the rate per acre as follows: pints caught × 20 = gallons per acre.

Pints of Spray Caught in 1 Minute	Rate (gal/acre)
¼	5.0
⅜	7.4
½	10.0
⅝	12.5
¾	15.0
1	20.0
1¼	25.0
1½	30.0
1¾	35.0
2	40.0

CALIBRATING AERIAL SPRAYERS

The first step in calibration is to select the nozzles or other dispensing devices to apply the application volume you select from the label recommendations.

Nozzle Selection

To select nozzles, you must know the ground speed you wish to fly and the approximate swath. You can then use the equation or the table below to determine the number of acres covered per minute.

$$\text{acres per minute} = \frac{\text{speed (mph)} \times \text{swath (ft)}}{495*}$$

Ground Speed (mph)	Acres per Minute per Swath Width (ft):						
	40	50	60	70	80	90	100
25	2.0	2.5	3.0	3.5	4.0	4.5	5.0
30	2.4	3.0	3.6	4.2	4.9	5.5	6.1
35	2.8	3.5	4.2	4.9	5.6	6.3	7.0
40	3.2	4.0	4.8	5.6	6.5	7.3	8.1
45	3.6	4.5	5.5	6.4	7.3	8.2	9.1
50	4.0	5.0	6.1	7.1	8.1	9.1	10.1
55	4.4	5.6	6.6	7.8	8.9	10.0	11.1
60	4.8	6.1	7.2	8.5	9.7	10.9	12.1
65	5.2	6.6	7.8	9.2	10.5	11.8	13.1
70	5.6	7.1	8.5	9.9	11.3	12.7	14.1
75	6.1	7.6	9.1	10.6	12.1	13.6	15.1
80	6.5	8.1	9.7	11.3	12.9	14.5	16.1
85	6.9	8.6	10.3	12.0	13.7	15.5	17.1
90	7.3	9.1	10.9	12.7	14.5	16.4	18.2
95	7.7	9.6	11.5	13.4	15.4	17.3	19.2
100	8.1	10.1	12.1	14.1	16.1	18.2	20.2
110	8.9	11.2	13.3	15.5	17.8	20.0	22.2
120	9.7	12.1	14.5	17.0	19.4	21.8	24.2

* For simplicity use 500, which results in an error well below 1%.

CALIBRATING SOIL FUMIGATORS

Two basic types of multipurpose soil fumigants exist as far as calibration is concerned: liquids under pressure and those liquids not under pressure.

1. *Liquids under pressure* (methyl bromide, chloropicrin, or various combinations of these materials). Because of the innate toxicity and volatility of these materials, they *cannot* be calibrated by conventional techniques. Rather, follow the label instructions concerning tractor speed, orifice diameter, and pressure to attain desired rates per acre. Additionally, fumigate an area of known size and compare the final weight of the bottle with the original weight to determine if the correct rate is being discharged. Flow meters are available for pressurized formulations so that the rate of application can be monitored and changed if necessary. For a complete understanding of flow rates of these materials and equipment used, see Dow Chemical Company's manual, "Field Pressurization and the Application of Methyl Bromide Soil Fumigants."

2. *Liquids not under pressure* (Telone, Vapam, Vorlex, etc.). These materials are calibrated using the "catch method," with chisel equipment moving through the soil and the chemical being caught simultaneously from the tubes temporarily disconnected from the chisel assembly. *Wear suggested protective clothing* (gloves, mask, etc.) *while calibrating.* The labels of these materials often present rates for 100 or 1000 linear feet of row for both broadcast and row applications for calibration purposes. By adjusting tractor speed and orifice sizes in the manifold of the applicator, the proper flow rate is achieved. Manufacturers of fumigant applicators have prepared tables on the rate of flow for various orifice sizes when used at different tractor speeds and for various row spacings. *Follow label rates!*

Appendix C:
Calculating Land Areas

Rectangle, square. The most common shape of a turf area is that of a rectangle or square. A rectangle is a four-sided figure (Figure C.1) with opposite sides parallel in which adjacent sides make angles of 90° with each other. A square is a rectangle with all sides equal. To compute the area of a rectangle, multiply the length by the width, as follows: Assume in Figure C.1 a length of 125 ft and a width of 85 ft.

$$\text{area} = 125 \times 85 = 10,880 \text{ sq ft}$$

$$\text{area in acres} = \frac{10,880}{43,560} = 0.25 \text{ acre}$$

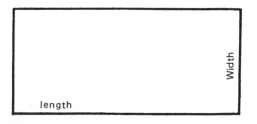

Figure C.1

Four-sided figure with two sides parallel. The area is found by multiplying the average length of the parallel sides (P_1, P_2), by the perpendicular or shortest distance between them (h) (Figure C.2).

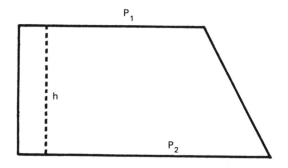

Figure C.2

$$\text{area} = \frac{P_1 + P_2}{2} \times h$$

Assuming that P_1 measures 280 ft, P_2 measures 350 ft, and h measures 180 ft:

$$\text{area} = \frac{280 + 350}{2} \times 180 = 43{,}700 \text{ sq ft}$$

$$\text{area in acres} = \frac{43{,}700}{43{,}560} = 1.003 \text{ acres}$$

Right triangle. The area of a right triangle (Figure C.3) is

$$\frac{\text{base} \times \text{altitude}}{2}$$

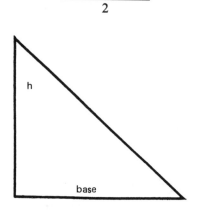

Figure C.3

Assume in Figure C.3 a base of 375 ft and an altitude of 450 ft.

$$\text{area} = \frac{375 \times 450}{2} = 84{,}375 \text{ sq ft}$$

$$\text{area in acres} = \frac{84{,}375}{43{,}560} = 1.937 \text{ acres}$$

Triangle. The area of a triangle (Figure C.4) is

$$\frac{\text{base} \times \text{altitude}}{2}$$

If the base is 500 ft and the height is 350 ft, then

$$\text{area} = \frac{500 \times 350}{2} = 87{,}500 \text{ sq ft}$$

or

$$\frac{87{,}500}{43{,}560} = 2.008 \text{ acres}$$

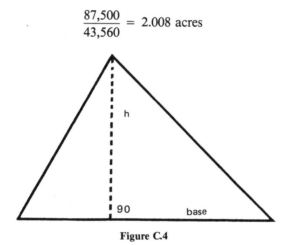

Figure C.4

Four-sided area; no sides parallel. This type of figure should be divided into two triangles by a diagonal (Figure C.5), and then the area of each triangle is computed. The area sum of both triangles will be the area of the figure.

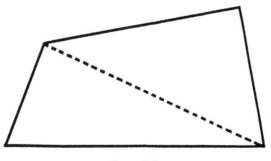

Figure C.5

Any number of sides. Any turf area bounded by more than four sides may be divided into a series of triangles by diagonal lines (Figure C.6) and the area of each triangle computed as before. The sum of the triangular areas is the area of the figure.

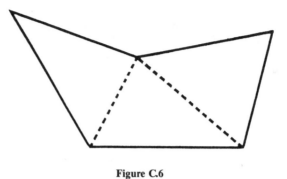

Figure C.6

Irregularly shaped area. The simplest way to measure an odd-shaped area (Figure C.7) is to reduce it to simple geometrical forms, then work out the different areas. The area of the triangle is the base multiplied by h divided by 2.

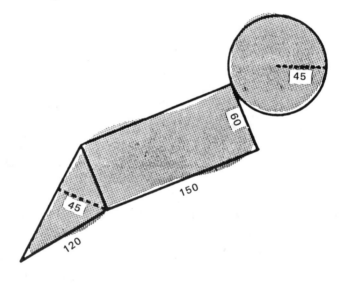

Figure C.7

$$\text{area} = \frac{120 \times 45}{2} = 2700 \text{ sq ft}$$

The area of the rectangle is length × width. Area = 150 × 60 = 9000 sq ft. The remaining area is almost a perfect circle. To measure its area, measure the radius (45 feet) and use the formula πr^2 (45 × 45), where the symbol π represents the number 3.14. (45 × 45 = 2025 × 3.14 = 6358.5 sq ft). Total area of circle, rectangle, and triangle = 2700 + 9000 + 6358.5 divided by 43,560 = 0.415 acre.

Appendix D:
Land-Grant Institutions and Agricultural Experiment Stations in the United States

For help in diagnosing and controlling turfgrass problems, write to the extension horticulturist or extension agronomist to answer questions on turfgrass management and weeds, the extension entomologist (insects, mites), and the extension plant pathologist (diseases). Write to the specialist at the College of Agriculture of your land-grant university or to your State Experiment Station. Turfgrass bulletins, circulars, "fact sheets," and spray schedules are often available free. Write to the Bulletin Room or Mailing Clerk, College of Agriculture, at your state university.

ALABAMA: Auburn University, Auburn, AL 36849.

ALASKA: University of Alaska, College, AK 99735; Experiment Station, Palmer, AK 99645.

ARIZONA: University of Arizona, Tucson, AZ 85721; University of Arizona Research Station, Route 1, Box 587, Yuma, AZ 85365.

ARKANSAS: University of Arkansas, Fayetteville, AR 72701; Cooperative Extension Service, P.O. Box 391, Little Rock, AR 72203; Southeast Research Center, P.O. Box 3508, Monticello, AR 71655.

CALIFORNIA: University of California, Berkeley, CA 94720; Riverside, CA 92521; Davis, CA 95616; Kearney Agricultural Center, 9240 S. Riverbend Ave., Parlier, CA 92648.

COLORADO: Colorado State University, Fort Collins, CO 80523.

CONNECTICUT: University of Connecticut, Storrs, CT 06268; Connecticut Agricultural Experiment Station, P.O. Box 1106, New Haven, CT 06504.

DELAWARE: University of Delaware, Newark, DE 19711.

DISTRICT OF COLUMBIA: University of the District of Columbia, Cooperative Extension Service, Washington, DC 20002.

FLORIDA: University of Florida, Gainesville, FL 32611; Agricultural Research & Education Center, 18905 SW 280 St., Homestead, FL 33031; Agricultural Research & Education Center, 3205 SW 70 Ave., Ft. Lauderdale, FL 33314; Agricultural Research & Education Center, P.O. Box Drawer A, Belle Glade, FL 33430.

GEORGIA: University of Georgia, Athens, GA 30602; Agricultural Experiment Station, Experiment, GA 30212; Rural Development Center, P.O. Box 1209, Tifton, GA 31793.

GUAM: University of Guam, Cooperative Extension Service, Box EK, Agana, GU 96910.

HAWAII: University of Hawaii, Honolulu, HI 96822; Hilo, HI 96720.

IDAHO: University of Idaho, Extension Service, Boise, ID 83702; Agricultural Experiment Station, Moscow, ID 83843; Research & Education Center, Kimberly, ID 83341; Research & Extension Center, Parma, ID 83660; Research & Extension Center, Caldwell, ID 83605; University of Idaho, 1330 Filer Ave. E, Twin Falls, ID 83301.

ILLINOIS: University of Illinois, Urbana, IL 61801.

INDIANA: Purdue University, West Lafayette, IN 47907.

IOWA: Iowa State University, Ames, IA 50011.

KANSAS: Kansas State University, Manhattan, KS 66506.

KENTUCKY: University of Kentucky, Lexington, KY 40546; Research & Education Center, P.O. Box 469, Princeton, KY 42445.

LOUISIANA: Louisiana State University, University Station, Baton Rouge, LA 70803.

MAINE: University of Maine, Orono, ME 04473; Aroostook County Extension Office, Houlton Road, Presque Isle, ME 04769.

MARYLAND: University of Maryland, College Park, MD 20742; Vegetable Research Farm, Quantico Road, Route 5, Salisbury, MD 21801.

MASSACHUSETTS: University of Massachusetts, Amherst, MA 01003.

MICHIGAN: Michigan State University, East Lansing, MI 48824.

MINNESOTA: University of Minnesota, St. Paul, MN 55108.

MISSISSIPPI: Mississippi State University, Mississippi State, MS 39762.

MISSOURI: University of Missouri, Columbia, MO 65201; Delta Center, Box 160, Portageville, MO 63873.

MONTANA: Montana State University, Bozeman, MT 59717.

NEBRASKA: University of Nebraska, East Campus, Lincoln, NE 68583; Panhandle Station, 4502 Ave. 1, Scottsbluff, NE; South Central Station, Box 66, Clay Center, NE 65833.

NEVADA: University of Nevada, Reno, NV 89557.

NEW HAMPSHIRE: University of New Hampshire, Durham, NH 03824.

NEW JERSEY: Rutgers, The State University of New Jersey, New Brunswick, NJ 08903; Rutgers Research & Development, R.R. #5, Bridgeton, NJ 08302.

NEW MEXICO: New Mexico State University, Las Cruces, NM 88003.

NEW YORK: Cornell University, Ithaca, NY 14853; Agricultural Experiment Station, Geneva, NY 14456; Highland Fruit Laboratory, Highland, NY 12528; Horticulture Research Laboratory, Riverhead, NY 11901.

NORTH CAROLINA: North Carolina State University, Raleigh, NC 27650; Mountain Horticulture Crops Research Station, Fletcher, NC 28732.

NORTH DAKOTA: North Dakota State University, Fargo, ND 58105.

OHIO: The Ohio State University, Columbus, OH 43210; Ohio Agricultural Research & Development Center, Wooster, OH 44691.

OKLAHOMA: Oklahoma State University, Stillwater, OK 74078.

OREGON: Oregon State University, Corvallis, OR 97331.

PENNSYLVANIA: The Pennsylvania State University, University Park, PA 16802; Fruit Research Laboratory, P.O. Box 309, Biglerville, PA 17307.

PUERTO RICO: University of Puerto Rico, Rio Piedras, PR 00927.

RHODE ISLAND: University of Rhode Island, Kingston, RI 02881.

SOUTH CAROLINA: Clemson University, Clemson, SC 29631; Edisto Experiment Station, Box 247, Blackville, SC 29817; Pee Dee Experiment Station, Box 5809, Florence, SC 29502; Sandhill Experiment Station, Box 528, Elgin, SC 29045.

SOUTH DAKOTA: South Dakota State University, Brookings, SD 57007.

TENNESSEE: University of Tennessee, P.O. Box 1071, Knoxville, TN 37901; Jackson, TN 38301.

TEXAS: Texas A & M University, College Station, TX 77843; Agricultural Experiment Station, Lubbock, TX 79401; Box 476, Weslaco, TX 78596; Uvalde, TX 78801; Fort Stockton, TX 79735; Stephenville, TX 76401; Dallas, TX 57252; Overton, TX 77684.

UTAH: Utah State University, Logan, UT 84322.

VERMONT: University of Vermont, Burlington, VT 05405.

VIRGINIA: Virginia Polytechnic Institute and State University, Blacksburg, VA 24061; Virginia Truck Experiment Station, Norfolk, VA 23501; Piedmont Fruit Research Laboratory, Charlottesville, VA 22903; Winchester Fruit Research Laboratory, Winchester, VA 22601; Southern Piedmont Research Center & Continuing Education, P.O. Box 448, Blackstone, VA 23824; Cooperative Extension Service, Virginia State University, Petersburg, VA 23803; Eastern Virginia Research Station, Warsaw, VA 22572; TR & CEC, Holland, VA 23437.

VIRGIN ISLANDS: College of Virgin Islands, Cooperative Extension Service, P.O. Box L, Kingshill, St. Croix, VI 00850.

WASHINGTON: Washingston State University, Pullman, WA 99163; Western Washington Research & Extension Center, Puyallup, WA 98371; Irrigated Agricultural Research & Extension Center, Prosser, WA 99350.

WEST VIRGINIA: West Virginia University, Morgantown, WV 26506; Fruit Experiment Station, Kearneysville, WV 25430.

WISCONSIN: University of Wisconsin, Madison, WI 53706; Peninsula Branch Experiment Station, Sturgeon Bay, WI 54235.

WYOMING: University of Wyoming, University Station, Laramie, WY 82071.

Glossary

Acaricide.   A pesticide used to kill mites (an insect relative). A miticide.

Acervulus (pl. acervuli).   Erumpent, saucer-shaped, cushionlike fruiting body of a fungus bearing conidiophores, conidia, and sometimes setae.

Acid soil.   A soil with a pH value of less than 7.0.

Active ingredient (AI).   The amount of actual pesticide in a formulation.

Acuminate.   Tapering to a slender point.

Acute.   Forming an acute angle or point.

Adjuvant.   A chemical added to a pesticide formulation or mixture to enhance its effectiveness.

Aeciospore.   Dehiscent, dikaryotic (N + N) spore from an aecium.

Aecium (pl. aecia).   Cuplike fruiting body of rust fungi.

Aeration, mechanical.   *See* Cultivation.

Alkaline soil.   A soil with a pH value greater than 7.0.

Allelopathic.   Substance produced by one plant which injures or suppresses the growth of another.

Alternate.   Leaves arranged singly at different heights and on different sides of the stem.

Amendment, physical.   Any substance added to the soil for the purpose of altering physical conditions (e.g., sand, calcined clay, peat, etc.).

Annual weed.   A weed that lives 1 year and is usually perpetuated only by seed. *See also* Summer annual and Winter annual.

400

Antagonism. The action of the combination of two or more pesticides that reduces the effectiveness of one or all of the pesticide components.

Anther. The pollen-bearing part of a stamen.

Antidote. A remedy used to counteract the effects of a poison.

Apical meristem. Terminal growing point.

Application rate. The amount of pesticide formulation applied to a given area.

Arthroconidium (pl. arthroconidia). Jointed conidium that is composed of more than one cell and that can become separated.

Ascocarp. Sexual fruiting body of an ascomycetous fungus.

Ascospore. Spore produced within an ascus.

Ascus (pl. asci). Saclike structure within an ascocarp in which ascospores are borne.

Auricle. Clawlike appendages occurring in pairs at the base of the leaf blade or at the apex of the leaf sheath.

Awn. Hairlike projection usually extending from the midnerve or section of a grass flower.

Axil. Upper angle formed between a leaf (or spikelet) and the stem axis.

B

Bactericide. A pesticide used to prevent, destroy, repel, or mitigate bacterial infection.

Bacterium (pl. bacteria). A microscopic, one-celled, nongreen plant that reproduces by dividing in half. Some bacteria attack plants, causing crown gall, wilts, cankers, rots, leaf spots, blights, and other plant diseases.

Basal whorl. Group of leaves attached at the same point at the base of a plant.

Basidiospore. Haploid sexual spore produced on a basidium.

Basidium (pl. basidia). Short, club-shaped, haploid promycelium produced by basidiomycetous fungi.

Bed knife. The fixed blade of a reel mower against which the rotating reel blades cut with a shearing action.

Bench setting. The height at which the bed knife of a mower is set above a firm, level surface.

Biennial weed. A weed that lives for more than 1 year but not more than 2 years.

Bifid. Two cleft or dividing into two points.

Biological control. Control of pests by means of living organisms such as predators, parasites, and disease-producing organisms.

Blade. The flattened portion of a grass leaf located above the sheath; the portion of the leaf that grows away from the stem.

Blend. A combination of two or more cultivars of a single turfgrass species.

Bract. Leaflike structure subtending a flower or occurring as scales on a bud.

Bulb. An underground perennial storage organ consisting of a stem axis and numerous overlapping scales.

Bulbil. Sclerotiumlike structure lacking a distinct rind layer.

Bulblet. A little bulb; usually applied to the bulblike structures produced by some plants in the axils of leaves or replacing the flowers.

Bunch-type growth. Plant development at or near the soil surface without production of rhizomes or stolons.

C

Calcined clay. Clay minerals, such as montmorillonite and attapulgite, that have been fired at high temperatures to obtain absorbent, stable, granular particles; used as amendments in soil modification.

Carbamate insecticide. A synthetic compound derived from carbamic acid. Carbamate insecticides are contact killers with relatively short-lived effects. Examples are carbaryl and bendiocarb.

Carbohydrate. Compound of carbon, hydrogen, and oxygen, as in sugar, starch, and cellulose.

Carrier. Inert material such as dust, clay, oil, water, and air that is mixed with the pesticide and provides for its more uniform dispersal.

Caryopsis. Dry, indehiscent, one-seeded fruit with a thin pericarp fused to the seed coat.

Castings, earthworm (wormcasts). Soil and plant remains excreted by earthworms that are deposited on the turf surface or in the burrow; forms a relatively stable soil granule that can be objectionable on closely mowed turf.

Chlamydospore. Thick-walled asexual spore formed via modification of a hyphal or conidial cell.

Chlorinated hydrocarbon insecticide. A synthetic pesticide that contains hydrogen, carbon, oxygen, and chlorine. Chlorinated hydrocarbon insecticides are persistent insecticides that kill insects mainly by contact action. They are insoluble in water and are decomposed by alkaline materials and high temperatures. Examples are DDT, aldrin, chlordane, dieldrin, heptachlor, lindane, toxaphene, and methoxychlor.

Chlorosis (adj. **chlorotic**). A yellow to white or gray condition of normally green plant tissue resulting from the partial to complete destruction of chlorophyll. Chlorosis is a common symptom of disease.

Ciliate. With marginal hairs.

Clamp connections. Bridges around the septa of a hypha; taken as evidence that the fungus is related to the basidiomycetes.

Cleistothecium (pl. **cleistothecia**). Closed, usually spherical ascocarp.

Clippings. Leaves and in some cases, stems cut off by mowing.

Cold water insoluble nitrogen (CWIN). Fertilizer nitrogen not soluble in cold water at 25°C.

Cold water soluble nitrogen (CWSN). Fertilizer nitrogen soluble in cold water at 25°C.

Coleoptile. Protective sheath of an embryonic shoot.

Collar. A light-colored band at the junction of the leaf blade and sheath on the outside of the leaf.

Colorant. A paintlike material, usually a dye or pigment, applied to (a) brown warm-season turfgrasses that are in winter dormancy; or (b) brown cool-season turfgrasses that are in summer dormancy; or (c) turfs that have been discolored by environmental stress, turfgrass pests, or the abuses of human beings. Its purpose is to maintain favorable green appearance.

Commercial pesticide applicator. A person who applies pesticides (for hire, not for hire, or public) to land or commodities.

Compatible chemicals. Chemicals that can be mixed together without decreasing their effectiveness against the intended pests.

Complete flower. One possessing all floral parts (i.e., sepals, petals, stamens, and pistils).

Compost. A mixture of organic residues and soil that has been piled, moistened, and allowed to decompose.

Compound leaf. One divided into two or more distinct leaflets.

Concentration. The amount of actual pesticide or active ingredient contained in a formulation or mixture. Expressed as percent, pounds per gallon, etc.

Conidiophore. Hypha differentiated to bear conidia.

Conidium (pl. **conidia**). Any asexual spore except sporangiospores or chlamydospores.

Conjugate. Joined; in two's.

Contact pesticide. A pesticide that kills on contact.

Cool-season turfgrass. Turfgrass species adapted to favorable or optimal growth during cool portions (60 to 75 °F) of the growing season.

Cordate. Heart-shaped; much wider at base, coming to a point.

Core aerification. A method of turf cultivation in which soil cores are removed by hollow tines or spoons to control soil compaction and to aid in the penetration and distribution of pesticides and water.

Corm. A short, underground organ for reproduction or food storage which is largely a thickened portion of the stem.

Culm. Stem of a grass plant.

Cultivar. An assemblage of cultivated plants distinguished by any characters (morphological, physiological, cytological, etc.) which, when reproduced sexually or asexually, retain their distinguishing features; a cultivated variety.

Cultivation. Applied to turf, cultivation refers to working of the soil and/or thatch without destruction of the turf; e.g., coring, slicing, spiking, or other means.

Cultural intensity. The time, money, and effort (mowing, fertilization, irrigation, cultivation, and pest control) needed to maintain a particular turfgrass.

Cyme. An inflorescence in which each flower is strictly terminal either to the main stem or to a branch.

D

Damage threshold level. The lowest pest population density at which damage occurs.

Damping-off.   Decay of seeds in the soil or young seedlings before or after emergence. Most evident in young seedlings that suddenly wilt, topple over, and die from rot at the stem base.

Desiccation.   Drying out.

Dethatching.   Removing excessive thatch from a turfgrass area by hand raking or with various types of machinery equipped with vertical knives or tines.

Dicot.   Plant having two cotyledons in the seed; as in broadleaf species.

Dikaryon (adj. **dikaryotic**).   Having two sexually compatible nuclei per cell.

Directed application.   A pesticide directed onto weeds or soil in such a manner as to avoid contact with the turfgrass.

Disarticulation.   Breaking or falling away from the plant.

Dissected.   Cut or divided into narrow segments; toothed with fine serrations; lobed, a partial division of an organ such as a leaf; the term generally applies to a division less than halfway to the base of the leaf.

Drift.   The movement of material by air outside the intended target area during or shortly after application.

Drouth or **drought.**   An extended period of dry weather that usually causes stress to turf.

Dust.   A formulation usually consisting of the active pesticide ingredient mixed with an inert material such as talc, powdered nut hulls, volcanic ash, and similar materials.

E

Economic injury level.   The lowest population density of pests that will cause economic damage.

Economic threshold level.   The density of pests at which control measures should be implemented to prevent an increasing pest population from reaching the economic injury level.

Eelworms.   Nematodes.

Endophyte.   A plant (such as a fungus) living within another plant.

Environment.   Soil, water, air, plants, animals, and human beings make up the environment.

Eradicant.   A fungicide or other chemical used to eliminate a pathogen from the host or environment.

Evapotranspiration.   Total loss of moisture through the combined process of evaporation and transpiration.

F

Field capacity.   The amount of moisture remaining in the soil after gravitational moisture has drained.

Flail mower.   A mower that cuts turf by high speed impact of inverted T-blades rotating in a vertical cutting plane relative to the turf surface.

Floret. A grass flower enclosed by a lemma and palea.

Flowable. A finely ground, wettable powder formulation that is sold as a thick suspension in a liquid. Flowables require only moderate agitation and seldom clog spray nozzles.

Foliar burn. Injury to shoot tissue caused by dehydration due to contact with high concentrations of chemicals, e.g., certain fertilizers and pesticides.

Formulation. The form in which a pesticide is offered for sale to the user (as emulsifiable concentrate, wettable powder, granule, dust, oil solution, etc.). Includes both the active and inert ingredients.

Fruiting body. A complex fungus structure containing or bearing spores.

Fumigant. A pesticide that as a gas kills destructive microorganisms, animals, and plants.

Fungicide. A pesticide used to prevent, destroy, repel, or mitigate fungal infections.

Fungistat. A pesticide that inhibits the growth of fungi but does not kill them.

Fungus. A small, many-celled, nongreen plant. Some fungi attack other plants and cause plant diseases such as rusts, smuts, mildews, wilts, and leaf spots.

G

Genus (pl. **genera**). A more or less closely related and definable group of plants or animals comprising one or more species. *See also* Species.

Germination. The development and growth of a shoot from a seed, bud, or spore.

Glabrous. Lacking pubescence, hairs; smooth.

Glumes. A pair of bracts usually present at the base of a grass spikelet.

Grade. To establish elevations and contours prior to planting.

Granules. A formulation in which the pesticide is attached to particles of an inert carrier such as clay or ground corncobs. Currently used granules range in size from 15 to 40 mesh.

Grass. Any plant that is a member of the family Gramineae (Poaceae).

Ground cover. Low-growing, nongrass plants used to cover the soil in areas where mowing is impractical or turf will not grow.

H

Haustorium (pl. **haustoria**). A specialized hypha of a fungus that penetrates a host plant, makes intimate contact with the host cell's protoplast, and absorbs food. Powdery mildews, downy mildews, and rusts produce haustoria.

Hazard. The likelihood that an injury will result from the use of a pesticide. A hazard consititutes both toxicity and exposure.

Herbaceous. Soft, lacking woody tissue.

Herbicide. A pesticide used to prevent, destroy, or mitigate plants that grow where they are not wanted.

Host. Any plant or animal that is invaded by a parasite and from which the parasite obtains its food.

Hot water insoluble nitrogen (HWIN). Fertilizer nitrogen not soluble in hot water at 100°C. Used to determine activity index of ureaforms. *See also* Nitrogen activity index.

Humus. The organic fraction of soil in which decomposition is so far advanced that its original form cannot be distinguished.

Hybrid. Product of a cross between individuals of unlike genetic constitution.

Hydroseed. To seed in a water mixture by pumping through a nozzle that sprays the mixture onto a seedbed. The water mixture may also contain amendments such as fertilizer and certain mulches.

Hypha (pl. **hyphae**). Single filament that constitutes the body (mycelium) of a fungus. Hyphae may be divided into cells by cross walls or be one long cell.

I

Inert ingredients. Ingredients of a pesticide formulation that are not active, such as water, sugar, dust, wetting and spreading agents, emulsifiers, propellants, etc.

Infectious disease. A disease caused by a pathogen that multiplies and can be transmitted from plant to plant.

Inflorescence. The flowering portion of a shoot, including the spikelets and any supporting axis or branch system.

Inoculum. Pathogen or its parts that infects (e.g., fungus spores, mycelium, nematodes, virus particles).

Insect. A term used to describe numerous small invertebrate (no backbone) animals, such as true insects, spiders, mites, ticks, centipedes, and millipedes. In the adult stage, true insects usually have six walking legs, wings, and three body divisions.

Insecticide. A pesticide used to prevent, destroy, repel, mitigate, or attract insects and their relatives.

Integrated pest management (IPM). Controlling pest populations through chemical, physical, cultural, biological, and regulatory methods.

Internode. Portion of a stem between the nodes or growing points.

L

Label. A printed statement affixed to the pesticide container by the manufacturer listing the contents, directions for use, and precautions. A pesticide label must be approved and registered by the U. S. Environmental Protection Agency and the State Department of Agriculture.

Lanceolate. Shaped like a lance head; much longer than wide and widest below the middle.

Larva. The immature or worm stage (caterpillar, maggot, grub) of an insect that passes through four stages (egg, larva, pupa, adult) in its development.

Larvacide. An insecticide used to kill larvae of insects.

Lateral shoot. A shoot originating from a vegetative bud in the axil of a leaf or from the node of a stem, rhizome, or stolon.

Layering, soil. Undesirable stratification within the A horizon of a soil profile; can be due to construction design, topdressing with different textured materials, inadequate on-site mixing of soil constituents, or blowing and washing of sand on other soil constituents.

Leaching. The washing of soluble materials from the soil by the downward movement of water (deep irrigation or rain).

Leaflet. Secondary division of the compound leaf.

Leaf margins. Edge of leaf or leaflets.

Lemma. Lowermost of the two bracts enclosing the flower of a grass floret.

Lesion. A localized area of diseased tissue.

Ligule. A membranous or hairlike appendage on the inside of the grass leaf at the junction of the leaf and blade.

Localized dry spot. A dry spot of sod amid normal, moist turf that resists rewetting by normal irrigation and rainfall; associated with a number of factors including thatch, fungal activity, shallow soil over buried material, or elevated sites in the terrain.

M

Macroconidium (pl. **macroconidia**). Long or large conidium relative to microconidia.

Melting-out. A disease (primarily of Kentucky bluegrass) caused by the fungus *Drechslera poae*. It is characterized by the appearance of dark leaf spots, often followed by the killing of irregular areas of turf.

Meristem (adj. **meristematic**). Plant tissue that functions principally in cell division and differentiation.

Metabolism. The complex of physical and chemical processes involved in the maintenance of life.

Microconidium (pl. **microconidia**). Small conidium relative to macroconidia; microspore.

Microorganism. Minute living organism such as a bacterium, fungus, nematode, or protozoan.

Midrib. The central vein of a grass leaf extending from the stem to the leaf tip.

Mixture. A combination of two or more species.

Mold. Any fungus with conspicuous mycelium or spore masses; often saprophytic. Grows most commonly on damp or decaying matter and on the surface of plant tissues.

Mottle. An irregular pattern of light and dark areas.

Mowing frequency. The number of times a turfgrass community is mowed per week, month, or growing season. (The reciprocal of mowing frequency is mowing interval—the number of days, weeks, etc. between successive mowings.)

Mowing height. The distance above the ground surface at which the turfgrass is cut during mowing.

Mowing pattern. The patterns of back and forth travel while mowing turf. Patterns may be changed regularly to distribute wear and compaction, to avoid creating "grain," and to create visually aesthetic effects, especially for spectator sports.

Mulch. Any nonliving material (straw, sawdust, leaves, plastic film, etc.) spread on the soil surface to protect it.

Mycelium (pl. **mycelia**). The mass of interwoven filaments (hyphae) that makes up the vegetative body of a fungus. The mycelia of fungi show great variation in appearance and structure.

Mycoplasma. A bacterialike organism that lacks a rigid cell wall and is variable in shape. Mycoplasmas cause certain plant diseases of the "yellows" type.

N

Necrosis (adj. **necrotic**). Death, usually accompanied by darkening or discoloration.

Nematicide. A pesticide used to prevent, repel, destroy, or mitigate nematodes.

Nematodes. Generally microscopic, unsegmented roundworms that usually live free in moist soil, water, or decaying matter, or as parasites of plants and animals.

Nitrification. Formation of nitrates and nitrites from ammonia by soil microorganisms.

Nitrogen activity index (AI). Applied to ureaformaldehyde compounds and mixtures containing such compounds, the AI is the percentage of cold water insoluble nitrogen that is soluble in hot water.

$$AI = \frac{\% \text{ CWIN} - \% \text{ HWIN}}{\% \text{ CWIN}} \times 100$$

Node. The joint of a stem; the region of attachment of leaves to a stem.

Noninfectious disease. A disease (or disorder) that is caused by unfavorable growing conditions and cannot be transmitted from plant to plant.

Nontarget organism. A plant or animal other than the one against which a pesticide is applied.

Nozzle. A device for metering and dispersing a spray solution.

Nursery, turfgrass. A place where turfgrasses are vegetatively propagated for increase and planting as stolons or sprigs or where sod is grown for later transplanting by sodding or plugging. Sometimes also used for experimentation.

Nutlet. A small nut or small fruit similar to a nut.

Nymph. The immature stage (resembling an adult) of an insect that passes through three stages (egg, nymph, and adult) in its development.

O

Obligate. Necessary; obliged. An obligate parasite is an organism or agent that can live only on or in living matter.

Off-site mixing. The mixing of soil and amendments during root zone modification at a place other than the site where they are to be used.

Oospore. A thick-walled, resting fungus spore; a fertilized female sex organ (*oogonium*).

Opposite. Leaves attached precisely opposite each other on a stem.

Opposite leaves. Those paired at each node.

Organic matter. Plant or animal material capable of undergoing breakdown and resynthesis (in the soil).

Organic phosphorus insecticide. A synthetic compound derived from phosphoric acid. Organic phosphorus insecticides are primarily contact killers with relatively short-lived effects. They are decomposed by water, pH extremes, high temperatures, and micro-organisms. Examples are malathion, diazinon, chlorpyrifos, Aspon, phorate, isofenphos, trichlorfon, dimethoate, and fenthion.

Orifice. An opening in a nozzle tip, duster, or granular applicator through which the spray, dust, or granules flow.

Ostiole. Pore; opening of a perithecium or pycnidium.

Ovate. Round in shape, generally more broad than long.

Overseed. To seed onto an existing turf, usually with temporary turfgrass, to provide green, active grass growth during dormancy of the original turf, usually a warm-season turfgrass.

Ovule. An immature seed contained within the ovary.

P

Palea. Uppermost of two bracts enclosing the flower of a grass floret.

Palmate. Three or more lobes, leaflets, or veins arising from one point.

Panicle. Type of inflorescence in which the spikelets are not directly attached to the main axis.

Parasite. An organism (fungus, bacterium, virus, nematode, etc.) that obtains its food from another organism. An obligate parasite is one that can develop only in living tissues (e.g., a virus or plant-parasitic nematode).

Parasitic insect. An insect that lives in or on the body of another insect.

Pathogen. An organism or agent capable of causing disease.

Pedicel. The stalk of a single grass floret.

Perennial weed. A weed that lives for 2 or more years.

Pest. Any insect, mite, rodent, nematode, fungus, weed, or other plant or animal (except those microorganisms in or on other living humans or animals) that is injurious to the health of human beings, animals, and plants or to the environment.

Pesticide. A chemical or mixture of chemicals used to destroy, prevent, mitigate, repel, or attract any animal, plant, or plant disease considered a pest. Examples are insecticides, miticides or acaricides, herbicides, fungicides, nematicides, disinfectants, bactericides, and chemical defoliants.

Petal. Portion of a flower surrounding the stamen and pistil; sometimes colorful or showy.

Petiole. The stalk of a leaf.

pH, soil. A numerical measure of the acidity or hydrogen ion activity of a soil. A pH of 7 indicates neutrality; above 7 is basic (alkaline), while below 7 is acidic.

Phloem. Food-conducting tissues in plants.

Photosynthesis. Process by which carbohydrates are produced from carbon dioxide, water, and light energy in chlorophyll-containing plants.

Phytotoxic. A pesticide that is injurious or poisonous to plants.

Pinnate. Having branches, lobes, leaflets, or veins; attached or arranged on two sides of a stem.

Pistil. Female structures of a flower; usually consisting of an ovary and one or more stigmas and styles.

Plasmodium (pl. **plasmodia**, adj. **plasmodial**). Motile multinucleate mass or protoplasm resulting from fusion of uninucleate amoeboid cells.

Plug. To propagate turfgrasses vegetatively by means of plugs or small pieces of sod.

Postemergence herbicide. A herbicide that is applied after emergence of the crop or weed.

Predatory or predaceous insect. An insect that feeds on other insects.

Preemergence herbicide. A herbicide that is applied before emergence of the crop or weed.

Preplant herbicide. A herbicide that is applied before the crop is planted.

Private pesticide applicator. A person certified to use or supervise the use of a restricted use pesticide on property owned, leased, or rented by himself or herself or by his or her employer on no more than two neighbors' properties, as exchange labor, for the purpose of producing an agricultural commodity primarily intended for sale, consumption, propagation, or other use by human beings or animals.

Procaryotic (n. **procaryote**). Without internal membrane-bound organelles.

Promycelium. Basidium; initial structure produced upon teliospore germination.

Protectant. A pesticide used to prevent infection by an organism.

Protoplasm. Living material of a cell.

Psi. Pressure; measured in pounds per square inch.

Pupa (pl. **pupae**). The resting state of an insect that passes through four stages (egg, larva, pupa, and adult) in its development.

Pure live seed (PLS). Percentage of the content of a seed lot that is pure and viable.

Pustule. A small, raised, blister- or pimplelike swelling that may rupture the epidermis to expose the causal agent (e.g., rust or smut).

Pycnidium (pl. **pycnidia**). A closed, flasklike fruiting structure (or variously shaped cavity) of certain fungi (e.g., *Septoria, Ascochyta*) that are speck-sized and contain conidia. Commonly found in diseased tissue.

Pycniospore. Haploid, sexually derived spore formed in a pycnium.

Pycnium (pl. **pycnia**). A flask-shaped structure in which pycniospores are formed.

R

Race (or strain).   A subgroup or biotype within a species of a pathogen that differs in virulence, symptom expression, or host range—limited to certain species, varieties, hybrids, or cultivars—from other races and the rest of the species.

Raceme.   Type of inflorescence in which the spikelets are borne on short stems (pedicels) attached directly to the main axis.

Rachilla.   The axis of a grass spikelet.

Rachis.   The axis of a spike or raceme.

Radicle.   The primary root of the grass embryo.

Recuperative potential.   The ability of a turfgrass to recover from injury through vegetative growth.

Reestablishment.   Rebuilding a lawn by complete removal of any existing turf, followed by site preparation and planting.

Renovation, turf.   Turf improvement involving replanting into existing live and/or dead vegetation.

Residual.   The property of a pesticide for persisting after application in amounts sufficient to kill pests for several days to several weeks or even longer.

Residue.   The amount of pesticide present following application.

Resistant species.   Pests that survive relatively high rates of pesticide application.

Resting spore.   A spore, usually thick-walled, that may remain alive in a dormant state for months or years, later germinating and capable of causing infection.

Rhizome.   A usually horizontal, elongated underground stem that produces leafy shoots above and roots below.

Root zone.   The upper 6 to 8 in. of soil in which most of the turfgrass roots are concentrated.

Rosette.   A basal, circular cluster of leaves not separated by evident internodal stem elongation.

Runoff.   Pesticide material that is carried away from an area by the flow of surface water. Also used to describe the rate of application to a surface—"spray to runoff."

S

Salinity.   An excess of soluble salts in the soil; turfgrass growth and quality are impaired.

Saprophyte.   An organism that obtains its food from dead organic matter, as opposed to a parasite that feeds on living tissue. *See also* Parasite.

Scald.   A condition that exists when a turfgrass collapses and turns brown under conditions of intense sunlight, high water temperatures, and standing water, usually of a relatively shallow depth.

Scalp.   To remove an excessive quantity of functioning, green leaves at any one mowing; results in a shabby, brown appearance caused by exposing crowns, stolons, dead leaves, and even bare soil.

Sclerotium (pl. **sclerotia**). A small, compact, often hard interwoven mass of fungus hyphae, usually more or less spherical or flat, and dark in color.

Scum. The layer of algae on the soil surface of thinned turfs; drying can produce a somewhat impervious layer that can impair subsequent shoot emergence.

Sedge. A grasslike plant with triangular stems that spreads by rhizomes and overwinters as tubers.

Seed blend. A combination of seeds of two or more cultivars of the same turfgrass species.

Seedhead. Floral development; in the case of grasses, usually a fruiting cluster or spike.

Seed mixture. A combination of seeds of two or more turfgrass species.

Selectivity. The ability of a pesticide to kill some pests but not others.

Septum (pl. **septa**, adj. **septate**). Cross wall in a hypha.

Serrate. Toothed along the margin; the apex of each tooth is sharp and directed forward.

Sessile. A leaf or flower attached directly to the axis without a stem.

Seta (pl. **setae**). Stiff, hairlike appendage.

Settling, soil. A lowering of the soil surface resulting from a decrease in the soil volume of a soil previously loosened by tillage; occurs naturally, and can be accelerated mechanically by tamping, rolling, cultipacking, or watering.

Sheath. The tubular, basal portion of the leaf that encloses the stem.

Shoot density. The relative number of shoots per unit area.

Slicing. A method of turf cultivation in which rotating, flat tines slice intermittently through the turf and the soil.

Slime mold. Primitive organisms whose plasmodium "flows" over low-lying vegetation like an amoeba.

Slit trench drain. A narrow trench (usually 5 to 10 cm wide) backfilled to the surface with a porous material such as sand, gravel, or crushed rock; used to intercept surface or lateral subsurface drainage water.

Slowly available fertilizer. Designates a rate of dissolution less than that obtained for completely water-soluble fertilizers; may involve compounds that dissolve slowly, materials that must be decomposed microbiologically, or soluble compounds coated with substances highly impermeable to water. Used interchangeably with delayed release, controlled release, controlled availability, slow acting, and metered release.

Sod. Plugs, squares, or strips of turfgrass with the adhering soil which is used in vegetative planting.

Sodding. Planting turf by means of sod.

Soil mix. A prepared mixture used as a growth medium for turfgrass.

Soil modification. Alteration of soil characteristics by adding soil amendments; commonly used to improve physical conditions.

Soil probe. A cylindrical soil sampling tool with a cutting edge at the lower end.

Soil reaction. *See* pH, soil.

Soil sterilant. A pesticide that completely prevents the growth of plants and micro-organisms.

Soil sterilization. Treating soil by heat or chemicals to kill living organisms.

Solubility. The maximum amount of a liquid or solid that will dissolve in a liquid.

Soluble powder. A powder formulation that dissolves and forms a solution in water.

Solution. A mixture in which a pesticide is dissolved in a liquid. The pesticide is evenly dispersed as individual molecules among the molecules of liquid.

Sorus (pl. **sori**). Compact fruiting structure of rust and smut fungi.

sp (pl. **spp**). Species; a genus name followed by sp. means that the particular species is undetermined; spp. after a genus name means that several species are being referred to without being named individually.

Species (pl. **species**). A group of closely related individuals resembling one another in certain inherited characteristics.

Spike. Type of inflorescence in which the spikelets are directly attached to the main axis with no connecting stem (pedicel).

Spikelet. The basic unit of the grass inflorescence, consisting of two glumes and one or more florets.

Spiking. A method of turf cultivation in which solid tines or flat, pointed blades penetrate the turf and soil surface.

Spiroplasma. A spiral-shaped, bacterialike organism.

Spoon, coring. A method of turf cultivation by which curved, hollow, spoonlike tines remove small soil cores and leave a hole or cavity in the sod.

Sporangium (pl. **sporangia**). Flasklike fungal structure whose contents differentiate into asexual spores.

Spore. A microscopic, one- to many-celled body of a fungus or other low plant that may become free, germinate, and give rise to a new plant.

Sporidium (pl. **sporidia**). Basidiospore.

Sporocarp. Body in or on which spores are borne.

Sporulate. To produce spores.

Spot. Limited, chlorotic or necrotic, circular to oval area on leaves or on other plant parts.

Spot treatment. Application to a restricted or small area.

Spray deposit. The amount of wet pesticide initially deposited per area of plant or other surface.

Spreader. Material added to a spray preparation to improve contact between the chemical and the plant surface.

Sprig. A single turfgrass stem (stolon, rhizome, or tiller), usually with some attached roots, that is used in vegetative propagation.

Sprigging. Vegetative planting by placing stolons, rhizomes, or tillers in furrows or small holes.

Sprigging, broadcast. Vegetative planting by broadcasting stolons over a prepared soil and, in most cases, covering by topdressing or press rolling.

Spring green-up. The initial seasonal appearance of green shoots as spring temperature and moisture conditions become favorable for chlorophyll synthesis, thus breaking winter dormancy.

Stamen. The male organ of the flower, consisting of a pollen-bearing anther on a filament.

Stand. The number of established individual shoots per unit area.

Stigma. The feathery portion of the pistil that receives the pollen for fertilization.

Stolon. An elongated horizontal stem (or shoot) that grows above the soil surface and roots at the nodes. It is used to propagate certain grasses.

Stoma (pl. **stomata**). A minute opening in the epidermis of a leaf or stem through which gases are exchanged.

Strain. Descendants of an isolated organism; biotype; race.

Streak. Necrosis along vascular bundles in leaves or stems of grasses.

Stroma (pl. **stromata**). Compact mass of mycelium (with or without host tissue) that supports fruiting bodies.

Style. The contracted portion of the pistil between the ovary and the stigma.

Stylet. Stiff, slender, hollow feeding organ in plant-parasitic nematodes.

Subgrade. The surface grade of a turf site prior to the addition of topsoil.

Summer annual. Plant that completes its life cycle from seed in one growing season.

Summer dormancy. The cessation of growth and subsequent death of shoots of perennial plants due to heat and/or moisture stress.

Surfactant. A material that reduces surface tension between two unlike materials such as oil and water. A spreader or wetting agent used to increase coverage of the surface being sprayed.

Susceptible. Not immune; lacking resistance; prone to infection.

Susceptible species. Pests readily killed by relatively low rates of pesticide application.

Suspension. A mixture in which the pesticide in a solid form (tiny particles) is suspended in water.

Swarm spore. Zoospore, as in *Pythium* spp.

Symptom. The reaction of a plant or animal to a pest's activities.

Synergism. The action of two pesticides that produces a greater cumulative effect when the pesticides are used together than when they are used individually.

Synergist. A chemical that, when mixed with a pesticide, increases its toxicity. The synergist may or may not have pesticidal properties of its own.

Syringe. To spray turf with small amounts of water; usually on a hot, dry windy day to reduce water loss (transpiration).

Systemic. Pertaining to chemicals or pathogens that spread throughout plants as opposed to remaining localized.

Systemic pesticide. A pesticide that is absorbed by treated plants or animals and translocated (moved) to most tissues.

T

Taproot. The primary descending root of a plant.

Teliospore. Thick-walled resting spore of rust and smut fungi that germinates to form a basidium.

Telium (pl. **telia**). Pustule containing teliospores.

Thatch. A tightly intermingled layer of undecomposed or partially decomposed organic residues situated above the soil surface and generally below the green portions of the turf.

Thatch control. The process of (a) preventing excessive thatch accumulation by cultural manipulation and/or (b) reducing excess thatch from a turf by either mechanical or biological means.

Tiller. A lateral stem (or shoot), usually erect, that develops from the central crown.

Tip burn. A whitening of the leaf tip resulting from a lethal internal water stress caused by wind desiccation or salt.

Tolerance. The amount of pesticide deemed safe and permitted by law on an agricultural product.

Topdressing. A prepared soil mix added to the turf surface, and usually incorporated into the soil by raking or irrigating.

Toxicity. The capacity of a pesticide to cause harm to a living organism.

Toxin. A poison produced by a plant or animal.

Transitional climatic zone. The suboptimal zone between temperate and subtropical climates.

Translocated pesticide. *See* Systemic pesticide.

Translocation. Movement of foods and wastes within a plant.

Transmission. Spread of virus or other pathogens from plant to plant.

Truncate. With edge transversely straight or nearly so, as if it were cut off.

Tuber. A swollen, usually underground stem with numerous buds.

Turfgrass community. An aggregation of individual turfgrass plants that have mutual relationships with the environment as well as among the individual plants.

U

Umbel. Type of inflorescence with a group of terminal flowers meeting at a single point on the stem; can be compound with subsets of umbels.

Ureaformaldehyde. A synthetic, slowly soluble nitrogen fertilizer consisting mainly of methylene urea polymers of different lengths and solubilities; formed by reacting urea and formaldehyde.

Urediospore, uredospore, or **urediniospore.** Binucleate, dikaryotic, asexual rust spore.

V

Variety. *See* Cultivar.

Vascular. Pertaining to conductive (xylem and phloem) tissue.

Vector. Agent that transmits inoculum.

Vegetative propagation. Asexual propagation using pieces of vegetation, i.e., sprigs or sod pieces.

Venation. The arrangement of veins in a leaf.

Vertical mower. A mechanical device whose vertically rotating blades cut into the face of a turf for the purpose of reducing thatch, grain, and surface compaction.

Virulence (adj. **virulent**). Degree of pathogenicity; capacity to cause disease.

Virus. A submicroscopic entity (parasite) capable of producing mosaics, ringspots, flower breaking, growth malformations, and other plant diseases. Viruses are capable of reproducing only in living plant or animal cells.

Volatility. The rate of evaporation of a pesticide.

W

Warm-season turfgrass. Turfgrass species adapted to an optimal growth during warm portions (80 to 95 °F) of the growing season.

Water-soaked. Pertaining to plants or lesions that appear wet, dark, and usually sunken and translucent.

Weed. Any plant growing in a place where it is not wanted.

Wettable powder. A powder formulation containing a wetting agent that causes the powder to form a suspension in water.

Wet wilt. Wilting of turf in the presence of free soil water when evapotranspiration exceeds the ability of roots to take up water.

Wilt. Loss of turgor and drooping of plant parts caused by insufficient water in the plant.

Wind burn. Death and browning most commonly occurring on the uppermost leaves of semi-dormant grasses caused by atmospheric desiccation. *See also* Winter desiccation.

Winter annual. An annual plant that usually initiates growth in the fall, lives over winter, and produces seed the following spring.

Winter desiccation. The death of leaves or plants by drying during winter dormancy.

Winterkill. Any injury to turfgrass plants that occurs during the winter period.

Winter overseeding. Seeding cool-season turfgrasses over warm-season turfgrasses at or near their start of winter dormancy; practiced in subtropical climates to provide green, growing turf during the winter period when the warm-season species are brown and dormant.

X

Xylem. Water-conducting tissue in plants.

Z

Zonate. Targetlike; appearing in concentric rings.

Zoospore. A swimming spore or swarm spore capable of independent movement; especially in the lower fungi (*Pythium*).

Index

417

Index

Index

Index   **435**

Index

446

Index

Index